Special Report 211

Effects on Highways and Highway Safety

Transportation Research Board
National Research Council
Washington, D.C. 1986

Transportation Research Board Special Report 211
Price $25.00

mode
1 highway transportation

subject areas
24 pavement design and performance
51 transportation safety
53 vehicle characteristics

Transportation Research Board publications are available by ordering directly from TRB. They may also be obtained on a regular basis through organizational or individual affiliation with TRB; affiliates or library subscribers are eligible for substantial discounts. For further information, write to the Transportation Research Board, National Research Council, 2101 Constitution Avenue, N.W., Washington, D.C. 20418.

Printed in the United States of America

Library of Congress Cataloging in Publication Data
National Research Council. Transportation Research Board.

Twin trailer trucks.

(Special report, ISSN 0360-859X; 211)
1. Tractor trailer combinations. 2. Traffic safety. 3. Roads. I. National Research Council (U.S.). Transportation Research Board. II. Series: Special report (National Research Council (U.S.). Transportation Research Board); 211.
TL230.T85 1986   363.1'259   86-16466
ISBN 0-309-04050-7

COMMITTEE FOR THE TWIN TRAILER TRUCK MONITORING STUDY

KENNETH W. HEATHINGTON, University of Tennessee, Knoxville, *Chairman*
ROBERT G. ADAMS, California Department of Transportation, Sacramento
CHARLES N. BRADY, American Automobile Association, Falls Church, Virginia
THOMAS W. BROWNE, The Woodlands, Texas
WILLIAM N. CAREY, JR., Bethesda, Maryland
RALPH V. DURHAM, International Brotherhood of Teamsters, Washington, D.C.
ROBERT D. ERVIN, University of Michigan, Ann Arbor
JOHN W. FULLER, University of Iowa, Iowa City
WILLIAM D. GLAUZ, Midwest Research Institute, Kansas City, Missouri
RONALD L. HUTCHINSON, Vicksburg, Mississippi
MARGARET HUBBARD JONES, Golts, Maryland
JOHN H. LEDERER, DeWitt, Sundby, Huggett and Schumacher, Madison, Wisconsin
HUGH W. MCGEE, Bellomo-McGee, Inc., Vienna, Virginia
JOHN K. MLADINOV, New York State Department of Transportation, Albany
HAROLD W. MONRONEY, Illinois Department of Transportation, Springfield
NATHANIEL H. PULLING, Liberty Mutual Insurance Company, Hopkinton, Massachusetts
BILLY ROSE, Raleigh, North Carolina
C. MICHAEL WALTON, University of Texas at Austin
MATTHEW W. WITCZAK, University of Maryland, College Park

Liaison Representatives

ARTHUR J. BALEK, Federal Highway Administration, U.S. Department of Transportation
WILLIAM T. DRUHAN, American Association of State Highway and Transportation Officials, Washington, D.C.
CHRISTINE HEALEY, Office of Representative Barbara B. Kennelly, U.S. House of Representatives
KAREN BORLAUG PHILLIPS, Senate Committee on Commerce, Science and Transportation
GEORGE W. RING III, Transportation Research Board

Preface

Through the Surface Transportation Assistance Act of 1982, the U.S. Congress required states to permit truck-tractors pulling twin 28-ft trailers on Interstate highways and other principal roads. Recognizing that the use of twin trailer trucks might have varied and unpredictable consequences, Congress directed the National Research Council to monitor the effects of twin trailer trucks, "determining the effects of the use of such vehicle combinations on highways and highway safety in urban and rural areas and in different regions of the country. . ."

With support from the Federal Highway Administration, the National Research Council assembled a committee of 19 members with experience in the many areas involved, including vehicular safety, trucking operations, highway administration, highway design, economics, statistics, law, insurance, traffic engineering, and vehicle handling and performance.

The Committee for the Twin Trailer Truck Monitoring Study examined potential impacts of twin trailer trucks on trucking industry productivity, traffic operations, pavement wear, and bridge loadings, but devoted particular attention to highway safety. The committee made judgments about the comparative safety of twin trailer trucks, but more definitive conclusions must await further data. Because the trucking industry has been adopting twins gradually, and will continue to do so over a number of years, it was difficult to observe directly the full impact of twins during the first few years of nationwide use. Potential differences in safety performance from one region to another were noted in a preliminary way, but because route structures and shipment characteristics may create regional disparities in the use of twins that are not currently documented, more detailed regional comparisons of accident experience were not possible.

The safety performance of twin trailer trucks compared with that of other large trucks tends to be obscured by confounding factors, including differences in typical driver qualifications, highway routes, loadings, fraction of nighttime driving, and carrier safety practices. Making a well-founded judgment about the comparative safety of twins requires reliance on the totality of available information, not on any single statistic. Vehicle-handling studies, driver reactions, accident and use statistics, and trucking-company experience each offer useful insights, and all were considered by the committee in making its judgments.

The findings presented here are based on experience with twins operating chiefly on principal roads. The observations made about the comparative safety of specific vehicle configurations apply mainly to these roads and may not apply to roads built to lesser design standards. Similarly, the safety findings are based on twins carrying general freight, their predominant use, and do not assess the potential risks involved should twins be used to transport hazardous materials.

In addition, the committee considered the effects of 48-ft semitrailers and 102-in. wide trucks, which were also legalized for nationwide use at the same time. Because these trucks were not used much before 1983, projections cannot be made with the benefit of a historical record. However, the committee was able to draw general conclusions about the potential use of these vehicles and their impacts.

The study benefited from data and assistance provided by state highway agencies, trucking companies, safety research organizations, trade organizations, and the Federal Highway Administration. This report presents the committee's conclusions and summarizes underlying data developed over a two-year period under the chairmanship of Dr. Kenneth W. Heathington, Associate Vice President for Research, University of Tennessee.

The study was performed under the overall supervision of Dr. Damian J. Kulash, Assistant Director for Special Projects. Robert E. Skinner, Jr., and Joseph R. Morris directed the project staff. Stephen R. Godwin, Dr. John A. Deacon, and Richard Margiotta made significant contributions.

Finally, special appreciation is expressed to Nancy A. Ackerman, TRB Publications Manager, and Naomi Kassabian, Associate Editor, for editing the final report and to Marguerite Schneider and Margaret M. Sheriff for typing the many drafts and the final manuscript.

Contents

Executive Summary

INTRODUCTION

Truck-tractors pulling twin 28-ft trailers are using the nation's highways increasingly as a result of the Surface Transportation Assistance Act of 1982, which required states to permit these vehicles on Interstate highways and on other principal roads. The act also legalized other larger trucks for nationwide use on these routes, and directed the National Academy of Sciences to monitor the effect of twin trailer trucks on highways and highway safety.

Truck safety is a serious concern. Public awareness of the hazards of large trucks and press and television attention to the topic have never been higher. Truck crashes are frequently spectacular and severe, can cause massive traffic tie-ups, and commonly receive media coverage. Motorists are aware that freight trucks are getting bigger and more common, and may feel intimidated when driving in truck traffic. Responding to public demands, government regulators and trucking industry spokesmen have declared truck safety to be at the top of their priorities and have announced new programs for attacking the problem. The perception that highway safety has deteriorated as a consequence of more and larger trucks has been a principal basis for opposition to liberalized truck size limits. The Twin Trailer Truck Monitoring Study closely examined the potential safety effects of the new federal truck size rules. The study also addressed other

1

important effects of the new rules on highway transportation. The effects were estimated in these areas:

- Trucking industry use of twins,
- Safety consequences of using twins,
- Pavement wear and other highway features affected by twins, and
- Safety and pavement wear affected by 48-ft long semitrailers and 102-in. wide trucks.

The study also made recommendations for further monitoring of truck activity and for continued safety improvement.

TRUCKING INDUSTRY USE

The use of twin trailer trucks will be concentrated within certain segments of the trucking industry. In particular, the general freight common carriers are rapidly integrating twins into their operations, replacing tractor-semitrailers (combination trucks with only one trailer). Most of these trucking companies specialize in shipments that are less than a full truckload, transported in trucks loaded with multiple shipments. Such firms account for about 15 percent of combination-truck travel in the United States. They can take advantage of the added volume capacity of twins and the flexibility that dividing loads into smaller trailers allows to reduce mileage and terminal handling costs. These firms will perform about 70 percent of their intercity combination-truck travel with twins by 1990.

In the other segments of the trucking industry—for-hire carriers who transport freight in truckload-sized shipments and private carriers such as manufacturers or retail trade firms that maintain their own truck fleets to transport their goods—opportunities for using twins advantageously are limited. Some private carriers are making experimental use of twins, and in the Far West, twins sometimes carry agricultural and other bulk commodities, but outside the general freight common carrier segment of trucking, twins will constitute a small share of all truck travel for the foreseeable future.

By 1990, twins will account for about 11 percent of nationwide combination-truck miles, up from about 4 percent in 1982. Nearly 90 percent of this increase will occur outside the western states where twins were common before 1983. General freight common carrier conversion to twins will be largely complete by 1990 and will account for most of the growth between 1982 and 1990.

As a result of increased capacity and greater flexibility in operations, general freight common carriers adopting twins will achieve on average a 9 percent reduction in combination-truck miles of travel in the portion of their freight hauling that is switched from tractor-semitrailers to twins. Cost savings from twins are not expected to stimulate any appreciable new combination-truck travel. Consequently, because of the nationwide use of twins, by 1990 combination-truck travel will total about two-thirds of a percent less than it would have been otherwise.

Because of these travel reductions and the equally important savings from reduced handling that twins allow, truckers adopting twins are increasing productivity. General freight common carriers specializing in less-than-truckload freight will achieve cost reductions of roughly $500 million annually, 2 percent of their total costs, compared with costs using pre-1983 equipment and operating practices, when twins are fully integrated into their operations.

Neither the current scope of the highway network open to twins nor existing restrictions on access to that network will ultimately have much impact on travel by twins. In general, the network allows carriers to operate twins on the Interstates and major primary routes that account for the bulk of combination-truck traffic. State restrictions on access to the network have slowed the introduction of twins in some areas, but these restrictions have generally lessened with time.

SAFETY CONSEQUENCES

The increased use of twins will have little overall effect on highway safety because a reduction in miles of truck travel will approximately offset the small possible increase in accident involvements per mile traveled.

Twins probably have slightly more accident involvements per mile traveled than tractor-semitrailers operated under identical conditions at highway speeds. Although the information available for comparing the relative safety of twins and tractor-semitrailers is imperfect, this conclusion is supported by two independent lines of evidence: studies of the performance and handling characteristics of large trucks using experimental vehicle testing and simulations, and analyses of historical twin trailer truck and tractor-semitrailer accident and travel experience.

Studies of the performance and handling characteristics of large trucks show that compared with tractor-semitrailers, twins are prone to experiencing rear-trailer rollover in response to abrupt steering maneuvers, provide less sensory feedback to the driver about trailer stability, tend slightly more to encroach on outside lanes or shoulders on curves at highway speeds, and undergo greater rear-end sway during routine operations. At low speeds, as when traveling on city streets, twins are more maneuverable than tractor-semitrailers because the rear wheels of a twin trailer truck track the path of the front wheels more closely when making turns. Such differences in handling are corroborated by professional truck drivers surveyed, who report experiencing these characteristics of twins and generally prefer to drive tractor-semitrailers rather than twins.

Taken together, these special handling characteristics are mechanisms that could lead to a higher accident rate for twins operating at highway speeds. However, it is not possible to tell from vehicle handling observations alone how differences in handling affect the frequency of accidents in on-the-road experience. To predict changes in accidents, actual accident and travel data are necessary.

Analyses of historical accident and travel experience before the nationwide adoption of twins in 1983 indicate that twins had slightly more accident involvements per mile of truck travel than did tractor-semitrailers similarly operated on rural highways. The three most reliable pre-1983 analyses comparing accident involvement rates for twins and tractor-semitrailers on rural highways estimated rates for twins that were 2 percent less, 6 percent more, and 12 percent more than the rates for tractor-semitrailers. In the three most reliable analyses of involvements in accidents resulting in fatalities, rates for twins of involvement in fatal accidents were estimated to be 7 percent less, 5 percent more, and 20 percent more than the rates for tractor-semitrailers. Comparisons of accident rates for twins and tractor-semitrailers are necessarily imprecise because they must be made between the two vehicle types operating under very similar conditions—for example, similar routes, drivers, and times of day—if they are to reflect safety differences between the vehicles rather than safety effects of the operating conditions. Even these relatively reliable accident rate analyses were unable to fully allow for the effects of these extraneous factors, and in no single analysis was the difference measured between twins and tractor-semitrailers large compared with the inherent uncertainty of the estimates.

The safety consequences of twins depend not only on their relative accident rates, but also on the reduction in truck travel that accompanies their expanded use. The 9 percent reduction in truck miles in operations that are converted from tractor-semitrailers to twins approximately offsets the possibly higher rate of accident involvements per mile that twins exhibit. Hence the likely net safety impact of expanded use of twins will be slightly fewer miles of truck travel with slightly more accidents per mile of travel, resulting in very little change in the number of accidents. When all factors are considered, despite the uncertainty in comparing accident rates of twins and tractor-semitrailers, twins clearly appear to be about as safe a method of hauling freight per ton-mile of travel as the tractor-semitrailers they replace.

Experience since 1982 shows an increased share of accident involvements for twins that is roughly the same as their increased share of miles traveled.

Collectively, the recent data are still too fragmentary to confirm or revise the results of pre-1983 analyses that estimated the accident rates of twins relative to those of tractor-semitrailers, but they show no surprising changes in truck accident experience that could be attributed to twins.

These safety findings are based on twins carrying general freight, their predominant use, and do not assess the potential risks involved should twins be used to transport hazardous materials.

PAVEMENT WEAR AND OTHER HIGHWAY FEATURES

Compared with the tractor-semitrailers they replace, twins accelerate pavement wear and will increase pavement rehabilitation costs. Three characteristics of twins and the loads they carry increase pavement wear:

● Twins typically weigh more than the tractor-semitrailers they replace. Twins carry higher average payloads, and they weigh more when empty, but they typically have the same number of axles as tractor-semitrailers. Pavement wear increases sharply with axle load: a 20,000-lb single axle causes 12 times more wear per mile traveled than the same axle loaded to 10,000 lb.

● The loads on twins are usually distributed less uniformly among their five axles than tractor-semitrailer loads. Uniform loading minimizes pavement wear, again because wear increases exponentially with increasing load.

● Twins transfer their loads to the pavement with an axle arrangement (five single axles) different from that of tractor-semitrailers (usually one single axle and two pairs of closely spaced axles called tandem axles). On asphalt pavements, a tandem axle causes less wear than two single axles equally loaded. On portland cement concrete pavements, however, a tandem axle causes more wear than two single axles equally loaded.

These factors are partially offset because greater use of twins reduces combination-truck travel, but with all factors considered, on asphalt pavements twins will on average cause about 90 percent more pavement wear than the tractor-semitrailers they replace, whereas on portland cement concrete pavement twins will cause about 20 percent more pavement wear on average than the vehicles they replace. Although twins cause more wear than comparably loaded tractor-semitrailers, the typical twin is not the most damaging vehicle in legal use on the U.S. highways—for example, the average tractor with hopper semitrailer carrying agricultural commodities on Interstates causes more wear than the average for twins.

Nationwide, at the expected 1990 level of twins use, the additional wear twins will cause would cost roughly $50 million annually to repair, about 2 percent of current highway rehabilitation expenditures by states and 10 percent of the expected 1990 annual productivity gains in trucking. More reliable estimates of the pavement costs attributable to twins and other large truck types will not be possible until pavement wear and rehabilitation costs can be related more explicitly to vehicle loads and environmental factors that vary from region to region and highway to highway. The Long-Term Pavement Performance Study, a part of the planned Strategic Highway Research Program sponsored by the American Association of State Highway and Transportation Officials, will be collecting the data needed to estimate these relationships—data on pavement condition, vehicle loads, environment, and maintenance on sampled roads throughout the country over a 20-year period.

Twins will have no effect on the rate of deterioration of existing bridges nor require any change in design procedures for new highway structures. The forces created in bridge components by fully loaded twins are about the same or less than those created by equally loaded tractor-semitrailers.

The nationwide use of twins probably will not affect overall highway congestion and traffic delay. Because twins operate with heavier loads and are longer, a twin trailer truck will cause some degradation of traffic flow compared with the typical tractor-semitrailer it replaces, but this degradation will be somewhat offset by a reduction in combination-truck miles of travel. The better low-speed turning maneuverability of twins will be of some aid to traffic flow.

Expanded use of twins will not require changes to geometric design policies and practices for highways. Because twins are more maneuverable at low speeds than the tractor-semitrailers they replace, they can more easily negotiate interchange ramps, intersections, and other roadway facilities that are designed to accommodate combination-truck turning movements.

SAFETY AND PAVEMENT WEAR AFFECTED BY 48-FT LONG SEMITRAILERS AND 102-IN. WIDE TRUCKS

The federal law that legalized nationwide use of twins also permitted use of trucks with 48-ft semitrailers and 102-in. wide trucks on the same network of roads. In contrast to twins, 48-ft semitrailers and 102-in. wide trucks had seen little use before 1983. Consequently they do not have a historical record on which to base definite projections of their ultimate effects on highway safety, freight productivity, or pavement wear. Nonetheless, the available information does support some general conclusions about the potential extent of use of these vehicles and their impacts.

The 48-ft semitrailer is particularly appealing to private carriers and truckload for-hire carriers who could use added volume capacity but do not have a potential for savings in handling costs through use of twins. Of new van trailer sales, the 48-ft length accounts for almost 60 percent and is becoming the industry semitrailer standard, replacing the 45-ft semitrailer. The safety effects of 48-ft semitrailers have not yet been established. Compared with the combination trucks with shorter semitrailers that they replace, which usually also have shorter wheelbases, combination trucks with 48-ft semi-trailers are less maneuverable and therefore more likely to have accidents on turns. However, they will travel fewer miles to carry a given quantity of freight because of their greater cubic capacity.

Widespread use of 48-ft semitrailers will accelerate deterioration of high-way shoulders and roadside signing and guardrails to a small extent in some locations and will probably require changes in highway design standards. Because they are less maneuverable than the shorter semitrailers they replace, 48-ft semitrailers are more likely to override shoulders and curbs during turns and at curves. So far, 18 states have made or plan to make changes in their design policies to better accommodate these vehicles.

Most new van trailers (70 percent in 1984) are purchased with widths of 102 in. instead of the older 96-in. standard. Of new twins, about 90 percent are purchased with the 102-in. width. As with 48-ft semitrailers, the safety consequences of increasing truck widths to 102 in. have not yet been demonstrated. Although wider trucks may be more hazardous on roads with narrow lanes, the added width increases stability and reduces the possibility of overturn, provided that the trailer is equipped with wider axles matching the increased width of the cargo space. Moreover, the added width increases the payload per trip on average and therefore reduces miles of travel required to transport a given amount of freight.

The use of 102-in. wide trucks and 48-ft semitrailers increases pavement wear, because these vehicles generally weigh more on average than the ones they replace. The greater weight increases net pavement wear despite the accompanying reduction in miles traveled.

RECOMMENDATIONS

Monitoring Truck Use and Its Effects

Closer coordination among the various data producers and users who participate in the programs that collect nationwide information on truck travel, safety, and highway impacts would greatly enhance the ability of these programs to provide reliable data addressing key truck-related policy questions. The following actions would help to provide this coordination and fill critical data gaps:

• The U.S. Department of Transportation should work with state agencies to improve the quality and consistency of state-collected data through oversight and technical assistance.

• The U.S. Department of Transportation should establish a forum for communication among truck data users and producers to more effectively direct the expenditure of data collection resources. Such a forum would embrace organizations within the Department, other federal agencies, state governments, and industry.

• The state governments should adopt more uniform practices in the collection of travel and accident data, including adoption of traffic monitoring procedures recommended by the U.S. Department of Transportation and consistent vehicle classification systems for accident reporting.

• The Federal Highway Administration should continue the twin trailer truck monitoring activities begun in this study for at least 4 more years.

• The Long-Term Pavement Performance Study should consider coordination with other highway monitoring programs and adopt a research plan that examines the effects of axle type and spacing on pavement wear.

• Research studies sponsored by the U.S. Department of Transportation are needed to develop trucking cost relationships for size and weight policy analysis and to examine relationships between safety and truck dimensions and between safety and driver characteristics.

Opportunities for Improving Truck Safety

Although on the basis of past experience twins can be expected to have little overall effect on highway safety, truck safety remains a serious public concern that demands attention. Improving truck safety involves not simply deciding what kinds of vehicles to allow, but also how these vehicles are to be designed and operated, how roadways are to be designed and maintained, and how drivers are to be licensed and monitored. Several potential means for improving safety for twins, other combination trucks, and large trucks generally should be vigorously pursued:

• Improved safety for twins through appropriate equipment specifications, operating practices, and driver training.

• More stringent driver controls. The greatest gains in combination-truck safety may lie in stricter requirements for their drivers.

• Improved truck controllability. There is a need for development of new technology and broader application of existing technology in the design of trucks and trailers for improved controllability. Opportunities for improved performance exist in the areas of brake performance, coupling devices, suspensions, and chassis design. Trucks or trailers built with the 102-in. body width should be required to be equipped with axles of the matching width to take advantage of this opportunity for improved stability. When considering any change to truck size and weight laws, government regulators should seek opportunities to link the change with vehicle requirements that assure that highway safety is maintained or improved in the process.

• Upgraded geometric design of highways. State highway agencies should periodically reexamine truck volumes and accident statistics to identify locations prone to combination-truck accidents and take corrective measures where cost-effective.

• Dedication to comprehensive safety management by trucking firms through monitoring and training of drivers, equipment maintenance, employment of safety professionals, accident data acquisition, and a policy placing safety before short-term cost considerations. Small firms may have more difficulty in establishing comprehensive safety management programs, but many of these activities are within the capability of trucking firms regardless of their size.

• More effective federal, state, and local enforcement of truck safety regulations. The Bureau of Motor Carrier Safety and the responsible state and local agencies must have the resources necessary for enforcement and monitoring programs to evaluate whether their efforts are effective.

1
Introduction

Twin trailer trucks—truck-tractors pulling two trailing units (Figure 1-1)—are appearing more frequently on roads in many parts of the United States as a result of the Surface Transportation Assistance Act of 1982 (enacted January 1983). This act provided that the states cannot prohibit the operation of twin trailer trucks on the Interstate highway system and on a system of other principal roads designated by the Secretary of Transportation.[1]

Before passage of the act, twin trailer trucks were illegal in 14 eastern states.[2] These trucks have been common for many years, however, on the roads of a number of states, mainly in the West. For example, twins made up 30 percent of all travel by combination trucks (trucks or truck-tractors pulling one or more trailers) on rural Interstates in California and 14 percent in Washington and Oregon in 1982. Three years after the effective date of the act, use of these vehicles has increased substantially on major rural

---

[1]See the glossary for definitions of truck and highway terms.

[2]Maine, Vermont, New Hampshire, Massachusetts, Connecticut, Rhode Island, New Jersey, Pennsylvania, West Virginia, Virginia, North Carolina, South Carolina, Georgia, and Alabama. Twins also were prohibited in the District of Columbia. New Jersey did not specifically ban twins, but the state's 55-ft truck length limit effectively barred the industry-standard 65-ft twin. Massachusetts allowed combinations with two trailers on its turnpike with a special permit, but the two trailers had to be disconnected and pulled separately once they left the turnpike. Several states other than these 14 restricted twins to certain designated roads (1,2).

roads nationwide, and they account for one combination truck in 30 on principal roads in the 14 eastern states that barred twins before 1983 (*3*).

Their use in these 14 states is limited to the 9,000 mi of Interstate highways in these states, 8,000 mi of other primary roads (15 percent of non-Interstate primary road mileage in these states) designated by the federal government (*4*), and state-designated access routes to terminals and rest stops.

In addition to permitting twins with individual trailer lengths of 28 ft, the 1983 act also required the states to allow 48-ft long semitrailers and vehicles 102 in. wide on major roads and 80,000-lb trucks on nearly all Interstates. Semitrailers 40 to 45 ft long and 96 in. wide had previously been the industry standard. Semitrailers 48 ft long were in use, but not common, in some parts of the country before the federal law; 102-in. wide trucks had been illegal in all but 10 states; and 80,000-lb trucks had been barred from the Interstate highways of 3 states.

The intent of the new truck size and weight limits was to increase the efficiency of freight transportation. Compared with the most commonly used combination trucks, twins and the longer and wider semi-

FIGURE 1-1   Twin trailer truck and tractor-semitrailer.

trailers offer the advantages of increased volume capacity, and twins allow greater flexibility in handling and routing cargo in some types of trucking operations. The new federal limits sought to improve productivity by allowing larger trucks than had been legal in many states and by providing more uniform size and weight regulations on a network of major national roads in place of the varying individual state regulations in effect previously.

The new federal truck size and weight limits were controversial for several reasons. They preempted state regulations in an area where federal involvement had historically been minimal: federal standards in effect before 1983 set only maximum weight and width limits (the states were free to set lower limits) applicable to Interstate highways only. The safety of the larger vehicles was questioned, and use of heavier trucks accelerates pavement deterioration. Following the U.S. Department of Transportation's publication in 1983 of a proposed designated network of roads where the larger trucks would be allowed, five states (Alabama, Florida, Georgia, Pennsylvania, and Vermont) took legal action to block the designations on the grounds that the federal network included roads that the states had requested to be excluded because of safety concerns (5). Connecticut passed a law in conflict with the federal legislation reaffirming its ban on twins (6), and five other states protested specific route designations (7). Legal action brought by the Center for Auto Safety, a private safety advocacy group, forced the federal government to undertake a more detailed examination of the characteristics of the roads it had designated in some states.

These early controversies have been resolved, and twin trailer trucks, 48-ft semitrailers, and 102-in. wide vehicles are operating on at least some major roads in each state. Nevertheless, the states and the federal government are today facing many decisions that depend on questions of the costs and benefits of allowing use of these trucks and of what roads are suitable for their operation. For example, the trucking industry is urging federal and state action to relax restrictions on the larger trucks in areas where their use is most constrained; the states now have authority (through an amendment to the original legislation) to influence federal route designations; the change in federal truck size and weight laws has stimulated several states to make parallel revisions in their own size and weight laws affecting many miles of roads beyond the federally designated network; and some states have instituted procedures for ongoing additions and alterations to the network of major roads and access routes where these trucks may operate. In addition, proposals for further revisions to the regulations governing truck dimensions and configurations are receiving serious consideration in federal and state government agencies. The states and the federal government will therefore continue to confront the problem of balancing the benefits of freight cost savings against the potential safety, maintenance, and road construction costs of larger trucks.

ORIGIN AND SCOPE OF THE STUDY

Recognizing that the use of twin trailer trucks was controversial in some parts of the country and that there were uncertainties about the effects of their expanded use, Congress in the act that authorized use of twins also directed the National Academy of Sciences to monitor their effects (8):

> SEC. 144. (a) The Secretary of Transportation shall undertake to enter into appropriate arrangements with the National Academy of Sciences to monitor the effects on the National System of Interstate and Defense Highways of the use of trucks with two trailing units, in light of the amendments made by this Act providing that no State shall prohibit the use of such vehicle combinations. Such monitoring shall include, but need not be limited to, determining the effects of the use of such vehicle combinations on highways and highway safety in urban and rural areas and in different regions of the country, taking into account differences in age and design features of highways on the Interstate System.
>
> (b) The Secretary of Transportation shall request the National Academy of Sciences to submit a report to the Secretary and the Congress of such monitoring, not later than two years after appropriate arrangements are entered into under subsection (a). The Secretary shall furnish to the Academy, at its request, any information which the Academy deems necessary for the purpose of conducting such monitoring.

In response to this mandate, the Transportation Research Board of the National Academy of Sciences assembled a committee including researchers and administrators with expertise in the trucking industry, highway safety, pavement design, and highway maintenance and operations. The findings of the committee are in three areas:

● *Safety*: Twins and the longer and wider semitrailers possess some differences in handling, maneuvering, and dynamic properties compared with the trucks they are replacing. The possibility of degrading highway safety now dominates the debate about these vehicles.

● *Highway costs*: Greater use of twin trailer trucks and of longer and wider semitrailers may increase pavement wear, create increased interference with other traffic, and alter design requirements for the geometric layout of road construction and reconstruction projects. Because these vehicles are heavier on average than the trucks they replace and because of the way in which the load of a twin trailer truck is distributed across its axles, pavement wear will be moderately accelerated. Increasing the length, width, and weight of trucks can impede the flow of traffic, especially on congested roads. In the design of new pavements and the rehabilitation of existing ones, the pavement thickness, the dimensions of intersections, the lane widths, and the grades must make allowance for the largest vehicles that will commonly use them; thus, accommodating large trucks can add to construction costs.

● *Productivity*: More widespread use of twins and of longer and wider semitrailers reduces the cost of moving goods by truck. Productivity improves because the volume capacity of these vehicles is greater than the capacity of the trucks they are replacing and also because in some types of trucking operations, replacing one large trailer with the two smaller twin trailers can reduce the number of times that a shipment must be loaded and unloaded between its origin and destination and allow shipments to travel more direct routes. Greater productivity means fewer miles of truck travel to carry a given quantity of freight. This reduction in travel would cause a reduction in the frequency of highway accidents and in the amount of pavement wear if twins and longer, wider semitrailers were identical to the vehicles they replace in their safety and pavement effects on a vehicle-to-vehicle basis and would counteract, at least partly, any safety or highway cost disadvantages of twins and longer, wider semitrailers.

In evaluating the safety, highway costs, and productivity of twins and of longer and wider semitrailers, it is important to make systemwide comparisons rather than focus on the comparative performance of individual vehicles. Such systemwide impacts depend not only on the characteristics of the vehicles, but also on the total volume of traffic of the vehicles, the characteristics of the roads they are using, and the kinds of firms and trucking operations that are employing them.

In addition, the committee has proposed improvements to the government's capabilities for long-term monitoring of the impacts of large trucks. A reliable, well-designed program of monitoring could substantially assist deliberations on new truck size, weight, and configuration regulatory questions that will surely face public officials in the future.

The committee studied the effects of twins and longer and wider semitrailers legalized for nationwide use by the 1983 act. It did not assess the effects of other combination-truck types such as turnpike doubles, Rocky Mountain doubles, or triple trailer trucks, which are permitted on some roads by individual states or toll road authorities.

METHOD OF THE STUDY

The full impact of the 1983 liberalization of truck size and weight rules cannot be observed during the law's first few years. Adoption of new vehicle sizes and configurations will be gradual, occurring over a period of years, for several reasons: a substantial stock exists of older trucking equipment with remaining useful life, uncertainty and controversy continue over the extent of the routes where the larger trucks may operate, investment funds in trucking have been scarce because of economic shocks to the industry from deregulation and the severe recession in the early 1980s, and time is required for experimentation with various operating practices using twins.

Because the full effects of the 1983 legislation cannot yet be directly observed, two steps were taken to estimate them in this study. First, the committee reviewed past experience with twin trailer trucks. Because twins have been in use for many years in some parts of the country, a record of their performance exists that has been valuable in helping to predict the full effects of their use nationwide. This record must be used with caution, however, because the size and weight laws controlling twins use in the past differed from those enacted in 1983 and because characteristics of the highway system and the trucking industry that affect the impacts of twins vary among regions of the country.

Second, the committee monitored the initial experience with nationwide twins use. This short-term monitoring has provided information about changes in the volume of traffic in twins, the characteristics of the roads they are using, the kinds of trucking operations that are using twins and the benefits they are realizing, and the frequency and circumstances of recent accidents involving twins. Because the characteristics of twins are advantageous only in certain types of trucking operations, they will always account for only a minority of large-truck traffic, so information on the current and probable future extent of twins' share of the trucking market is critical to assessing their impacts.

The sources for the short-term monitoring included data on truck use and accidents that are regularly collected by government and private organizations and three surveys conducted to support the Twin Trailer Truck Monitoring Study:

- A survey of all state highway agencies concerning their experiences with twins and their regulations governing twins use, conducted by the American Association of State Highway and Transportation Officials;
- A survey of 180 professional truck drivers, conducted by five local drivers' unions, to learn of their perceptions of performance differences between twins and tractor-semitrailers; and

• A series of interviews with trucking companies using twins and with trailer manufacturers to learn the extent of expansion of twins use and the benefits and drawbacks of twins.

ORGANIZATION OF THE REPORT

In Chapter 2 the history and rationale of truck size and weight regulation, the size and weight provisions of the Surface Transportation Assistance Act of 1982, and the policy debate that preceded and followed passage of those provisions are outlined. In the next three chapters each of the major categories of impact identified earlier is addressed: in Chapter 3, trucking cost impacts and the characteristics of twins use; in Chapter 4, the safety effects of twins; and in Chapter 5 the impact of twins on highway condition, operations, and design practices. In each of these chapters there is a review of past experience and research related to the effects of twins, a summary of the evidence from short-term monitoring of the impact of the new twins traffic generated by the change in the federal law, and finally a projection of the probable overall magnitude of the effect of twins nationally and regionally. Each also addresses the impacts of the longer and wider semitrailers that were legalized at the same time as twins.

The committee's assessment and recommendations concerning needs for long-term monitoring of large-truck effects are presented in Chapter 6, and Chapter 7 gives a summary of findings and recommendations concerning truck safety.

REFERENCES

1. J. Galligan and D.M. DiNunzio. "Rules and Regulations." *Commercial Carrier Journal*, April 1983.
2. B. Mertz. *Legislative History of 65 Foot Twin Trailers*. American Trucking Associations, Washington, D.C., July 2, 1971; April 28, 1983.
3. *Annual Truck Weight Study* (magnetic tape). FHWA, U.S. Department of Transportation, annual.
4. *Highway Statistics 1983*. FHWA, U.S. Department of Transportation, 1984.
5. "Truck Size." *Federal Register*, Vol. 48, No. 170, Aug. 31, 1983, p. 39592.
6. "Brief of the Council of State Governments [et al.]." *State of Connecticut et al. v. United States of America*, 83-870, U.S. Supreme Court, 1983.
7. "Truck Size and Weight; Proposed Rulemaking." *Federal Register*, Vol. 48, No. 179, Sept. 14, 1983, p. 41276.
8. Public Law 97-424 (Jan. 6, 1983), *Surface Transportation Assistance Act of 1982*, 96 Stat. 2097.

2
Historical and Regulatory Background

The new federal rules governing the use of twin trailer trucks and other larger combination trucks are only one recent development in a 70-year history of state and federal regulation of motor vehicle size and weight. Throughout this period, as automotive and highway technologies have developed, vehicles have become progressively larger and legal size limits have been revised to accommodate them. With each revision of size limits, governments have been faced with similar problems of balancing increased highway construction and maintenance costs and possible safety consequences against efficiency of freight transportation. Most recently, a new balance was struck when expanded use of twin trailer trucks and longer and wider semitrailers was permitted by the Surface Transportation Assistance Act of 1982 (enacted in 1983).

The question of the costs and benefits of twin trailer trucks must be viewed in the context of this historical evolution of truck size and weight. Each successive change in legal limits and in truck sizes has produced only small incremental impacts on highway costs and freight transportation. However, the cumulative results have been that many highways are today exposed to much heavier, longer, and wider trucks and to greater volumes of large-truck traffic than their designers envisioned, and that trucking has grown to be the largest freight transport mode in terms of the cost of providing its services. The 1983 federal law takes on new significance when seen as one step in this trend rather than as an isolated occurrence.

In the first section of this chapter the history of state and federal truck size and weight regulations is reviewed from the enactment in 1913 of the first state limits through 1982. During this time the states had the dominant role in setting size limits. The diversity of state regulations gave rise to calls for more uniform nationwide rules to promote efficiency in trucking and in highway design, but federal involvement remained minimal.

In the second section developments in highway transportation that accompanied the trend to greater size and weight limits are described: the growth of trucking as a major freight carrier, large increases in the dimensions of trucks on the road, and improvements in the highway system that have made operation of bigger trucks feasible. These developments have been the source of pressures for liberalized size limits. The trends in truck involvements in highway accidents are also described.

The 1983 federal size and weight limits are summarized in the final section. The new federal limits were a departure from the historical federal role in truck size and weight regulation—they were the first to require the states to change their existing rules and were the first federal rules to apply to roads other than the Interstates.

Appendix A contains the text of the sections of federal law pertaining to size limits, and in Appendix B the status of implementation of the 1983 federal law today is given: the extent of the road network designated for use by the federally authorized trucks, the provisions for access between the designated roads and the origin and destination points of shipments, and the changes in some state size and weight laws that have been stimulated by the federal action.

TRUCK SIZE AND WEIGHT LAWS BEFORE 1983

State and local governments have regulated truck dimensions, weights, and allowable configurations since shortly after the first motor trucks appeared. The purpose of these limits has been to control four public costs associated with large trucks:

- *Road maintenance*: The wear on pavements, shoulders, and bridges due to traffic increases with greater vehicle weights.
- *Construction*: Vehicle dimensions dictate requirements for the dimensions of the roadway—lane width must accommodate the widest vehicle normally using the road, the longest vehicle must be able to negotiate the sharpest curve, and so forth. Thus the states need to be able to predict the dimensions of the vehicles to be accommodated when new roads are designed and have an interest in limiting these dimensions as a control

on construction costs. Similarly, vehicle weights also influence the structural design of new roads. If more heavy-truck traffic is expected, pavements and bridges may need to be made stronger.

• *Congestion*: Large vehicles are often less maneuverable than small ones and may cause congestion, particularly in mountainous terrain, where the power needs and braking requirements of heavy vehicles may slow down other traffic.

• *Safety*: Accidents involving a large truck and an automobile are more severe on average than those involving only automobiles because of the greater mass of the truck. The special handling and stability properties of some types of large trucks may increase the likelihood of accidents. Large trucks create special hazards on highways not designed to handle them— roads with steep grades, sharp curves, and narrow lanes and shoulders.

Against these potential costs of allowing larger vehicles on the road, regulators have had to balance the economic benefits of improved productivity in freight transportation. (Size limits also constrain the dimensions of passenger buses, but the major economic significance of the regulations is their effect on freight-carrying trucks.) Using larger trucks allows a given quantity of freight to be hauled at a lower cost in labor, fuel, and equipment and gives carriers new options in routing and handling freight that can also reduce costs. The reduction in miles of travel required to handle a given quantity of freight in larger trucks directly alleviates the public costs of allowing their use.

These concerns—the effects of large trucks on the costs of building and maintaining roads, the performance and safety of roads, and the cost of moving freight—have been central to all previous evaluations of truck size limits and are the impacts evaluated in this study.

Regulation of vehicle dimensions, weights, and configurations historically has been primarily a responsibility of state governments. Federal limits were first enacted in 1956, and their scope was greatly extended by the 1983 federal size and weight law. In the next section the history of state regulation is described, followed by a discussion of the federal role before 1983.

State Regulations

In 1913 the first laws setting statewide vehicle size restrictions were enacted: weight limits in Maine, Massachusetts, and Washington and weight and width limits in Pennsylvania. The last state to enact a weight limit, in 1933, was North Dakota. The laws were passed to stem the severe damage to the earth- and gravel-surfaced roads then prevalent by the iron and solid rubber wheels of heavy trucks. State involvement in road construction and maintenance was expanding at this time, in part because under the terms of the federal-aid highway program created in 1916, state governments were responsible for administering federal road funds. Therefore state governments had a strong interest in controlling maintenance costs.

Limits on length, width, and height were adopted somewhat later than weight restrictions, but by 1929 the majority of states restricted all these dimensions as well as weight. Most early state regulations made no specific provisions for combination trucks, but as these vehicles became more common in the 1920s and 1930s, separate weight and length limits were established for straight trucks and combination trucks (1).

The scope of state regulations established during this early period has persisted until the present. The dimensions usually limited are

- Weight on any single axle or tandem axle (a pair of closely spaced axles);
- Gross weight of the total vehicle—either as an absolute maximum or through application of a formula relating the maximum weight to the spacing and number of axles;
- Length of straight trucks, combination trucks, and trailers;
- Number of trailers allowed;
- Width; and
- Height.

Some states impose separate limits for different classes of roads, and some allow local jurisdictions to set limits within their boundaries.

Throughout the history of size and weight regulations, limits have tended over time to allow larger and heavier vehicles [Figure 2-1 (2–5)], have changed frequently, and have varied widely from state to state. The median weight limit for combination trucks was less than 40,000 lb in 1927 (for a straight truck towing a full trailer, the most common combination truck at the time), rose to 48,000 lb in 1948 (for a four- or five-axle tractor-semitrailer), 72,000 lb in 1964 (five-axle tractor-semitrailer), and 80,000 lb in 1982.[1] Length limits were made more stringent for a time in the 1930s, but the median 1949 limit of 50 ft for a combination truck was

---

[1]See the notes for Figure 2-1, which explain the assumptions for determining the maximum practical gross weights in the figure. According to these assumptions (which are necessary for comparability over the 55-year period), the median 1982 practical limit would be 76,000 lb, but under the more reasonable assumption of a 12,000-lb loading of the steering axle, the 1982 median becomes 80,000 lb.

increased to 55 ft by 1964 and 65 ft by 1982. Width limits have been the most stable and uniform regulation, with most states agreeing on 96 in. from the earliest enactments until 1982.

A 1941 federal study of motor vehicle size and weight (*1*) documented 300 changes in individual state size and weight laws between 1913 and 1941, or about one change every 4 years per state, and the rate of change probably has been similar since then. Thus size and weight limits have undergone continual revision in order to accommodate developments in trucking equipment and improvements to the road system.

State-to-state variation in some limits has narrowed over time. For example, the spread between the lowest and highest single-trailer combination weight limits was 50,000 lb in 1927 (not considering the three states with no limit), 38,000 lb in 1949, 11,000 lb in 1964, and 8,000 lb in 1982. However, uniformity of combination-truck length limits has not improved; the 20-ft spread between the lowest and highest limits in 1949 (45 to 65 ft, not including one state with no limit) rose to 30 ft in 1982 (55 to 85 ft). The full scope of variations among state limits is even greater than the range of statutory limits suggests. The specific dimensions regulated and their definitions vary from state to state, as do the tolerances allowed in enforcement. Many states have special rules applying to particular vehicle types, roads, or industries; noncomplying vehicles are allowed to operate regularly with special permits in some areas; and the states differ in the stringency of enforcement of their limits.

Legalization of twin trailer trucks at the pre-1983 industry-standard length of 65 ft spread gradually among the states, generally from West to East, from the 1950s to 1982 [Table 2-1 (*6*)]. Legalization of 65-ft twins came about in some states as a result of lifting restrictions on the number of trailers allowed and in others as a byproduct of increasing the length limit. Twins shorter than 65 ft were in use in a number of states at earlier dates than those shown in Table 2-1.

The recommended policies of the American Association of State Highway and Transportation Officials (AASHTO) on dimensions and weights have provided a model for many state limits [Table 2-2 (*7–10*)]. AASHTO first adopted a policy in 1932 and revised it seven times between 1942 and 1980. From its first policy, AASHTO urged the states to adopt uniform regulations in order to allow standardized highway design and to promote efficiency and safety in highway transportation. Although the AASHTO policies have influenced state and federal regulations, their appeal for uniformity clearly has had a limited effect.

The 1983 federal size and weight rules superseded many state limits, at least as they applied to the designated network where trucks meeting the federal standards may operate. At the end of 1982, 65-ft long twin

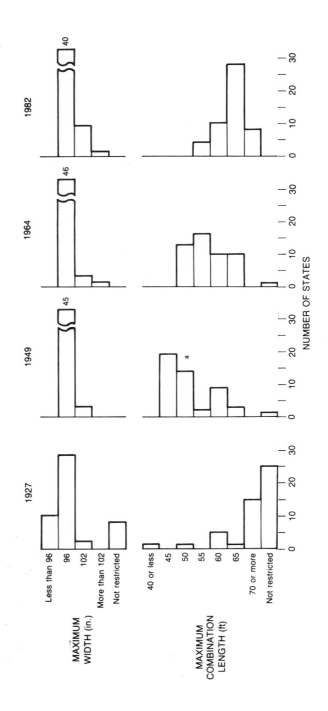

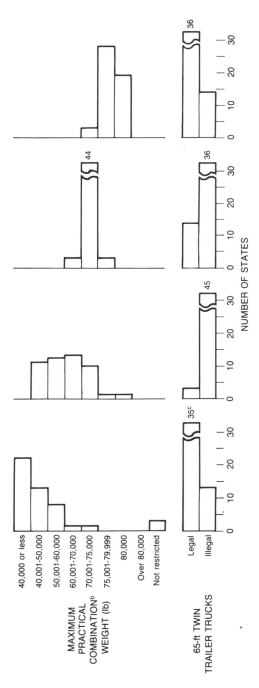

FIGURE 2-1 Evolution of state size and weight limits, 1927–1982 (1,2–5).

aIncludes one state at 48 ft.

bIn 1982, 1964, and 1949, the maximum weights are for a combination truck with a three-axle tractor and a two-axle semitrailer. In 1949, five-axle tractor-semitrailers were impractical for most purposes in the 19 states with a 45-ft length limit; however, in none of these states would a five-axle combination have been subject to a different practical weight limit than a four-axle combination. In 1927 the maximum weight is for a two-axle straight truck with a two-axle full trailer (the most common combination-truck type at the time) except in the few states that had a specific limit for tractor-semitrailers. Only half the states had specific weight provisions for combinations in their laws in 1927; the practice in most states without such limits apparently was to apply the single-unit limit separately to the truck and the trailer. The maximum weights tabulated take into account axle weight limits, gross weight formulas or tables (bridge formulas), and length limits, as well as specific gross weight limits. The steering-axle load is assumed to be 8,000 lb.

cIn 1927, 65-ft twin trailer trucks presumably were rare but would have been legal in most states because length limits were liberal or nonexistent at the time. By 1935, 46 states had enacted length limits, and 65-ft twins would have been illegal in 44 states.

TABLE 2-1   Dates of State Legalization of 65-ft Twin Trailer Trucks Before 1983 (6)

State	Date	Route Restrictions
Arizona	NP	
Nevada	NP	
Idaho	1937	
New Mexico	1955	
Hawaii	Pre-1956	
California	1959	
Montana	1959	
Oregon	1959	
Utah	1959	
Colorado	1961	
Washington	1961	
Wyoming	1961	
Illinois	1963	Designated highways only
South Dakota	1963	
Indiana	1965	
Kansas	1965	
Missouri	1965	Designated highways only
Nebraska	1965	
North Dakota	1965	Designated highways only
Oklahoma	1965	
Texas	1965	
Alaska	1966	
Kentucky	1966	Designated highways only
Michigan	1966	Designated highways only
Arkansas	1967	
Delaware	1967	
Maryland	1967	Four-lane highways and direct routes to terminals
Ohio	1967	
Louisiana	1972	Four-lane highways plus 10 mi access
Minnesota	1973	Designated highways only
Wisconsin	1978	Four-lane highways only
Florida	1979	Four-lane highways only
Iowa	1980	Designated highways only
New York	1981	Four-lane highways plus 1 mi access
Mississippi	1982	Four-lane highways plus 12 mi access
Tennessee	1982	Interstates and designated access roads

NOTE: NP = never prohibited.

trailer trucks were allowed on at least some roads in 36 states (Figure 2-2).[2] Fourteen states restricted the use of twins to designated highways in 1982 (Table 2-1), and several required special permits for their operation.

---

[2]Massachusetts, one of the 14 states not allowing twins, allowed the longer turnpike doubles (nine-axle combinations typically 105 ft long) on its turnpike with a special permit, but the two trailers had to be disconnected and pulled separately as soon as the vehicle left the turnpike. These restrictions made the use of twins impractical. In addition, 17 states where twins were used also allowed turnpike doubles or Rocky Mountain doubles.

TABLE 2-2 AASHTO Recommended Policies on Motor Vehicle Dimensions and Weights, 1932–1980 (7–10)

Size or Weight Provision	1932	1946	1964	1974	1980
Maximum width (in.)	96		102^a		
Maximum height (ft)	12.5		13.5		
Maximum length (ft)					
Tractor-semitrailer	35	50	55		60
Other combination^b	45	60	65		
Trailer	Not restricted		40		45
Maximum single-axle load (lb)	16,000	18,000	20,000		
Maximum tandem-axle load (lb)	32,000			34,000	
Maximum practical gross vehicle weight, five-axle tractor-semitrailer (lb)^c	49,000–72,000^d	61,490	72,000	76,000	
Multitrailer combinations	Not permitted		Two trailers permitted		

NOTE: Values are shown under the year in which the limit was changed or was first introduced. A blank indicates that previous limit remained in effect.
^{a}Provided that the state's highway system is predominantly of lane width to safely accommodate.
^{b}Straight truck with full trailer and multitrailer combinations.
^{c}Limit determined by formulas relating maximum weight to number and spacing of axles. Practical limit shown assumes 8,000-lb load on steering axle and maximum weight consistent with length limit and weight limits on other axles.
^{d}The formula specified permits states discretion in setting gross weight limit below the maximum imposed by the axle limit.

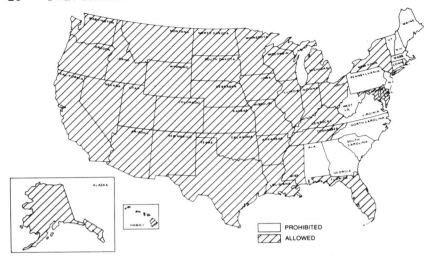

FIGURE 2-2   States allowing 65-ft twin trailer trucks on December 31, 1982 (2,5).

Semitrailers 48 ft long were legal and practical within overall length limits on at least some roads in 35 states in 1982 (Figure 2-3),[3] and 10 states allowed 102-in. wide trucks (Figure 2-4). The federal requirement that no overall length limit be imposed on motor vehicles operating in tractor-semitrailer or tractor-semitrailer-trailer combinations overturned such limits in all 50 states.

Federal Regulations

The Federal-Aid Highway Act of 1956 contained the first federal size and weight limits enacted. The act established maximum limits on Interstate highways for vehicle width (96 in.), axle weight (18,000 lb for a single axle and 32,000 lb for a tandem axle), and gross weight (73,280 lb).

[3]The classification of states according to legality of 48-ft semitrailers in Figure 2-3 is based on reports of the states to AASHTO during 1982 (5), the state survey conducted by AASHTO to support this study, and a tabulation of state laws by a trade journal (2). These three sources disagree for several states, and the question of legal trailer lengths before 1983 has become controversial because of the grandfather provision of the 1983 federal law that required that each state continue to allow the operation of the longest trailers that were legal in the state during 1982.

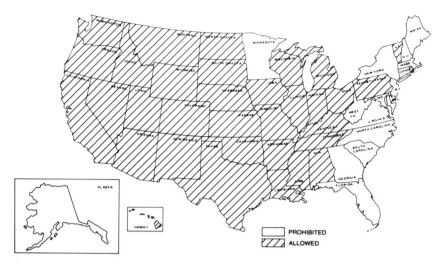

FIGURE 2-3   States allowing 48-ft long semitrailers on December 31, 1982 (*2,5*). [NOTE: In California, 48-ft (or longer) trailers were allowed provided fifth-wheel to rear-axle length did not exceed 38 ft; in Connecticut, 48-ft trailers were allowed with a permit; in Washington, no trailer length limit was specified for certain tractor-semitrailers that were allowed to operate at over 65-ft overall length.]

These limits followed the 1946 AASHO recommended policy. Length, height, and number of trailers were not addressed. The states could enforce lower limits on the Interstates if they chose and any limits they wished on roads other than Interstates, and a grandfather provision allowed higher state weight and width limits that existed at the time the federal law was passed to remain in effect.

The intent of the federal weight limit, according to Congressional reports at the time, was to control heavy-truck damage to the growing federal investment in roads (*7*). The 1956 act also established the Interstate system, with 90 percent federal funding, and created the Highway Trust Fund as the financing mechanism for the federal-aid highway program. Federal highway aid to state governments grew from $670 million in 1955 (14 percent of all state highway funding) to $3 billion in 1959 (41 percent of state funds) (*11*).

The limited scope of the 1956 federal limits and the exceptions they allowed suggest that their objective was not to obtain the potential eco-

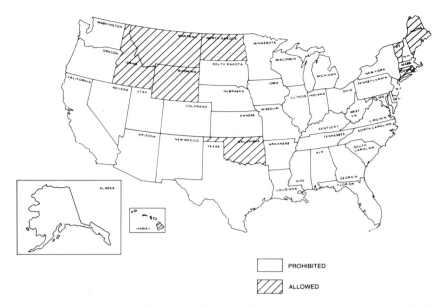

FIGURE 2-4   States allowing 102-in. wide trucks on December 31, 1982 (*2,5*). [NOTE: Buses 102 in. wide were allowed on Interstates in all states by federal law.]

nomic benefits (from improved trucking efficiency and standardization of highway design) of nationwide uniformity in size and weight regulation. Congress did in the 1956 act commission a study by the Secretary of Commerce to determine and recommend to Congress the maximum desirable dimensions and weight of vehicles operated on the federal-aid highway system. This report, delivered in 1964 (*7*), endorsed the concept of nationwide uniformity and recommended repeal of the grandfather clause; and indeed as early as 1941 a Congressionally commissioned study on the same topic had recommended that the federal government overrule state limits where they interfered with interstate commerce (*1*).

Despite these recommendations, Congress took no action to increase federal control of truck size and weight between 1956 and 1983. Federal limits were revised in 1975 (permitting gross weights up to 80,000 lb and introducing a formula that controlled the maximum weight allowed on any group of axles as a function of the number of axles and their spacing) and in 1976 (allowing the states to permit buses up to 102 in. wide on

Interstates), but these revisions left intact the features of the federal rules that permitted the states to retain wide latitude in setting standards: they applied to Interstates only, more liberal preexisting state limits were allowed to stand, and the states could choose lower limits than the federal ones (Table 2-3). It was not until the Surface Transportation Assistance Act of 1982 that the federal government actually required states to change existing limits in the interest of uniformity.

TABLE 2-3 Federal Motor Vehicle Size and Weight Regulations, 1956–1983

Size and Weight Provision[a]	Year of Legislation			
	1956	1975	1976	1983
Maximum width	●	●	●	●
Maximum height	○	○	○	○
Length				
Combination truck	○	○	○	●
Trailer	○	○	○	●
Maximum axle load	●	●	●	●
Maximum gross vehicle weight	●	●	●	●
Number of trailers	○	○	○	●
Enforcement certification required[b]	●	●	●	●
Roads where limits apply[c]				
Interstates	●	●	●	●
Federally designated non-Interstate	○	○	○	●
Grandfather provisions				
More restrictive prior state limits preempted	○	○	○	●
More liberal prior state limits preempted[d]	○	○	○	○

KEY:
● Federal legislation in that year included the provision or earlier provision remained in effect.
○ No federal provision in effect.
SOURCE: Federal-Aid Highway Act of 1956, Federal-Aid Highway Amendments of 1974 (signed January 5, 1975), Federal-Aid Highway Act of 1976, and the Surface Transportation Assistance Act of 1982 (signed January 6, 1983, amended in 1983 and 1984).
[a]The limits are as follows: width—1956, 96 in.; 1976, 102 in. for buses only; 1983, 102 in.; vehicle length—1983, states forbidden to restrict overall length on Interstates and other designated roads; trailer length—1983, 48 ft for semitrailer, 28 ft for one trailer of a twin trailer truck; axle weight—1956, 18,000-lb single axle and 32,000-lb tandem axle; 1975, 20,000 and 34,000 lb; gross weight—1956, 73,280 lb; 1975, 80,000 lb subject to formula limiting weights on short-wheelbase vehicles.
[b]Each state is required to certify annually to the federal government that it is enforcing its size and weight laws on all federal-aid roads.
[c]With the 1983 law, federal weight limits still apply only to Interstates, but states are required to grant access to terminals and service stops to trucks meeting the federal limits. All other federal limits apply to Interstates and other federally designated roads.
[d]Higher state gross weight limits in effect before July 1, 1956; more liberal formulas restricting weights on axle groups in effect before January 4, 1975; and Hawaii's 108 in. width limit were allowed to stand. States are required to allow trailers longer than the federal limits legally in use on December 31, 1982, to remain in use.

Summary Points: Truck Size and Weight Laws Before 1983

- Legal limits on truck size and weight are necessary to control road construction and maintenance costs, to control traffic congestion, and to keep unsafe vehicle types off the roads.
- State governments historically have taken principal responsibility for size and weight regulation. State limits have changed frequently, almost always in the direction of allowing larger trucks. For example, the median state practical gross weight limits (for five-axle tractor-semitrailers) and length limit (for any vehicle) in 1949, 1964, and 1982 were as follows:

	1949	1964	1982
Weight (lb × 1,000)	61	72	80
Length (ft)	50	55	65

- Size and weight limits have always varied greatly from state to state. Lack of uniform limits has created inefficiency in trucking operations and has complicated enforcement.
- Federal truck size and weight limits were first enacted in 1956. Until 1983, federal rules limited weight and width only, applied only on Interstates, and permitted states to enact more restrictive limits than the federal maximums. Federal rules allow more liberal pre-1956 state weight limits to remain in effect.

TRENDS IN TRUCK USE AND SIZE, HIGHWAY DEVELOPMENT, AND ACCIDENTS

Beginning in the early 1900s and continuing to the present, trucking has grown to become a primary component of the freight transportation system and the average size of freight trucks in use has continuously increased. During the same period U.S. roads have greatly improved but can adapt only slowly to the changing traffic burdens they carry. A 1918 Bureau of Public Roads report described these trends up to that time (12):

> Single light units expanded into great fleets, then grew into heavier units that, in turn, developed into long trains. From horse-drawn vehicles with concentrated load of probably 3 tons at most, traveling at the rate of 4 miles an hour, sprung almost overnight the heavy motor truck with a concentrated load of from 8 to 12 tons, thundering

along at a speed of 20 miles an hour. The result? The worn and broken threads that bind our communities together.

The rates of growth of truck travel and truck sizes have slowed since 1918, and roads are now better suited for heavy trucks, but the patterns established in the early highway era have continued. These concurrent trends have provided the impetus for raising truck size limits and have themselves been accelerated at times by the evolution of state truck regulations. These trends in trucking industry growth, truck size and weight, and highway development are outlined to show where the demand for higher limits has originated and how trucking has responded to past changes in limits. As trucking has grown, so has the role of trucks in highway accidents. This trend is also described, because opposition to liberalized truck size limits has in many instances reflected a perception that trucks are a major and growing part of the highway safety problem.

Growth of the Trucking Industry

Trucking's share of domestic intercity freight transportation grew from 3 percent of total ton-miles in 1929 to 32 percent in 1983[4] (Figure 2-5) (*13,14*). To carry this freight, combination trucks (the most important type of intercity freight truck) traveled 66 billion mi on U.S. roads in 1983, 4 percent of all motor vehicle travel (Figure 2-6) (*11,15*). Truck traffic volume is comparatively heavier on intercity routes, accounting for 9 percent of travel on all major rural roads in 1983 and 14 percent of travel on rural Interstates. Combination-truck travel has increased 13-fold since 1936, but its share of all road travel has only doubled over the same period.

Figure 2-5 shows that the period of most rapid growth in trucking's share of the freight market was 1945 to 1960. During this period legal restrictions on size and weight were stringent by today's standards, and construction of the Interstate highway system, which today carries most intercity truck freight, was just beginning. Highway development and relaxation of truck size limits in the past 25 years do not appear to have caused much change in the share of freight traffic carried by trucks; rather, once trucking became a major transportation mode, incentives were strong to allow greater efficiency through larger trucks and better roads.

---

[4]These percentages and those in Figure 2-5 exclude shipments of petroleum and petroleum products, nearly all of which are carried by pipeline and water transport and which account for a very small share of truck and rail freight.

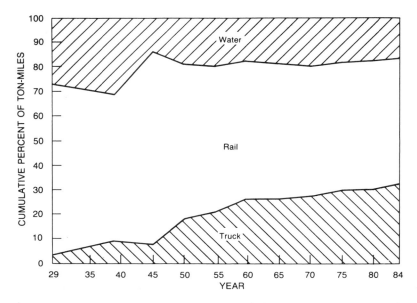

FIGURE 2-5   Growth of trucking's share of domestic intercity freight, 1929–1984 (*13,14*). [NOTE: Transportation of petroleum and petroleum products (which is almost entirely by pipeline and water) has been excluded for all modes. Air freight makes up less than 0.5 percent of ton-miles in all years.]

Trucks today are the preferred mode for most shipping of high-value manufactured goods (*16*), and expenditures for intercity trucking, $108 billion, accounted for 70 percent of all intercity freight transportation costs in 1983 (*13*). Even marginal improvements in trucking efficiency can therefore produce large economic benefits.

Truck Size and Weight Trends

Historically the trucking industry has taken advantage of higher legal limits by increasing the size of its trucks and the load per truck, but average truck sizes have lagged behind legal limits. For example, the average gross weight of loaded combination trucks on main rural roads doubled (30,000 to 60,000 lb) between 1936 and 1983 (Figure 2-7), but throughout this period the average weight was about 25 percent below typical legal maximums (*11,15,17–21*). There is a lag for three reasons: carriers of

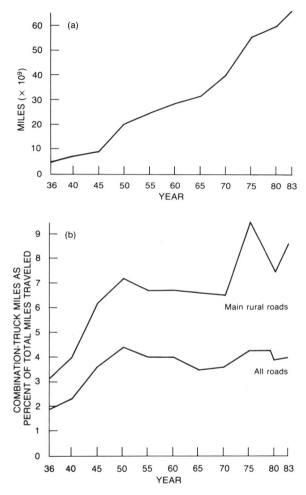

FIGURE 2-6 (*a*) Miles traveled annually and (*b*) share of total vehicle miles traveled for combination trucks, 1936–1983 (*11,15*).

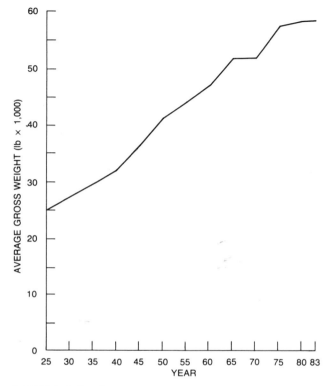

FIGURE 2-7   Gross weight of loaded combination trucks on main rural roads, 1925–1983 (*11,15,17–21*).

low-density freight are constrained by length and width limits rather than by weight, many carriers' loads are dictated by the size of a shipment or by delivery schedules rather than by legal limits, and large trucks have long useful lives—8 years for tractors and 12 years for trailers on average (*22*)—so adoption of new equipment occurs gradually.

Data on the length of trucks in use have never been systematically collected, but new-trailer sales data (*23*) show that the most popular trailer length increased from 24 ft in 1946 to 45 ft in 1973 and to 48 ft in 1984 (Figure 2-8). Not surprisingly, dimensions of new equipment purchased have tracked changes in state size and weight limits more closely than have the sizes of vehicles in use.

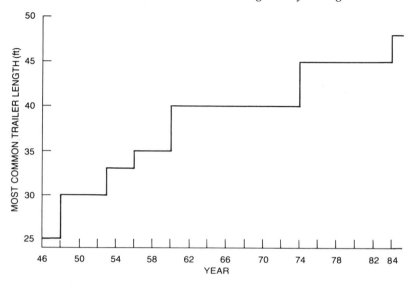

FIGURE 2-8   Length of new van trailers sold, 1946–1984 *(23)*.

As with weight limits, changes in legal lengths are more important to some segments of the trucking industry than to others. Today, greater lengths benefit mainly carriers and shippers of low-density cargoes, whereas carriers of high-density goods (for example, crushed stone or dry chemicals in hopper trailers or coiled steel on flatbeds) are constrained by the weight limit and have no use for added length. During the 1940s and 1950s, however, increases in length limits from 45 to 50 or 55 ft in many states had the effect of allowing heavier trucks by making it practical for truckers to replace four-axle combinations with five-axle ones.

The adoption of heavier and longer vehicles has been accompanied by changes in the standard configuration of trucks. Tractor-semitrailers replaced straight trucks as the predominant intercity freight vehicle in the 1930s. Until the early 1950s the most common combination was a three-axle tractor-semitrailer (two-axle tractor with a single-axle semitrailer) *(19,20,24–27)*. From the 1950s to about 1960 the four-axle tractor-semitrailer was the most common. By the early 1960s most states had length limits of 50 ft or more and weight limits over 70,000 lb, and as a result the five-axle tractor-semitrailer (a three-axle tractor with a two-axle semitrailer) became the standard truck for intercity freight, which it remains today (Figure 2-9).

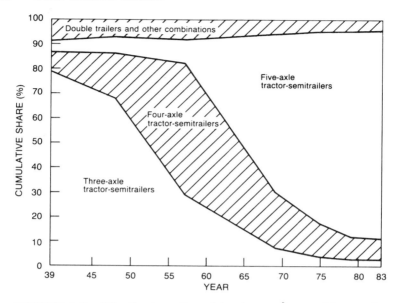

FIGURE 2-9   Distribution of combination-truck travel by configuration type, main rural roads, 1939–1983 (*19,20,24–27*).

State length and weight limits allowed five-axle tractor-semitrailers much earlier in the West than in the East. The popularity of that vehicle in the West, together with the promise of some savings in pavement wear from distributing truck loads over more axles, presumably influenced the eastern states to adjust their limits to permit five-axle combinations (*28*). This pattern in which new truck types and sizes appeared first in the West and then expanded eastward was repeated in the 1960s and 1970s with twins.

Highway Development Trends

The extent and capacity of the U.S. road system and the employment of road design features that enhance safety have increased dramatically in the past half-century. Better roads have made trucks a more attractive and efficient means of transporting freight and have made large trucks safer to operate.

The extent of paved roads in the United States has increased 10-fold since the 1920s, to over 2 million mi today (Figure 2-10). Of state-

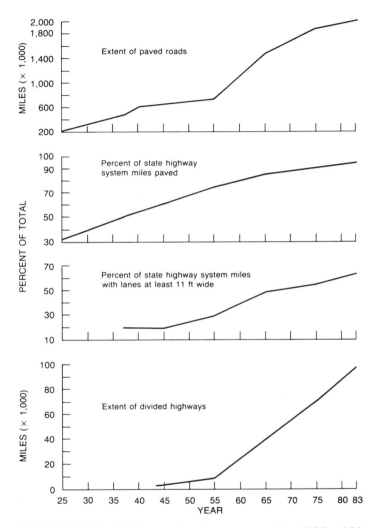

FIGURE 2-10   Highway development trends, 1925–1983
(*11,15*).

maintained roads (generally the major rural routes in each state) less than one-third were paved in 1925; today nearly all are. Improved designs for new and reconstructed roads have incorporated wider lanes, more gradual curves and grades, and separation of conflicting traffic by means of divided highways and access control. The fraction of all state-maintained paved roads with lanes at least 11 ft wide has increased from 20 percent in 1937 to over 60 percent at present. Miles of divided highways increased from 2,600 in 1944 to 100,000 today, including 42,000 mi of Interstates built, for the most part, to the highest design standards. Although they constitute only 2 percent of paved-road mileage, the Interstates carry 20 percent of all motor vehicle travel (15).

The development of the road system has stimulated the growth of trucking by opening all parts of the country to service by truck, by providing roads that can physically accommodate bigger trucks and higher speeds, and by improving the safety of large-truck operations. However, it would be an oversimplification to say that the construction of the modern road system created today's trucking industry—cause and effect have operated in both directions. The damage done by heavy trucks to earth and gravel roads was a principal motive for beginning to pave rural roads in the 1920s (12), and the requirements of large-truck traffic have always dictated the structural features of road design—the strength of pavements and the load-bearing capacity of bridges. Defense needs for material and equipment transportation were a major justification for building the Interstate system. Demands for better roads to serve trucks have influenced highway development as much as better roads have stimulated trucking.

Although the average design standards of roads have improved in recent decades, road conditions are highly diverse, and the system today contains many miles of roads not up to current standards, constraining the size of trucks that may practically and safely be operated. The question of appropriate size and weight limits on these roads of older design has been the critical issue in selecting the designated network of roads where twins and the other recently federally authorized trucks are permitted.

Truck Accident Trends

In this section the available data on trends in the number of large-truck accidents are presented first, followed by trends in large-truck accident rates.

Lack of data hinders development of a complete picture of large-truck accident trends. Comprehensive nationwide statistics on fatal accident involvements classified by vehicle type have been compiled only since 1975 by the National Highway Traffic Safety Administration (NHTSA)

Fatal Accident Reporting System (*29*), although the National Safety Council has published rough estimates of combination-truck accidents, based on reports from a few states, since 1968 (*30*). There is little reliable historical nationwide information on injuries or nonfatal accidents involving large trucks; NHTSA's National Accident Sampling System (*31*) has compiled such data since 1979, but the sample size for large trucks in that program is small, so the estimates are uncertain. The Federal Highway Administration (FHWA) has since 1936 estimated annual combination-truck miles traveled (*32*), which is essential for computing accident rates, but these estimates are derived indirectly by piecing together data from a variety of sources, and their validity is unknown.

Frequency

In 1983, combination trucks' shares of vehicle registrations, miles traveled, and accident involvements were as follows (*29,31–33*):

	All Vehicles	*Combinations*	
		No.	*Percent*
Vehicles registered	169.4 million	1.3 million	0.7
Vehicle miles traveled	1,649 billion	66 billion	4.0
Vehicles involved in all police-reported accidents	9.9 million	220,000	2.2
Vehicles involved in fatal accidents	55,000	3,600	6.6

In addition to combination trucks, about 400 heavy (over 26,000 lb gross weight) single-unit trucks were involved in fatal accidents. Of the 42,600 people killed in highway traffic accidents in 1983, 4,200 died in accidents involving combination trucks, and another 500 died in accidents involving heavy single-unit trucks. About 50,000 to 75,000 nonfatal injuries occurred in heavy-truck accidents. Property damage in heavy-truck accidents was roughly $500 million to $1 billion (*34*).

According to NHTSA (*29*), the number of combination trucks involved each year in fatal accidents increased slightly between 1975 and 1983, and the fraction of all vehicles involved in fatal accidents that were combination trucks increased from 5.6 percent in 1975 to 6.6 percent in 1983 (Figure 2-11).

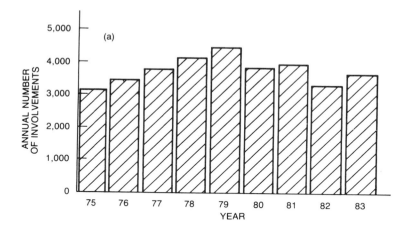

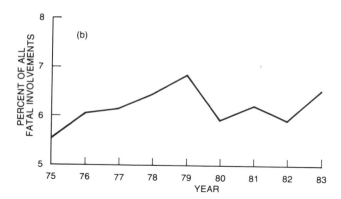

FIGURE 2-11   Fatal accident involvements of combination trucks, 1975-1983: (*a*) annual frequency and (*b*) proportion of all fatal involvements (*29*). [NOTE: The Fatal Accident Reporting System data file for 1975 shows 2,878 combination-truck involvements. The value plotted (3,099) contains an adjustment of 221 additional involvements as an estimate of missing accidents in six states where reported heavy-truck involvements were implausibly low in 1975.]

Involvement Rates per Mile Traveled

Virtually all data sources available indicate that heavy trucks and combination trucks (which account for nearly 90 percent of heavy-truck travel) have higher fatal involvement rates than other vehicles. This relationship appears to hold for all road classes (e.g., Interstates and non-Interstates), in both urban and rural areas, and in data reported for individual states and sample road segments as well as in aggregate nationwide statistics. According to NHTSA accident data and FHWA travel estimates, 1983 nationwide rates were 5.5 fatal involvements per 100 million mi for combination trucks and 3.3 for all vehicles.

Total accident involvement rates for combination trucks apparently are lower than those for other vehicles, although this comparison is uncertain because data on involvements by road class are sparse and because of widely varying definitions of accidents. Nationwide rates for 1983 from NHTSA data for accident involvements and FHWA travel data were 332 involvements per 100 million mi traveled for combination trucks and 620 for all vehicles.

Aggregate involvement rate comparisons tend to show combination trucks in a more favorable light than comparisons under similar operating conditions, because a relatively high share of combination-truck travel is on Interstates and in rural areas, where accident rates for all vehicles are lower than those on other road classes.

The consequences of accidents involving heavy trucks differ on average from those when no heavy truck is involved. The average number of fatalities per fatal accident (*29*) and the ratio of fatal involvements to fatal and injury involvements (*33*) are higher for heavy trucks than for other vehicles. Eighty-three percent of the fatalities in 1983 heavy-truck accidents were not heavy-truck occupants (*29*).

Trends in Involvement Rates

Combination-truck involvement rates from NHTSA fatal and all-accident involvement data and FHWA travel estimates show rising rates in the late 1970s and a decline in the early 1980s (Figure 2-12). This pattern may be partly explained by the effect of economic cycles on accident rates. The pattern of rising rates in the late 1970s and falling or level rates in the 1980s holds on both Interstate and non-Interstate roads, according to NHTSA involvement data for heavy trucks and FHWA travel estimates by road class.

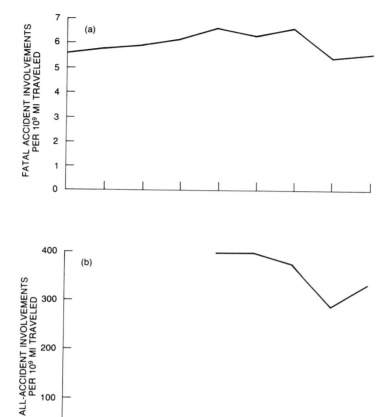

FIGURE 2-12   (a) Fatal accident involvement rate and (b) all-accident involvement rate of combination trucks, 1975–1983 (29,31,32).

The trend in the ratio of the combination-truck involvement rate to the all-vehicle involvement rate shows a moderate rise throughout the period 1975–1983 (Figure 2-13).

Data from National Safety Council Fleet Safety Contest (30) allow an independent check on the trends computed from NHTSA involvement data

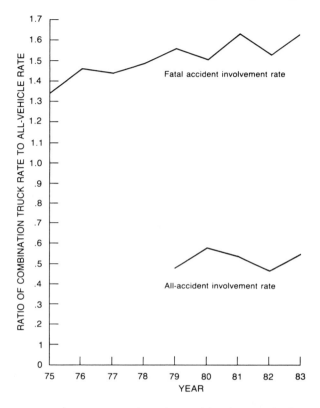

FIGURE 2-13   Ratio of combination-truck involvement rate to all-vehicle involvement rate, 1975–1983 *(29,31,32)*.

and FHWA travel estimates and indicate trends over a longer time span. The Council has compiled annual motor carrier accident rates since 1929. The rates have generally declined throughout this period (Figure 2-14). Although the experience of the self-selected group of carriers participating in the contest may be unrepresentative of the experience of all combination trucks in any given year, it is plausible that the long-term trend in the contest results parallels the trend for all heavy trucks.

Involvement Rates per Ton-Mile

Even if incremental increases in the sizes of heavy trucks led to higher accident costs per truck or per truck mile, the net effect of increased

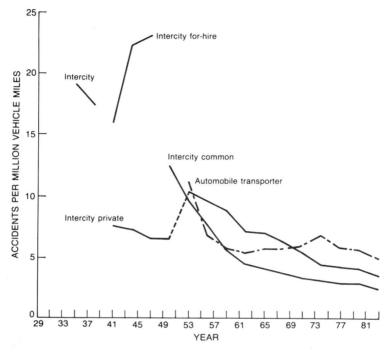

FIGURE 2-14   Fleet accident rates reported to NSC, 1933–1983 (*30*). [NOTE: Data reported are 3-year averages for all intercity fleets participating for 1933–1937, for intercity for-hire and intercity private fleets in 1938–1947, for intercity private and intercity common carriers in 1948–1951, and for various categories of intercity for-hire carriers (including common and automobile transporter) and private carriers since 1951.]

size on highway safety would be positive if a reduction in the number of trucks on the road (because of greater capacity per truck) could offset higher safety costs per truck. The trend in accident involvement rates per ton-mile of freight carried may therefore be a more meaningful measure than rates per vehicle mile for determining whether the overall safety performance of motor freight transportation is deteriorating.

The cargo load carried by combination trucks has increased more or less continuously since these trucks were first introduced. From 1969 to 1983 the average load of combination trucks on the nation's roads (including empty truck miles) increased 15 percent, from 8.7 to 10 tons (*26,27,24*). During this period, FHWA-estimated vehicle miles increased 80 percent, implying a 108 percent increase in combination-truck ton-miles.

If combination-truck ton-miles estimated by multiplying average load by FHWA miles traveled is used for the exposure measure, fatal-accident involvement rates (involvements per ton-mile) during 1975–1983 grew more slowly (or declined more rapidly) than did rates of involvement per mile traveled (compare Figures 2-15 and 2-12).

The following table gives a comparison of the total percentage change in combination-truck fatal accident involvement rates per vehicle mile and per ton-mile and all-vehicle fatal involvement rate per vehicle mile for three periods: the full terms for which data are available, the period

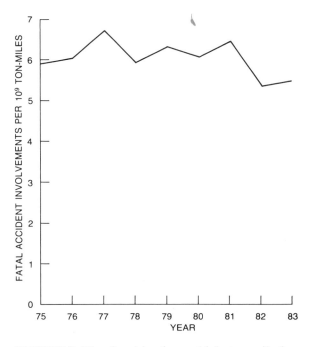

FIGURE 2-15   Combination-vehicle ton-mile fatal accident involvement rate, 1975–1983 (*26,27,29,31,32*).

in which the combination-truck rate appears to have been increasing rapidly (1975–1981), and recent experience (1981–1983):

	Change in Fatal-Accident Involvement Rate (%)		
	Combination Trucks		All Vehicles
Period	Per Vehicle Mile Traveled	Per Ton-Mile	per Vehicle Mile Traveled
Total (1975–1983)	− 1	− 7	− 20
Rapid increase (1975–1981)	18	10	− 3
Recent experience (1981–1983)	− 16	− 15	− 17

The two combination-truck series agree in showing an overall decline in the fatal involvement rate for the full period of the data, an increase in 1975–1981, and a decrease in recent years. In every time period, the change in safety performance for combination trucks is less favorable than the change for all vehicles.

Summary

Intercity trucking has grown from a minor transport mode in the 1920s to one of critical importance, and today it is a $100-billion-a-year industry. Therefore the benefits from improvement in trucking efficiency are large. The trucking industry has responded to changes in size limits by employing ever larger vehicles, but most freight trucks on the road are well below legal limits and incremental changes in limits usually directly affect only a particular segment of the industry. A common historical pattern has been that once a new or larger truck type becomes established and popular in one part of the country, pressures are created to allow its use nationwide. Although improvements to road design have to some extent kept pace with the growth of truck sizes and traffic volumes, many links in the road network have not been upgraded to modern standards and pose problems for the operation of the largest legal trucks.

Heavy trucks are involved in fatal accidents about twice as often per mile traveled as other vehicles when accident rates for the two classes of vehicles on similar roads are compared. The heavy-truck total accident involvement rate (that is, involvements in property-damage, injury, and fatal accidents combined) per mile traveled is lower than the rate for other vehicles but this difference is in large part because heavy trucks travel a higher percentage of time on Interstates and on rural roads.

The long-term nationwide trend (over the past 50 years) in heavy-truck accident involvement rates certainly has been downward—accident involvement rates for intercity freight trucks reported in the 1930s were as much as five times higher than rates typical today.[5] Heavy-truck accident involvement rates increased in the late 1970s and stabilized or fell in the early 1980s. The available data on the frequency of truck accidents and on the miles traveled by trucks are of poor quality, so following trends in truck accident rates or comparing truck rates with those of other vehicles is difficult and entails much uncertainty.

Summary Points: Trends in Truck Use and Size, Highway Development, and Accidents

---

- As the states have gradually liberalized size and weight limits, trucking has grown to become a primary component of the freight transportation system, the average size of trucks in use has increased, and U.S. roads have been greatly improved. These concurrent trends have influenced state decisions on size and weight limits and have themselves been accelerated by the evolution of state truck size regulations.
- Trucking's share of intercity freight transportation grew from 1936 through 1983:

	1936	1983
Combination-truck miles traveled ($\times 10^9$)	5	66
Share of intercity freight ton-miles (%)	7	32

- Truck size and weight limits have also increased over the same period:

	1936	1983
Average length of combination trucks (ft)	36	58
Average weight of loaded combination truck (lb $\times$ 1,000)	30	60

---

[5]A variety of factors like better roads and better brakes contributed to this decline in accident involvement rates. Imposition of the 55 mph nationwide speed limit in 1974 probably contributed as well.

- State highway development shows the following trends:

	1937	1983
Miles paved (%)	49	94
Miles with lane width at least 11 ft (%)	20	64
Miles of divided highways (%)	—	12

- Combination-truck accidents and rates since 1976 (according to NHTSA and FHWA data) show the following trends:

	1976	1983
Fatal involvements	3,400	3,600
Fatal involvement rate (per 10^8 mi)	5.7	5.5

THE 1983 FEDERAL TRUCK SIZE AND WEIGHT PROVISIONS

The Surface Transportation Assistance Act of 1982 (35), passed by Congress in December 1982 and signed into law in January 1983, expanded the federal role in motor vehicle size and weight regulation. For the first time, states were required to raise limits that were more restrictive than the federal ones, and for the first time federal limits applied to some roads other than Interstates. The act continued federal regulation of weight and width and added rules on length and the allowable number of trailers—two vehicle dimensions not previously subject to federal controls.

In the sections that follow, a description is given of the content of the new regulations, their origins and objectives, why they have been controversial, and revisions to the original law. In Appendix B the characteristics of the network of roads designated for use by the larger vehicles and administrative procedures governing this network are described.

Content

The size and weight provisions of the act are reproduced in Appendix A, and are summarized and contrasted with previous federal and state limits as follows:

- *Weight limits* (Section 133 of the act): States were required to allow on the Interstate system single-axle weights of 20,000 lb and tandem-axle weights of 34,000 lb and a gross weight of 80,000 lb overall on vehicles with five or more axles, subject to a restriction imposing lower gross weight limits on heavy trucks with short wheelbases. The states also were prohibited from enacting new laws setting limits higher than these, but the grandfather exemptions of the 1956 and 1974 federal weight standards were retained. The states were prohibited from denying reasonable access from the Interstates to terminals and to food, fuel, repair, and rest facilities. Noncomplying states would have their federal highway aid apportionments withheld.

These weight limits were the same as those under previous law, but for the first time states were prohibited from imposing a lower limit. Three states with limits of less than 80,000 lb were affected (Arkansas, Missouri, and Illinois). The access provision was new and would have been irrelevant under the old law (because no state had been required to allow higher weights on Interstates than those that it allowed on non-Interstate roads).

• *Trailer length* (Sec. 411a): States were prohibited from limiting the length of the semitrailer in a single-trailer combination to less than 48 ft or each trailer of a combination with two trailers to less than 28 ft on the Interstates and on certain other roads in the federal-aid primary system to be designated for use by vehicles of the authorized dimensions by the Secretary of Transportation.

There had previously been no federal length limit. This provision overruled semitrailer length limits below 48 ft (or overall length limits that effectively barred 48-ft semitrailers) in 35 states (Figure 2-3) on the affected roads.

• *Overall combination-vehicle length* (Sec. 411b): The states were prohibited from enacting any overall length limit on tractor-semitrailers or combinations with two trailers.

The length limits of all 50 states on the designated roads were overruled. Although the wording of this provision did not restrict its application to any particular class of roads, the U.S. Department of Transportation has interpreted the provision as applying only to the designated network where the federal trailer length limits apply [23 Code of Federal Regulations, Sec. 658.13 (a)]. Vehicle lengths are constrained in practice by the trailer length limits.

• *Prior length limits* (Sec. 411b): The states were prohibited from enforcing any reduction of trailer size limits that would have the effect of banning trailers that were legal and actually in use before 1983.

This provision was a strong form of grandfather clause, because not only did it allow the states to retain higher existing length limits, it required them to do so.

• *Twin trailer trucks* (Sec. 411c): States were required to allow use of combinations consisting of a tractor and two trailing units on the Interstates and the network of primary roads to be designated by the Secretary of Transportation.

This provision together with the one concerning trailer lengths in effect required all states to permit twin trailer trucks with each trailer at least 28 ft long. Fourteen states had barred twins with the previous industry standard of 27-ft trailers and 65-ft overall length (Figure 2-2). Although some twin 28-ft trailers had been in use before 1983, they generally employed a short tractor and narrow spacing between trailers (which required modified trailer ends to allow turning) to conform to a 65-ft overall length limit, the most common pre-1983 limit on twins. With the federal prohibition of state overall length limits, twins today typically have overall lengths greater than the previous 65-ft limits.

• *Designated network* (Sec. 411e): The Secretary of Transportation was to designate as roads where the states would be required to allow 48-ft semitrailers and twins (in addition to the entire Interstate system) those federal-aid primary highways capable of safely accommodating the allowed vehicle lengths. An initial determination of roads was to be made within 3 months, a final determination within 9 months, and the Secretary could revise the designations as necessary.

• *Reasonable access* (Sec. 412): The states were prohibited from denying reasonable access by twins and 48-ft semitrailers from the Interstates and designated primaries to terminals; facilities for food, fuel, repairs, and rest; and points of loading and unloading for household goods carriers.

• *Enforcement* (Sec. 412): The Secretary of Transportation was to institute civil action for injunctive relief if necessary to assure state compliance with the federal rules (other than the weight limit).

• *Vehicle width* (Sec. 416): The states were required to allow vehicles up to 102 in. wide on Interstates and federal-aid highways designed for 12-ft lanes and designated by the Secretary. (This provision was originally passed earlier, in 1982. It was incorporated by amendment into the Surface Transportation Assistance Act, and its effective date and enforcement mechanism made consistent with those of the other size provisions in April 1983.)

The previous federal limit was 96 in., applicable only on Interstates. Width limits were superseded in 40 states (Figure 2-4).

Another major provision in the 1983 act was an increase in taxes on highway users, with the revenues devoted to federal aid for highways and transit. The increases for heavy trucks were substantial. The federal tax on diesel fuel and gasoline was raised from 4 to 9 cents per gallon, the excise on sales of new heavy trucks and trailers was increased from 10 percent of factory price to 12 percent of retail price, the excise tax on heavy tires was increased, and the federal heavy-vehicle use fee (an annual tax on heavy trucks that increases with the gross weight of the truck) was to be raised incrementally over 4 years so that eventually the fee on an 80,000-lb truck would be increased from $240 annually under the old law to $1,900 annually.

The new federal rules created a nationwide network of major routes where trucks of the specified dimensions could operate, and these dimensions included the longest vehicles then in widespread use, with the exception of multitrailer combinations over 80,000 lb. Nonetheless, the new rules did not impose stringent nationwide uniformity. The grandfather provisions exempting states with higher weight limits were retained; the states were barred from rolling back preexisting higher trailer length limits; and weight limits off the Interstates and all limits on roads other than Interstates and the federally designated primary roads were left at the discretion of the states, except for the reasonable-access requirement.

Origins

In the history of federal involvement in truck size and weight regulation until 1982, a strong reluctance to preempt the traditional authorities of the states is shown. Congress had acknowledged some concern for the problem of nonuniform state regulations by commissioning several studies on national size and weight limits, but for 26 years the principal federal limit in effect specified maximum weights on the Interstates.

One key event that finally stimulated federal action toward uniformity was the fiscal crisis facing the highway program in the late 1970s. The inflation, slow economic growth, and fuel shortages of the period combined to depress highway revenues and accelerate construction and maintenance costs, and highway agencies found that they were unable to keep pace with the backlog of maintenance and expansion needs. Higher road user taxes were needed to reverse the trend, and the consensus formed that heavy trucks would have to pay a substantial share of the added tax burden. The size and weight limits and the tax increases in the 1983 act thus made up a unified package, with the liberalized federal size and weight rules serving as compensation to the trucking industry for the increased tax burden.

Two studies commissioned by Congress in the 1978 highway act, one on truck size and weight and one on road user taxation, supplied the technical basis for the package of greater size limits and higher taxes. In the truck size and weight study, the U.S. Department of Transportation (DOT) was to examine "the need for, and desirability of, uniformity in maximum truck size and weight limits throughout the United States. . ." [36,Sec.161(a)]. DOT's study (37,p.III-1), transmitted to Congress in October 1981, was a comprehensive benefit-cost analysis of the likely effects of various alternative nationwide uniform weight limits (at 80,000 lb gross weight in most cases analyzed) and length limits (requiring the states to allow at least 65 ft), and nationwide legalization of twins on the Interstates or on all Interstates and federal-aid primary roads. It concluded that with nationwide uniformity at limits that were then common in many states, "transport cost savings (from improved truck productivity) could overwhelm the associated costs of increased highway and bridge wear and tear and truck accident costs" (37,pp.5-7). Net savings of several billion dollars annually were predicted. The report stressed the significance of several Midwestern "barrier states" with weight limits lower than those of the states to their east and west as a particularly costly case of non-uniformity impeding efficient freight movement.

The conclusions of the size and weight study contained an important qualification. The report warned that many pavements and bridges would have to be upgraded to carry heavier loads to achieve the full benefits predicted and that the required investments were beyond the means of the state highway agencies.

In the second study Congress directed DOT to determine the federal-aid highway program costs attributable to each of the various classes of users and vehicles and to recommend a tax structure to "achieve an equitable distribution of the tax burden among classes" (36,Sec. 506). Congress had commissioned a similar study when it created the current federal user-tax-based highway finance system in 1956. DOT submitted the new highway cost allocation study to Congress in May 1982 (38). It concluded that tax revenues from heavy trucks were less than the costs allocated to them.

The cost-allocation study and the truck size and weight study together demonstrated the need for coordination between size and weight regulation and highway-user taxation. The size and weight study had emphasized this linkage when it warned that the states were financially unable to undertake the investments in highway improvements necessary to gain the greatest net benefits from higher uniform truck size limits, and the cost-allocation study established the relationship between the sizes of trucks and their cost responsibilities.

The connection between the size and weight provisions and truck tax provisions of the 1983 act was clearly acknowledged in the proceedings before its enactment. In hearings on the bill, the then Secretary of Transportation commented (39,p.24):

> I think it is only fair to point out that the gains as we see them conservatively to this industry will be about $3.8 billion annually and the taxes imposed about $1.7 billion. So this industry is going to receive about a two to one return.

With the framework of the 1983 act thus established, the specifics of the size and weight rules were worked out in a series of compromises among the affected parties. The background of each of the major provisions is described in the following paragraphs.

Truck Weight

The weight limits of the act were the same as the existing federal limits; requiring the states to allow trucks meeting the federal limits on their Interstates was to eliminate the barrier-state situation highlighted in the truck size and weight study.

Twin Trailer Trucks

Obtaining nationwide rights to use twins had been a top priority of general freight common carriers, a segment of the industry that includes the largest for-hire trucking firms. In suits by trucking firms against the states, 1978 and 1981 U.S. Supreme Court decisions struck down restrictions on the operation of twin trailer trucks in Wisconsin and Iowa. The court found that the state regulations were a substantial burden on interstate commerce, discriminated in favor of shipments to or from the states over freight passing through them, and, on the safety question, that "the state failed to present any persuasive evidence that 65-foot doubles are less safe than 55-foot singles" (*40,41*).

The court decisions provided a strong argument for federal legislation allowing twins. During hearings on the 1983 law, a Senate supporter of the bill concluded (*39*,p.2):

> There is absolutely no doubt that under this Supreme Court ruling Federal courts will be striking down these laws [state laws prohibiting twins] one by one. All we are doing in this bill is saving the enormous legal fees that would be generated by the litigation that is inevitable.

Combination-Truck Length

The most common state length limit in 1982 was 65 ft, and Congress considered enacting this limit as the federal standard. However, the International Brotherhood of Teamsters, representing unionized drivers, objected to this form of length limit on grounds that it created safety problems. Specifically, the Teamsters objected to the use of cab-over-engine tractors (in which the driver's compartment is located above the engine rather than behind it as in the conventional design), which had been adopted by the industry in order to obtain the greatest possible semitrailer length in states that regulated the overall length of tractor-semitrailer combinations but not the length of the semitrailer itself. Use of a cab-over-engine tractor rather than the conventional design allows up to about 7 ft more of semitrailer length within a given overall vehicle length limit. In testimony at hearings on the 1983 law, the union argued that many cab-over-engine tractors were unsafe and uncomfortable for drivers, and recommended as a remedy that length regulations apply only to the semitrailer and not to the overall vehicle or that both lengths be regulated but that 15 ft be provided for the tractor (*42*). Trucking industry spokesmen objected to any semitrailer length limit less than 48 ft. The length limit enacted— that states must allow at least 48-ft long semitrailers and unlimited overall length for either twins or single-trailer combinations—responded to both industry and labor concerns.

The 28-ft limit for each trailer of a twin trailer truck was 1 ft longer than the most common trailer length in twins at the time, although some 28-ft trailers were then in use.

Vehicle Width

AASHTO had recommended a 102-in. width limit on Interstates and other roads with adequate lane width since 1964, and the federal limits had allowed 102-in. wide buses on Interstates since 1976. Paralleling the AASHTO recommended policy, the 1983 act (before amendments) specified that 102-in. wide vehicles were to be permitted only on Interstates and on other roads with 12-ft lanes.

The Designated Network

Congress devised the designated-network concept as a compromise between limiting the allowed vehicles to the Interstate system, an approach that would have removed most objections to the new size limits on safety grounds but would have severely curtailed the utility of the larger vehicles, and permitting them on all major federal-aid routes (the federal-aid primary system), an approach that would have imposed few practical limits on the use of the vehicles. One senator supporting the bill, in hearings before its passage, described this purpose (*39*, p. 2):

> It is important, therefore, to include all the highways of major interstate commerce. Limiting this to the interstate highway system alone will not do the trick. I think we have found a way to include the major arteries of interstate commerce, but still exclude those roads

where the new standards would cause unsafe conditions, and I feel we can do this with a minimum of regulation and bureaucracy.

Controversy over Implementation

On April 5, 1983, FHWA published in the *Federal Register* a list of the federal-aid primary routes it had selected as an interim designated network, and the truck size and weight provisions of the Surface Transportation Assistance Act of 1982 became effective. Because the act produced major changes in the existing system of size and weight regulation, it is not surprising that its implementation created controversy; state highway agencies, the trucking industry, and other interested parties objected to many specific provisions of the act or to FHWA's interpretation of them.

The States' Positions

Opinions varied among state agencies, because the act constituted a much more drastic alteration of existing limits in some states than in others. The principal concerns raised by at least some states included the following (*43*):

• Some of the specific limits were considered too high. Twins were the major concern in the East and some central states where they had not been common, but in other parts of the country the 48-ft semitrailer provision attracted the greatest objections. The states knew that many of the curves and intersections in their systems were designed with much shorter combinations than a tractor and a 48-ft semitrailer in mind and feared safety problems from introduction of the longer trucks.

• Several states contested the routes selected by FHWA for the network, especially roads with lanes less than 12 ft wide or alignment difficult for long vehicles to negotiate. Some states also argued that parts of their Interstate systems, which Congress had opened to the larger trucks without exception, were substandard and therefore unsuitable for the new trucks.

• More generally, the states objected to the scope of federal preemption of their authority over size and weight limits, arguing that the states need to retain control over the use of their highways especially where safety concerns exist, because they have the legal responsibility for their safe operation.

The April 1983 interim network comprised 137,000 mi of non-Interstate federal-aid primary roads, 54 percent of all roads in that system. In addition, under the provisions of the law the entire 42,000-mi Interstate system was opened to the allowed truck sizes. FHWA had previously requested that the states propose routes for inclusion in the system, but the April 1983 network included routes in a number of states (which totaled

40,000 mi) beyond those that the states had proposed. FHWA stated that these additional routes were necessary for continuity and to connect the network to major economic centers (44).

In April and May five states (Alabama, Florida, Georgia, Pennsylvania, and Vermont) brought suit in U.S. District Court to enjoin FHWA from designating the routes that the states had not nominated. Five other states disputed specific designations and in one state, Connecticut, the legislature passed a law, in direct conflict with the federal legislation, reiterating the state's ban on multitrailer trucks. In the following months FHWA revised the network repeatedly, mainly on the basis of consultations between the states and FHWA's state offices, and reached negotiated settlements with most of the objecting states. In all, nine notices of interim, proposed, or final route designations appeared in the *Federal Register* between April 5, 1983, and June 5, 1984, the date of the final rule (45).[6] FHWA successfully sued Connecticut to overturn the state's conflicting law (46).

An as-yet-unresolved federal-state conflict arose over the grandfather clause of the 1983 law prohibiting the states from adopting any limits that would make illegal semitrailers longer than 48 ft or individual trailers over 28 ft in a twin trailer combination if longer trailers were actually and lawfully operating on December 1, 1982, within a 65-ft overall length limit in the state. States with no trailer length limit in their laws but with an overall length limit that would in principle have permitted semitrailers over 48 ft argued that this provision was unenforceable because they had no way of determining what the longest legal trailer in the state was on a particular date. In several states industry claims that longer trailers had been in use and legal were disputed by the highway agency. It was not until March 1985 that FHWA proposed a rule listing 21 states with grandfathered semitrailer length limits greater than 48 ft (47), and several of these states disputed the federal determination.

Trucking Industry Positions

The overriding objection to the 1983 act from the trucking industry was the tax increase, especially the heavy-vehicle use tax. The industry disputed the methods used in the highway cost-allocation study to estimate the heavy-truck share of highway cost responsibilities (48). It also asserted that DOT's analyses overestimated by a factor of 2 the productivity savings from the new size and weight limits and that DOT overestimated by a

---

[6]Appendix B describes the current extent and condition of the federally designated network and other roads where the federally authorized vehicles may also operate and describes administrative procedures governing designation and access.

factor of 4 the net trucking cost savings after taxes (*49*). Truckers also argued that the costs and benefits of the law were inequitably distributed, because all large trucks would pay higher taxes but only certain segments of the industry would benefit from the new size limits. They claimed that most of the benefits would accrue to shippers and carriers of low-density commodities in the East, where size limits had been most restrictive and twin trailer trucks had been banned, but that shippers of high-density freight and shippers and carriers in the West, where limits had already been high, would receive little benefit (*43*, p. 326). Owner-operators, another segment of the industry who believed that the new size limits were of little practical importance to them, staged a strike in 1983 protesting the tax increases (*50*).

The industry also expressed frustration at the slowness with which the designated network and access provisions of the law were being implemented by FHWA and the states, the limited extent of the network in some states, and the access problems encountered, especially by 48-ft long by 102-in. wide semitrailers (*51*). Finally the industry pointed out an omission in the legislation's access requirements: Congress had specified that the states must give access between the designated network and terminals for 48-ft semitrailers, 102-in. wide vehicles, and twin trailer trucks, but made no requirement that the states allow use of the 102-in. by 28-ft individual trailers of a twin trailer truck for local pickup and delivery between terminals and shippers. The ability to use a 28-ft trailer in this manner is a major operational advantage of twins, and the industry claimed that without federal assurance that this use would be allowed, local restrictions could negate the practical benefits of twins (*52*).

Positions of Private Highway Safety Groups

In addition to the states and the trucking industry, several private organizations involved in highway matters were active in the debate over implementation of the new truck size rules. The American Automobile Association and affiliated state automobile clubs urged a conservative approach to designating routes and access for large trucks in order to guarantee that safety would not be downgraded. They also urged Congress to drop the provisions protecting trucks heavier and longer than the federal minimums, arguing that the grandfather provisions of the act actually exacerbated the problem of nonuniformity and would lead to a reemergence of complaints about barrier states and pressures on states with low limits to raise them to match more liberal limits in surrounding states (*43*, p. 287).

Another private group, the Center for Auto Safety, a nonprofit highway safety advocacy organization, sued FHWA to block its route designations on the grounds that FHWA had not adequately evaluated the safety of operating longer and wider trucks on the routes and had ignored the law's provision that the roads designated for 102-in. wide vehicles be highways "with traffic lanes designed to be a width of twelve feet or more" (*35*, Sec.416). FHWA's interim designation specified a single network for all of the new-dimension vehicles, which included roads with lanes less than 12 ft wide.

In a March 1984 preliminary ruling, the U.S. District Court stated that the Center for Auto Safety suit would probably be successful in its argument that the designation of roads that have lanes less than 12 ft wide for use by 102-in. wide trucks was contrary to the law (*53*); but Congress removed this difficulty by dropping the 12-ft lane width requirement in the 1984 Tandem Truck Safety Act (*54*), described in the following section.

Revisions

Some of the issues raised by the states, truck operators, and the other interested parties were resolved in the Tandem Truck Safety Act of 1984 (*54*), enacted in October. The following provisions were included:

● A procedure for the governor of a state to request that the Secretary of Transportation exempt segments of the Interstate system from one or more of the federal truck length and width requirements if the state first consulted with the governments of affected local communities and neighboring states and declared that it had found the segment unsafe for use by the larger truck sizes.

● A requirement that DOT could not designate any more roads for use by 102-in. wide vehicles without approval of the states in which the roads were located.

● An amendment to the original provision regarding 102-in. wide vehicles, dropping the requirement that designated roads be designed to be a width of 12 ft or more and replacing it with the requirement that the Secretary of Transportation designate roads for 102-in. wide trucks "if the Secretary determines that such designation is consistent with highway safety," language similar to the requirement for 48-ft semitrailers and twin trailer trucks.

● A requirement extending the reasonable-access provision to cover single trailers from a twin trailer truck used individually. However, the act affirmed the right of state or local governments to impose "any reasonable restriction, based on safety considerations" on the use of these 102-in. wide trailers.

The 1984 act thus further relaxed some restrictions on the use of the larger vehicles and at the same time gave the states a greater role in defining the designated network.

Congress also was sympathetic to the tax complaints of the trucking industry, which had been hard hit by the 1980–1983 recessions and was experiencing dislocations as a result of economic deregulation. A July 1984 law (55) reduced the heavy vehicle use tax to between $100 and $550 a year, depending on weight, and exempted all trucks below 55,000 lb. At the same time the diesel fuel tax was increased from 9 to 15 cents per gallon. The new tax was supposed to have no net effect on revenues, but tended to make the tax incurred by a truck more dependent on the miles it travels and less dependent on its weight.

Summary Points: The 1983 Federal Truck Size and Weight Provisions

- The major new federal limits enacted in 1983 and the federal limits they replaced were as follows:

	1983 Federal Law	*Previous Federal Law*
Weight	Trucks up to 80,000 lb allowed on all Interstates	States permitted to enact any limit less than 80,000 lb
Semitrailer length	States required to allow trailers 48 ft long on federally designated routes and access roads	None
Width	Vehicles up to 102 in. wide allowed on federally designated routes	Maximum of 96 in. applied to Interstates only
Twins	States required to allow on federally designated routes	None

- The 1983 limits expanded the federal role in regulating truck size and weight. They were the first federal rules that forced states to change their own existing size and weight limits and the first to apply to roads other than Interstates.
- The objectives of expanding federal control over size and weight were to remove barriers to efficient freight movement created by nonuniform state size and weight limits and to compensate truckers, through more liberal limits, for higher road user taxes enacted at the same time.

REFERENCES

1. U.S. Congress. House. Interstate Commerce Commission. *Federal Regulation of the Sizes and Weight of Motor Vehicles*. H. Doc. 354, 77th Congress, 1st Session, Aug. 14, 1941.

2. J. Galligan and D.M. DiNunzio. "Guide to Trucking Rules and Regulations." *Commercial Carrier Journal*, April 1983.

3. *The Truck Weight Problem in Highway Transportation*. HRB Bulletin 26. Highway Research Board, National Research Council, Washington, D.C., July 1950.

4. "State Legal Maximum Dimensions and Weights of Motor Vehicles Compared with AASHO Standards." *Public Roads*, Vol. 33, No. 1, April 1964.

5. *Legal Maximum Dimensions and Weights of Motor Vehicles Compared with AASHTO Standards, December 1, 1981*. American Association of State Highway and Transportation Officials, Washington, D.C., 1982.

6. B. Mertz. *Legislative History of 65 Foot Twin Trailers*. American Trucking Associations, Washington, D.C., July 2, 1971; April 28, 1983.

7. *Maximum Desirable Dimensions and Weights of Vehicles Operated on the Federal-Aid Systems*. Bureau of Public Roads, U.S. Department of Commerce, Aug. 1964, pp. 9–10.

8. *Gross Weight, Dimensions, and Speed for Vehicles Operating on the Highways*. American Association of State Highway Officials, Washington, D.C., Nov. 17, 1932.

9. *Policy Covering Maximum Dimensions, Weights, and Speeds of Motor Vehicles to be Operated over the Highways of the United States*. American Association of State Highway Officials, Washington, D.C., 1946.

10. *Policy on Maximum Dimensions and Weights of Motor Vehicles to be Operated Over the Highways of the United States*. American Association of State Highway Officials, Washington, D.C., 1964, 1968, 1973, 1974, 1980.

11. *Highway Statistics Summary to 1975*. FHWA, U.S. Department of Transportation, 1977.

12. "The Highways of the Country and the Burdens They Must Carry." *Public Roads*, Vol. 1, No. 2, June 1918.

13. F. Smith. *Transportation in America*. Transportation Policy Associates, Washington, D.C., March 1985.

14. *Yearbook of Railroad Facts 1982*. Association of American Railroads, Washington, D.C., 1982.

15. *Highway Statistics* (annual). FHWA, U.S. Department of Transportation, 1946–1985.

16. *1977 Census of Transportation: Commodity Transportation Survey*. Bureau of the Census, U.S. Department of Commerce, 1977.

17. *Report of a Survey of Transportation on the State Highway System of Ohio*. U.S. Bureau of Public Roads; Ohio Department of Highways and Public Works, Columbus, 1927.

18. *Report of a Study of Highway Traffic and the Highway System of Cook County, Illinois.* U.S. Bureau of Public Roads; Cook County Highway Department, Ill., 1925.

19. J. Lynch and T. Dimmick. "Amount and Characteristics of Trucking on Rural Roads." *Public Roads*, Vol. 23, No. 9, July-Aug.-Sept. 1943.

20. T. Dimmick. "Traffic Trends on Rural Roads in 1945." *Public Roads*, Vol. 24, No. 10, Oct.-Nov.-Dec. 1946.

21. M. Kent and H. Stevens. "Dimensions and Weights of Highway Trailer Combinations and Trucks, 1959." *Public Roads*, Vol. 32, No. 12, Feb. 1964.

22. D. Anderson. *Forecasting Motor Carrier Traffic Demand and Equipment Requirements.* Data Resources, Inc., Washington, D.C., 1979.

23. *Van Trailer Size Report* (biennial). Truck Trailer Manufacturers Association, Alexandria, Va., 1982, 1984.

24. *Annual Truck Weight Study* (magnetic tape). FHWA, U.S. Department of Transportation, 1969-1984.

25. U.S. Congress. House. U.S. Department of Commerce. *Third Progress Report of the Highway Cost Allocation Study*, H. Doc. 91, 86th Congress, 1st Session, 1959.

26. P. Kent and M. Branes. *1975 National Truck Characteristic Report.* FHWA, U.S. Department of Transportation, April 1978.

27. P. Kent and M. Robey. *1975-1979 National Truck Characteristic Report.* FHWA, U.S. Department of Transportation, June 1981.

28. J. Lynch and T. Dimmick. "Axle-Load and Gross-Load Trends." *Public Roads*, Vol. 25, No. 12, Feb. 1950.

29. *Fatal Accident Reporting System* (annual). National Highway Traffic Safety Administration, U.S. Department of Transportation, 1976–1985.

30. *Accident Facts* (annual). National Safety Council, Chicago, Ill., 1930–1985.

31. *National Accident Sampling System* (annual). National Highway Traffic Safety Administration, U.S. Department of Transportation, 1980–1984.

32. *Highway Statistics* (annual). FHWA, U.S. Department of Transportation, 1955–1983.

33. *National Accident Sampling System 1983.* National Highway Traffic Safety Administration, U.S. Department of Transportation, Jan. 1985.

34. *Accidents of Motor Carriers of Property* (annual). Bureau of Motor Carrier Safety, U.S. Department of Transportation, FHWA, 1981–1985.

35. Public Law 97-424 (Jan. 6, 1983), *Surface Transportation Assistance Act of 1982*, 96 Stat. 2097.

36. Public Law 95-599 (Nov. 6, 1978), *Surface Transportation Assistance Act of 1978.*

37. *An Investigation of Truck Size and Weight Limits: Final Report.* U.S. Department of Transportation, Aug. 1981.

38. *Final Report of the Highway Cost Allocation Study.* U.S. Department of Transportation, May 1982.

39. U.S. Congress. Senate. Committee on Commerce, Science, and Transportation. *Highway Revenue Act of 1982,* Hearings. . . 97th Congress, Dec. 3, 1982 (Serial No. 97-144, p. 24).

40. *Raymond Motor Transportation, Inc., et al. v. Rice, Secretary, Wisconsin Department of Transportation,* 76-558, U.S. Supreme Court, February 21, 1978.

41. *Raymond Kassel et al. v. Consolidated Freightways Corporation of Delaware,* 79-1320, U.S. Supreme Court, March 24, 1981, p. 7.

42. U.S. Congress. Senate. Committee on Commerce, Science, and Transportation, *Uniform Motor Vehicle Standards Act,* Hearings. . . 97th Congress, Sept. 24, 1981 (Serial No. 97-74, p. 21).

43. U.S. Congress. Senate. Committee on Environment and Public Works. *Anticipated Economic Effects of the Surface Transportation Assistance Act of 1982,* Hearings. . . 98th Congress, 1983 (Serial No. 98-447).

44. "Truck Size." *Federal Register,* Vol. 48, No. 170, Aug. 31, 1983, p. 39592.

45. "Truck Size and Weight." *Federal Register,* June 6, 1984, pp. 23310–23311.

46. "Connecticut to Continue Quest to Defeat 'Twins'." *Traffic World,* Sept. 26, 1983, p. 12.

47. "Truck Size and Weight; Revisions." *Federal Register,* Vol. 50, No. 41, March 1, 1985, p. 8344.

48. CounselTrans, Inc. *A Primer on Highway Cost Allocation.* American Trucking Associations Foundation, Washington, D.C., undated.

49. *Analysis of the Department of Transportation's Claim of the Benefits Accruing to the Trucking Industry from the Surface Transportation Assistance Act of 1982.* American Trucking Associations, Inc., Washington, D.C., July 1983.

50. "Transportation 1984." *Traffic World,* Jan. 21, 1985, p. 106.

51. David J. Airozo. "American Trucking Associations Strives to Revitalize Its Image." *Traffic World,* Oct. 15, 1984, p. 19.

52. "Surface Transport Act Called 'Very Beneficial' to Trucks in Some Aspects." *Traffic World,* July 11, 1983, p. 30.

53. *AASHTO Journal Newsletter,* March 30, 1984, pp. 6–7.

54. Public Law 98-554, *Tandem Truck Safety Act of 1984.*

55. Public Law 98-369, *Tax Reform Act of 1984.*

3

Use Characteristics and Cost Impacts

The twin trailers and the wider and longer trailers permitted in the Surface Transportation Assistance Act of 1982 (enacted in 1983) offer motor carriers opportunities for major productivity gains. Haulers of light-density cargoes, for example, can transport 24 percent more freight in twin 28-ft trailers than in a 45-ft semitrailer of the same width. The potential national benefits of this productivity improvement are significant because of the size and importance of the motor carrier industry. The bill for transporting intercity freight by truck in the United States in 1984 amounted to over $100 billion (*1*). Even if the larger semitrailers and new twin trailer truck operations provided only modest productivity gains (in percentage terms), they would still reduce freight costs by hundreds of millions of dollars annually.

The reduction in the national freight bill depends on the amount of cargo carried in twin trailer trucks and 48-ft semitrailers. The growth in traffic of the larger trucks will determine the possible magnitude of the highway safety impacts, the effects on highway condition and performance, and the transport cost savings resulting from the nationwide legalization of twins.

The changes in and the characteristics of the new traffic of twin trailer trucks observed during the term of this study will not necessarily illustrate the ultimate impact of the new truck size regulations. The Surface Transportation Assistance Act of 1982 introduced new trailer dimensions at the same time that the motor carrier industry was caught up in the turbulence of deregulation. The industry had slipped into a major economic slump from which it had not emerged when the act was passed. The legislation also set off a sharp debate about which highways would be part of the designated network for 102-in. wide equipment; this debate was not resolved until 1984. These uncertainties delayed investment in new trailers, and, as a result, the full effects of the act will not be felt for several more years.

As a basis for developing an estimate of the future use of twins, four steps are taken in the following sections. After some background on the motor carrier industry, the historical use of twins in the states that have permitted their use for many years is examined to provide clues about the types of carriers that will use them, the highways they will depend on, and the loads they will carry. Next, trailer sales data supplemented with interviews with eight manufacturers are reviewed to determine who the buyers of the new equipment are. The plans of motor carriers to convert their fleets to twins, as determined through in-depth interviews with 16 carriers, are summarized. Finally, estimates from other major studies of the market penetration of twin trailer trucks and their impact on motor carrier productivity are reviewed before future twin trailer truck travel and freight cost savings due to use of more productive equipment are projected.

The information on truck traffic and the trucking industry in this chapter is taken mainly from data regularly collected by the federal and state governments, including vehicle count and truck weight data assembled by the Federal Highway Administration (FHWA) (2), surveys of truck operators (3), Bureau of Motor Carrier Safety accident records (4), and trucking industry economic and operating statistics and data collected by the Interstate Commerce Commission (ICC) (5–7). Recent special studies of twin trailer truck traffic undertaken by FHWA and several states (8,9) and some trucking industry and equipment supplier surveys produced by private organizations (10–13) have also been used.

STRUCTURE OF THE MOTOR CARRIER INDUSTRY

The new trailers legalized in 1983 will not appeal equally to all segments of the motor carrier industry. Instead, the shift to twin trailer trucks or to longer semitrailers will depend on the operating characteristics of the carriers themselves. The trucking industry is quite varied and the different types of carriers have correspondingly different needs for specific equipment.

The major carrier types in the industry are firms that transport goods for the public based on published rates (the common carriers), firms that transport goods for specific companies under contract (the contract carriers), individual owner-operators, and companies whose primary business is not trucking but who have their own fleets to move the goods they produce or sell (private carriers) (Figure 3-1).

The ICC began regulating the industry in 1935 and has had a powerful influence over the types of carriers that have evolved. With substantial deregulation of the industry, however, the distinctions among carrier types blurred. Continued evolution of the industry structure can be expected. For example, common carriers now frequently move goods under contract and private carriers have begun competing in markets from which they used to be excluded. Although the deregulation of the motor carrier industry has eroded the distinctions among segments, the available information about the industry is still classified in the traditional definitions. After a review of these definitions, the potential impact of deregulation on trucking and the adoption of the longer and wider vehicles permitted in the 1983 act will be discussed in greater detail.

Before Deregulation

The ICC regulated trucking according to how firms sold their service to the public, by the types of commodities they shipped, and by the routes on which they moved. Private carriers were not regulated. However, they could haul only their own products. Although included in the definition of the for-hire industry, movers of certain goods, particularly unprocessed agricultural commodities, were also largely exempt from ICC regulation. Companies that operated only within a single state were completely exempt from ICC regulation. As a result, little information about the number and size of these operators is available. The common and contract carriers, in contrast to the unregulated segments of the for-hire industry, were limited to providing specific types of service (Figure 3-1).

The ICC regulated who could enter the for-hire trucking industry, the rates a carrier could charge, the commodities each carrier could carry, the routes and territories it could serve, procedures for shippers' claims against carriers, insurance requirements, and other aspects of trucking businesses.

Private Carriers

Private carriers account for 44 percent of the total combination-truck miles [Table 3-1 *(3,14)*]. Many national wholesale and retail stores, leasing companies, large grocery chains, utilities, manufacturers, governments, and oil companies own and operate private fleets. These fleets vary widely in size, from one tractor-semitrailer to hundreds (and in some cases, thousands) of vehicles *(13)*.

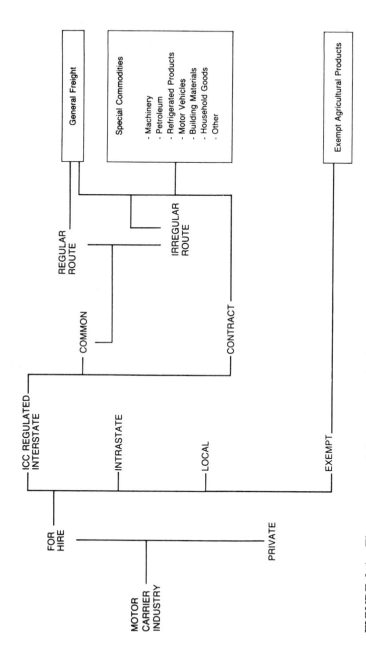

FIGURE 3-1 The structure of the motor carrier industry, 1984.

For-Hire Carriers

Unregulated   Independent owner-operators make up a relatively small but important share of the industry. Various estimates suggest that there may be as many as 100,000 independent operators and recent statistics indicate that owner-operators account for 11 percent of combination vehicle miles (*3,15*). Many of these individuals lease their services for temporary periods to larger carriers. They are also the principal motor vehicle transporters of exempt commodities. These commodities include unprocessed agricultural products such as vegetables, grains, and livestock, as well as fish and certain other seafoods. Agricultural cooperatives also own and operate trucking fleets for the movement of exempt commodities and are largely free of ICC regulation. Little information about these different unregulated carriers has been collected.

Regulated   In the regulated segment of the for-hire industry, firms generally specialize in offering shipping to the public according to established rates (common carriers) or moving goods for individual companies under contract (contract carriers).

Contract carriers mainly transport goods classified by the ICC as special commodities. Some of these goods tend to require a specific type of tractor-semitrailer combination, for example, motor vehicles, petroleum, and refrigerated products. In addition, these goods move from the factory, or point of origin, direct to destination in what are referred to as truckload lots. This means that a contract carrier picks up a single shipment of one commodity and moves it direct to its destination. Contract carriers account for about 11 percent of the combination vehicle miles of regulated carriers and about 6 percent of all combination vehicle miles (Table 3-1).

TABLE 3-1   Composition of Motor Carrier Industry, 1983 (*3,14*)

Carrier Type	Share	
	Miles ($\times$ 10^6)	Percent
For-hire		
Common	18,290	27.7
Contract	4,094	6.2
Exempt	2,245	3.4
Owner-operator	7,461	11.3
Private	29,252	44.3
Other (local, rental not reported)	4,688	7.1
Total	66,030	

Common carriers also transport special commodities and are the principal transporters of general freight. General freight is an ICC classification that includes most goods moved by truck except truckload-sized shipments of special commodities. General freight common carriers include most of the largest for-hire trucking firms. The major business of nearly all larger general freight common carriers is less-than-truckload (LTL) carriage, but most also carry truckload freight and a few specialize in truckload freight. An LTL carrier is a general freight common carrier that specializes in hauling small shipments of a size such that several can make up the full load of one truck. An LTL carrier must have a network of terminals located throughout its service area where shipments are consolidated, a local pickup and delivery fleet, and a fleet of combination trucks for line haul.[1]

Common carriers transport the majority of regulated truck freight (Table 3-1). Special commodities account for about one-half of common carrier vehicle miles; the balance of their mileage is for moving general freight (5). LTL general freight accounts for about 14 to 15 percent of total intercity combination vehicle miles.

Before deregulation the ICC designated specific highways (regular routes) over which certain common carriers could operate. This provided shippers with information about which carriers served specific routes but also limited competition and protected the market share of individual trucking firms. Contract carriers and certain truckload common carriers were allowed to operate freely (restricted to certain geographic areas) and were referred to as irregular route carriers. Route distinctions have become less meaningful recently as many carriers have received approval to operate on routes most suited to their needs.

The ICC also classifies regulated carriers by size according to their revenue. Since 1979, companies with over $5 million in revenue have been defined as Class I carriers, those with from $1 million to $5 million in revenue as Class II carriers, and those with less than $1 million as Class III carriers. The Class III designation has the most carriers (90 percent), but these firms account for a small share of miles traveled in the regulated segment of the industry. Indeed, the ICC regulated for-hire trucking industry is characterized by a few large companies surrounded by hundreds of medium-sized companies and tens of thousands of small firms. The 10 largest companies in terms of revenue in 1984 generated

---

[1]As will be observed in the next section, hauling LTL freight will be the major application of the twin trailer trucks brought into use as a result of the 1983 act. The users of these twins will often be referred to in this report as general freight common carriers, because virtually all LTL freight is hauled by this class of carrier and because in many data sources it is possible to identify general freight common carriers but not LTL carriers *per se*.

one-quarter of the total revenue of the entire regulated motor carrier industry. The share of revenue increases to 40 percent for the top 50 revenue earners and to just under 50 percent for the top 100 revenue earners (*16*).

After Deregulation

The Motor Carrier Act of 1980 lifted many of the regulatory constraints on the industry. Among the more important changes, the ICC simplified entry into the industry, allowed private fleets to operate more like for-hire carriers, expanded the classification of exempt commodities, and eased the requirement that common carriers operate on regular routes. These changes have further blurred the traditional distinctions among industry segments.

Even several years after the advent of deregulation the full effects on the industry remain unclear. The industry sank into a severe recession in 1980 (following the trend in the general economy) from which it had only partially emerged by 1985. During this period hundreds of trucking firms failed, among them some major, well-known companies (*17,18*).

These failures probably resulted from both the competitive pressures encouraged by deregulation and the decline in demand during the recession, but the changes ushered in with deregulation should have other, lasting effects. Transportation companies have been given more flexibility to provide shippers with more efficient service. The barriers erected by regulation to protect the market shares of rail and truck have been lowered. More trucking companies are merging to establish national networks, and truck-rail mergers between major companies are pending. These changes will continue to alter the shape of the industry in unpredictable ways.

Open Market Entry

One apparent consequence of deregulation to date has been a large number of new firms seeking authorization to enter the business. In 1982, a year with the lowest level of shipper demand in recent history, 6,000 firms applied to the ICC for permanent operating rights. This compares with only 700 new applicants in 1979 [Table 3-2 (*19*)]. Many of these firms may have operated as exempt carriers or owner-operators before deregulation.

The ICC no longer places heavy burdens on applicants to prove the need for new service. Instead, it routinely approves almost all applications. Many new applicants have entered the industry under contract carrier operating rights, but the majority have applied to enter the common carrier market (Table 3-2).

Deregulation has also allowed carriers to expand the areas they serve relatively freely. Expansion into additional markets by established carriers

TABLE 3-2   ICC Disposition of Permanent Operating Rights Applications (*19*)

Disposition	Fiscal year					
	1979	1980	1981	1982	1983	1984
All applicants						
Full/partial	12,333	22,125	27,475	14,786	7,294	13,577
Denied/dismissed	711	610	939	767	10	44
New applicants						
Full/partial	689	1,423	3,702	5,728	2,240	6,537
Denied/dismissed	59	38	80	438	3	30
New applicants by type						
Common carrier	—[a]	—[a]	3,381	—[a]	922	2,977
Contract carrier	—[a]	—[a]	1,546	—[a]	487	1,705
Broker	—[a]	—[a]	801	—[a]	319	1,255

[a]Data not available.

and entry of new carriers, coupled with stagnant demand, has kept prices down. "Everyone gets a 20 percent discount these days," said one corporate traffic executive in 1984. Discounts ran as deep as 50 percent for some freight (*17*). Under these conditions, many firms were forced to operate below cost and many failed as a consequence.

The largest for-hire companies have fared better than the industry as a whole and have been the first to show signs of improved profitability. The 10 carriers with the largest revenue increased their net operating income from 3.0 percent of their revenues to 7.0 percent between 1982 and 1984, and the remainder of the top 200 companies lagged behind. In 1984 the remainder of the top 200 companies showed a net operating income of only 3.5 percent (*16,20*).

The Class II companies (revenue from $1 million to $5 million annually) may have suffered the most since deregulation. The number of Class II carriers has declined 50 percent since 1977, whereas the number of Class I carriers has remained fairly constant [Table 3-3 (*21*)].

Class III carriers (revenue less than $1 million annually) have fared somewhat better through deregulation than the middle-sized firms. By the end of 1982, roughly 8 percent of Class III firms had failed, but an equal percentage of firms had improved their earnings and moved up to Class II (*22*). The number of Class III carriers grew from 13,000 in 1979 to 27,000 in 1984.

The changes within the for-hire segments of the industry could influence private trucking. With the cost of for-hire trucking dropping and with the increased flexibility and service being offered, some private companies may opt to divest their fleets. Many motor carrier executives foresee a strong growth in the contract carriage market as private companies begin

TABLE 3-3   Number of ICC-Regulated Motor
Carriers by Class Size (*21*)

Year	Class I	Class II	Class III	Total
1984	1,088	1,554	27,370	30,481
1983	1,139	1,631	24,411	27,517
1982	1,144	2,139	22,059	25,342
1981	1,031	2,293	—[a]	18,000
1980	947	2,164	—[a]	17,000
1979	992	2,754	13,337	17,083
1978	1,045	2,929	12,900	16,874
1977	1,052	3,101	12,453	16,606

NOTE: Class definitions last changed in 1979. Current definitions are Class
I, over $5 million annual revenue; Class II, $1 million to $5 million; Class
III, $1 million.
[a]The number of Class III carriers is not known for 1980 and 1981 (totals
shown were estimated by source).

purchasing services rather than providing their own (*23*). As a counter-
current, however, private carriers have new freedoms that may encourage
them to retain their truck fleets. Private companies can now set up trucking
subsidiaries that act as for-hire fleets. By mid-1984, 19 percent of private
fleets had received ICC authority to provide for-hire services and another
22 percent had applied to do so (*24*). Firms can also lease drivers and
equipment from others with fewer restrictions, which the majority of
private fleets are planning to do (*24*).

Effects of Greater Competition on Spending for New Equipment

Although these regulatory changes are still working their way through the
freight transportation industry, some implications for the future use of
twin trailer trucks and 48-ft semitrailers are clear. Intense competition is
forcing firms to aggressively market their services to provide shippers
with improved service, lower cost, or both.

The majority of for-hire carriers plan greater investments in cost-saving
technologies such as computerized business systems, more efficient engines, and the new trailer dimensions permitted by the 1983 act (*13*).
Carriers that transport LTL freight represent the major potential users of
twin trailer trucks because of the suitability of this equipment to their
operations. The average general freight LTL shipment has a density of
12 to 13 lb/ft^3 (*25,26*). At this density, a 45-ft semitrailer loaded to capacity
would still be 10,000 lb below the gross vehicle weight limit of 80,000
lb. With a set of twin trailers, a carrier can haul considerably more volume
and still not exceed the gross vehicle weight limit.

In addition, LTL carriers may also reduce handling costs by taking advantage of the flexibility of twin trailer trucks. To illustrate, LTL shipments transported in a standard semitrailer must be handled numerous times between the points of origin and destination (Figure 3-2). Twin trailer trucks offer an opportunity to bypass some of these steps. For example, a standard semitrailer might arrive at an intermediate terminal in Charlotte, N.C., and have part of its load removed for transport to Atlanta and the balance routed to Columbia, S.C. The space in the trailer bound for Columbia might be filled with other shipments to Columbia, and the shipments bound for Atlanta would be consolidated with others in a different trailer. In contrast, a twin trailer truck arriving at that same terminal could bypass this breakbulk operation. The shipments in the trailer bound for Atlanta would not have to be unloaded; instead, the trailers would simply be separated. In addition to direct dollar savings, time savings can also be gained because the shipments bound for Atlanta can also be dispatched immediately.

The benefits of lower line-haul and terminal costs are important. Line-haul costs for general freight common carriers account for 48 percent of total costs, and terminal and handling costs account for an additional 21 percent (5). For the LTL operations of general freight common carriers (the major line of business of most of these carriers), line-haul costs are a somewhat smaller percentage and terminal and handling costs a higher percentage of total costs. The current competitive environment has strengthened incentives to hold down or reduce costs. As more of the largest common carriers order new equipment, the rest of the carriers in this segment will have an incentive to invest in order to compete.

Summary Points: Structure of the Motor Carrier Industry

- General freight common carriers, the most likely future users of twin trailer trucks, account for roughly 15 percent of total intercity combination vehicle miles.
- A small number of firms set the pace for the regulated for-hire trucking industry. The top 10 revenue earners account for one-quarter of regulated industry revenues.
- Thousands of small firms are entering the common carrier market.
- Deregulation has intensified competition in trucking.
- Most carriers plan large investments in the trailers permitted in the 1983 act.

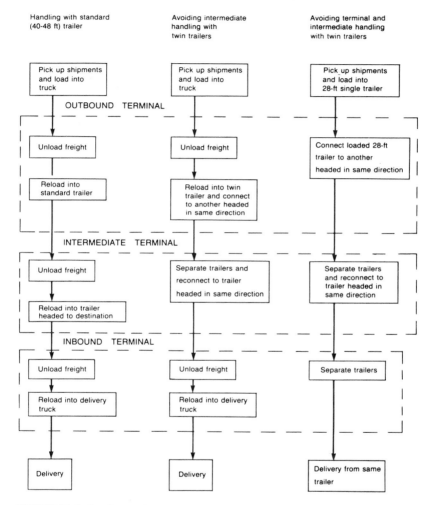

FIGURE 3-2 Potential handling eliminated by twin trailer trucks. [NOTE: Carriers are not able to avoid handling on every trip using twins. The third column shows the greatest possible effect on handling; carriers are rarely able to achieve all the handling savings shown within a single twins trip.]

HISTORICAL USE CHARACTERISTICS

Before 1983 most twin trailer truck travel occurred in the West, the bulk of it within California. Until the early 1970s, twin trailer trucks had a considerable gross weight advantage over tractor-semitrailer combinations because of the axle weight and length limits specified in California law. Twins are also particularly suited for use in certain of California's specialized agricultural operations. As a result of the widespread use of twins in California, this one state dominated national statistics on twins travel. Regional classifications used in comparing twin trailer truck travel with that of other combination trucks are given in Figure 3-3. In 1982, on the basis of FHWA vehicle count data collected from the states, 56 percent of all twin trailer truck vehicle miles occurred in California (Table 3-4). The remainder of the Western and Mountain states accounted for an additional 21.9 percent of total twins travel. Thus, before 1983, nearly 78 percent of all mileage for twins occurred in the West.

FIGURE 3-3   Regional classifications used in comparing twin trailer truck travel.

Even though twins were legal in 37 states before 1983, they made up a small share of combination-truck travel except in California. Only 9 other states (Arizona, Idaho, Montana, Nebraska, Nevada, Oregon, Utah, Washington, and Wyoming) had more than 4 percent of combination-truck traffic in twins (Figure 3-4).

Experience in the East has been considerably different. Indeed, in four of the eastern states in which twins were legal before 1983 (Delaware, Louisiana, Maryland, and Mississippi) (Figure 3-4), none were observed in the annual FHWA vehicle classification count. Throughout the East, twins represented less than one-half of 1 percent of total combination vehicle miles traveled before 1983.

Travel Patterns Before 1983

Most travel in twins occurred on main rural highways before 1983. Including California, 63 percent of total twins travel was on rural highways during that period (Table 3-4). Outside of California, that share increased from 63 to 75 percent. Interstates and primary highways carried the majority (80 percent) of total twins travel (Table 3-4). Most of this mileage (55 percent, including California) occurred on rural Interstates and primary highways. When California is excluded, rural Interstate and primary travel becomes even more predominant: 65 percent of all twins travel occurred on rural Interstates and primary highways, with rural Interstates carrying 43 percent and other rural primary highways another 22 percent.

In the last full year before the passage of the 1983 act, twin trailer trucks traveled approximately 2.3 billion vehicle-mi. This represents less than 4 percent of total combination vehicle miles traveled in the entire nation. In the following sections the users of twin trailer trucks are examined as another step toward predicting how much twin trailer truck travel will increase because of the new federal rules.

Users Before 1983

Although historical data on use of twins provides some guide to future use, national statistics can be misleading. As has been demonstrated, the statistics on twins travel are dominated by California, where twins once had a decided gross vehicle weight advantage over tractor-semitrailers. Because California's experience with twins has been atypical, in the fol-

TABLE 3-4 Estimated Total Vehicle Miles for All Combination Vehicles and Twins, 1982

Region and Trailer Type	Rural				Urban				Rural and Urban Total
	Interstate	Primary	Other	Total	Interstate	Primary	Other	Total	
California									
All	966	879	260	2,105	939	885	678	2,502	4,607
Twins	331	295	56	682	214	241	129	584	1,266
Other Western and Mountain									
All	2,124	1,298	588	4,010	419	256	434	1,509	5,519
Twins	214	104	78	391	33	48	23	104	495
Central and Plains									
All	8,822	7,841	1,716	18,379	4,511	1,579	2,033	8,123	26,502
Twins	212	117	12	341	59	27	63	149	490
East No twins									
All	3,989	3,412	1,444	8,845	3,043	1,838	707	5,588	14,433
Twins	0	0	0	0	0	0	0	0	0
East With twins									
All	3,292	2,516	958	6,766	1,290	1,490	1,103	3,883	10,649
Twins	5	5	1	11	1	0	0	1	12
U.S. total									
All	19,193	15,946	4,966	40,105	11,202	6,448	4,955	21,605	61,710
Twins	762	521	142	1,425	307	316	215	838	2,263

NOTE: Mileage is given in millions of vehicle miles.

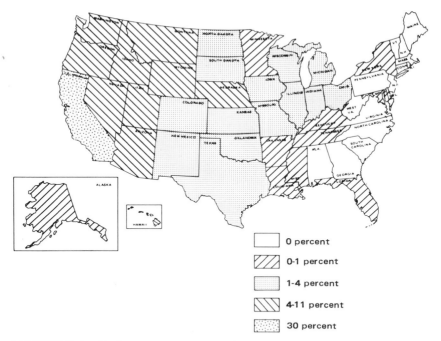

FIGURE 3-4   Twins as a percentage of rural interstate combination-truck traffic before 1983 *(2)*.

lowing discussion that experience is contrasted with that of other states to get a more representative picture of who the future users of twins might be.

The statistics on user characteristics that follow are presented for three geographic regions: (a) California, (b) Other Western and Mountain states (Alaska, Arizona, Colorado, Hawaii, Idaho, Montana, Nevada, New Mexico, Oregon, Utah, Washington, and Wyoming), and (c) the East and Central and Plains states (the remainder of the United States).

Major User Categories

ICC-regulated for-hire carriers (contract and common carriers) operated 93 percent of the twins observed in the eastern and central regions before 1983 compared with 63 percent of the five-axle tractor-semitrailer combinations (Table 3-5). These carriers accounted for 74 percent of twins

TABLE 3-5 Traffic in Twins and Tractor-Semitrailers Before 1983 by Carrier Class (2)

| | Percentage of Traffic by Region | | | | | |
| | California | | Other Western and Mountain | | East, Central and Plains | |
Carrier Class	Tractor-Semitrailer (N = 2,423)	Twins (N = 1,073)	Tractor-Semitrailer (N = 8,294)	Twins (N = 908)	Tractor-Semitrailer (N = 55,181)	Twins (N = 672)
Private	40	47	29	20	33	5
ICC for-hire	32	25	53	74	63	93
Other for-hire	28	28	19	6	4	2

NOTE: Data are for all trucks weighed and classified by carrier in the truck weight study for the latest year reported by each state before 1983. One year of data is used for each state; years vary between states. Rhode Island is excluded. Tractor-semitrailers include combinations with a three-axle tractor and two-axle semitrailer only. Five-axle twins only are included.

use in the Other Western and Mountain states but only 25 percent in California. These statistics do not distinguish between contract and common carriers, but other sources indicate that virtually all mileage in twins was produced by common carriers (*3*).

Nearly half the California doubles and one-fifth of those in the Other Western and Mountain states were privately operated. In 1983 Bureau of Motor Carrier Safety data, large private interstate users of twins tended to be retailers or producers of food and forest products (*4*).

Primary Cargo

Outside California, the most common cargoes in twin trailer trucks were mixed general freight and small package freight (Table 3-6). In California, by contrast, the commodities carried by twins were as varied as those in tractor-semitrailers; the largest percentage was in the category of agricultural and food products.

Predominant Body Type

Examining trailer body types gives another indication of who the users of twin trailer trucks were. As the previous tabulations would suggest, twins in the East and Central and Plains states and Other Western and Mountain region were mainly enclosed dry vans (weathertight, unrefrigerated vans, the most common type of van), whereas twin flatbeds and bulk commodity carriers (hoppers and tank trailers) were common in California (Table 3-7). There was no appreciable traffic in twin refrigerated vans or furniture moving vans in any region.

Gross Vehicle Weight Distributions

Because twin trailers have greater volume capacity than tractor-semitrailers, they can carry more light-density payload within the 80,000-lb gross weight limit. Weights and loads are relevant to the economic benefits of twins and are also necessary for estimating the consequences of increased vehicle weights on highway pavements (discussed in Chapter 5). Table 3-8 shows pre-1983 gross vehicle weight distributions for tractor-semitrailers and twin trailer trucks carrying general freight on primary (including Interstate) highways. The distributions are for general freight vans because the useful comparisons (for evaluating pavement impacts, for example) are between twins and the vehicles with which they compete for freight.

TABLE 3-6 Traffic in Twins and Tractor-Semitrailers Before 1983 by Commodity (2)

| | Percentage of Traffic by Region | | | | | |
| | California | | Other Western and Mountain | | East, Central and Plains | |
Commodity	Tractor-Semitrailer (N = 1,897)	Twins (N = 761)	Tractor-Semitrailer (N = 10,647)	Twins (N = 1,133)	Tractor-Semitrailer (N = 54,226)	Twins (N = 803)
Mining products	1	8	2	1	3	—
Agricultural and food products	39	42	22	7	26	2
Forest and wood products	13	7	18	2	5	—
Other manufacturing	37	23	20	12	43	5
Mixed general and small package freight	6	17	38	75	21	92
Other	3	3	1	1	2	1

NOTE: Data are for all loaded trucks weighed and with commodity reported in the truck weight study for the latest year reported by each state before 1983. One year of data is used for each state; years vary between states. Rhode Island is excluded. Tractor-semitrailers include combinations with a three-axle tractor and two-axle semitrailer only. Five-axle twins only are included.

TABLE 3-7 Traffic in Twins and Tractor-Semitrailers Before 1983 by Trailer Body Type (2)

Trailer Body Type	Percentage of Traffic by Region					
	California		Other Western and Mountain		East, Central and Plains	
	Tractor-Semitrailer (N = 2,451)	Twins (N = 1,085)	Tractor-Semitrailer (N = 15,870)	Twins (N = 1,400)	Tractor-Semitrailer (N = 93,431)	Twins (N = 988)
Enclosed dry van	34	33	25	70	44	94
Open van	2	1	3	2	3	1
Refrigerated van, moving van, or other enclosed van	24	2	18	2	14	1
Flatbed or platform	28	35	30	8	20	3
Tank or hopper	9	30	12	13	17	2
Other	2	—	12	6	2	—

NOTE: Data are for all loaded trucks weighed and with body type reported in the truck weight study for the latest year reported by each state before 1983. One year of data is used for each state; years vary between states. Rhode Island is excluded. Tractor-semitrailers include combinations with a three-axle tractor and two-axle semitrailer only. Five-axle twins only are included.

TABLE 3-8   Gross Vehicle Weight Distributions on Rural Interstates and Other Primary Highways Before 1983 (2)

| Weight Class (lb × 1,000) | Percentage by Combination Type | | | |
| | Twins | | Tractor-Semitrailer | |
	Empty	Loaded	Empty	Loaded
20–25	1.3	—	4.2	
25–30	35.1	0.6	52.7	3.0
30–35	63.6	1.8	43.1	8.3
35–40		3.9		7.3
40–45		5.2		9.2
45–50		8.2		11.2
50–55		11.4		11.9
55–60		14.1		12.8
60–65		15.5		12.1
65–70		18.3		12.1
70–75		14.9		8.9
75–80		6.1		3.3

NOTE: Distributions are for five-axle vehicles with van bodies. Loaded distributions are for vehicles carrying general freight. Vehicles weighing over 80,000 lb were excluded before the distributions were computed. Data are for all trucks for which the necessary information was reported in the most recent truck weight study by each state before 1983. National distributions produced by weighting each state observation by the state's share of total combination truck miles traveled.

Trends in Use of Twins

Before 1983

Before enactment of the new federal size rules, twins travel averaged 3 to 4 percent of all combination-truck miles traveled in the United States. This travel, as has been noted, was unevenly distributed among geographic regions. On rural Interstates, twins accounted for 30 percent of combination-truck travel in California, 10 percent in the Other Western and Mountain states, and less than 2 percent in the remainder of the nation (Figure 3-5). This level of use appears to have been fairly stable for the past 30 years; nationwide vehicle counts indicated that twin trailer trucks made up 3.2 percent of all combinations in 1957 (27) and 1.2 percent outside California in 1959 (28). During the 1970s, twins travel declined as a share of combination-truck travel in the West, presumably because in California twins lost their previous vehicle weight advantage. Twins travel grew in some of the Central and Plains states as more states opened their roads to these vehicles.

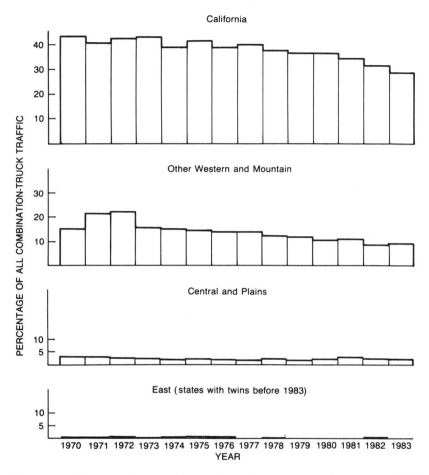

FIGURE 3-5   Trends in twins traffic volume on rural Interstates, 1970–1983 (2).

1983–1985

Data are not yet available to provide a comprehensive picture of the growth in twins traffic since the introduction of the new federal truck size rules in 1983, but the evidence so far indicates substantial increases—although from a small initial level—in the East and much smaller percentage increases in the remainder of the country. Among the 22 states that reported

1984 vehicle classification counts to FHWA, 18 indicated increases in the number of twins on rural Interstates (Figure 3-6). In the four reporting eastern states where twins had been legal in 1982 (Kentucky, Mississippi, New York, and Tennessee), twins traffic increased from an average of 0.2 percent of rural Interstate combination-truck traffic in 1980–1982 to

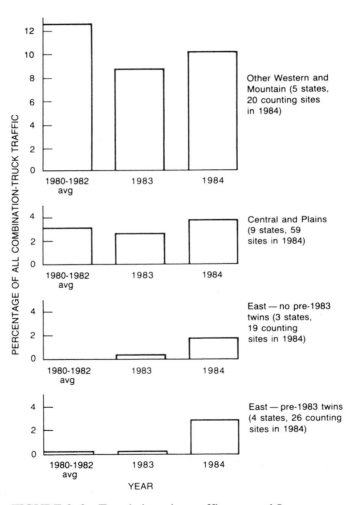

FIGURE 3-6   Trends in twins traffic on rural Interstates, 1980–1984 (2).

3.0 percent by the summer of 1984. In nine reporting Central and Plains states, it increased from 3.1 percent in 1982 to 3.8 percent in 1984, and in five Other Western and Mountain states (excluding California), it declined from 12.6 to 10.1 percent. The percentage increases represent small traffic volumes; the number of twins per day in the 1984 counts averaged 76, or 3 an hour, at 45 eastern rural Interstate counting sites out of an average 18,000 vehicles of all types daily. In 1985 counts available for a few states, the twins share of all combinations at rural Interstate sites in the East was 2.2 percent (up from 0.1 percent in 1980–1982) and 6.2 percent (up from 5.0 percent in 1980–1982) in the central and western states (excluding California).

Pennsylvania has reported monthly counts of twin trailer trucks at major border crossings since 1983 (Figure 3-7). The state's geographic location makes these counts a useful index of trends in twins traffic throughout the northeastern states. Twins traffic in the state expanded rapidly throughout 1983 and especially 1984, but growth appeared to have slowed in 1985. Twins traffic to and from the west and south was initially much heavier than traffic to and from the east, but this gap has gradually been narrowing.

The 16 LTL general freight common carriers interviewed for this study (discussed in more detail later) were operating twins for 48 percent of their line-haul miles by early 1985. This constituted a doubling of their pre-1983 use of twins and represented about 40 percent of the total amount of travel that these carriers projected they would be converting from tractor-semitrailers to twins between 1983 and 1990. If all LTL general freight common carriers were converting to twins at the same rate as these 16 and truckload uses of twins remained constant, the level of twins travel in early 1985 would have been equivalent to about 3.7 billion vehicle-mi annually, or a 60 percent increase over 1982 travel.

Summary

Use of twins in California before 1983 was as diverse as the use of tractor-semitrailers, but outside California, a different and fairly consistent pattern held. In the East and the Central and Plains region before 1983 twins were used primarily by general freight common carriers (virtually all of this use was presumably by LTL carriers). In the Other Western and Mountain region, twins use patterns reflected some spillover of California doubles traffic but were closer to the patterns of the East and Central and Plains region. Twins tended to be used by general freight common carriers who relied on major rural highways as their primary routes, and they tended to be more heavily loaded than comparable tractor-semitrailers.

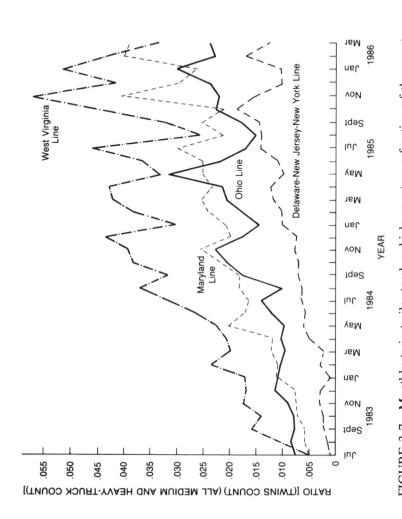

FIGURE 3-7 Monthly twin trailer truck vehicle count as a fraction of the count of all medium and heavy trucks at major border crossings in Pennsylvania, 1983–1986. SOURCE: Pennsylvania Department of Transportation. [NOTE: Combination trucks make up about 80 percent of all medium and heavy vehicles.]

Total travel in twin trailer trucks in 1982 made up a small share of total combination travel (3.7 percent), or about 2.3 billion vehicle-mi. General freight common carriers accounted for about 40 percent of total mileage in twins nationwide, but outside of California, twins used for general freight accounted for 78 percent of the total.

Available indicators show an upward trend in twins use since the new federal truck size rules, particularly in the East.

THE MARKET FOR TWINS

The new trailers permitted by the 1983 act have had a great effect on the motor carrier industry. Van trailer sales for 1984 were twice the annual sales of the previous 4 years as motor carriers, beginning to recover from the recession, jumped at the opportunity to invest in more productive equipment. Even this abrupt shift, however, does not fully portray the ultimate adoption of the newly permitted trailers by the motor carrier industry. The lingering dampening effect of the recession on capital investment in trucking, the changes in freight transportation under way due to deregulation, and the lack of clarity about the designated network of roads where the newly authorized equipment could operate all slowed the potential shift toward twin trailer truck use. In this section information on the current trends in the market for twins available from trailer sales data, interviews with trailer manufacturers, and interviews with carriers using twins is given. The section concludes with descriptions of use by non-LTL carriers and the characteristics of new twins equipment.

New-Equipment Sales

As noted earlier, 1984 was a strong year for trailer sales. Dry van sales, which account for about half of total trailer sales, jumped from about 60,000 units in 1983 to over 115,000 in 1984 (*21*). Sales statistics collected and published semiannually by the Truck Trailer Manufacturers Association reveal that the 48-ft by 102-in. wide trailer is the most popular choice (*10*):

Length	*Percentage of Sales*	
(ft)	*1982*	*1984*
27–28	8	22
45	75	15
48	1–2	56

The previous industry standard, the 45-ft semitrailer, dropped from 75 percent of total sales in 1982 to 15 percent in 1984. Sales of 48-ft trailers (practically negligible in 1982) increased to 56 percent of total sales. Meanwhile, sales of twin trailers (27- or 28-ft units) increased from 8 to 22 percent of total sales. About 70 percent of all 1984 trailer sales (28-ft and 48-ft) were for trailers 102 in. wide, an increase from nearly zero in 1982.

For analyzing the industry response to the availability of new truck configurations, trailer sales statistics can be misleading; the characteristics of trailers purchased in any given year do not necessarily represent the desired or ideal mix of trailer sizes. The 1984 sales data reflect the desire of some motor carriers who are in a position to acquire new equipment to rapidly convert part of their fleets from long semitrailers to twins. Other carriers may not be in a position to invest and those that do may not complete all investment plans in a single year.

The Truck Trailer Manufacturers Association data do not provide information about the purchasers of the equipment. To get an idea of the type of carriers investing in the new equipment and the expected level of investment, eight major trailer manufacturers were interviewed, as is discussed in the next section.

Manufacturer Interviews

The eight trailer manufacturers interviewed for this study were selected to provide a representative picture of sales in all regions of the country. Twin trailer trucks currently account for 5 to 30 percent of their market, and 48-ft semitrailers account for about 30 to 75 percent, figures that are generally consistent with the trailer sales figures discussed earlier. The manufacturers provided their assessment of the current and future market characteristics for twins, 48-ft long semitrailers, and 102-in. wide semitrailers.

Major Market for Twins

The manufacturers agree that general freight common carriers are the primary market for twins and that the larger general freight common carriers have accounted for the bulk of recent purchases of twins. Virtually all orders are for enclosed dry van trailers. The sale of twins has been strongest in the Midwest and in the southeastern states. In the Northeast, sales of twins have been sluggish. Marketing executives explain the slow penetration into the Northeast by citing small terminals in congested urban areas and shorter trip lengths, which diminish the advantages of added cubic capacity and operational flexibility of twins. In the West, sales have not greatly increased because twins have been permitted in most western states for some time. The firms that are buying more twins in the West are those that have operations that extend into the East. In addition to general freight common carriers, manufacturers report scattered sales to private and truckload for-hire carriers, mostly serving industries that move low-density commodities to many distribution points, like food and retail store chains. These experimental uses account for a small percentage of total sales.

The manufacturers report that, so far, carriers investing in twins for the first time are initially attracted to them because of the added cubic capacity. The operational flexibility that twins offer for reducing handling costs will be a less important factor, they believe, until carriers have had more experience with twins.

Some marketing analysts believe that twins are most advantageous to the largest general freight common carriers who are currently buying them and expect that the surge in twins sales will end shortly. Others expect that such sales will continue to be strong as smaller general freight common carriers and some truckload carriers adopt the use of twins.

New Standard Semitrailer Length

Manufacturers report that the 48-ft semitrailer is becoming the truckload industry standard. Although semitrailers over 48 ft long are now legal in many states through the grandfather provision of the 1983 act or state laws, the trailer manufacturers expect that sales of those longer than 48 ft will account for a small share of the market for the time being.

Wider Equipment

Manufacturers report that carriers tend to prefer 102-in. wide trailers over the previous 96-in. standard. About 70 percent of all sales in 1984 were for 102-in. wide equipment. Evidently many carriers want the largest trailer size they can purchase, but some firms, such as food store chains operating private fleets, prefer the 96-in. width because the pallets for their commodities are designed for this size. Overall, however, manufacturers expect 102-in. wide trailers to become increasingly popular in the industry.

Carrier Interviews

To determine the investment plans of carriers adopting twins, 16 general freight common carriers were selected for in-depth interviews. These firms were chosen on the basis of size, location, and extent of experience with operating twin trailer trucks. All specialize in LTL freight, but most also carry appreciable amounts of truckload freight. The group was intentionally weighted toward the largest companies. Although the 16 carriers interviewed account for a tiny fraction of the total number of carriers, they include the dominant for-hire trucking firms, which set the pace for other carriers. The firms interviewed alone account for one-quarter of for-hire trucking industry revenue.

The group includes firms from all regions of the country. Of the companies that operate nationwide, some had operated twins in the West, but several firms headquartered east of the Mississippi River had begun using them on a large scale for the first time in 1983. Two western firms that had operated twin trailer truck fleets for many years were included to review their perception of the advantage of such operations.

The companies were interviewed confidentially to encourage them to share plans that many companies are reluctant to divulge. All information provided by the companies that participated in the interviews is presented in aggregate form to avoid disclosure of information about an individual company.

Conversion to Twin Trailer Truck Fleets

Twin trailer trucks were already in use by some of the companies in the sample, particularly those headquartered west of the Mississippi River. In 1982 twins accounted for about one-quarter of the line-haul vehicle miles for the group as a whole. Two western regional general freight common carriers were already operating fleets made up almost entirely of twins. For national carriers headquartered in the central and western states, twins made up from one-quarter to one-half of total line-haul miles. Regional carriers in the East had virtually no mileage in twins before 1983. When visited in mid-1985 these eastern companies were generally undergoing massive fleet conversions by purchasing thousands of twin trailer trucks. By early 1985 the companies in the entire group had 48 percent of their line-haul miles in twins.

Aside from regional firms headquartered in the Northeast, all companies foresaw continued conversion of their fleets to twins. Most companies foresaw a conversion ranging from 65 to 100 percent twins. All the companies interviewed specialized in LTL freight, but those with relatively large amounts of truckload business also expected the bulk of their LTL freight to move in twins. The exception to these conversion plans occurs among regional firms headquartered in the Northeast. These companies have shorter line-haul distances and routes with relatively low volumes of freight traffic (i.e., often only a partial truckload or a few loads per day between most origin-destination pairs), both of which tend to diminish the line-haul advantages of twins. These northeastern carriers, however, tend to have small fleets. The largest companies in the group foresaw a conversion to 70 percent or more. Because the fleets of the largest companies are far larger than those of the smaller ones, their investment plans dominate the group. As a whole, the sample firms expect to have close to 80 percent of their line-haul vehicle miles in twin trailer trucks by about 1990.

Effect on Line-Haul and Freight Handling Costs

The company executives interviewed were enthusiastic about twin trailer trucks. They gave two reasons. First, the extra cubic capacity of twins means that fewer combination trucks are needed to carry the same amount of freight, which promises reductions in vehicle mileage and line-haul costs. Second, twins allow for more direct loading between origin and destination and reduce the number of times freight has to be handled, which promises reductions in handling costs and faster service, and saves additional miles.

The importance of these two benefits varied among the many companies in the sample. National companies with preexisting fleets of twin trailer trucks were already taking advantage of both benefits. Because large eastern carriers were just beginning to use twins, they tended to be running them between major breakbulk terminals where the additional cubic capacity would be put to best advantage.

Smaller regional firms regardless of geography were more interested in the flexibility of twins. For these companies the ability to transport more loads direct to destination reduces circuitous movement of freight, reduces handling, and provides faster service.

Estimates of the actual cost reductions attributable to twins varied. Nonetheless, most executives believed that twins would reduce tractor-semitrailer miles by 9 to 10 percent by allowing a substitution of 10 sets of twins for 11 tractor-semitrailers. Actual reductions in the routes with the heaviest traffic are greater for some companies. Systemwide, the estimates range from a 5 to 20 percent reduction in line-haul costs, with most estimates in the 10 percent range. Estimated handling cost benefits also varied but centered on a roughly 9 percent reduction in breakbulk handling costs.

Carrier executives noted that increasing the use of twins will increase some other costs. For example, because twins have to be separated at terminals and backed up twice for unloading, the cost of hostling (handling trailers within terminal yards) will increase as well. One major company that had increased its use of twins by 25 percentage points reported a 34 percent increase in hostling labor cost. Hostling costs, however, represent less than half of 1 percent of company expenses. Twins also require additional capital investment in terminals. More loading stations are required to handle the larger number of trailers, and because of the increased amount of hostling and parking, a larger paved yard around the terminal may be required. Maintenance costs will also be higher because of the increased number of trailers. For example, trailer doors tend to require regular maintenance and repair, and twins have two such doors. Carriers report paying from 7 to 25 percent more for a complete twin trailer truck combination than for a complete tractor-semitrailer combination. Capital costs represent the largest offset to the cost savings of twin trailer trucks. Some labor contracts specify slightly higher wages for the drivers of twins. All these cost disadvantages, however, are small compared with the potential benefits.

Use by Private and Truckload Carriers

Although the manufacturers of twin trailer trucks agree that LTL general freight common carriers account for the bulk of sales, they report that other carriers have begun to experiment with twins. For example, one manufacturer reports that a truckload common carrier serving a food distribution company has purchased refrigerated twin trailers. A major manufacturer of refrigeration units, however, revealed that the potential for this market is quite small. The company expects sales of fewer than 600 units each year and believes that many of these smaller refrigeration units are being used for short single trailers primarily for city delivery.

Trailer manufacturers cite other sales to firms transporting light-density products. For example, a western retail furniture chain has purchased a few twins to see whether they will fit into their operations. Furniture and household goods are among the lightest-density commodities. At least one household mover has purchased a number of 28-ft trailers to increase the cubic capacity of its trailers during the line-haul portion of the trip (29).

Some private carriers are also trying out twins. By the end of 1984, about 10 percent of private firms voluntarily providing data to a private truck trailer fleet data base reported that they had purchased twin trailer trucks as a result of the 1983 act (*30*). This survey does not reveal the number of purchases but serves to indicate interest in twins outside of the general freight common carrier market. As a comparison, over 50 percent of the firms in the survey reported having purchased 48-ft single trailers since 1982.

As an example of specialized uses of twins in the private market, one textile firm in the South has found the length of twins well suited to the 13-ft rolls of carpet it manufactures. The twins make four stacks of rolls possible compared with only three in either a 45- or 48-ft semitrailer. The twins are also useful for the LTL freight the company transports in its back-haul operations.

This experimentation with twins by private carriers does not reveal any discernible pattern. Companies moving a wide variety of different commodities appear to be trying out twins (*30*), but, as the manufacturers report, the number of trailers purchased by these carriers is small. In accident reports to the Bureau of Motor Carrier Safety few private carriers reported accidents involving twins in 1983 and 1984 who had not been using twins before 1983. These varied data sources suggest that some private companies and truckload for-hire carriers are finding specialized uses for twins; however, no major shifts from semitrailers to twins are yet evident outside the general freight common carrier segment of the industry.

Characteristics of New Equipment

Because of the uncertainty regarding use of 102-in. wide equipment, many carriers purchased equipment 96 in. wide in 1983. Subsequent investments, however, have been for 102-in. trailers. In almost all new investments, 102-in. dollies are matched with the wider trailers. However, for carriers with fleets of twins of mixed widths, there will be some mixing of wider semitrailers with dollies designed for 96-in. semitrailers.

All carriers have been buying trailers 28 ft (or in a few cases 28.5 ft) long. Only one carrier in the group had made a substantial investment in 48-ft semitrailers, and these were for the company's truckload business. Virtually all have purchased two-axle tractors to pull the trailers, with most carriers opting for engines with power ratings between 270 and 300 hp. Some carriers already operate their twins exclusively with two-axle tractors, and of those that do not, most plan to do so as they invest in more complementary equipment. Carriers varied considerably on whether they would purchase only conventional, rather than cab-over-engine, tractors.

The twin trailer trucks already in use before 1983 by the carriers in the group have an empty (tare) weight 3,000 to 5,000 lb greater than that of the tractor-semitrailers in their fleets. Newer twins, however, tend to have less of a tare weight disadvantage. Newer designs and lightweight materials have reduced trailer weights. Among eastern carriers whose twin fleets were exclusively new equipment, twins combinations were only 900 to 1,500 lb heavier when empty than the 45-ft semitrailers in their fleets. Tare weights for twins ranged from 27,500 to 36,000 lb.

Summary

General freight common carriers have already begun a massive and rapid conversion of their fleets to twin trailer trucks. Between 1982 and early 1985, the carriers interviewed for this study had increased twin trailer truck vehicle miles from about one-quarter of total line-haul miles to nearly 48 percent. By 1990, the carriers in the survey will have nearly 80 percent of total line-haul miles in twins.

MARKET PENETRATION STUDIES

The ultimate market penetration of twin trailer trucks depends in large measure on the productivity advantages these vehicles offer to freight carriers. Other studies estimating the future use of twins and their economic benefits are reviewed here as an additional source of information for estimating the probable increase in twin trailer truck use nationwide. Individual studies addressing these issues are summarized in more detail in Appendix C.

Previous Studies

A number of studies and analyses were undertaken in the late 1970s and early 1980s as part of the debate about the need for greater uniformity in federal and state regulation of truck size and weight. Three major studies analyzed a variety of possible uniform standards for the trucking industry, among them allowing 27- or 28-ft twin trailers to operate nationwide at a gross vehicle weight of 80,000 lb (25,31,32). In these studies it was argued that the lower weight limits of the barrier states and the prohibition against double trailers in the eastern states hampered trucking productivity by increasing line-haul costs. Because light-density cargoes frequently exceed the volume capacity of a semitrailer before they approach the weight limit, these studies noted that twin trailer trucks could increase trucking productivity by offering more volume without increasing the gross vehicle weight.

These studies assumed that the cubic capacity of twins was the primary incentive for shifting to this configuration, but some noted that twins also offer considerable operating efficiencies to LTL carriers by reducing the number of times that freight has to be handled. In the remainder of this section a review and analysis is presented of estimates in the literature of

- Cost advantages of twins,
- Carriers most likely to be attracted to increased use of twins, and
- Potential nationwide use of twins from other studies.

Cost Advantages of Twins

Cost advantages were identified in all studies of the option of allowing twins to operate nationwide. In a study done for the American Trucking Associations (*25*), it was estimated that line-haul cost per ton-mile for the average general commodity LTL shipment would decline between 16 and 19 percent in the regions not formerly permitting the use of twins. In the Truck Size and Weight Study (*26*) reductions of approximately 11 percent in line-haul costs per ton-mile were estimated. These estimates compared the productivity of twins with that of 45-ft tractor-semitrailers. With the introduction of the 48-ft trailers also permitted in the 1983 act, the comparative benefits of twins became somewhat smaller. Nonetheless, two 28-ft twin trailers still have 17 percent more cubic capacity than a 48-ft semitrailer.

A field study of pre-1983 use of 27- to 28-ft twin trailers in the states permitting them was commissioned by the Transportation Systems Center to provide estimates of the benefits of twin trailer trucks as an input to the Truck Size and Weight Study. This study (*33*) was unable to document the actual cost advantages but did stress the benefits of operating efficiencies that would reduce terminal and handling costs. The use of twin trailers eliminates some handling at intermediate breakbulk terminals. On the basis of this advantage, it was estimated in the Truck Size and Weight Study (*26*) that terminal costs would decline by 10 percent per ton handled. Other reports gave no estimates of the benefits in reduced handling costs because they relied on line-haul cost curves that only consider vehicle operating costs.

Carriers Benefitting

In all studies it was agreed that general freight common carriers would be the primary beneficiaries of nationwide operation of twins. However, in the field study done as part of the Truck Size and Weight Study (*33*) potential problems for these carriers were noted that may temper the attractiveness of twins. For terminals that lack a balance between inbound truckload and outbound LTL freight, a fleet made up of a mix of twins and tractor-semitrailers could become unbalanced, which would require substantial inefficient movement of empty trailers to allow the terminal operator to keep an appropriate number of single and twin trailer trucks on hand. This disadvantage of twin trailer trucks may help explain why use of twins in California for general commodity freight had not exceeded 50 percent of truck miles in the general freight category (*33*).

Market Penetration

The studies estimating the ultimate use of twins rely on different assumptions and methodologies. All were done before the passage of the 1983 act, and thus do not estimate market penetration for the exact vehicles or highway network designated in the legislation.

For example, in the Truck Size and Weight Study (*34*), it is assumed that only LTL general freight common carriers will switch to twins and it is estimated that travel by these vehicles (over all primary highways) will ultimately increase by 2.7 billion vehicle-mi. This estimate, however, excludes much intrastate combination-truck travel because of the interest in focusing on interstate impacts. For example, the total combination vehicle miles in the base case (1985) totals only 45.4 billion, far less than the 66 billion vehicle-mi reported by the FHWA for 1983. The Truck Size and Weight Study estimate of 6.4 billion total twin trailer truck vehicle-mi for 1985 represents 14 percent of the study's estimated total combination vehicle miles. Because intrastate and local combination-truck travel was excluded by the Truck Size and Weight Study, the 14 percent estimate is probably high as a percentage of all combination-truck travel. General freight common carriers tend to use twins between major break-bulk terminals; thus twins are more likely to represent a larger share of interstate travel. Intrastate and local travel of all types is more likely to occur in tractor-semitrailer combinations.

After publication of the Truck Size and Weight Study, the U.S. Department of Transportation had subsequent analyses done to estimate the increase in twin trailer truck traffic if they were limited to Interstate highways (with some provision for access to terminals via primary highways). This estimate showed an increase in twin trailer truck travel of 1.65 billion vehicle-mi (*35*). Limiting twins use to the Interstates is more restrictive than using the current designated network; hence this estimate is probably too low.

In a report by the American Trucking Associations (*25*), it was estimated that cubed-out freight (freight in which the truck is loaded to its volume capacity but weighs less than the legal weight limit) accounts for about 16 percent of all combination-truck mileage. A separate American Trucking Associations study (*36*) estimated that allowing twins to operate nationwide would increase twin trailer truck traffic by 2.03 billion vehicle-mi in the 18 states then prohibiting their use (about 13 percent of total combination vehicle miles in the affected states). Both studies depend on two assumptions: first, that half of all general freight cubes out and, second, that common carriers of general freight are estimated to represent 34 percent of intercity mileage. The former assumption appears accurate; however, the Truck Inventory and Use Survey (*3*) indicates that common carriers account for about 28 percent of total combination vehicle miles. In addition, common carriers of specialized commodities—carriers unlikely to shift to twins because of the special equipment they use—make up a large share of all common carrier miles (*5*). Thus, the assumptions in the American Trucking Associations study overstate the potential impact of twin trailer trucks by assuming that common carriers of general freight represent a larger share of total mileage than other studies indicate.

National Cooperative Highway Research Program Report 198 (*32*), a precursor to the Truck Size and Weight Study, used commodity-specific rather than carrier-specific assumptions, and on the basis of its commodity-flow model and the percentage of commodities assumed to shift to twins, it was estimated that annual twin trailer truck travel would increase by about 2.9 billion vehicle-mi. Combined with the study estimate of existing vehicle miles for twins, this would represent 14 percent of total combination vehicle miles.

This estimate is probably high because the study relies on a commodity-specific rather than carrier-specific assumption in assigning freight in its commodity-flow model. That is, the study assumed that shifts in commodities to different trailer types would be made regardless of whether they were carried by LTL or truckload firms. Most truckload carriers, however, would probably bypass the occasional cubic capacity advantage that a twin trailer truck would allow because of the extra labor costs involved in handling two trailers and a dolly and because the 48-ft semitrailer may represent a single optimal trailer type for the varied uses of truckload commodities.

Summary

Despite the different assumptions and analytic approaches, the studies discussed demonstrate a fair degree of agreement. In all it is agreed that

LTL general freight common carriers will be the primary users of twins. The estimates of total vehicle miles in twins, aside from the overly restrictive limitation to Interstates in one estimate, range from 12 to 14 percent of total combination vehicle miles. For the reasons noted, these estimates may be somewhat high; nonetheless, given the varied assumptions and approaches, the agreement among them is fairly surprising.

Summary Points: Market Penetration Studies

- LTL general freight common carriers will be the principal users of twins.
- Twins reduce line-haul costs 9 to 19 percent per ton-mile and reduce handling costs.
- Studies estimate that once twins are fully adopted they will account for between 12 and 14 percent of intercity combination vehicle miles.

FUTURE USE OF TWINS

Twin trailer trucks will be operated on the highways increasingly as LTL general freight common carriers complete their investment plans. This projection is supported by several sources. Past use of twin trailer trucks, aside from their atypical use in California, has mostly been by carriers of general freight. Trailer manufacturers report booming sales of twins and also indicate that general freight common carriers are the primary purchasers. The carriers surveyed for this study report that 80 percent of their line-haul vehicle miles will occur in twins by 1990. Previous studies estimating future use of twins agree that LTL carriers will be the primary users.

Projection by Region

The use of twins will vary somewhat by region. In California, where 47 percent of general freight common carrier vehicle miles was in twins in 1982, twins' share of LTL general freight mileage will increase to 60 percent. The estimate of 80 percent line-haul vehicle miles by 1990 made by the carriers in the study sample is higher because it is restricted to line-haul miles, whereas the 60 percent projection includes all combination pickup and delivery mileage.

The 60 percent projection is also applied to all Other Western and Mountain states and to all Central and Plains states. Use in the East will lag behind that of other regions for some time. In the eastern states where twins had formerly been prohibited (Vermont, Maine, Massachusetts, Connecticut, Rhode Island, Pennsylvania, New Jersey, Virginia, West Virginia, North Carolina, South Carolina, Georgia, and Alabama), 40 percent of LTL general freight vehicle miles (equivalent to somewhat over half of all LTL line-haul miles) will occur in twins by 1990. In other eastern states that had formerly allowed limited use of twins (Mississippi, Tennessee, Kentucky, Florida, Maryland, Delaware, and New York), twins will account for 50 percent of LTL general freight vehicle miles (equivalent to two-thirds of their line-haul miles). The percentage increases over the base case in each region in twins are given in Table 3-9. Estimates of vehicle mileage are given in Tables 3-10 and 3-11.

Projection of Total Combination Vehicle Miles

The estimate of vehicle miles in twins developed for this study is derived from two sources. State reports of vehicle counts and weights were used to estimate shares of vehicle types on each class of highway. These shares were applied to FHWA estimates of total combination vehicle miles for each class of highway, and total combination vehicle miles for 1990 were projected assuming annual growth in combination-truck traffic equal to the average for the preceding 7 years (about 1.5 percent a year). Increases in twin trailer traffic are based on the projected twins shares of LTL general freight vehicle miles given in Table 3-9.

TABLE 3-9   Projected LTL Twin Trailer Truck Vehicle Miles in 1990

Region	Percentage of LTL Vehicle Miles in Twins	
	Base Case	Projected for 1990
California	47	60
Other Western and Mountain	24	60
Central and Plains	10	60
East		
No twins before 1983	0	40
With twins before 1983	0.3	50

NOTE: Base case assumes no change in twins use (i.e., the percentages are estimated actual pre-1983 percentages). Projected percentages reflect change in use resulting from nationwide legalization of twins.

TABLE 3-10 Projected Vehicle Miles for All Combination Vehicles in 1990

Region	Rural				Urban				Rural and Urban Total
	Interstate	Primary	Other	Total	Interstate	Primary	Other	Total	
California									
Base	1,132	1,030	305	2,467	1,101	1,037	795	2,933	5,400
Change	−2	−1	0	−3	−1	−1	0	−2	−5
Other Western and Mountain									
Base	2,501	1,529	692	4,722	493	773	511	1,777	6,500
Change	−22	−11	−8	−41	−3	−5	−3	−11	−52
Central and Plains									
Base	10,452	9,290	2,033	21,776	5,345	1,871	2,409	9,624	31,400
Change	−79	−70	−15	−164	−40	−18	−18	−72	−236
East									
No twins before 1983									
Base	4,726	4,042	1,711	10,479	3,605	2,178	838	6,621	17,100
Change	−30	−25	−11	−66	−30	−18	−8	−56	−122
With twins before 1983									
Base	3,895	2,977	1,133	8,006	1,526	1,763	1,305	4,594	12,600
Change	−32	−25	−9	−66	−9	−10	−8	−27	−93
U.S. total									
Base	22,704	18,863	5,874	47,442	13,251	7,628	5,861	25,558	73,000
Change	−165	−132	−43	−340	−83	−52	−37	−168	−508

NOTE: Mileage is given in millions of vehicle miles. Base case shows total combination travel assuming no change in travel due to twins. The change represents the decline in tractor-semitrailer miles from the base assuming growth in twins travel given in Table 3-11. Columns and rows may not add to totals shown due to rounding.

TABLE 3-11 Projected Vehicle Miles for Twins in 1990

Region	Rural				Urban				Rural and Urban Total
	Interstate	Primary	Other	Total	Interstate	Primary	Other	Total	
California									
Base	392	349	66	807	253	285	153	691	1,498
Change	+12	+11	+2	+25	+8	+9	+5	+22	+47
Other Western and Mountain									
Base	253	123	86	463	39	57	27	123	586
Change	+227	+110	+78	+415	+35	+51	+25	+111	+526
Central and Plains									
Base	251	138	14	404	70	32	75	176	580
Change	+799	+710	+155	+1,664	+404	+141	+182	+727	+2,391
East									
No twins before 1983									
Base	0	0	0	0	0	0	0	0	0
Change	+301	+258	+109	+668	+310	+187	+73	+570	+1,238
With twins before 1983									
Base	6	6	1	13	1	0	0	0	14
Change	+325	+249	+95	+669	+92	+106	+79	+277	+946
U.S. total									
Base	901	616	167	1,686	363	374	253	991	2,677
Change	+1,664	+1,338	+439	+3,441	+849	+494	+364	+1,707	+5,148

NOTE: Mileage is given in millions of vehicle miles. Base case shows twins travel assuming no change in twins share of combination travel. The change represents the projected increase in twins travel from the base resulting from nationwide legalization of twins. Columns and rows may not add to totals shown due to rounding.

If there were no change in vehicle miles of twins, it is projected that total combination vehicle miles would increase to 73 billion by 1990 (Table 3-10).

In the forecast, vehicle miles in twins will increase from about 2.7 billion in 1982 to about 7.8 billion by 1990, representing a net increase of 5.1 billion vehicle-mi (Table 3-11). Almost all of this increase (97 percent) will be general freight common carrier mileage. A small additional increase is assumed to account for some specialized uses of twins outside of the common carrier segment of the industry. The estimate of 7.8 billion total miles in twins represents 11 percent of total combination vehicle miles. This is consistent with—though slightly lower than—the projections by other studies discussed in the preceding section.

The increased reliance of LTL general freight common carriers on twin trailer trucks will reduce total tractor-semitrailer miles by 493 million vehicle-mi. This corresponds to the substitution by general freight common carriers of 10 twin trailer trucks for 11 tractor-semitrailers. In addition, a small amount of mileage will be saved by conversion from tractor-semitrailers to twins in truckload sectors. Thus, in the forecast, all combination vehicle miles would total 72.5 billion vehicle-mi rather than the base-case forecast of 73 billion vehicle-mi (Table 3-10). The net reduction in miles has two sources: twins' greater volume capacity, which allows more freight to be carried on each trip that is fully loaded, and the flexibility of twins, which allows LTL freight to avoid circuitous routings through breakbulks and reduces mileage of partially loaded trucks.[2]

The estimates of travel by road type indicate that most future twins traffic will occur on rural Interstates and primary highways (57 percent of the total). Nearly 67 percent of all twins travel will occur on rural highways. Almost all travel (85 percent) will occur on urban and rural Interstates and primary highways (Table 3-11).

Mode Diversion and Generated Traffic

The travel forecast developed for this study depends on the prediction that very little freight will be diverted to LTL general freight carriers from other modes as a result of the increased use of twins. The projections also assume that generation of entirely new freight traffic (as opposed to diverted traffic) as a result of freight price reductions following productivity savings from twins will be negligible. The basis for this conclusion is that there is no close substitute for LTL freight service. Several possible sub-

---

[2]This forecast does not incorporate any prediction of changes in travel because of increased use of 48-ft semitrailers.

stitutes are available, but none is closely comparable with LTL in terms of both price and service attributes. The alternatives are discussed in the following paragraphs.

Conventional Rail Service

The railroads today carry virtually no small-shipment freight other than in piggyback operations (discussed in the next paragraph). Total rail loadings of less-than-carload freight in 1984 were 11,000 carloads (*37*), equivalent to less than 1 percent of truck LTL freight. Analysts with both trucking industry and railroad perspectives agree that the interface of competition between rail and truck today involves truckload freight services versus rail carload and piggyback service (*38,39*).

Rail Piggyback

Piggyback rail carloadings (including both road trailers loaded on rail flatcars and containers on flatcars) have grown substantially since deregulation, from 1.9 million in 1979 to 2.7 million in 1984 (*37*), roughly equivalent in ton-miles to 15 percent of all truck line-haul freight. Little information is available on the composition of piggyback freight, but it is believed that freight diverted from conventional rail service accounts for much of the recent growth, although some freight has been diverted from truckload motor carriers.

Some LTL freight moves for part of its journey by piggyback, but the quantities are small and piggyback is not yet a serious competitor because it cannot match LTL service. Most of the costs in an LTL operation are in pickup, delivery, consolidation, and routing of freight at terminals. Line haul, the only part of the LTL operation for which piggyback can substitute, may be as little as a third of total LTL costs. If LTL moves by piggyback for line haul, handling at origin and destination must be provided or arranged by the railroad (directly through a trucking subsidiary or through contracts with local trucking or warehousing firms), by an LTL trucking company, by a shipper's agent (an agent who accepts freight from shippers and arranges for its transport), by the owner of the container, or by the shipper itself. None of these channels is well developed for getting LTL freight on piggyback, and consequently piggyback cannot match LTL service for speed or reliability of delivery schedules. Cargo damage in piggyback is high compared with that in through-truck LTL service, responsibility for cargo damage is vaguely defined, shipment-tracing services are unavailable, and on the whole, most of the essential aspects of LTL service are missing (*40–42*). The shipper gives up these service qualities in return for a relatively small cost saving, because handling, the largest LTL cost item, is unaffected. Piggyback often cannot even offer a lower freight rate than LTL service on short- and medium-haul shipments.

Some of the difficulties with piggyback service from the shippers' point of view are circumvented when the LTL carrier arranges the piggyback haul to replace its own line haul. Almost all the LTL carriers interviewed for this study use piggyback in this manner, but in all but one case, piggyback use was very limited in extent, and the carriers reported without exception that they did not expect increased use of twins to affect the volume of their piggyback traffic. The reason for this response is that with the exception of one large carrier, the LTL operators do not use piggyback as a routine cost-cutting tool but only in special circumstances where cost is not the key issue:

• To handle exceptional seasonal peaks in traffic volume,

• Use of piggyback by a regional carrier to offer service into a region outside the carrier's usual service area, often by arrangement with another carrier in the receiving region (these services were usually offered primarily as a marketing tool and produced small amounts of revenue); and

• For service to an area from which backhaul loads are unavailable (the trailer or container holding the freight on the rail leg usually does not belong to the LTL carrier).

Truckload Freight

Some diversion of freight from truckload to LTL operations may be occurring because of the introduction of just-in-time inventory systems and other changes in production and distribution practices. When a shipper shifts from truckload to LTL service, he is selecting a mode with much higher shipping rates (two to three times higher to move a given quantity of freight), presumably in return for substantial inventory cost savings. In such a cost calculation, the 2 percent cost reduction in LTL operations from twins use can play only a minor role.

Although cost savings from twins will not divert any substantial amount of freight from truckload carriers, it is nonetheless possible that LTL twins traffic in 1990 will be substantially higher or lower than that projected in this report. This eventuality would have little net impact on the conclusions of the study, because all costs and benefits would change roughly in proportion with the unpredicted change in twins travel.

More rapid growth of twins traffic would mean that trucking productivity benefits of twins would be greater than predicted in exactly the same proportion if the growth in LTL traffic is unaffected by the cost savings due to twins. If twins were to directly stimulate LTL growth by encouraging shifts from truckload carriers, the freight productivity benefit would be more than proportionately larger.

Similarly, pavement wear costs would also be proportionately greater if the growth in LTL traffic is not caused by twins. If twins were to stimulate LTL growth at the expense of truckload freight, the net pavement cost of the diverted traffic might be smaller because truckload vehicles tend to be more heavily loaded than LTL vehicles.

If safety impacts are close to zero given the predicted twins travel (as the following chapter will conclude), under the assumption of higher-than-predicted LTL traffic and no diversion attributable to twins, they will remain close to zero. If twins were to stimulate diversion from truckload to LTL operations, this effect probably would result in some small safety gains, because truckload carriers operate more miles empty and often have substantially higher accident rates than LTL carriers.

Air Freight

Some diversion from air freight to LTL service is conceivable, but the volume of domestic air freight traffic is small compared with that for LTL operations, and differences in rates and service characteristics are great, so a marginal change in LTL rates will have little effect.

Net Effect of Diversion and Generated Traffic

Despite the unique characteristics of LTL service, price reductions resulting from twins will stimulate some additional LTL traffic, either by diversion from other modes or by generating entirely new shipments. The foregoing descriptions of competing modes illustrate why the price elasticity of demand for LTL service is expected to be small. Many studies have estimated price elasticities of trucking demand, although the estimates usually apply to all of trucking or to broad commodity categories rather than to functional segments such as LTL carriers. These estimates are typically in the range of -1 to -2 (*31,43–45*). However, elasticity estimates in the literature for commodity categories with a composition similar to that of LTL freight (high-value manufactured products) tend to be among the lowest, in the range of 0 to -0.5. The major demand response observed in all these studies was undoubtedly shifts of bulk commodities and truckload-sized shipments between rail and private or truckload for-hire trucking operations. For the reasons cited earlier, rail is a much poorer substitute for LTL than for truckload service, so the price elasticity of demand for LTL service is probably in the low range of these estimates, − 0.5 to 0.0.

The cost and travel projections of this chapter predict a 2 percent average cost reduction in LTL service and anticipate a 6 percent reduction in total miles of LTL line-haul travel as a result of use of twins (assuming that modal diversion and new traffic generation are negligible). An elasticity of − 0.5 would imply new traffic equal to only one-sixth of the reduction of mileage for existing traffic. Most likely, the effect is even smaller.

Because the total costs (including transportation) of the products of the sectors of the U.S. economy that rely on LTL carriers will be reduced slightly by the productivity benefits of twins, demand for these products will increase somewhat. Because such growth stimulated by twins is believed to be negligible, the study did not estimate the benefits of increased productivity and expanded output to the U.S. economy as a whole, or to sectors reliant on LTL carriers, that might result.

Estimated Vehicle Weight Distributions

The general freight twins operating in 1990 will weigh somewhat more than the vehicles they replace. The highway impacts of heavier twins discussed in Chapter 5 assume that the weight differential in 1990 between semitrailers and twins will be the same as the observed weight differential in the truck weight data available for the most recent year before the 1983 act (these distributions were given earlier in Table 3-8).

REDUCED FREIGHT TRANSPORTATION COSTS

The shift to twins in the LTL general freight segment of the industry will reduce freight transportation costs and provide better service to many customers. Cost savings from the shift to twins, especially savings in handling costs, are extremely difficult to estimate because they depend strongly on individual carrier circumstances and variable market factors. The estimates presented in the following sections are rough, but suffice as reasonably reliable indicators of the order of magnitude of the savings. Major cost reductions will occur in two major areas of carrier costs: line haul and freight handling.

Line-Haul Costs

On the basis of the projections in Tables 3-10 and 3-11, tractor-semitrailer vehicle miles in the LTL general freight segment of the industry will decline 493 million vehicle-mi by 1990. The elimination of this mileage, at the approximate industry line-haul cost of $1 per mile, represents a gross line-haul cost reduction of $493 million.

The savings will not be quite this large because twin trailer truck miles cost about 2 cents more per truck mile than the tractor-semitrailer miles they will replace. Most carriers in the survey report paying drivers an additional penny a mile for driving twins; this is a standard provision in labor contracts. Assuming that this extra pay compensates for greater effort, skill, or experience required to drive twins, it represents a real cost rather than a transfer of some of the benefits of twins to drivers. In addition, twins require somewhat more fuel per mile because of the greater operating weight, and will increase maintenance costs slightly because most trailer maintenance costs are proportional to the number of units maintained. Assuming a total 2-cent/truck-mile operating cost penalty for twins from higher fuel and labor costs, the line-haul operating cost savings for 1990 (before consideration of capital cost differences) are closer to $400 million than $500 million (in 1985 dollars) (Table 3-12).

Handling Costs

Twin trailer trucks will reduce handling costs when carriers are able to bypass breakbulk terminals through direct loading. The carriers in the survey estimated that handling costs on freight shifted to twins would decline by roughly 9 percent. The mileage projections indicate that 75 percent of LTL line-haul miles will be in twins in 1990. This would represent a net change of 66.5 percentage points from the 8.5 percent of

TABLE 3-12 Projected Line-Haul Cost Savings in 1990

	LTL Line-Haul Mileage (mi × 10^6)	×	Average Cost Per Truck Mile ($/mi)	=	Total Cost ($ × 10^6)
Base case					
Tractor-semitrailer	8,455	×	1.00	=	8,455
Twins	1,050	×	1.02	=	1,072
Total					9,527
Projected for 1990					
Tractor-semitrailer	2,972	×	1.00	=	2,972
Twins	6,040	×	1.02	=	6,040
Total					9,133

Gross savings ($ × 10^6): 9,527 (base case) − 9,133 (change) = 394.

NOTE: Costs are in 1985 dollars.

total LTL general freight in twins in 1982. Thus handling costs in the general freight common carrier segment of the industry should decline on the order of 6 percent ($0.665 \times 0.09 = 0.059$).

Terminal and handling expenses for general freight common carriers account for 21 percent of total expenses (5). Although this category of carriers includes some truckload as well as LTL operations, most revenues in the category, and nearly all terminal handling costs, are in LTL operations. Very little LTL freight is excluded by ignoring the smallest (Class III) general freight carriers. Reducing this 21 percent share of costs by 6 percent implies that total costs by common carriers would decline by 1.3 percent. Expenses for Class I and II general freight common carriers totaled $21 billion in 1982 (5). By 1990 these expenses will increase in proportion to the increase in general freight mileage, resulting in a total of $25 billion. A 1.3 percent reduction in this cost results in savings of roughly $300 million.

These savings would be reduced by the higher capital cost associated with twin trailer trucks. The carriers in the survey reported paying more per complete combination truck for twins. The equivalent of about 50,000 new twin trailer rigs will be in operation by 1990 as a result of nationwide twins use (the forecast 5 billion annual miles of additional twins travel divided by 100,000 mi per year per truck). The carriers reported average added equipment costs equivalent to about $10,000 per rig, allowing for the reduction in the total number of trucks achieved through twins' greater efficiency and the fact that the carriers need more than two twin pups per rig or more than one full-sized semitrailer per rig to make up for trailer idle time. Assuming a 5-year payback period, additional capital costs for equipment amount to $100 million annually.

An additional capital cost of using twins is expansion of terminal facilities. Handling more trailers requires a greater number of doors (loading stations) at terminals. Also, more yard space surrounding terminals may be needed to move and store pup trailers, and some costs may be incurred in accommodating the greater width of the new trailers. Partially offsetting the need for more terminal space to handle twins will be the reductions in the average number of handlings per shipment and in the total number of combination trucks necessary to handle a given quantity of LTL freight.

If each of the 50,000 new twin trailer rigs gives rise to a requirement for one-third of a new terminal door, 17,000 new doors will be required. According to the carrier interviews, terminal construction costs are about $30,000 per door. Thus a total capital outlay on the order of $500 million will be necessary to expand terminals. Again assuming that carriers demand a 5-year payback, added capital costs for terminals will reduce the net benefit of twins by $100 million per year.

Thus, line-haul and handling costs for the LTL general freight common carriers will decline by roughly $700 million (1985 dollars) by 1990, offset by an added annual capital cost of $200 million for equipment and terminals. The net annual savings will be $500 million, 2 percent of these carriers' projected total costs.

REFERENCES

1. *Transportation in America: A Statistical Analysis of Transportation in the United States.* Transportation Policy Associates, Washington, D.C., 1984.
2. *Annual Truck Weight Study* (magnetic tape). FHWA, U.S. Department of Transportation, 1970–1984.
3. *Truck Inventory and Use Survey.* Bureau of the Census, U.S. Department of Commerce, 1980, 1985.
4. *Motor Carriers of Property Accident Master* (magnetic tape). FHWA, U.S. Department of Transportation, 1982, 1984.
5. *Trinc's Blue Book of the Trucking Industry,* 1982 ed. Trinc Transportation Consultants, 1983.
6. *1982 Financial Analyses of the Motor Carrier Industry.* American Trucking Associations, Washington, D.C., 1983.
7. *Cost of Transporting Freight by Class I and Class II Motor Common Carriers of General Commodities.* Interstate Commerce Commission, U.S. Department of Commerce, 1979, 1981.
8. *Monitoring Operations of Longer Dimension Vehicles.* FHWA, U.S. Department of Transportation, 1984.
9. *Tandem-Trailer Monitoring Program Monthly Summary of Key Information.* Pennsylvania Department of Transportation, Harrisburg, 1984.
10. *Van Trailer Size Report.* Truck Trailer Manufacturers Association, Alexandria, Va., 1982, 1984.
11. *FS-20: Selected Types of Motor Vehicles: Factory Sales from Plants in the United States.* Motor Vehicle Manufacturers Association of the U.S., Inc., 1982–1984.
12. *The National Motor Transport Data Base.* Transportation Research and Marketing, Inc., undated.
13. R. Cross. "Private Fleets." *Commercial Carrier Journal,* July 1984.
14. *Highway Statistics, 1983* (Table VM-1). FHWA, U.S. Department of Transportation, 1984.
15. D. Maister. *Management of Owner-Operator Fleets* (Table 1-2). Lexington Books, Lexington, Mass., 1980.
16. C. Glines. "Top 100: Trucking Industry Begins to See a Few Long Distance Swimmers." *Commercial Carrier Journal,* July 1984, p. 65.
17. "Presser's Push to Halt the Slide in Unionized Trucking." *Business Week,* Jan. 21, 1985, pp. 90–91.

18. L. Arbruzzese. "The Drive to Survive." *Commercial Carrier Journal*, July 1984, pp. 95–97.

19. R. Ross. "The New Era of Motor Carrier Marketing: Meeting the Challenge." *Proceedings of the 24th Annual Meeting of the Transportation Research Forum*, Vol. 24, 1983, pp. 193–200.

20. C. Glines. "1982: A Disastrous Year." *Commercial Carrier Journal*, June 1983, pp. 84–87.

21. J. Standley. "Industry Trends and Statistics." *Commercial Carrier Journal*, July 1985.

22. Mandex, Inc. *A Survey of Class III Motor Carriers of Property*. Office of Industrial Policy, U.S. Department of Transportation, July 1984.

23. *Motor Carrier Executive Survey Report: Strategies for Success in the Motor Carrier Industry*. Booz-Allen and Hamilton, Bethesda, Md., June 1984.

24. R. Cross. "Private Fleets." *Commercial Carrier Journal*, July 1984, pp. 105–119.

25. R. Kolins. *General Freight Common Carrier Productivity and the Liberalization of Truck Size and Weight Statutes*. American Trucking Associations, Washington, D.C., 1981.

26. R. Kochanowski and D. Sullivan. Truck and Rail Cost Effects of Truck Size and Weight Limits. In *An Investigation of Truck Size and Weight Limits* (Vol. 2), U.S. Department of Transportation, 1980.

27. U.S. Congress. House. U.S. Department of Commerce, Bureau of Public Roads. *Third Progress Report of the Highway Cost Allocation Study*. H. Doc. 91, 88th Congress, 1st Session, 1959.

28. M. F. Kent and H. Stevens. "Suspensions and Weights of Highway Trailer Combinations and Trucks, 1959." *Public Roads*, Vol. 32, No. 12, Feb. 1964.

29. *Traffic World*, Sept. 9, 1985, p. 22.

30. *Private Fleet Cost Index: 1984 Survey Results*. A.T. Kearny, Inc. and Private Truck Council of America, Inc., 1984.

31. *An Investigation of Truck Size and Weight Limits: Final Report*. U.S. Department of Transportation, 1981.

32. R.J. Hansen and Associates. *State Laws and Regulations on Truck Size and Weight*. NCHRP Report 198. Transportation Research Board, National Research Council, Washington, D.C., 1979.

33. Gordon Fay Associates and Traffic and Distribution Services. Carrier, Market and Regional Cost and Energy Tradeoffs, Part 2. In *An Investigation of Truck Size and Weight Limits* (Tech. Suppl. Vol. 7), U.S. Department of Transportation, 1982.

34. D. Maio. Carrier, Market and Regional Cost and Energy Tradeoffs, Part 1. In *An Investigation of Truck Size and Weight Limits* (Tech. Suppl. Vol. 7), U.S. Department of Transportation, 1982.

35. System Design Concepts, Inc. *Additional Truck Size and Weight Analyses: Impact of Allowing Doubles on the Full Interstate System and Using Only*

the Bridge Formula (B) to Limit Gross Weight. Office of the Secretary, U.S. Department of Transportation, April 1982.

36. R. Kolins and R. Selva. *Potential for Conserving Fuel Through Modern Truck Size and Weight Regulations*. American Trucking Associations, Washington, D.C., 1981.

37. *Railroad Facts: 1985 Edition*. Association of American Railroads, Washington, D.C., Aug. 1985.

38. L.R. Batts, R.N. Kolins, and R.T. Silva. *Increased Truck Weights: Their Impact on Relative Costs of Motor Carriers and Railroads and Potential Modal Diversion*. American Trucking Associations, Inc., Washington, D.C., Jan. 1982.

39. F.M. Larkin and K.E. Wolfe. *Rail-Competitive Truck Characteristics, 1977-1982*. Association of American Railroads, Washington, D.C., 1984.

40. "Shipper Agents Ponder Next Moves as Intermodal Growth Tapers Off." *Traffic World*, April 28, 1986.

41. "The Shifting Lines of Responsibility in Intermodalism." *Traffic World*, March 17, 1986.

42. R. Delaney. "Managerial and Financial Challenges Facing Transport Leaders." *Transportation Quarterly*, Jan. 1986.

43. C. Winston. "A Disaggregate Model of the Demand for Intercity Freight Transportation." *Econometrica*, July 1981.

44. T.H. Oum. "A Cross Sectional Study of Freight Transport Demand and Rail-Truck Competition in Canada." *Bell Journal of Economics*, Autumn 1979.

45. G.W. Wilson. *Economic Analysis of Intercity Freight Transportation*. Indiana University Press, Bloomington, 1980.

4
Safety Impacts

Nationwide use of twin trailer trucks has been controversial primarily because of fears that twins will cause more highway traffic accidents than the vehicles they replace. Concern for safety was the major justification used by states for laws banning twins and the principal argument supporting the legal challenges to implementing the 1983 federal law allowing nationwide use of twins. In mandating the Twin Trailer Truck Monitoring Study, Congress specifically directed the committee to observe the effects of twins on highway safety in urban and rural areas and in different regions of the country.

To respond to this charge, the committee has estimated the change in the frequency of highway accidents and in the losses due to accidents that can be expected from the increased use of twins resulting from the 1983 law. This change in accidents will be determined by

1. The intrinsic safety of twin trailer trucks compared with that of tractor-semitrailers, that is, the difference in accidents per mile traveled due solely to the physical properties of the two combination trucks that would be observed when the two vehicles were driven in identical operating environments (the same road types, driver qualifications, traffic volume, time of day, etc.);

2. Changes in the total miles traveled by twins and by tractor-semitrailers due to the 1983 law; and

3.   Any net changes in the operating environment—how truck travel is distributed across the various types of roads, kinds of drivers and firms that operate trucks, and so forth—that will result from increased use of twins.

The first objective in this chapter is to assess the intrinsic safety of the twin trailer truck compared with that of other combinations. The safety of 48-ft semitrailers and 102-in. wide vehicles is also examined. The intrinsic safety question probably is the most difficult of the three determinants to evaluate, because traffic accident rates are highly sensitive to many variables in addition to the types of vehicles involved. The effect attributable to the mechanical differences between two vehicle types must be isolated from the large effects of road conditions, driver skills, and other conditions before conclusions about the safety of a particular kind of vehicle can be drawn from historical accident and travel data.

In Chapter 3 estimates are presented of the second and third determinants—the changes in twin trailer truck travel and in travel of other combination trucks and changes in the environment of combination-truck travel—that will result from nationwide legalization of twins. The final objective of this chapter is to synthesize the estimates of all three determinants to project the total impact on highway accidents of the expanded use of twins.

In the first section of this chapter, the range of conditions that influence the accident experience of large trucks is described and the difficulty of isolating the effects of any one factor, such as truck configuration, when accident histories are examined is illustrated. Next the intrinsic safety of twins is evaluated. This evaluation relies on three kinds of evidence: the results of research measuring the handling and stability of various truck types in controlled circumstances, studies of large-truck impacts on traffic operations, and statistical studies of accident rates. Results of this evaluation are checked for consistency with recent twin trailer truck accident experience, including state accident data and a driver opinion survey. In the final section the conclusions about the intrinsic safety of twins and the estimates of changes in truck travel from Chapter 3 are drawn together to determine the likely nationwide safety impacts. Although emphasis is on the impact of twin trailer trucks, the evidence on safety implications of 48-ft semitrailers and 102-in. wide vehicles is reviewed also.

FACTORS AFFECTING LARGE-TRUCK ACCIDENTS

An accident typically is a complex event with several factors contributing to its occurrence and consequences. These factors may be grouped into those relating to the characteristics of the driver, the vehicle, and the environment (Table 4-1). Attempts to assign a singular cause may cloud the true nature of the event; more often than not, a combination of interacting conditions determines the outcome. It is important to keep in mind the complexity of accident causation in evaluating the safety consequences of twins, because observed differences in accident rates between two classes of vehicles (e.g., twins and tractor-semitrailers) will almost invariably reflect differences in their operating environment that affect safety as well as physical differences in the behavior of the vehicles themselves.

Some illustrative research results indicate the relative importance of factors other than vehicle configuration in determining accident rates:[1]

● Various studies (1) show that young drivers are involved in a disproportionately high share of large-truck accidents. Drivers under 30 make up less than 15 percent of all large-truck drivers but account for 30 percent of the drivers of large trucks involved in accidents.

● A recent study by the California Department of Transportation (2) illustrates the significance of road and traffic characteristics in truck accidents. Combination-vehicle accident involvement rates over a 5-year period on each of 18 road segments differ by a factor of 6 between the roads with the highest and lowest rates. The road with the lowest rate is a rural Interstate, the highest rural rate is for an undivided highway, and the highest rate overall is for an urban non-Interstate freeway.

● Characteristics of the firms operating trucks are also correlated to accident rates. In a survey by the Bureau of Motor Carrier Safety (BMCS) of companies reporting truck accidents in 1982, firms operating between 45 and 1,000 trucks report 20 percent higher accident rates than firms operating over 1,000 trucks (3). In another survey (4) fleets with fewer than 50 trucks had an average fatal accident involvement rate more than twice that of fleets with 50 or more trucks.

None of these accident rate comparisons was measured in a completely controlled experimental situation; that is, the conditions surrounding the groups being compared probably differ in many respects other than the single feature highlighted in the comparison. Nonetheless, they strongly imply that a variety of factors may be more important than trailer configuration in explaining differences in accident rates.

What are the special characteristics of twin trailer trucks that might make them more or less safe than the vehicle configurations they are

---

[1]See also Appendix F for a review of research on the effects of the operating environment on accident rates.

TABLE 4-1 Some Factors Contributing to the Accident Pattern

Category	Factor	Category	Factor
Driver	Education and training	Environment	Visibility
	Experience		Time of day
	Age		Pavement surface
	Maturity and		condition
	temperament		Weather
	Health and medical		Temperature
	condition		Traffic
	Fatigue		Volume
	Alcohol or drug use		Composition
			Speed
Vehicle	Configuration and		Density
	hitching		Roadway
	Size		Roadside features
	Weight		Geometric features
	Power		Cross-sectional
	Cab style		features
	Body type		Pavement surface
	Chassis design		features
	Crashworthiness		Roadway type
	Conspicuity		Location
	Inspection and maintenance		Traffic control
	Human engineering		Intersections and
	Driver's cab environment		interchanges
	Integrity of design and		Regulation and
	manufacture		enforcement
	Cargo		
	Weight		
	Density		
	Hazardousness		
	Restraint and liquid slosh		
	Loading pattern		

replacing? The evidence on physical differences between twins and tractor-semitrailers is analyzed in the sections on handling and stability and traffic operations that follow. Because of their two extra articulation points, greater length, and different load distribution, twins have different handling characteristics than tractor-semitrailers. Because of the difference in length, passing twins takes slightly longer than passing a tractor-semi-trailer.

In addition to differences in physical performance, the twins traffic resulting from the 1983 act differs from the bulk of tractor-semitrailer traffic on the road because the changes in equipment use are greatest in a single segment of the trucking industry—the less-than-truckload general freight common carriers. The drivers, trucking firms, routes, and cargoes in this segment are in some ways uncharacteristic of the industry as a whole. For the most part, the twins traffic generated by the less-than-truckload carriers is identical in these respects to the less-than-truckload tractor-semitrailer traffic being replaced; however, the specialized nature of this industry segment complicates the comparison of accident rates for twins and other vehicles.

Understanding the origins of observed differences in the safety performance of twins and of other combination trucks compared with that of other vehicles (related to how they are used and who uses them as well as to the mechanical characteristics of the vehicles) is essential for formulating effective policies for reducing losses from combination-vehicle accidents. Regulation can influence not only the size and configuration of vehicles operated but also the qualifications of drivers, the practices of carriers regarding vehicle maintenance and driver supervision, the characteristics of the roads used by trucks, traffic rules for trucks, and truck design and manufacturing. The best mix of truck safety regulatory policies will depend on the magnitude of the influence of each of these factors on accident rates, the amenability of each to regulatory control, and the impacts of alternative regulations on the efficiency of motor freight transportation.

SAFETY OF TWINS AND OF LONGER AND WIDER TRACTOR-SEMITRAILERS COMPARED WITH OTHER COMBINATIONS

Analysis Approach

This analysis of the intrinsic safety of twins is primarily a synthesis and critical review of prior research and experience. Such an approach is possible because twins have been in extensive use for many years, so a record of experience and research that can establish their relative safety impacts has accumulated.

The studies reviewed examine the safety of combination trucks from three perspectives:

• *Truck handling and stability studies*: These studies use both track testing and vehicle simulations to estimate and compare the handling and stability properties of large trucks. Because of the controlled nature of these experiments, they are useful for in-depth examination of vehicle characteristics that may contribute to traffic accidents. Results cannot, however, be easily translated into comparative accident levels or accident rates. Truck performance evaluations can sometimes be used effectively to explain or interpret the findings of statistical accident analyses.

• *Traffic operations studies*: These studies measure interactions among vehicles in the traffic stream, such as following distances, closure rates, speed differences, conflicts, and passing behavior. As with truck performance evaluations, the results can only suggest possible accident impacts.

• *Accident analyses*: These studies use accident and exposure data to estimate accident rates for twin trailer trucks and other vehicle types, usually expressed in terms of accidents or accident involvements per mile traveled. Their advantage is that they attempt to measure directly the question of primary interest: how safe are twin trailer trucks relative to other trucks? The major disadvantage of these studies is that the data often do not contain sufficient information for isolating the effects of truck configuration from the variety of driver and the environmental and other truck characteristics that also influence accident rates.

The review of truck handling and stability studies, summarized next, indicates how these properties of twins and of longer and wider semitrailers will differ from those of tractor-semitrailers of typical pre-1983 dimensions and suggests how such differences may affect the safety of their operations. The traffic operations studies are then summarized to show what changes in traffic operations affecting safety can be anticipated as a result of increased use of longer and wider trucks. Research on the accident experience of twins and tractor-semitrailers is reviewed, and finally conclusions are presented.

Handling and Stability

The handling and stability properties of large trucks have an important bearing on the safety of their operations. For example, if a truck does not respond quickly to emergency braking or if it is unable to maintain the driver's intended path or to resist overturning while negotiating sharp turns, it is reasonable to assume that the truck is more likely to become involved in accidents than vehicles with better performance. Thus, handling and stability studies represent an important supplement to accident statistics for examining the safety impact of large-truck operations. They are particularly useful for identifying vehicle-related factors that may contribute to traffic accidents and for making initial assessments of the potential safety consequences of new classes or configurations of trucks.

The handling and stability characteristics most related to safety that are influenced by truck weight, size, or articulation are the following:

• *Offtracking*: A condition in which the paths of the trailing wheels of a turning vehicle are offset from those of the leading wheels. In a turn at low speed, the paths of the trailing wheels of the offtracking vehicle are offset inward from those of the leading wheels (Figure 4-1). In high-speed offtracking, the paths of the trailing wheels of the turning vehicle are offset outward from those of the leading wheels. Offtracking can cause potentially hazardous encroachment by the rear of a trailer into the lane next to the one it is traveling in, can stimulate disruptive maneuvering by the truck driver or other drivers nearby, and can cause stationary roadside objects (e.g., signs and curbs) to be struck.

• *Response to rapid steering*: On combination trucks having more than one hitch coupling (such as twin trailer trucks and triple trailer trucks) the rear trailer may exhibit an exaggerated, whiplike response to rapid steering such that rear-trailer rollover results.

• *Sensory feedback*: To properly control a rapidly moving vehicle, the driver must be able to sense quickly the dynamic forces acting on it, but articulation delays and attenuates the driver's sensation of motions at the rear of the vehicle, decreasing his ability to react effectively to critical situations.

• *Braking*: Large trucks are unable to respond as quickly as other vehicles in emergency braking situations, and articulated vehicles are more likely to experience instability during braking than nonarticulated vehicles.

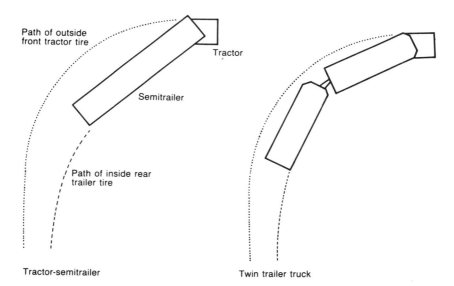

FIGURE 4-1   Offtracking at low speed. [NOTE: Drawings represent a 90-degree turn at low speed and are not to exact scale.]

• *Oscillatory sway*: Trailers of articulated vehicles can oscillate in response to small perturbations while traveling on a straight road. Sway usually does not jeopardize vehicle control but may distress the driver of the truck or other motorists.

• *Rollover in steady turns*: Large trucks are more prone than most other vehicles to roll over during steady turns, a condition exacerbated by high centers of gravity, excessive speeds, and sharp turns.

• *Yaw stability in steady turns*: Yaw stability refers to the quality of a vehicle's response to the driver's steering inputs in a steady turn. Large trucks tend to exhibit a mildly unstable yaw response in turns (that is, the vehicle may become difficult to control because of a greatly increased sensitivity to steering) when traveling fully loaded at high speeds.

In general, any combination truck will perform worse with respect to these handling and stability characteristics (that is, will be more difficult to handle) than smaller single-unit vehicles. The question addressed in this section is whether track testing and simulation research have shown the performance of twins and combination trucks with 48-ft semitrailers or with 102-in. wide trailers to be any worse than that of the conventional tractor-semitrailer 96 in. wide and with a 40- or 45-ft semitrailer. Results of the review are detailed in Appendix D. The conclusions are summarized in the following discussion. These conclusions apply to twins in which the trailers are connected together with a single-drawbar dolly, the usual practice in the United States (see Glossary, Figure G-3). In Appendix D a discussion of how different dolly design might alter the handling and stability of twins is presented.

Offtracking

Twins demonstrate significantly less offtracking at low speeds but slightly greater offtracking at highway speeds (where the centrifugal effect influences the path of the rear tires) than conventional tractor-semitrailers. Offtracking is more likely to be a problem for twins than for conventional tractor-semitrailers at moderate to high speed on freeway exit ramps.

Semitrailers 48 ft long encounter serious offtracking problems when negotiating at-grade intersections or similar sharp turns at low speeds. A tractor with a 48-ft semitrailer usually has a 3-ft greater distance between the fifth-wheel connection and the rear axle than does a tractor with a 45-ft semitrailer; therefore offtracking is a more serious problem with 48-ft semitrailers. At highway speeds, an increase in trailer length from 45 to 48 ft slightly reduces offtracking.

The amount of offtracking (measured in terms of the maximum lateral distance that the path of the rear tires diverges from the path of the front tires) is not influenced by vehicle width, although its consequences may be slightly exaggerated because of reduced clearances resulting from wider trucks.

Response to Steering

Both field testing and computer simulations have shown that twins behave much differently from tractor-semitrailers in their response to quickly applied evasive steering. In particular, there is a greater delay between the response of the tractor and the response of the rearmost trailer, and rapid evasive steering causes the rear trailer to experience amplified motion that can cause rollover. This whiplike behavior, referred to as rearward amplification, may explain the high frequency of rear-trailer rollover in twin trailer truck accidents and is probably the most important physical feature that affects the relative safety of twins and tractor-semitrailers. Twins and tractor-semitrailers do not respond much differently to gradually applied steering.

The responses of longer or wider combination trucks to abrupt steering are not appreciably different from those of 45-ft semitrailers.

Sensory Feedback

Because of the greater number and flexibility of trailer couplings in twins, their drivers are less well able than those of tractor-semitrailers to sense impending trailer instability and prevent related accidents. Impaired sensory feedback therefore may affect the relative safety of twins and tractor-semitrailers.

Although direct comparisons of longer and shorter tractor-semitrailers and wider and narrower combination trucks have yet to be undertaken, little or no difference in sensory feedback is expected as a result of small length or width changes.

Braking

The effect of truck configuration on braking performance has been the subject of intense investigation using both simulation techniques and field testing. With properly designed, maintained, and adjusted brakes, comparably loaded twins and tractor-semitrailers have been found to have similar emergency stopping distances. Of equal importance, little difference in controllability under emergency braking has been observed. One operating condition that may become rather prevalent with twins, however, involves the coupling of an empty trailer behind a full one to facilitate trailer movement between terminals. Under such conditions, the wheels on the empty rear trailer are severely overbraked and controllable braking is hampered.

No significant change in emergency braking is expected with increased use of 48-ft semitrailers and 102-in. wide combination trucks.

Oscillatory Sway

Although twins commonly exhibit some noticeable rear-trailer sway, limited observations of twins in service reveal that sway resulting from minor road disturbances causes only small-amplitude motions. The occurrence of sway has been associated with driver inexperience, slack in the hitch connections, improper trailer loading, and poorly maintained equipment. These factors are avoidable through proper operating practices. Oscillatory sway is a potential hazard only to the extent that other motorists may take anomalous action to avoid operating near a swaying twin.

The semitrailer in a tractor-semitrailer combination does not normally undergo any sway, regardless of the semitrailer's length and width.

Rollover in Steady Turns

One of the most significant findings of the truck handling and stability studies is the substantial improvement in roll stability, and consequently safety, that can be realized by the use of 102-in. wide trucks, provided that these trucks have the wider axles and greater spring-base widths to match the width of the truck bed. These studies have also shown that under steady turning maneuvers, roll stability is similar for twins and tractor-semitrailers and is unaffected by length of the trailing units.

Yaw Stability in Steady Turns

When turns are entered at high speed, a vehicle may become difficult to control because of a dramatically increased sensitivity to steering. That is, small increments in steering will tend to yield increasingly severe responses. If the control challenge is great enough, the driver may be unable to prevent the vehicle from spinning around, running off the road, or rolling over. Because the yaw stability level is lower on the shorter-wheelbase tractors that are typically employed with twins, there may be a mildly greater potential for such unstable yaw response with twin trucks. The significance of such a distinction has not been explored, however.

Vehicles 102 in. wide have better yaw stability than 96-in. wide vehicles.

Summary

As a complement to statistical accident evaluations, truck handling and stability studies are a particularly useful means for identifying vehicle-related factors that may contribute to traffic accidents. Among the handling and stability properties examined, differences in braking, oscillatory sway, and yaw stability in steady turns are small and unlikely to have significant safety implications for twins relative to tractor-semitrailers.

However, the increased number of articulation points in twin trailer trucks causes a significant degradation in their response to evasive steering, more greatly impaired sensory feedback, and slightly more high-speed offtracking compared with tractor-semitrailers, all of which probably affect accident patterns for twins by increasing the frequency of rear-trailer rollovers. Because they offtrack less under tight, low-speed turns, twins should be less frequently involved in collisions while turning.

Several of the handling and stability characteristics of combination trucks described in this section are more likely to create problems at high speeds. For both tractor-semitrailers and twins, yaw stability in turns deteriorates at higher speeds, increasing the chance of loss of control. For twins, oscillatory sway and the amplified, whiplike response of the rear trailer to sudden evasive steering become more severe at higher speeds. Because of these behaviors, the safety consequences of increasing speed are more serious in twins than in a tractor-semitrailer.

The one area in which the performance of 48-ft and 45-ft semitrailers differs significantly is low-speed offtracking. The increased offtracking of the longer semitrailer in intersection turns will increase its rate of involvement in intersection accidents.

A significant improvement in roll stability is realized by the increases in axle length and spring-base width permitted on 102-in. wide trucks. Because of the definitive correlation between rollover accidents and roll stability, increased use of wider trucks will avoid some accidents.

Summary Points: Handling and Stability

- **Twin trailer truck versus 45-ft semitrailer**   Twins show a poorer response to evasive steering and impaired sensory feedback, but superior low-speed offtracking; therefore, the rate of rear-trailer rollover accidents is likely to be higher and the rate of intersection accidents to be lower.
- **48-ft versus 45-ft semitrailer**   48-ft semitrailers exhibit worse low-speed offtracking; therefore, the rate of intersection accidents is likely to increase.
- **102-in. versus 96-in. width**   102-in. wide vehicles show significantly improved roll stability; therefore, the rate of rollover accidents is likely to be lower.

Traffic Operations

The safety of combination trucks is a function not only of their handling and stability properties but also of the influence of their presence in the traffic stream on the operations of other vehicles. For example, large trucks can obstruct the vision of nearby motorists and when they are carrying heavy loads on steep upgrades can impede the free flow of traffic. The following traffic operations effects of large trucks can have adverse safety impacts:

- *Speed*: Large trucks often travel at reduced speeds on grades, requiring following vehicles to react in ways that may increase the risk of an accident.
- *Passing*: The passing of large trucks by other vehicles on two-lane, two-way roadways is made more difficult by width increases that reduce the sight distance of overtaking motorists and by length increases that increase overtaking times and distances.
- *Freeway merging and lane changing*: Longer and heavier trucks experience greater difficulty in freeway merging. Their ability to safely enter the through traffic stream is impeded by their reduced acceleration capability and also by their increased length, which reduces the frequency of gaps into which they can safely move. The difficulties experienced by large trucks in lane changing are similar to those in merging.
- *Splash and spray*: Large trucks generate more splash and spray on wet roadways than cars or light trucks, thereby increasing the risk of accidents due to visual impairment.

● *Aerodynamic buffeting*: The likelihood of potentially hazardous aerodynamic buffeting as small vehicles approach and pass large trucks is increased as the size of the truck increases.

● *Blockage of view*: Large trucks can block the view of nearby motorists, thereby increasing the accident risk.

● *Lateral placement*: As vehicles meet or pass wider trucks, they must be positioned closer to the truck or to the pavement edge, or both, which reduces the margin of safety.

The following summary of the literature review in Appendix E describes the anticipated influence of increased use of twins, 48-ft semitrailers, and 102-in. wide combination trucks on the foregoing operational features.

Speed

The speed differential between large trucks and other vehicles has been reduced over time as a result of the 55-mph speed limit, continual improvements to highways, and the use of higher-powered trucks. Nevertheless, large trucks continue to travel more slowly than other traffic on severe grades, which suppresses the average travel speed, intensifies passing requirements, and increases the risk of accidents.

Because of their increased weight and the increased aerodynamic resistance of wider vehicles, twins, 48-ft semitrailers, and 102-in. wide vehicles are expected to travel more slowly than conventional tractor-semitrailers on grades where maximum power is required to maintain speed. According to the carrier interviews, twins users do not usually consider the greater weight of these vehicles to warrant increasing tractor power specifications.

Passing

The reduced speeds of large trucks on grades increase the number of overtakings by higher-performance vehicles. Safety can be diminished because of braking by other vehicles to reduce their speed and the increased risk associated with passing maneuvers. On multilane highways, the opportunities to pass are frequent except under severe congestion, and the lane-change maneuver entails little risk. On two-lane, two-way highways, on the other hand, passing is inherently more risky, and the degree of risk is influenced by truck size. Wide trucks restrict the sight distance of trailing motorists, and long trucks increase the distance and time during which the passing vehicle is at greatest risk. Because of these effects, passing twins, 48-ft semitrailers, or 102-in. wide vehicles in the face of oncoming traffic entails slightly more hazard than passing 45-ft semitrailers, although all the effects are small.

Freeway Merging and Lane Changing

The increases in truck length and weight that are anticipated are not likely to have a significant adverse effect on merging and lane changing. Past studies of the effects of trucks on merging and lane changing are inconclusive, although there are prior arguments that suggest that increased truck size and weight may have detrimental effects on the ease and safety of these maneuvers. The length and limited acceleration capability of large trucks may increase their difficulty in finding a suitable gap in which to merge without interrupting the flow of either main-line or ramp traffic. When a large truck is operating at reduced speeds in the outer lane of a freeway, the length of the truck combined with a backup of closely trailing vehicles may tend to block the entry of merging vehicles. In addition, increases in truck length and width may impair the rearward view of the truck driver as well as his ability to judge the safety of a lane change.

It is probable, therefore, that twins, 48-ft semitrailers, and 102-in. wide trucks will more greatly affect merging and lane-changing operations than will conventional semitrailers. However, past operational studies have not recorded serious disruption by large trucks nor have they identified significant differences among trucks of different lengths and weights, and it is likely that any differences of this nature will be small.

Splash and Spray

In wet weather, large trucks splash water, slush, or snow, creating, at the least, an inconvenience to nearby motorists and pedestrians. Further, the splashed droplets hit the underside of the truck, breaking up and causing a cloudlike spray that can impair the vision of motorists and increase the risk of accidents. Both controlled field testing and observations of trucks in service suggest that the extent to which the vision of other motorists is obscured will be reduced by increased use of twins. This is explained primarily by the different axle configurations of twins and tractor-semitrailers: the closely spaced tandem axles used on the latter generate more spray than the separated single axles of twins. On the other hand, it is also argued that the greater length of twins means that a motorist will be exposed to the spray longer when passing, which somewhat counters the advantage of the less dense spray.

The differential effects of the longer 48-ft semitrailers and the wider 102-in. combinations have not been documented in the literature, but there is no reason to suspect that these vehicles will generate any more or less splash and spray than 45-ft by 96-in. semitrailers.

Aerodynamic Buffeting

The aerodynamic forces acting on a moving vehicle are suddenly altered when it overtakes or passes a large truck traveling in an adjacent lane. Unless appropriate steering adjustment is quickly made, the small vehicle may suffer a rapid and potentially hazardous lateral displacement.

Primarily as a result of their increased length, twins and 48-ft semitrailers create more disturbance than conventional semitrailers, but only when the disturbed vehicle is on the leeward side in a crosswind. The differential effect, which is quite small, is not expected to increase the hazard of highway travel.

Wider trucks conceptually pose a greater hazard—more air is displaced at the front of the moving truck and the disturbed vehicle passes closer to the body of the truck. Both with and without crosswinds, however, these effects have been found to be negligible for the small width increase from 96 to 102 in.

Blockage of View

One of the potentially adverse safety impacts of large trucks is that they may block the line of sight of nearby motorists, temporarily depriving them of information essential to safe vehicle operation. The effects of increasing truck size have not been examined by studies reported in the literature, but the larger dimensions of twins, 48-ft semitrailers, and 102-in. wide trucks can be expected to marginally degrade visibility for other motorists.

Lateral Placement

Adequate clearances between vehicles traveling in adjacent lanes are necessary for safe traffic operations. The presence of large trucks not only reduces lateral clearances but also may require oncoming and overtaking vehicles to shift their paths of travel, moving them closer to the pavement edge and reducing the margin for driver error. The extent to which large trucks are detrimental to safety in this respect depends primarily on the width of the trucks and the lane and secondarily on shoulder width and type. Increasing truck width from 96 to 102 in. decreases clearance between the truck and a vehicle in the adjacent lane, although by less than the full 6 in. because both vehicles tend to move closer to the shoulder to compensate. Regardless of lane width, wide paved shoulders allow increased lateral separations and reduce the accident hazard.

Summary

Traffic operations are influenced by the presence of large trucks. Findings of prior studies, although not as conclusive as might be desired, indicate that twins, 48-ft semitrailers, and 102-in. wide trucks can have generally adverse but marginal effects on traffic operations compared with 45-ft semitrailers. One possible exception is a marginal reduction in the splash-and-spray hazard accompanying use of twins. It must be kept in mind that these comparisons are on a truck-to-truck basis, before allowance for the net reduction in combination-truck travel that will accompany expanded use of twins.

Summary Points: Traffic Operations

- **Twin trailer truck versus 45-ft semitrailer**   Twins may reduce spray but may be somewhat inferior in impact on traffic operations otherwise.
- **48-ft versus 45-ft semitrailer**   48-ft semitrailer may be somewhat inferior in its impact on traffic operations.
- **102-in. versus 96-in. width**   102-in. wide vehicle may be somewhat inferior in its impact on traffic operations.

Accident Rates

Although truck performance and traffic operations studies are useful, the evaluation of historical accident patterns is essential for ascertaining the influence of large trucks on highway safety. The number and severity of accidents are the definitive measures of safety. Meaningful comparisons of the accident experiences of twins and tractor-semitrailers are possible because twins have been in use long enough to have established a reliable accident record. The nationwide data used in Chapter 2 to describe trends in large-truck accidents and travel are not sufficiently detailed or reliable to establish the accident rates of particular combination-truck types such as twins. However, a number of special studies, using data for particular collections of roads or of truck operators, have estimated the accident rates and accident severities for twins relative to tractor-semitrailers.

In the following section two topics are addressed: first, a summary of the review of studies reporting accident rates for twins or other multitrailer combinations compared with tractor-semitrailers and, second, a summary of the literature review and of an analysis of BMCS accident records conducted for this study concerning the relative severity of twin trailer truck accidents compared with accidents of other combination vehicles. Appendix F gives a literature review of truck accident rates; Appendix G gives the literature review of accident severity and an analysis of BMCS accident reports.

The accident experiences of 48-ft semitrailers and 102-in. wide trucks are not yet well established. These trucks have been used less extensively than twins, and few sources of accident records identify the length and width of trucks involved. Consequently, the literature review identified no research or historical data sources that allow comparisons of accident rates of the longer and wider vehicles with those of other combination vehicles.

Accident Involvement Rate and Severity

The relative accident rates of twins and tractor-semitrailers as reported by the studies reviewed appear on first inspection to be extremely variable and conflicting. Among all the studies, the reported rates for double-trailer combination trucks ranged from about one-half the rate for tractor-semi-trailers to more than six times as large. The objective of the literature review was to narrow this range of uncertainty in relative accident rates by identifying the studies that were most successful in measuring accident rate differences that are genuinely attributable to vehicle configuration rather than to the confounding influences of environmental factors. In the review the following questions were answered, to the extent possible, for each study:

● Were there any obvious, debilitating flaws or errors in the underlying data and analysis methods?
● Was there adequate control for factors other than configuration that could affect the relative accident rates observed; that is, was the reported difference in accident rates likely to be due predominantly to intrinsic differences in the performance of the two vehicles or was it possibly due in part to difference in the environments (road conditions, driver skills, time of day, traffic conditions, etc.) where the two vehicle types were operated?
● Because no study can be perfectly controlled, what environmental factors that were not controlled for might account for part of the apparent differences in accident rates?
● To what operating conditions do the measured accident rates most directly apply (do they reflect primarily rural or urban road conditions, large common carriers or all types of carriers, etc.) and are these conditions

not so narrow or unusual as to invalidate generalization from the reported results to other situations?

Of the 14 studies reporting relative accident rates for twins and tractor-semitrailers that are reviewed in Appendix F, five stood out as studies that were the most nearly free from obvious methodological flaws, that made reasonable attempts to minimize the obscuring effects of the operating environment, and that reflect accident experience under conditions that are typical of many roads throughout the nation (Table 4-2).[2] All five of the better studies have shortcomings—uncertainties related to the accuracy of the underlying data, to the representativeness of the roads where the travel and accidents occurred, or to the possibility that environmental factors not accounted for in the study design or analysis could explain part of the apparent difference between accident rates. The principal such uncertainties are described in the following discussion of the five studies.

Chirachavala and O'Day (5)   Data for this study were taken from accidents reported to the BMCS for 1977, and exposure estimates were derived from the 1977 Truck Inventory and Use Survey of the Bureau of the Census. Reasonable similarity between roadway types, temporal distribution of operations, commodity types and densities, and carrier operating practices was achieved by limiting comparisons to intercity operations of van trailers by ICC-authorized carriers.

The accident data were carrier-reported and hence might be suspected of some bias. The nationwide estimates of miles traveled by each truck type are based on a small sample (less than 300 vehicles) for twins. Because of the nature of the truck use survey from which the travel estimates were derived, it was not possible to control for the effects on relative accident rates of differences in the travel distribution of twins and tractor-semitrailers across regions or road classes.

Glennon (6)   Accident and mileage data furnished by a large general freight carrier (Consolidated Freightways) allowed comparison of accident rates for about 300,000 pairs of similar trips by a tractor-semitrailer and a twin trailer truck. Each pair of trips comprised a tractor-semitrailer and a twin trailer truck operating on the same day over identical routes. Matched-pair study design, concentration of movements on main intercity highways,

---

[2]This group excludes studies that reported the extreme estimates of relative accident rates cited earlier. The study reporting a total accident involvement rate for double-trailer combination trucks of about half the tractor-semitrailer rate was excluded because the type of doubles and the special permit toll operation involved were not typical of twins and their nationwide use. The study reporting a casualty rate for twins of more than six times the tractor-semitrailer rate was excluded because the underlying exposure (miles traveled) estimates were unreliable (Appendix F).

TABLE 4-2 Summary of Comparative Accident Rate Studies

Study	Vehicles and Roads Represented	Years of Data	Involvement-Rate Ratio: Twins to Tractor-Semitrailers		
			Fatal Accidents	Casualty Accidents	All Accidents
Chirachavala and O'Day (5)	Nationwide, intercity van trailers, ICC-authorized carriers	1977	—	—	0.98[a]
Glennon (6)	Consolidated Freightways, nationwide	1976–1980	—	—	1.06[a]
Yoo, Reiss, and McGee (7)	Rural roads, California	1974	1.05	0.94	—
BMCS[b] (8)	Interstate carriers, nationwide	1969–1980	1.20	1.08	—
Graf and Archuleta[c] (2)	{ Rural roads, California	1979–1983	0.93	1.03	1.12
	{ Urban roads, California	1979–1983	2.29	0.82	0.79

[a]Ratio reported not to be statistically significantly different from 1. Significance tests were not reported in the other studies shown, but the uncertainties in all studies probably are dominated by possible systematic biases rather than random error.
[b]Ratio of average number of deaths or casualties per mile traveled for 10 carrier periods. See Appendix F.
[c]Data from multiple sites have been combined to compute the rates shown with weights equal to total (semitrailer plus multitrailer) mileage at each site. See Appendix F.

and validation of similar day and night distribution of operations and similar driver age and operational experience indicate exceptional control for operating environment effects.

Because this was a carrier-sponsored study, it might be subject to some skepticism; however, it did withstand close scrutiny in litigation. Certainly its results apply only to the safety experience that can be expected for twins operated by large general freight carriers in intercity operations.

Yoo, Reiss, and McGee (7) The accident measures were the total number of accident involvements of twins and other combination trucks reported to the California Highway Patrol in 1974. Relative travel by twins and other combination trucks was estimated from the frequencies of the vehicle types at counting stations at 15 locations around the state. Although no effort was made to control for possible differences in the operating environments for the two truck configurations, in the aggregate such differences are likely to be small in California because of the extensive use of a wide variety of twins there.

Estimates of the relative travel of twins and tractor-semitrailers based on limited counting at only 15 locations are highly uncertain, because the proportions of the two vehicles vary greatly according to the location, time of day, and season of the year and because the 15 counting sites were not chosen as a probability sample. By comparing all twins with all tractor-semitrailers (rather than limiting the comparisons to general freight carriers as did Glennon, Chirachavala and O'Day, and BMCS) the study fails to take into account the possible effects on accident rates of differences between the two populations in driver characteristics, trailer body type, frequency of empty trips, distribution of travel by time of day, and other factors that influence safety and are correlated with class of carrier. Because of the extensive use of twins in California, such differences in the typical uses of twins and tractor-semitrailers are of less significance than in other states, where uses of twins are more specialized. However, this unique character of the population of twins in California also prevents unqualified extrapolation to other regions of safety records of twins measured in California.

BMCS (8) A panel of 12 carriers, each operating both twins and tractor-semitrailers, reported annual miles, number of vehicles, accidents, injuries, and deaths for each vehicle type annually over a 12-year period. The BMCS data are less amenable to control for operating environment effects than the three previous studies. However, limitation to over-the-road movements by carriers operating both twins and tractor-semitrailers suggests reasonable similarity in carrier operating practices.

Carriers operating both twins and tractor-semitrailers presumably use them for different purposes, which are dictated by operating requirements, or in different parts of the country according to state restrictions on twins use. Therefore, some significant differences almost certainly exist between the operating environments of twins and tractor-semitrailers in these data. Also, the possibility of reporting bias in unaudited data reported by carriers cannot be ruled out.

Graf and Archuleta (2)   Miles traveled by twin trailer and semitrailer combination trucks on 18 sample road segments in California were estimated from a vehicle count station on each segment, and accidents by vehicle type on the 18 segments for a 5-year period were compiled from highway patrol records. Control for possible operating environment effects was achieved by limiting the analysis to roadway segments for which reliable accident and exposure estimates could be made. The site-by-site data reported by Graf and Archuleta may be used to make accident-rate comparisons limited to specific road classes (rural freeways and urban freeways).

Limiting the analysis to accidents and travel on 18 road segments was an attempt to circumvent the problem of the uncertainty of statewide travel estimates in the earlier California study [Yoo, Reiss, and McGee (7)] and to ensure that observed accident rate differences between vehicle types were not due to differences in the roads on which they travel. However, some of the road segments, which had only one counting station each, were very long (up to 120 mi) and included intersections, so the travel estimates must still be regarded as uncertain, especially in urban areas. Also, the same problems of the earlier California study arising from comparison of all multitrailer vehicles with all other combination trucks hold: there is no way to isolate the effect of configuration from the effects of differences in type of carrier. In fact, twins at the 18 counting stations performed a higher proportion of their travel at night than other combination trucks and were more often vans operated by general freight carriers, suggesting that operational differences between the two vehicle types may have been great enough to influence accident-rate differences. The peculiar nature of California twins traffic compared with the new twin trailer truck traffic that is appearing in other parts of the country as a result of the 1983 federal law is probably the most important shortcoming of both California studies as guides to the relative safety performance of this new twin trailer truck traffic. The California comparisons apply to twins of diverse body styles and types of operation, whereas the new traffic in twin trailer trucks is almost uniformly vans operated by general freight common carriers.

The California urban results are included in Table 4-2 for completeness but are based on a small sample (e.g., 10 twins fatalities were observed), and the urban exposure estimates are especially uncertain because entering and exiting traffic within the segments is presumably highest in urban areas (urban segments were each up to 70 mi long). The results from other studies in Table 4-2 reflect predominantly intercity rural experience, so the California rural results are the ones most comparable with the others.

Accident Severity

The matter of relative accident severity was also considered in a literature review (Appendix G). This is an important aspect of traffic accidents and one that is easier to examine than accident-rate comparisons because estimates of exposure are not required. The differences in accident severity between the two configurations reported in the literature were generally quite small and often statistically insignificant. The studies suffered from many of the same shortcomings as the accident-rate investigations, in particular failure to adequately control for possible effects of operating environment.

Because definitive findings regarding relative accident severity could not be reached from the review of published studies, the study committee undertook an original investigation of accident severity by using the records of accident involvement reported to the BMCS (Appendix G). Comparisons were limited to five-axle combination trucks carrying general freight in van trailers and operated by ICC-authorized carriers. To control for possible operating environment influences, the data, aggregated over the period 1976–1981, were partitioned into 32 categories representing all possible combinations of four regions, four highway types, and two land uses. The severity measures analyzed in most detail were the fraction of involvements in accidents resulting in injury and the fraction in accidents resulting in death.

Overall, twins were involved in 7.5 percent fewer injury accidents (statistically significant) and 15.0 percent fewer fatal accidents (not statistically significant) than would be expected if the fraction of twins accident involvements resulting in injury and death had been identical to those of tractor-semitrailers. The difference in injury involvement was attributable primarily to accidents on divided highways of four or more lanes in rural areas. Regional differences, if any, were not pronounced.

Perhaps the most notable difference between accidents involving twins and those involving tractor-semitrailers was that a significantly higher proportion of twins accidents were single-vehicle accidents (that is, involved no vehicle other than the truck), a factor partially explaining the reduced overall severity of twins accidents. In automobile-truck accidents, differences in severity between accidents involving twins and those involving tractor-semitrailers were small and in no case statistically significant.

Summary

Historical accident records have been used in a number of studies to investigate the relative safety of twins and tractor-semitrailers. The apparent contradictions in their findings are due primarily to various methodological and data shortcomings. In particular, most studies were not designed to isolate the effects of truck configuration from possible confounding effects of the operating environment, and few attempted to ensure that the twins and tractor-semitrailers that were being compared had been operated in similar environments, that is, by similarly qualified drivers, on similar roads, in similar weather and light, and in similar kinds of freight operations. However, five studies that were able to compare twins and tractor-semitrailers under reasonably similar conditions found ratios between the involvement rate of twins and that of tractor-semitrailers for all accidents of 0.98, 1.06, and 1.12 (in the three that measured the all-accident involvement rate) and ratios of 0.93, 1.05, and 1.20 for fatal-accident involvement rates (in the three studies that measured this rate). Because of the data sources used in this most plausible group of accident studies, this comparison pertains primarily to intercity operations over rural roads by general freight carriers.

Differences in the severity of twins and tractor-semitrailer accidents are small, and neither configuration is consistently associated with a more severe accident pattern.

A significantly higher fraction of twin trailer truck accidents reported to BMCS are single-vehicle accidents (involving only the twin trailer truck) than are tractor-semitrailer accidents. This difference appears to hold when other factors influencing accident characteristics (region, road class, urban or rural area) are held constant, and may reflect the handling difficulties of twins described earlier. Differences in the severity of twins and tractor-semitrailer accidents remain small when separate comparisons are made for single-vehicle and multivehicle accidents.

No historical data exist that allow comparisons between the accident rates of 48-ft semitrailers or 102-in. wide vehicles and those of shorter semitrailers or narrower vehicles.

Summary Points: Accident Involvement Rate and Severity

- **Twin trailer truck versus 45-ft semitrailer** Twins accident rates in general appear slightly higher than those for tractor-semitrailers. There is no significant difference in accident severity. A higher fraction of twins accidents are single-vehicle accidents.
- **48-ft versus 45-ft semitrailer** There are no studies available.
- **102-in. versus 96-in. width** There are no studies available.

Summary

The results of comparative truck performance and traffic operations studies do not point toward a major degradation in highway safety through the substitution of twins, 48-ft semitrailers, or 102-in. wide trucks for conventional tractor-semitrailers. Truck handling and stability studies, however, suggest that twins are more difficult to control than tractor-semitrailers and exhibit a greater tendency for instability, particularly during evasive maneuvering. Except for low-speed offtracking, the performance characteristics of twins may approach but are seldom more favorable than those of tractor-semitrailers. The handling and stability characteristics of 48-ft semitrailers are similar to those of 45-ft semitrailers except for increased low-speed offtracking by the longer combination, which may increase the frequency of intersection accidents. The wider vehicles have significantly improved roll stability, but otherwise their performance is similar to that of 96-in. wide vehicles. Larger and heavier trucks will marginally degrade traffic operations, although the degradations are small when these trucks are operated on roads with high design standards. The evidence from the truck handling and stability and traffic operations studies suggests that widespread use of twins, 48-ft semitrailers, and 102-in. wide trucks will produce small incremental degradations in truck accident rates.

Studies that have tried to measure the difference in accident rates between twins and tractor-semitrailers have produced conflicting results. Even the studies that have done the best job of controlling for the many factors other than vehicle configuration that affect accident rates are not completely consistent, but on rural highways they generally indicate that twins accident involvements per mile traveled are equal to or slightly more frequent than those of tractor-semitrailers.

RECENT TWIN TRAILER TRUCK SAFETY EXPERIENCE

The available data on trends in the number of twin trailer truck accidents from before 1983 to the present provide a check that the potential safety impacts of twins described in the preceding section are reasonable. Because this report includes estimates of both current travel and accident frequencies for twins and tractor-semitrailers, in principle it would appear to be possible to compute accident rates for each vehicle type and measure the safety impacts of twins directly. However, the uncertainties in the estimates of travel and accidents are large compared with the plausible range of differences in the accident rates of the two vehicles, so the following assessment of the trends in accident frequency will be qualitative only.

Recent data on accidents involving twins and tractor-semitrailers are available from four sources:[3]

● The National Highway Traffic Safety Administration Fatal Accident Reporting System (9),

● BMCS accident reports (10),

● Data from a few states reported with the state highway agency survey conducted for this study by the American Association of State Highway and Transportation Officials, and

● A special safety monitoring program organized by FHWA that is compiling accident and travel data for the federally designated networks in seven states.

These are each summarized in the following paragraphs. In addition to the accident data, results are summarized from an opinion survey of professional truck drivers conducted for this study during 1985, which asked the drivers to compare the performance and safety of twins and tractor-semitrailers. The survey included both new and experienced twins drivers.

No data are available on accidents for 48-ft long or 102-in. wide trailers. Only two states (Georgia and Virginia) reported that they collect any accident data by trailer dimensions, and these two have only recently begun to record this information.

Fatal Accident Reporting System

The number of multitrailer vehicles involved in fatal accidents in 1984 was 184, an increase of 25 percent over the average 147 annual involvements in 1980-1982 (Table 4-3). During this period multitrailer vehicles rose from 4.0 percent of all combination vehicles involved in fatal acci-

---

[3]Several of the motor carriers interviewed provided accident and travel data for twins and tractor-semitrailers in their fleets. However, some of the carriers did not have the data available, and a small number of carriers were unwilling to provide accident data that were in existence. Because the data are incomplete and unaudited, no carrier safety data collected during the interviews are reported here.

TABLE 4-3 Annual Multitrailer Fatal Accident Involvements, 1975–1985

Region	1975	1976	1977	1978	1979	1980	1981	1982	1983	1984	1985[a]
California											
No. of involvements	83	101	89	95	134	89	94	73	105	96	88
Fraction of all combination-truck involvements	.359	.461	.346	.352	.425	.295	.330	.289	.345	.267	.273
Other Western and Mountain											
No. of involvements	9	36	41	38	30	33	39	40	33	40	35
Fraction of all combination-truck involvements	.026	.095	.095	.083	.057	.077	.088	.106	.087	.104	.088
Central and Plains											
No. of involvements	21	19	16	14	21	31	20	15	35	33	31
Fraction of all combination-truck involvements	.017	.013	.010	.008	.011	.019	.011	.011	.024	.022	.022
East											
No pre-1983 twins											
No. of involvements	9	14	1	2	0	0	1	4	2	7	5
Fraction of all combination-truck involvements	.014	.016	.001	.002	0	0	.001	.005	.002	.007	.006
Pre-1983 twins											
No. of involvements	5	27	2	3	1	1	0	2	3	8	11
Fraction of all combination-truck involvements	.012	.058	.003	.005	.002	.002	0	.004	.005	.014	.020
U.S. total											
No. of involvements	127	197	149	152	186	154	154	134	178	184	170
Fraction of all combination-truck involvements	.041	.058	.040	.037	.042	.041	.040	.039	.050	.049	.048

NOTE: Nearly all multitrailer combination trucks involved in accidents are twins.
SOURCE: Unpublished data, U.S. Department of Transportation, National Highway Traffic Safety Administration Fatal Accident Reporting System.
[a]Preliminary data.

dents to 4.9 percent. Outside California, multitrailers involved in fatal accidents increased from an annual average of 62 (1.8 percent of all combinations involved in fatal accidents) in 1980-1982 to 88 (2.6 percent) in 1984. Preliminary 1985 data from the Fatal Accident Reporting System show 170 multitrailer involvements, about the same proportion of all combination involvements as in 1984. In 1984, 67 percent of all twins fatal accident involvements was on rural roads and 12 percent was on rural Interstates compared with 70 percent and 16 percent for all combination trucks and 58 percent and 4 percent for all vehicles.

The recent multitrailer fatal accident involvement trend appears consistent with the recent travel estimate in Chapter 3.

The Fatal Accident Reporting System does not distinguish between twins and longer doubles, and until 1984 did not distinguish between double and triple trailers. Judging from BMCS accident reports, twins are involved in at least 93 percent of all multitrailer accidents.

The Fatal Accident Reporting System data are known to contain fairly frequent miscoding of combination-truck types (*11*). Because of the uncertainty in vehicle identification, recent apparent increases in multitrailer involvements in some states may be spurious. Many state agencies (which are the sources of the fatal accident data) have given increased care to identifying twins since 1983, but in some states, multitrailers involved in accidents may still be misidentified as tractor-semitrailers.

BMCS Accident Records

Truck accidents reported to the BMCS also show a trend that appears consistent with the recent growth in twins traffic. Federal law requires truck operators subject to federal motor carrier safety regulations to submit a report to BMCS for each involvement of one of their trucks in an accident leading to death, injury, or property damage of $2,000 or more. Because of the criteria for who must report accidents, the accident reports are dominated by interstate for-hire carriers. Private carriers, intrastate carriers, and small carriers of all types appear to be underrepresented compared with their share of travel. A large portion of California intrastate twins traffic apparently is excluded from BMCS reporting. Nevertheless, the reports include most fatal and injury accidents involving twins outside California and are another source for observing recent trends in accidents involving these vehicles.

The number of twins involvements reported to BMCS increased from an average of 1,062 annually in 1980-1982 (3.8 percent of all combination involvements reported to BMCS) to 1,452 (4.5 percent) in 1984 and 1,574 (5.1 percent) in 1985 (Table 4-4). Outside California, the increase was from an average annually of 846 in 1980-1982 (3.1 percent of all com-

TABLE 4-4 Annual Twin Trailer Truck Accident Involvements Reported to the Bureau of Motor Carrier Safety, 1976–1985

Region	1976	1977	1978	1979	1980	1981	1982	1983	1984	1985
California										
No. of involvements	266	272	315	248	223	245	182	179	202	207
Fraction of all combination-truck involvements	.266	.245	.234	.185	.186	.187	.147	.154	.147	.155
Other Western and Mountain										
No. of involvements	326	374	427	442	413	366	440	418	465	379
Fraction of all combination-truck involvements	.138	.142	.133	.131	.118	.113	.132	.131	.139	.125
Central and Plains										
No. of involvements	369	458	525	566	392	418	415	461	572	686
Fraction of all combination-truck involvements	.038	.039	.039	.039	.032	.033	.032	.038	.041	.051
East										
No pre-1983 twins										
No. of involvements	8	19	21	34	8	11	12	38	119	174
Fraction of all combination-truck involvements	.001	.003	.003	.004	.001	.002	.002	.005	.014	.022
Pre-1983 twins										
No. of involvements	13	14	19	15	12	11	27	40	94	115
Fraction of all combination-truck involvements	.004	.004	.004	.003	.003	.003	.007	.010	.019	.024
U.S. total										
No. of involvements	983	1,137	1,307	1,304	1,042	1,051	1,076	1,136	1,452	1,574
Fraction of all combination-truck involvements	.044	.044	.044	.042	.038	.037	.038	.041	.045	.051

NOTE: Twins are identified as a tractor with two trailing units and a total length of 77 ft or less. Regions do not always sum to U.S. total because total includes some accidents for which the location was not reported.

Accidents reportable to the Bureau are those involving injury or death or those with property damage of $2,000 or more. Because the property damage threshold is not changed from year to year, inflation will impart some degree of upward bias to the trend in reported accidents over a period of years. This bias has no effect on the ratio of twins involvements to all combination-truck involvements.

SOURCE: Unpublished Bureau of Motor Carrier Safety accident report data.

bination involvements) to 1,250 in 1984 (4.1 percent) and 1,367 (4.6 percent) in 1985.

State Accident Data

Because every state maintains some form of statewide computer-based accident records system, monitoring recent trends in twins accidents might appear to be a simple task. However, most of these data systems have historically recorded few details about the types of trucks involved in accidents, and in the state highway agency survey conducted for this study only 16 respondents were capable of providing statewide counts of the number of multitrailer combination-truck accidents or accident involvements for a recent year. In the seven states providing all the data necessary to make the comparison, twins accidents increased from 3.2 percent of all combination-truck accidents in 1982 to 3.8 percent in 1984. These states (Missouri, North Dakota, Ohio, South Dakota, Montana, Nevada, and Wyoming) all had appreciable pre-1983 twins traffic, so, once again, the magnitude of the change in twins accidents is consistent with the estimated change in twins traffic.

In two eastern states that have closely monitored the safety impacts of the new twins traffic (Pennsylvania and North Carolina), the trend in quarterly number of twins accidents gives a good indication of the rate at which twins have appeared in the East (Figure 4-2). After almost no activity in 1983, twins accidents rose rapidly in 1984 and began to stabilize in 1985.

In the survey of state highway agencies, officials were asked whether they had observed any special safety problems related to the dimensions or configuration of twins or longer, wider semitrailers. One state, North Carolina, reported that it had observed what it regarded as a characteristic or recurring safety problem with twins: an apparently high frequency of separation of the rear trailer of a twin trailer combination during an accident. Of the 71 twins accidents reported to police in North Carolina between August 30, 1983, and March 9, 1986, 18, or 25 percent, involved separation of the rear trailer.

An examination of police accident reports determined that in 7 of these 18 North Carolina accidents the separation appeared to have been a precipitating event in the occurrence of the accident. In at least 2 of these 7 cases, and in several others among the 18 accidents, there were some indications that the separation occurred during a sudden steering maneuver (for example, during passing) of the kind that can stimulate the exaggerated whiplike response in the rear trailer described in the previous section on handling characteristics of twins. In the remaining 11 trailer separation

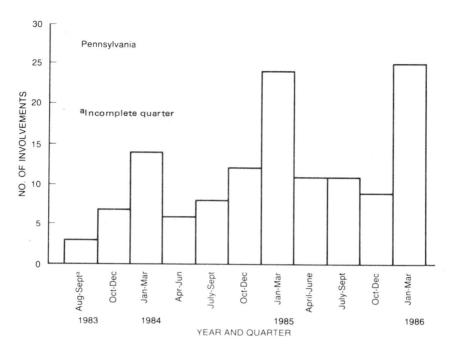

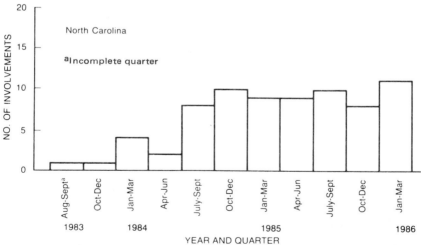

FIGURE 4-2 Quarterly number of twin trailer truck accident involvements reported to state authorities in Pennsylvania and North Carolina, 1983–1986.

accidents, the separation appeared to have occurred as a consequence of some other event (for example, rollover of the rear trailer) during the accident, and did not appear to have contributed to causing the accident. The police accident reports do not always show whether a rollover began before the disconnection, so it is possible that among the accidents where the disconnection appeared to be a precipitating event, in fact a rollover caused the disconnection.

Police reports of twin trailer truck accidents from other sources show roughly similar proportions of trailer separations. For example, in Pennsylvania, of the 60 twins accidents between August 1983 and January 1985, 12 (20 percent) involved trailer separation, and in 3 of these 12 the separation may have been a precipitating factor. Among 82 police reports of twins accidents between June 1983 and January 1986 collected by the National Highway Traffic Safety Administration for its nationwide accident data programs, 12 (15 percent) involved trailer separation. In these two sets of accident reports, as in the North Carolina reports, the separation was usually a consequence of loss of control of the vehicle, and often occurred as the trailer was rolling over.

Determination of the circumstances of accidents from police accident report forms is highly uncertain and dependent on judgment. Nevertheless, it appears that the phenomenon of rear-trailer separation in twins may be a factor contributing to a higher accident rate for twins, and may increase the severity of any accidents that occur. Although firm conclusions are not yet possible, this accident pattern may be further evidence that the rearward amplification in response to sudden steering motions observed in vehicle handling studies is reflected in actual accident experience.

FHWA Special Monitoring

In 1983 FHWA recruited the assistance of seven states (Illinois, Missouri, Nevada, Utah, Washington, West Virginia, and Wisconsin) in collecting data on miles of travel and involvements in fatal and injury accidents for multitrailer and single-trailer combinations and all vehicles on segments of the federally designated network. Most states have been reporting semi-annually, and the program is scheduled to run at least through reporting of 1985 data. Missouri, Nevada, Utah, and West Virginia are reporting data for the entire designated network in their states; Illinois, Washington, and Wisconsin are reporting for sample road segments only.

The monitoring results so far show lower involvement rates for multitrailer combination trucks than for either single-trailer combination trucks or other vehicles on all road classes (Table 4-5).

TABLE 4-5 Involvement Rates for Single-Trailer and Multitrailer Combination Trucks and Other Vehicles from FHWA Accident Rate Monitoring

Road Class	Vehicle Miles of Travel ($\times 10^6$)			Fatal and Injury Involvements			Involvement Rate (per 10^8 mi)		
	Single-Trailer Combination	Multi-trailer Combination	Other Vehicle	Single-Trailer Combination	Multi-trailer Combination	Other Vehicle	Single-Trailer Combination	Multi-trailer Combination	Other Vehicle
Rural Interstate	2,433	233	10,863	596	24	4,200	24.5	10.3	38.7
Other rural	1,112	115	12,220	461	25	8,889	41.5	21.8	72.7
Urban Inter-state	683	49	12,459	389	17	9,736	56.9	34.8	78.1
Other urban	125	7	4,808	96	3	7,777	76.6	40.8	161.7

SOURCE: Unpublished 1983–1985 accident and travel data for the federally designated network reported by seven states to FHWA.

The results supply some further confirmation that serious safety problems are not arising from expanded use of twin trailer trucks. However, the involvement rates reported for both single-trailer and multitrailer combinations appear to be extremely low when compared with other sources of accident rate estimates, and the quantity of data is still small. Therefore, the results of the FHWA monitoring so far cannot be taken as a conclusive indication of the magnitude of twins safety impacts.

Truck Driver Opinions

A survey of professional drivers conducted by five local unions at the request of the study committee provided another source of information about the handling and performance of twins and an opportunity to identify any problems that the drivers perceived with twins safety. The questionnaire (Appendix H) was completed by 178 drivers who had experience with long-distance driving in both twins and tractor-semitrailers.

Most questionnaires were distributed at regularly scheduled union meetings, completed by all or nearly all the drivers present who had driven twins and tractor-semitrailers, and returned at the meeting. The local unions that were asked to participate were selected to represent regions where twins had been recently introduced as well as regions where they had been used for some time. The five participating locals were in Indiana, North Carolina (two locals), Oregon, and Pennsylvania.

The typical driver responding was in his forties and had over 20 years' experience driving tractor-semitrailers (Table 4-6). Nearly all drove for large common carriers and, of course, all were union members. When the responses were divided into three groups according to the fraction of the respondent's driving career during which he had been operating twins, the drivers in the group with low twins experience averaged 2 years' experience with twins, drove 42 percent of their miles in the previous year in twins, and were mainly from North Carolina and Pennsylvania. The drivers in the groups with medium and high twins experience had driven twins a higher percentage of the time in the past year and most were from Indiana and Oregon.

In general, the drivers expressed a clear preference for tractor-semitrailers over twins, but this preference was considerably weaker among the drivers with the most experience in twins (Table 4-7). Most drivers in all three experience categories responded that the tractor-semitrailer is the safer truck and that it performs better on the road.

In the questionnaire the drivers were asked to compare the ease of operating a twin trailer truck and a tractor-semitrailer in a variety of situations. The ranking of situations according to the percentage of drivers

TABLE 4-6 Truck Driver Opinion Survey: Respondent Profile

	All Respondents	Amount of Twins Experience		
		Low	Medium	High
Age[a] (years)	49	51	49	47
Driving experience[a] (years)				
Combination trucks	24	27	25	22
Twins	10	2	10	18
Distance driven annually[a]				
(miles × 1,000)	100	97	105	96
Past year's mileage in twins[a] (%)	68	42	72	88
Employed by large[b] common				
carrier (%)	84	86	79	84
Distribution by domicile				
(no. of respondents)				
North Carolina	48	36	10	2
Indiana	94	11	40	43
Pennsylvania	18	13	5	0
Oregon	18	1	3	14

[a]Average values.
[b]Over 500 tractors.

TABLE 4-7 Truck Drivers' Overall Comparisons of Twins with Tractor-Semitrailers

	Respondents Selecting "Semi"[a] (%)			
Question	All	Low Twins Experience	Medium Twins Experience	High Twins Experience
If you had the choice on your current job, which truck would you prefer to drive?	63	80	57	49
Which truck is safer to operate?	77	87	75	67
Which truck performs better on the road?	71	85	68	58

[a]Choices on questionnaire were "Twin," "No Difference," "Semi," and "Don't Know."

stating that tractor-semitrailers are easier to operate (Table 4-8) shows an ordering that is consistent overall with the findings of the vehicle handling and stability studies summarized earlier in this chapter. Situations relating to the control of the vehicle on slick pavement, when braking, and in crosswinds were those for which the drivers in all experience categories most strongly preferred tractor-semitrailers. Twins were favored more often than tractor-semitrailers only for operating on city streets and turning

TABLE 4-8   Truck Drivers' Comparisons of Ease of Operation of Twins and Tractor-Semitrailers

	Respondents Selecting "Semis Easier"[a] (%)			
	All	Low Twins Experience	Medium Twins Experience	High Twins Experience
Operating on slick pavement	88	93	90	79
Operating under severe crosswinds	87	90	84	85
Controlling truck in emergency braking	86	92	88	78
Hitching and unhitching a trailer	85	100	83	73
Stopping quickly in emergency	81	90	79	72
Operating empty truck	80	87	81	73
Passing slow vehicles on two-lane road	71	80	69	64
Operating on very rough pavement	69	84	64	60
Operating truck having poorly adjusted brakes	65	79	72	43
Operating truck having worn or mismatched tires	63	68	65	56
Controlling loaded truck on long steep downgrade	63	67	66	54
Changing lanes on freeway	57	74	53	44
Passing slow vehicles on freeway	54	69	48	43
Operating on steep, curved off ramps	53	75	49	33
Merging onto freeway	45	60	38	37
Maintaining speed on long steep upgrade	37	51	34	26
Operating on city streets	33	61	24	14
Turning sharp corners	11	23	9	2

[a]The choices were "Twins Easier," "No Difference," "Semis Easier," and "Don't Know."

sharp corners. The drivers with the greatest experience in twins generally agreed in their rankings with the majority but preferred twins to tractor-semitrailers on steep, curved off ramps as well as on city streets and sharp corners.

The drivers were also asked to compare how often twin trailer trucks and tractor-semitrailers were associated with several potentially risky situations (Table 4-9). Here again, responses were in accord with the vehicle

TABLE 4-9 Truck Drivers' Comparisons of Frequency of Adverse Situations

	Respondents Selecting "More Often with Twins"[a] (%)			
	All	Low Twins Experience	Medium Twins Experience	High Twins Experience
Trailer swaying on open roadway	88	90	89	84
Magnified trailer movement in response to abrupt steering	81	80	84	80
Poor trailer load distribution interferes with handling	78	85	82	66
Following motorists hesitate to pass on two-lane roadways	73	82	66	70
Difficulty detecting quickly when trailer starts unusual motion	72	77	71	66
Hitch malfunction	67	76	61	64
A trailer feels like it is about to roll over	63	60	66	64
The truck feels like it is about to jacknife	62	60	67	59
Difficulty seeing rear of the truck	59	66	65	48
Brakes malfunction	51	53	56	43
Vehicles approaching on two-lane roads encroach on shoulder	43	58	39	33
Passing motorists pull in too quickly	39	53	29	33

[a]The choices were "More Often with Semis," "No Difference," "More Often with Twins," and "Don't Know."

handling and stability research. Trailer sway was the situation that the drivers most frequently associated more with twins than with tractor-semitrailers, followed by rearward amplification of steering motions and handling problems due to load distribution. Experienced twins drivers agreed for the most part with the majority, although they tended to see less difference between twins and tractor-semitrailers in most situations.

In the final section of the questionnaire drivers were asked for their own ideas about how to improve the safety and performance of twins and also for their overall opinions of 48-ft semitrailers and 102-in. wide trucks compared with the previous standard sizes. The suggestions most often mentioned concerning twins related to load distribution (even loading or placing the heavier trailer in front), proper alignment of all units in the combination, and adjustment, maintenance, or specification of brakes. Regarding 48-ft semitrailers, the most frequent comments were that they perform about the same as the semitrailers that the drivers had previously pulled, followed by comments referring to difficulties in cornering. The comments on 102-in. wide trucks most commonly referred to poor visibility.

Summary

The data available for monitoring recent experience with twins safety all show increases in the frequency of accidents involving twins. However, this increase is parallel to the expanded twins traffic that has occurred, and these accidents still account for only a few percent of all combination-truck accidents. Collectively, the recent data are still too fragmentary to confirm or revise the results of the pre-1983 accident analyses summarized in the preceding section. Professional drivers recently assigned to twins reported some problems with the handling of these vehicles in the truck driver opinion survey. More experienced twins drivers had less strongly negative opinions of twins, but regardless of experience, drivers more often chose tractor-semitrailers as the safer and better-performing vehicle.

Most of the available information on the relative safety of twins, from the recent safety experience data as well as the vehicle handling research and the pre-1983 accident rate studies, points the same way: twins have slightly more accident involvements per mile traveled than tractor-semitrailers operated under identical conditions at highway speeds. This conclusion is based on the following key findings:

● Twins are somewhat more difficult to drive than tractor-semitrailers. Field tests and simulation studies show that twins are more prone to experiencing rear-trailer rollover in response to abrupt steering maneuvers, provide less sensory feedback to the driver about trailer stability, tend to encroach slightly more on outside lanes or shoulders on curves, and undergo greater rear-end sway during routine operations.

● Professional truck drivers say that they find twins harder to handle than tractor-semitrailers, although they learn to cope with the handling differences of twins over time, according to the driver survey made for this study.

● The more reliable accident rate studies tend to measure higher involvement rates for twins than for comparable tractor-semitrailers on rural roads. The historical data also show that a higher fraction of twins accidents are single-vehicle accidents.

● The one available accident rate study that used accident and travel experience of a single trucking company and compared twins and tractor-semitrailers operating under identical conditions (6) tends to bear out twins' higher accident rate, although the difference measured was not statistically significant. Some carriers may experience lower accident rates for twins than for tractor-semitrailers in their fleets, but such results are likely to inflict differences in how the two vehicle types are used rather than intrinsic differences between the twins and tractor-semitrailer configurations.

● State highway agencies, with one exception, reported no special safety problems with twins in operation on their roads.

No single one of these findings unambiguously demonstrates the relative safety of twins compared with the vehicles they replace. However, the various sources of evidence considered as a whole all reinforce the conclusion that twins have a slightly higher accident involvement rate than tractor-semitrailers operated under identical conditions at highway speeds. The handling characteristics of twins suggest a physical basis for a higher rate for twins. Driver observations and accident rate studies also lend support to a higher rate, but not a substantially higher one. Neither state highway agency reports nor data on truck accidents and travel since 1982 show evidence that safety problems consistent with a substantially higher rate are emerging. A slightly higher rate for twins is also consistent with the observed pattern that a somewhat higher proportion of twins accidents involves no vehicle other than the truck.

SYSTEMWIDE SAFETY EFFECTS

The conclusions of the preceding sections imply that if a fraction of all the tractor-semitrailers on the road was simply replaced by twins on a one-for-one basis, with no change in miles driven or other characteristics of truck travel, then the net effect on safety would be small but probably negative. However, in addition to changing the dimensions and configurations of trucks, the new federal truck size rules have affected the volume and patterns of truck travel. The total safety impact of the new size rules depends on all three factors: the truck-to-truck comparative accident rates of twins, longer and wider tractor-semitrailers, and other combination trucks when operated under identical conditions; the change in exposure (miles traveled) for each truck type; and any net changes in the operating environment where truck travel occurs.

In Chapter 3 estimates are presented of the change in truck travel and in travel patterns due to the new truck size rules. In summary, four factors determine the change in total miles traveled:

- The extent to which carriers adopt the new equipment,
- The greater capacity of twins and larger tractor-semitrailers compared with the vehicles they are replacing and the extent to which carriers can utilize the increased capacity in practice,
- The effect of designated network restrictions on the road mileage between points served by the larger trucks, and
- Any new freight traffic attracted from rail to truck because of the efficiency gains from use of the larger trucks.

For the most part, the carriers using twins will operate them exactly as they operated the tractor-semitrailers replaced by twins; however, net changes in the operating environment of combination-truck travel may occur because of two factors:

- Restrictions on routes where the longer trucks can travel, diverting some truck traffic away from poorer roads (though at the expense of increasing trip mileage) and
- Effects on competition—if larger carriers could utilize the larger equipment better than small carriers and thereby gain greater cost savings, some freight would shift from small to large carriers, possibly a beneficial impact from the standpoint of safety.

In Chapter 3 it was concluded that the effect of the federal rules allowing expanded twins use on combination-truck miles traveled will be a 9 percent reduction on average in trucking operations that are converted entirely from conventional tractor-semitrailers to twins and somewhat less than a 1 percent reduction in overall combination travel compared with travel volumes if no expansion in twins use occurred and that the net change in the operating environment of combination-truck travel will be insignificant except in a few areas where the designated network is highly restrictive. In the paragraphs that follow, an estimate is given of what these travel changes, together with the intrinsic safety characteristics of twins, mean for highway safety. The use of 48-ft long, 102-in. wide semitrailers allowed by the new federal rules will also save truck miles, and the handling and performance characteristics of these vehicles, as described in the preceding section, give some grounds for concern about their safety impacts. However, no basis exists for quantifying the safety impacts of 48-ft by 102-in. semitrailers in terms of accident rate differences, so no estimate has been made of their overall effect on number of accidents.

Nationwide Changes in Accidents

Assuming a range of possible changes due to twins in combination-truck travel by 1990 according to the projection in Chapter 3 and the range of possible ratios of twins accident involvement rates to tractor-semitrailer rates established in this chapter, the net changes in annual highway accident losses by 1990 will be as follows:

	Net Change According to Percentage of Tractor-Semitrailer Miles Replaced by Twins	
Relationship of Twins Involvement Rate to Tractor-Semitrailer Rate	*8 Percent*	*4 Percent*
Twins have same rate as tractor-semitrailers		
Fatalities (no.)	− 30	− 15
Injuries (no.)	−470	−235
Property damage ($ × 10^6)	−5.4	−1.7
Twins have 10 percent higher rate		
Fatalities (no.)	0	0
Injuries (no.)	0	0
Property damage ($ × 10^6)	0	0
Twins have 20 percent higher rate		
Fatalities (no.)	+ 30	+ 15
Injuries (no.)	+470	+235
Property damage ($ × 10^6)	+5.4	+1.7

Thus if 8 percent of the travel now in tractor-semitrailers switches to twins by 1990 and the resulting new twins traffic has an accident rate equal to that of the tractor-semitrailers replaced, then the number of 1990 highway fatalities is expected to decline by 30 as a result of the decrease in total combination-truck travel accompanying the switch to twins. Similarly, a decline of 470 nonfatal injuries and $5.4 million in property damage from highway accidents is expected. However, if the ratio of twins involvement rate to tractor-semitrailer rate equals 1.1, there will be no net change in the number of accidents (because the reduction in accidents from lower combination-truck travel is exactly offset by the increase in accidents due to the higher accident rate of the new twins traffic). If the involvement-rate ratio is 1.2, then annual fatalities will increase by 30 and injuries and property damage by 470 and $5.4 million, respectively. If only half of the forecast change in twins travel holds (4 percent of tractor-semitrailer miles replaced by twins), the impacts in each case are reduced by half.

These estimates of safety impacts of changes in twins traffic depend on the following assumptions:

1. Combination-truck travel in 1990 is projected as follows:

Percentage of Tractor-Semitrailer Miles Switched to Twins	Miles ($\times 10^6$)	
	All Combination Trucks	Twins
8	72,500	7,800
4	72,700	5,300
No shift	73,000	2,700

The 8 percent switch to twins is the projection of probable 1990 twins traffic described in Chapter 3. The 4 percent switch is simply half this projection, to establish a range.

2. Combination-truck involvements in fatal accidents are projected to be 4,000 in 1990 if no shift to twins from their pre-1983 share occurs. This number of involvements implies the same rate in 1990 as that which occurred in 1983 (5.48 combination fatal involvements per 100 million mi traveled).

3. The following average ratios are assumed constant:

1.11 fatalities per combination-truck fatal involvement
15.7 injuries per fatality in combination-truck accidents
Property damage proportional to fatalities

These ratios are averages from 1983 combination-truck accident statistics reported by the Fatal Accident Reporting System (9), the BMCS (10), and the National Accident Sampling System (12). They are assumed to hold for both twins and tractor-semitrailers; that is, the two vehicle types are assumed to have equivalent accident consequences or severities.

4. The ratio of the twins rate to that of tractor-semitrailers is the same for fatal, injury, and property-damage-only involvement rates.

5. The average accident rate for the tractor-semitrailer mileage that is replaced by twins is the same as the average rate for all tractor-semitrailer travel, and the accident rate for the new twins traffic is the same as the average rate for all twins travel.

Several oversimplifications are embodied in these assumptions. However, the small magnitude of the projected changes in accidents (amounting to less than 1 percent of all combination-truck accidents) together with the uncertainties in the underlying accident rate and travel estimates suggest that a more complicated approach is not warranted.

The final assumption in the foregoing—that the accident rate for the travel diverted from tractor-semitrailers to twins is the same as the average for all tractor-semitrailer travel—is particularly imprecise and may have the effect of exaggerating the impact of the shift to twins. The shifted traffic will be made up mainly of general freight common carriers and will be more concentrated on the Interstates than other combination-truck travel. The effect of these two characteristics together might reduce the potential safety impacts by as much as half, that is, to a change of 15 instead of 30 fatalities in the extreme cases.

Regional and Urban Safety Impacts

The safety impacts of the increase in twins traffic will be distributed among regions of the country and between urban and rural areas roughly in proportion to the distribution of the additional twins travel due to the 1983 federal truck size rules. From Chapter 3, the percentage distribution of additional twins travel in 1990 (and, for comparison, the regional distribution of all combination vehicle miles of travel) will be as follows:

Region	New Twins Travel (%)			All Combination-Truck Travel (%)
	Rural Roads	Urban Roads	Total	
California	1	—	1	7
Other Western and Mountain	8	2	10	9
Central and Plains	33	14	47	43
East				
No pre-1983 twins	13	11	23	23
Pre-1983 twins	13	5	18	17
U.S. total	67	33	100	100

Nearly half the increase in twins mileage, and consequently the same proportion of changes in the number of accidents, is projected to occur in the Central and Plains states, and nearly as much will occur in the East. However, outside California, the impact is distributed about in proportion to each region's share of total combination-truck travel. Only in California, where half of pre-1983 twins travel occurred, is the impact of expanded use of twins small in comparison with the state's share of all combination-truck travel.

One-third of the additional twins travel will be on urban roads, and most of this will be on urban Interstates. As the literature review summarized earlier in this chapter showed, there are virtually no data or accident research results to support any inference about whether the relative safety of twins and tractor-semitrailers on urban roads is any different than that on rural roads. One accident study listed in Table 4-2, conducted in California, compared accident rates of twins and tractor-semitrailers on urban freeways and found some substantial apparent differences. However, the data were limited to five road sections, travel estimates were highly uncertain because of entering and exiting traffic at intersections within the segments, and the number of observations of fatal twins accidents was small; so the California study presents insufficient information to support conclusions about the relative safety of twins in urban areas.

The handling properties of twins may actually give them some safety advantages in urban areas. Twins offtrack less at low speeds than 45-ft or 48-ft semitrailers, making them easier to drive through intersection turns or other sharp turns at city driving speeds. Twins should therefore be less frequently involved than tractor-semitrailers in collisions while turning.

The survey of twin trailer truck drivers conducted for this study confirmed that twins possess certain operating advantages in city driving. When asked to compare the ease of operation of twins and tractor-semitrailers in a variety of situations, drivers rated turning sharply and operating on city streets to be easier in twins, and the most experienced twins drivers thought that operating on an off-ramp was also easier in twins.

The state highway agency survey (described in Chapter 1 and Appendix B) also requested information about the safety and operational problems on urban access routes of the federally authorized vehicles. Although states frequently cited problems in urban areas with 48-ft semitrailers (due to offtracking), no state reported observing any special problems for twins on urban roads.

Another possible urban safety advantage from increased use of twins is the replacement of full-sized semitrailers with single 28-ft pup trailers for urban pickup and delivery runs. Most of the carriers interviewed for this study are using pups in this way in place of longer trailers, and some expected that a reduction in pickup and delivery accidents would result, because the shorter trailer is more maneuverable. Any potential safety benefits from use of pups for pickup and delivery may be in part offset by their greater width and height compared with some older pickup-and-delivery trailers, and by any increase in miles of pickup-and-delivery travel due to their smaller capacity.

Summary

Taken together, the evidence shows that twins probably have slightly more accident involvements per mile traveled than tractor-semitrailers operated under identical conditions at highway speeds. However, the 9 percent reduction in truck miles in operations that are converted from tractor-semitrailers to twins approximately offsets the higher rate of accident involvements per mile that twins exhibit, with the net result of very little change in the number of accidents. Overall, twins clearly appear to be about as safe a method of hauling freight as the tractor-semitrailers they replace. This conclusion applies in the aggregate to the highway system as a whole; on individual roads, on which design and traffic conditions may be more or less suited to operation of twins or tractor-semitrailers and which may experience varying amounts of change in the volume and composition of truck travel as a result of nationwide introduction of twins, the consequences may differ from the average.

REFERENCES

1. J.P. Eicher, H.D. Robertson, and G.R. Toth. *Large Truck Accident Causation*. Report DOT-HS-806-300. National Center for Statistics and Analysis, NHTSA, U.S. Department of Transportation, July 1982.
2. V.S. Graf and K. Archuleta. *Truck Accidents by Classification*. California Department of Transportation, Sacramento, Feb. 1985.
3. *Calendar 1982 Accident Frequency and Severity Rates for Department of Transportation Reportable Accidents by General Vehicle Configuration*. Bureau of Motor Carrier Safety, FHWA, U.S. Department of Transportation, July 5, 1983.
4. K.L. Campbell and O. Carsten. *Fleet Accident Evaluation of FMVSS 121*. Highway Safety Research Institute, University of Michigan, Ann Arbor, March 1981.
5. T. Chirachavala and J. O'Day. *A Comparison of Accident Characteristics and Rates for Combination Vehicles with One or Two Trailers*. Highway Safety Research Institute, University of Michigan, Ann Arbor, Aug. 1981.
6. J.C. Glennon. "Matched Pair Analysis." *Consolidated Freightways Corporation v. Larson et al.*, 81-1230, U.S. District Court, Middle District of Pennsylvania, Aug. 12, 1981.
7. C.S. Yoo, M.L. Reiss, and H.W. McGee. *Comparison of California Accident Rates for Single and Double Tractor-Trailer Combination Trucks*. Report FHWA-RD-78-94. BioTechnology, Inc., Falls Church, Va., March 1978.

8. *Safety Comparison of Doubles versus Tractor-Semitrailer Operation.* Bureau of Motor Carrier Safety, FHWA, U.S. Department of Transportation, June 1983.

9. *Fatal Accident Reporting System* (annual). NHTSA, U.S. Department of Transportation, 1976–1985.

10. *Accidents of Motor Carriers of Property 1982.* Bureau of Motor Carrier Safety, FHWA, U.S. Department of Transportation, May 1983.

11. A.C. Wolfe, L.D. Filkins, and J. O'Day. *Factbook on Combination Vehicles in Fatal Accidents, 1975–1981.* Transportation Research Institute, University of Michigan, Ann Arbor, April 1983.

12. *National Accident Sampling System* (annual). NHTSA, U.S. Department of Transportation, 1980–1984.

5
Highway Condition, Operations, and Design Impacts

The nationwide introduction of new, larger combination trucks, as authorized by the Surface Transportation Assistance Act of 1982, could potentially harm U.S. highways by accelerating their deterioration, reducing their operating efficiency, and requiring more costly designs and construction.

These and other possible highway effects of twins and the longer and wider semitrailers were investigated in this study. The findings are organized into the following impact categories:

* *Deterioration of highway facilities*—The introduction or increased use of larger, heavier trucks may accelerate highway deterioration and increase costs on existing highways. The highway elements of particular concern are

Pavements, on which heavier loads, different axle configurations, or both may increase wear rates;

Bridges and culverts, on which heavier loads, different axle configurations, or both may increase deterioration rates;

Shoulders and roadside appurtenances, for which larger vehicle dimensions, different handling characteristics, and different axle configurations may increase either the frequency of excursions onto shoulders and roadsides or the degree of damage to shoulder surfaces or roadside appurtenances resulting from such excursions.

* *Highway operations*—The increased use of combination trucks with larger dimensions and different handling properties may affect the inter-

157

action between these trucks and other vehicles. In some circumstances, the effective highway capacity may be reduced and vehicle delay increased so that overall highway efficiency declines.

● *Highway design and construction*—The use of larger trucks may require that highways be constructed, or reconstructed, with thicker pavements, heavier structures, or more forgiving geometry (e.g., wider lanes) than would otherwise be the case.

● *Environment*—The introduction of new heavy truck configurations with different operating characteristics presents the possibility that highway related noise and air pollutants may increase, particularly in localities adjacent to corridors with heavy-truck traffic.

For each of these categories, possible theoretical and empirical bases for different effects due to twins or other new truck types are reviewed and a description is given of what sort of impact might be expected at the level of an individual vehicle or on an individual highway segment under realistic conditions. When there is evidence suggesting a substantial or measurable impact, the extent of such an impact on a nationwide (or systemwide) basis is evaluated, given the observed use of twins and other new vehicle types or their expected long-term use.

Impacts were evaluated wherever possible in quantitative terms relative to the effects that might have been expected had twins and other vehicle types not been legalized on a nationwide basis. However, quantitative evaluation was not always possible. Some impacts, those related to design or administrative practices, for instance, do not lend themselves to quantitative analysis and therefore were addressed qualitatively. Regardless of whether quantitative analysis was possible, some context is provided for each impact assessment to give an indication of its seriousness.

DETERIORATION OF HIGHWAY FACILITIES

Pavements

Highway pavements deteriorate in a number of ways that require repair, rehabilitation, or even replacement. For instance, flexible pavements, which are usually constructed with asphalt concrete, can develop ruts, transverse cracks, weblike "alligator" cracks, potholes, and surface roughness. Rigid pavements, constructed with portland cement concrete, also develop various forms of cracking and surface roughness and exhibit joint-related problems as well. These forms of pavement deterioration or distress are caused by a variety of factors acting both independently and in combination:

1. Load and vehicle characteristics
   a. Total gross vehicle weight (GVW)
   b. Number, type, and spacing of axles
   c. Weight distribution on axles
   d. Tires per axle
   e. Suspension
   f. Tire pressure
2. Traffic characteristics
   a. Volume
   b. Composition by axle or weight class
3. Environmental conditions
   a. Temperature
   b. Moisture
4. Subgrade earth and rock conditions
   a. Strength
   b. Drainage
   c. Compactibility
5. Pavement design and construction
   a. Pavement design or specifications
   b. Materials (base, subbase, and pavement)
   c. Construction quality
   d. Surface smoothness
   e. Subdrainage systems
   f. Shoulder characteristics
6. Pavement maintenance practices
7. Pavement age
8. Other (exposure to deicing chemicals)

Studies of pavement performance have focused on pavement design and vehicle loads, the way in which these loads are transferred to highway pavements (i.e., axle and wheel configurations), and the accumulations of loads over time (i.e., load repetition) to explain pavement deterioration. So far, researchers have had little success in relating environmental conditions and maintenance practices to pavement performance.

Although twin trailer trucks must operate with the same axle load and GVW limits as tractor-semitrailers do, the increased use of twins might nevertheless accelerate pavement wear and thereby increase maintenance requirements for the following reasons:

● *Twins weigh more on average than the tractor-semitrailers they replace.* The added cubic capacity of twin trailer trucks allows heavier average payloads, and the empty (tare) weight of twins is typically greater than the empty weight of tractor-semitrailers. Heavier average payloads imply fewer trips, which tends to compensate for any increase in pavement wear per trip, but pavement design relationships suggest that the incremental effect on pavement deterioration increases sharply as the load increases. For instance, when a single axle is loaded to 20,000 lb, it will do more than 12 times the damage than if it were loaded to 10,000 lb.

● *The weight of twins is distributed less uniformly than the weight of tractor-semitrailers*. Because the payloads in twin trailer trucks are divided between two trailers, the possibility of uneven loading between available axles is greater than it is for tractor-semitrailers. Pavement damage per vehicle is minimized by uniform loading.

● *Twins transfer their weight to highway pavements with a different axle arrangement than the one used by tractor-semitrailers*. Typically, a twin operates with five single axles (all with four wheels except the front steering axle), whereas a tractor-semitrailer operates with one single axle (the steering axle) and two tandem axles (each axle again has four wheels). For flexible pavements, studies show that the use of single axles is more destructive than the use of tandem axles at equal loads, thus favoring tractor-semitrailers over twins. On rigid pavements, the relative advantages of single axles versus tandem axles are reversed, but the differences are not as great.

A fourth possibility exists—that twins would increase pavement wear by diverting shipments from rail or other nonhighway modes—but this appears unlikely for reasons discussed in Chapter 3. Each of the remaining possibilities can be initially addressed by examining empirical and theoretical relationships between vehicle and axle loadings and pavement deterioration and applying these relationships for typical vehicle and axle loads.

First, existing pavement analysis and design procedures will be reviewed. Then the likelihood that twins will increase pavement wear because of heavier loads, less uniform loading, or different axle configurations will be examined. In a subsequent section the cumulative effect of these factors will be projected.

Pavement Performance and Design Relationships

Pavement performance is related to the nature and extent of imposed traffic loading—the numbers of vehicles of varying types and weights that pass over a given pavement section. For simplicity and manageability, pavement design and analysis techniques typically express the destructive effects of complex traffic patterns in terms of a single measure, the equivalent number of applications of a base or reference load and axle type. The conversion from the volumes and weights of different vehicle types to equivalent applications of the base axle uses load-equivalency factors, defined as the number of repetitions of a base load and axle configuration that is equivalent in pavement wear to one application of a different load and axle combination. Depending on the type of pavement distress selected, load-equivalency factors vary (*1*).

The best known and most commonly applied pavement design procedure is based on the results of a major research effort of the American Association of State Highway Officials (AASHO) completed in the early 1960s—the AASHO Road Test (*2*)—which involved accelerated testing of flexible and rigid pavements under carefully controlled traffic conditions. It was conducted by the Highway Research Board (now the Transportation Research Board) under the sponsorship of AASHO, now the American Association of State Highway and Transportation Officials (AASHTO) (*2*). The Road Test developed statistical relationships that link observed pavement performance with amounts of vehicular traffic, including trucks with different loads and axle configurations. It did not measure the effects of different environmental conditions and maintenance practices and did not explicitly consider more particular load and vehicle characteristics such as dynamic versus static loading, truck suspension systems, uneven loading of axles grouped in tandem, and tire pressure. The Road Test relationships define pavement performance in terms of a present serviceability index that combines multiple measures of pavement condition into a single parameter. These relationships are incorporated into pavement design procedures endorsed by AASHTO (*3*). For its load-equivalency factors, the AASHTO procedure uses an 18,000-lb single axle as the base load; any single- or tandem-axle load can be expressed in terms of 18,000-lb equivalent single-axle loads (ESALs) by using AASHTO procedures, basically derived from Road Test results.

For both flexible and rigid pavements, the AASHTO design procedures show that the effect on pavement wear of a given load increment increases significantly as total load increases. For a single axle on flexible pavements, for instance, the effect on pavement wear increases approximately as a fourth-power function of the axle load (Figures 5-1 and 5-2).[1] Other

---

[1]AASHTO design procedures report load-equivalency factors based on axle configuration, load, terminal serviceabilty (p_t), and a measure of pavement thickness—structural number (*SN*) for flexible pavements and slab thickness (*D*) for rigid pavements. Throughout this report, pavement wear comparisons are based on a terminal serviceability value of 2.5 and mid-range values for structural number (*SN* = 3) and slab thickness (*D* = 9 in.). Strictly speaking, equivalency factors should be calculated on the basis of the characteristics of a particular pavement, but the difference in pavement wear between two vehicle types, as measured by equivalency factors, is quite insensitive to pavement thickness. For example, for flexible pavements a structural number of 5 is probably more appropriate for the thicker pavements on primary routes where twins travel is most likely. If a structural number of 5 is used instead of 3, the rough estimate of added nationwide pavement repair costs reported later in this chapter is unchanged. (The raw results for the two structural numbers differ by 2 percent, and this difference is lost when the estimates are rounded.)

design procedures, such as those of the Asphalt Institute (4) for asphalt pavements and those of the Portland Cement Association (5) for portland cement concrete pavements, also indicate that the effect on pavement wear increases as a power function of load. Empirical and theoretical pavement design procedures in use in other parts of the world also reflect a power function relationship between axle load and pavement wear (6).

In its study of highway cost allocation, the Federal Highway Administration (FHWA) related traffic loads to different forms of pavement distress (e.g., cracking, rutting, and joint deterioration) for which rehabilitation costs were estimated (7, Appendix D). To do this, existing theoretical and empirical models were used to relate load to overall pavement serviceability loss (similar to the present serviceability index used in the AASHTO procedure) and a variety of specific forms of deterioration for flexible and rigid pavements (8). Generally, the resulting relationships also show that most forms of pavement distress are related exponentially to load and that overall serviceability loss closely follows the AASHTO design relationships.

For its analysis of pavement wear, the study used AASHTO load-equivalency factors to compare the relative effects of heavier loads, less uniform weight distribution, and different axle arrangements. The AASHTO method is not universally accepted, largely because the original testing

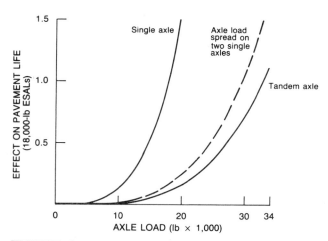

FIGURE 5-1   Effect of axle load on pavement life: flexible pavement (3) (equivalency factors based on SN = 3 and p_t = 2.5).

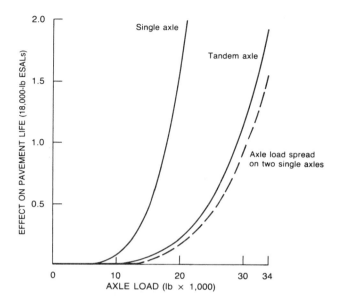

FIGURE 5-2   Effect of axle load on pavement life:
rigid pavement (*3*) (equivalency factors based on *D* =
9 in. and p_t = 2.5).

did not measure the effects of different environmental conditions and
maintenance practices. However, the AASHTO load-equivalency factors
are the best and most widely accepted means available to compare the
relative load-related effects on pavement wear of different vehicle configurations.

Effect of Heavier Loads

Compared with the tractor-semitrailers they replace, empty twins typically
weigh more (2,000 to 4,000 lb) and carry somewhat heavier cargo loads
on average (1,000 to 4,000 lb). As described earlier, pavement performance relationships indicate that increases in load exponentially increase
the effect on pavement life per vehicle.

To illustrate the effect of a heavier load alone, consider a 60,000-lb
tractor-semitrailer replaced by a 66,000-lb tractor-semitrailer. The
AASHTO design procedures show that the increase in total weight of
6,000 lb (10 percent) increases the effect on pavement wear by over

40 percent on flexible pavements and about 55 percent on rigid pavements (Appendix I).

Depending on the portion of such a weight increase that is attributable to added cargo (as opposed to higher vehicle tare weight), this increased effect on pavement wear will be partially offset by a reduction in the number of trips needed. But because the effect on pavement wear increases exponentially with load increases, the added cargo per trip will not fully compensate for the increase in pavement wear per trip.

Continuing with the example of a 60,000-lb tractor-semitrailer replaced by a 66,000-lb tractor-semitrailer, if the heavier truck carries more cargo and makes 9 percent fewer trips on average, it still will increase the net effect on pavement wear by 30 percent on flexible pavements and 42 percent on rigid pavements (Appendix I). Thus, regardless of any other differences between twins and tractor-semitrailers, twins will produce a net increase in pavement wear compared with the tractor-semitrailers they replace simply because they carry somewhat heavier loads on average and have somewhat higher tare weights.

Effect of Less Uniform Weight Distribution

Because of the exponential relationship between pavement wear and axle loads, pavement wear per vehicle may be minimized by spreading the GVW uniformly over available axles. Although trucks are seldom loaded with perfect uniformity, twins are generally loaded less evenly on average than tractor-semitrailers at equal GVWs, in part because payloads are often divided between trailers on the basis of destination rather than weight and in part because loads cannot be easily redistributed once trailers are loaded.

For instance, in the GVW range of 60,000 to 65,000 lb, FHWA truck weight survey data show that the average ratio of the heaviest to lightest tandem-axle load for a tractor-semitrailer is about 1.20 whereas a roughly comparable ratio for twins (the sum of the second and third axle loads divided by the sum of the fourth and fifth axle loads or vice versa, depending on which is higher) is about 1.32.[2] For a 60,000-lb tractor-semitrailer, a change in weight distribution of this order between the tandem axles can increase the effect on pavement wear by about 3 percent on flexible pavements and 7 percent on rigid pavements (Appendix I).

---

[2]Data are from TRB summaries of most recent state weigh station data reported to FHWA up to 1982 for loaded van trailers carrying general freight; individual state observations are weighted by state sample size and state combination-truck vehicle miles for national averages.

Therefore, even if twins carried the same loads and had the same axle arrangement as the tractor-semitrailers they replace, they would increase pavement wear somewhat because of less uniform loading.

Effect of Axle Arrangement

Both twins and the tractor-semitrailers they replace rely on four axles under the trailers (or trailer) to carry the bulk of the vehicle load. They differ in how these axles are spaced. On twins the axles are spaced relatively far apart (generally no closer than 9 ft). On tractor-semitrailers the axles are grouped into pairs, or tandem axles, where the space between axles is just 4 ft (see Glossary).

Pavement design and performance relationships indicate that such differences in axle spacing affect pavement wear. For example, the AASHTO load-equivalency factors for tandem axles differ from what would be expected if the load were divided between two widely spaced single axles (Figures 5-1 and 5-2). For flexible pavements, this difference favors the use of tandem axles—the combined load-equivalency factors for two single axles are generally 40 to 50 percent greater than that for the tandem axles. This relationship was established empirically and is incorporated into both AASHTO and Asphalt Institute design procedures, but a theoretical basis exists. The pattern of distress-causing strains induced in pavements by a loaded single axle is often sinusoidal, with the strain decaying from the maximum value beneath the center of the loading and reversing in type (e.g., from tensile to compressive) at some distance from the center. When two single axles are close together, as they are in tandem axles, the compressive strains caused by one axle can offset the tensile strains caused by the other, effectively reducing the net pavement strain (*6, 9*).

The extent of such strain interaction is dependent on the characteristics of the pavement and the axle spacing. For flexible pavements a compensating effect exists at typical tandem-axle spacings, whereas for stiffer pavements, the strains from the two axles may reinforce each other, increasing the net pavement strain. The AASHTO load-equivalency factors as well as the Portland Cement Association (*5*) design procedures suggest that the latter phenomenon occurs with rigid pavements. The combined load-equivalency factors for two single axles are about 10 to 20 percent less than that for the comparable tandem axles.

Thus, because of different axle spacings alone, a difference between twins and tractor-semitrailers with equal GVWs and load distribution is expected in pavement wear—a difference that favors tractor-semitrailers on flexible pavements and twins on rigid pavements. For example, on the basis of the AASHTO load-equivalency factors, a 60,000-lb twin trailer truck will have a 40 percent greater effect on flexible pavement wear than a 60,000-lb tractor-semitrailer with the same weight distribution on its axles. On rigid pavements, however, twins reduce the effect on pavement wear by 18 percent (Appendix I).

Overall Effect on Pavement Wear

To illustrate the cumulative effect of higher GVW, less uniform loading, and different axle arrangements, again consider a 60,000-lb tractor-semi-trailer that is replaced by a 66,000-lb twin trailer truck that carries 3,000 lb more payload, weighs 3,000 lb more when empty, and makes 9 percent fewer trips because of the increased payload and added operational flex-ibility of two trailers. On each vehicle, the GVW is distributed on available axles as observed in truck weigh station data. On flexible pavements and with an adjustment for fewer trips, twins will nearly double (91 percent increase) the net effect on pavement wear compared with tractor-semi-trailers on the basis of the AASHTO pavement design relationships (Ap-pendix I). Of this increase, the added weight accounts for about one-third and the difference in axle arrangement accounts for nearly one-half.

On rigid pavements and with an adjustment for fewer trips, twins will increase the net effect on pavement wear by 31 percent. In this case, the increase is attributable to the combined effects of increased weight and less uniform loading, which more than offset the favorable effect of axle configuration.

What these differences mean for pavements on the nation's highways depends on the number and weight characteristics of the new twins and the characteristics of the trucks they replace. In Chapter 3 rough estimates are presented of the annual vehicle mileage for tractor-semitrailers in 1990 that will be replaced by new twins once most carriers have had the op-portunity to switch. These estimates are based on a 9 percent reduction in vehicle miles because of the greater cubic capacity and operational flexibility of twins. Chapter 3 also presents estimates of the expected GVW distributions of twin trailer trucks and tractor-semitrailers developed from the most recent pre-1983 truck weight data reported for general freight carriers using van trailers (Table 3-8).

With these weight data, weighted average ESALs per vehicle were estimated for new twins and the tractor-semitrailers they replace by using the AASHTO procedures (Table 5-1). When these data were adjusted to reflect the lower mileage by twins compared with that of the tractor-semitrailers they replace, twins were found to cause about 90 percent more pavement wear on flexible pavements and about 20 percent more on rigid

TABLE 5-1 Average ESALs for Twins and Tractor-Semitrailers

Truck Type	Average Gross Vehicle Weight (lb)	ESALs by Pavement Type	
		Flexible	Rigid
Van Trailer Carrying Full or Partial General Freight Payload			
Tractor-semitrailer	53,900	0.80	1.15
Twin trailer	60,100	1.67	1.50
Empty Van Trailer			
Tractor-semitrailer	29,700	0.11	0.09
Twin trailer	30,800	0.14	0.09

NOTE: Data are from TRB summaries of most recent state weigh station data reported to FHWA up to 1982; ESALs calculated for each axle are weighted by using AASHTO design procedures (*3*) (p_t = 2.5, SN = 3, and D = 9 in.) and according to combination-truck vehicle miles by state. Data are not adjusted for fewer trips by twins.

TABLE 5-2 Estimated Increase in 1990 Pavement Loads from Nationwide Use of Twins

Region	Increase in Loads (ESAL-mile $\times$ 10^6) by Road Class			
	Interstates	Other Primary	Other	Total
California	5	13	6	24
Other Western and Mountain	164	112	73	349
Central and Plains	498	535	244	1,277
East				
No pre-1983 twins	290	306	129	726
Pre-1983 twins	208	237	124	569
Total	1,165	1,203	576	2,945

NOTE: Data were developed from average ESALs (Table 5-1), assuming 10 percent empty vans and 1990 vehicle-mile estimates reported in Chapter 3. Pavement type was estimated from *Highway Statistics, 1983 (10)* by state and road class.

pavements. Heavier loads and less uniform load distribution account for about one-third of this increase on flexible pavements. On rigid pavements, where the axle arrangement of twins has a favorable effect, heavier loads and less uniform load distribution would increase pavement wear by about 35 percent without the offsetting effect of axle arrangement. These results were used in turn to estimate the net increase in pavement loadings (in ESAL-miles) by road class (Table 5-2) and region. The Central and Plains region accounts for almost 45 percent of the increase, followed by the portion of the eastern region in which twins were prohibited before 1983. With regard to road class, the increase is concentrated on Interstates, which account for about 40 percent of the total increase.

Because of these added loads, affected pavements must be resurfaced either more often or more thickly if pavement condition is not to drop below the level that would have occurred otherwise. Either of these strategies involves additional pavement resurfacing and rehabilitation costs. Several studies have reported pavement rehabilitation unit costs in terms of ESAL-miles, but the estimates and underlying methods vary widely:

● Wong and Markow (*11*) reported average pavement rehabilitation and routine maintenance costs of 0.9 to 4.9 cents/ESAL-mi for Interstate highways, with different values depending on region (values in the Southwest are greater than those in the Northeast), pavement type (flexible usually more than rigid), and location (rural greater than urban). In addition, they estimated marginal rehabilitation and routine maintenance for the same highway groups ranging from 0.7 to 2.9 cents/ESAL-mi.

● FHWA in its last highway cost-allocation study (*7*, Appendix E) cited illustrative average unit costs of 5 cents/ESAL-mi for rural Interstates, 15 cents/ESAL-mi for urban Interstates, 13 cents/ESAL-mi for rural arterials, and 41 cents/ESAL-mi for urban arterials.

● FHWA, in its recent study of longer combination trucks (*12*), cited a figure of 14.8 cents/ESAL-mi for additional pavement investment.

Rather than using any of these estimates to put the additional costs resulting from the use of twins in perspective, the study used a rough cost per ESAL-mile for rural Interstates based on national highway statistics. Rural Interstates alone will account for about one-third of the travel by twins.

Federal-aid apportionments for Interstate resurfacing, restoration, rehabilitation, and reconstruction (4R) work in 1984 totaled $1.9 billion. If this figure is prorated to rural Interstates based on 1983 federal-aid Interstate spending and adjusted to include state funds used for matching federal aid and undertaking non-federal-aid projects, total spending for rural Interstate 4R work is about $1.6 billion annually.[3] Of this, it is assumed that 70 percent actually is used for pavement repairs instead of geometric or roadside improvements.[4] It is further assumed that of pave-

---

[3]The factors used to prorate costs between urban and rural Interstates, as well as those used to adjust costs upward to include non-federal-aid projects, were developed from 1983 expenditure data for 44 states presented in *Highway Statistics, 1983* (*10*, pp. 77-83).

[4]Interstate 4R expenditures include not only costs for pavement resurfacing but also costs for added lanes, improved geometrics, and roadside improvements. It is assumed here that these other costs account for 30 percent of 4R expenditures on rural Interstates.

ment rehabilitation costs, 70 percent can be attributed to load as measured by ESALs, a figure that matches the conclusions of the last FHWA highway cost-allocation study.[5] Thus, of the $1.6 billion, about half, $800 million, is spent on load-related Interstate pavement rehabilitation. FHWA statistics indicate that the total annual loading on rural Interstates amounts to about 50 billion ESAL-mi, for an average load-related pavement rehabilitation cost of 1.6 cents/ESAL-mi.

The 1.6-cent average cost per ESAL-mile is based on the assumption that the 1984 Interstate 4R apportionment is just adequate to keep pace with pavement deterioration. The condition of Interstate pavements worsened between 1975 and 1983, which suggests that the 1.6-cent average cost may be understated. On the other hand, the 1984 apportionment is almost 2.5 times the 1983 apportionment, which is itself much greater than apportionments for previous years. Thus, it is also possible that the 1.6-cent figure may overstate average cost appreciably.

Nevertheless, applying this figure to the added ESAL-miles expected because of twins on all roads by 1990 (Chapter 3) yields a rough estimate of $50 million per year in added pavement rehabilitation costs, which is roughly 2 percent of 1983 highway rehabilitation expenditures by states[6] and less than 10 percent of the expected 1990 annual productivity gains to the trucking industry (Chapter 3).

Although twins cause more wear than the tractor-semitrailers they replace, the typical twin trailer truck is not the most damaging vehicle in legal use on U.S. highways. For example, on the basis of TRB summaries of weigh station data reported to FHWA, the average tractor with hopper semitrailer carrying agricultural commodities on Interstates causes more wear than the average for twins (this excludes empty trucks in both cases).

Other New Truck Types

Concentrating on twins, the study did not estimate the nationwide pavement effects of other vehicle types legalized by the 1983 act—the 48-ft semitrailer and 102-in. wide trucks of all types. These vehicles will also

---

[5] In the FHWA highway cost-allocation study (*7*, p. IV-50) it was found that the relationship between axle loads and pavement condition varies depending on the type of pavement, region, and pavement distress under consideration. As the authors of the study point out, however, the overall allocation of pavement rehabilitation costs is very close to that which would be obtained by assuming that 70 percent of costs are related to ESALs and that the remaining 30 percent are unrelated to load.

[6] In FHWA's *Highway Statistics, 1983* (*10*) total capital disbursements by state highway agencies of $14.8 billion are reported of which resurfacing, restoration, and rehabilitation projects account for about one-fourth ($3.7 billion).

accelerate pavement deterioration, principally because their added cubic capacity and tare weight will tend to increase average GVWs. No differential effects due to load distribution or axle configuration are expected. As a result, the change in pavement loadings per vehicle will be substantially less for these trucks than the change expected for twins. However, more 48-ft semitrailers and 102-in. wide trucks of all types will be introduced than twins, so the nationwide effect may equal or exceed the effect of twins.

Summary Points: Pavement Wear

- **Twins versus 45-ft semitrailers** Twins increase net pavement wear per vehicle on flexible and rigid pavements. Nationwide pavement rehabilitation costs will increase by roughly $50 million per year by 1990.
- **48-ft versus 45-ft semitrailers** 48-ft tractor-semitrailers increase net pavement wear per vehicle. Nationwide effects have not been estimated.
- **102-in. versus 96-in. width** 102-in. wide trucks increase net pavement wear per vehicle. Nationwide effects have not been estimated.

Bridges and Culverts

State highway agencies spend over $400 million annually to maintain highway structures, and the federal government provides nearly $1.5 billion annually to replace and rehabilitate existing bridges (*10*). Although less visible than bridges, culverts—pipelike drainage structures that carry surface water transversely beneath highways—are far more common and account for about one-sixth of all highway construction spending (*13*,p.424).

Bridges deteriorate and become less serviceable for a variety of reasons, generally related to how they are used, how they are maintained, or the environmental setting in which they are located. In addition, the quality of the original construction and the materials used have an effect on the rate of deterioration. The magnitude and frequency of loads placed on bridges by traffic, especially large trucks, is a primary use-related cause of bridge deterioration, and the expected use by heavy trucks is an important factor in bridge design. Similarly, highway loading is one of a number of factors that may contribute to the deterioration of culverts.

Because most recently constructed bridges and culverts were designed to withstand forces greater than those produced by trucks loaded to the legal GVW limit, imposition of higher (or different) loads through modest changes in legal truck weights and configurations will not appreciably increase the risk of collapse (catastrophic failures of new bridges have occurred only when bridges were grossly underdesigned or improperly constructed). But such changes in load may reduce remaining service life through repetitive load applications that can cause fatigue failure. The safety issue is of greater concern for older bridges, which may have been constructed to lower standards, and is usually handled by posting of special weight limits by state and local highway agencies. When new vehicle configurations are introduced without increases to either the maximum legal GVW or maximum loads on axles and axle groups, the risk of collapse of unposted bridges should not increase, regardless of age, but fatigue damage might be accelerated, thereby shortening useful bridge life.

The nationwide introduction of twins was not accompanied by any changes in federal load limit maximums, but as with pavements, bridge and culvert damage might conceivably be accelerated. Compared with the tractor-semitrailers they replace, twins have higher GVWs, distribute their loads on available axles less uniformly, and transfer their loads to supporting structures differently. Prior studies that have examined the effects of different truck classes on highways, such as the U.S. Department of Transportation Truck Size and Weight Study (*14*) and FHWA's highway cost allocation study (*7*), have not generally related bridge and culvert deterioration and resulting maintenance costs to specific heavy-vehicle types. Nevertheless, relevant studies and design procedures with respect to major bridge elements and culverts were reviewed and it was concluded, as in earlier studies, that no change in bridge and culvert deterioration will occur because of the nationwide introduction of twins or other new truck types. In brief, the reasons for this conclusion are outlined in the following paragraphs.

Bridge Substructures

The dimensioning of piers, abutments, and other foundation structures that support a bridge and constitute its substructure is dictated primarily by the weight of the bridge itself. Changes in traffic loading, even when the GVW limit on trucks is modestly increased, would usually have an inconsequential effect on existing bridge substructures.

Bridge Superstructures

Longitudinal bridge girders, trusses, or arches and transverse floor beams that form the superstructure are designed to withstand forces that would be induced by hypothetical truck loading patterns. Provided that actual forces from in-service trucks do not exceed these design levels, no practical effect on bridge service life exists, unless truck volumes are very much greater than those expected at the time of design. Because the introduction of twins and other new truck types will tend to reduce truck traffic, the key concern is how the forces induced by these vehicles compare with those of the hypothetical vehicles used for design. At span lengths where single vehicle loads govern design, the forces created by fully loaded (80,000-lb) twins are less than those created by the hypothetical loading pattern (HS 20-44) used for Interstate bridges and other bridges with substantial truck traffic, and in addition are generally less than the forces induced by comparably loaded 45-ft semitrailers. At longer span lengths where multiple truck-loading patterns govern design, trains of fully loaded twins create lower forces generally than trains of fully loaded tractor-semitrailers. The forces produced by 48-ft semitrailers on bridge super-structures are no greater than those induced by the 45-ft semitrailer at the same GVW, and the added axle length on 102-in. wide trucks will have inconsequential effects.

Bridge Decks

Bridge decks and roadways are designed to withstand the same hypo-thetical loading patterns as bridge superstructures, and as is the case for superstructures, fully loaded twins and 48-ft semitrailers will generally create forces that are well below those induced by the hypothetical design loads and lower than or about the same as those of fully loaded 45-ft semitrailers. Similarly, the increase in width to 102 in. will have no practical effect.

Culverts

Culverts are designed with respect to the same hypothetical truck loading patterns as bridges, and these loads are at least as severe on buried culvert structures as those from fully loaded twins or 48-ft semitrailers. Theo-retically, single axles used on twins are somewhat more destructive than tandem axles used on tractor-semitrailers for heavy loads, but the differ-ences are of no practical consequence except for shallow culverts that are constructed with less than 2 ft of cover, an uncommon practice on Interstate and major primary highways.

Detailed explanations of these findings are presented in Appendix J.

Summary Points: Bridges and Culverts

- **Twins versus 45-ft semitrailers** There is no difference between fully loaded trucks. No systemwide differences are expected.
- **48-ft versus 45-ft semitrailers** There is no difference between fully loaded trucks. No systemwide differences are expected.
- **102-in. versus 96-in. width** There is no difference between fully loaded trucks. No systemwide differences are expected.

Shoulders and Roadside Appurtenances

Highway vehicles make minor, unintended excursions onto shoulders during normal operation and make more deliberate movements onto shoulders during emergency situations. In addition, shoulders are used for a variety of other purposes—heavy trucks routinely park on shoulders to check loads or mechanical conditions; vehicles often use shoulders to turn or pass at intersections; vehicles sometimes use shoulders as full running lanes in congested, high-volume situations; and some states permit slow-moving vehicles to operate on shoulders to allow faster vehicles to pass more easily (*15*). All of these maneuvers raise obvious safety concerns (see Chapter 4) but in addition can damage highway facilities and appurtenances located beyond the travel lanes. More specifically, heavy vehicles can cause deterioration of shoulder surfaces, which often are not constructed in the same manner or with the same load-bearing capability as roadway pavements. When vehicles encroach on roadsides while turning, they can strike signing, curbs, traffic islands, and roadside protective devices (e.g., guardrails), sometimes (particularly at low speeds) not severely enough to disable the vehicle or even force it to stop but enough to require repair or replacement of the highway appurtenance.

In comparison with the tractor-semitrailers they replace, twins and other vehicles legalized by the 1983 act might accelerate such effects on shoulders and roadside appurtenances because their performance characteristics or greater width increases the frequency of shoulder encroachments or because their axle and loading configuration is more destructive to shoulder surfaces. In this study available evidence was examined concerning the possibility of such impacts on the following:

- *Full-strength paved shoulders*, constructed with the same load-bearing capacity as that of adjacent lanes;
- *Gravel, turf, and thinly paved shoulders*, constructed without the load-bearing capacity of adjacent lanes; and
- *Roadside appurtenances*, such as signs, guardrails, and curbs.

In summary, the introduction of twins and other larger vehicles is unlikely to cause the deterioration of full-strength paved shoulders. For gravel, turf, and weakly supported paved shoulders, the added width of 102-in. tractor-semitrailers and twin trailer trucks will increase the frequency of minor shoulder encroachments that erode shoulder material, create rutting, or damage pavement edges, but the magnitude of this increase and its consequences on maintenance needs are not now known and will be difficult to measure even over the long term. For roadside appurtenances, the nationwide introduction of twins will have little effect, whereas 48-ft semitrailers will increase the possibility of collisions during low-speed turning maneuvers. Again the magnitude of any increase and its maintenance implications are not known. Such collisions are related to the degree of vehicle offtracking; that is, during low-speed turns the rear wheels of a vehicle follow a path to the inside of the path of the front wheels, "cutting" the corner. Twins offtrack less than 45-ft semitrailers do, but 48-ft semitrailers offtrack more than 45-ft ones. The 102-in. truck width slightly exacerbates offtracking of any vehicle.

Further discussion of study findings in these areas is presented in Appendix K.

Summary Points: Shoulders and Roadside Appurtenances

- **Twins versus 45-ft semitrailers**   Twins are less likely to damage roadside appurtenances during low-speed turns. Systemwide effects are unknown.
- **48-ft versus 45-ft semitrailers**   48-ft semitrailers are more likely to damage roadside appurtenances during turns. Systemwide effects are unknown.
- **102-in. versus 96-in. width**   102-in. vehicles are more likely to damage gravel, turf, and thinly paved shoulders. Possibility of damage to roadside appurtenances is exacerbated by greater width. Systemwide effects are unknown.

HIGHWAY OPERATIONS

A primary consideration in the provision and upgrading of streets and highways, in addition to structural, geometric, and roadside features, is the ability to accommodate travel without excessive congestion and delay. Each highway is limited in its ability to efficiently handle traffic by design features such as the number and width of lanes. The maximum traffic flow rate, usually expressed as vehicles per hour, that can reasonably be accommodated is termed highway capacity. The quality of flow in the traffic stream significantly deteriorates as volume approaches capacity: as a result, pressures mount for facility expansion or new construction.

Although highways are designed to serve a mix of vehicle types, the effects of various types of vehicles on capacity are not uniform. In particular, the presence of large trucks, because of their increased lengths and lower accelerative and speed-maintenance capabilities, reduces highway capacity. The effect of each large truck is measured in terms of passenger-car equivalents, the number of passenger cars that has the same impact as one truck. The normal range in passenger-car equivalents is from a low of about 2 to a high of about 12, depending on such factors as the number of lanes, topography or gradient, and the extent of truck usage [Appendix E, Tables E-2 (*16*) and E-3 (*17*)].

To illustrate the effects of large trucks on capacity, consider a highway that can accommodate 2,000 vehicles per hour providing that it carries no large trucks. If conditions were so favorable that the passenger-car equivalent of each large truck was 2, this same highway could accommodate only about 1,740 vehicles per hour when 15 percent of the traffic stream was composed of large trucks. Under more unfavorable conditions for which the passenger-car equivalent was 12, the capacity of this highway with 15 percent large trucks would be only 755 vehicles per hour.

As summarized in Appendix E, the passenger-car equivalents of large trucks are sensitive to numerous factors, including several associated with the trucks themselves. The detrimental effects of large trucks are much more pronounced on two-lane than on multilane highways and in terrain having greater relief. They are particularly severe on long, steep upgrades on two-lane highways. Because longer trucks occupy more roadway space, they reduce capacity more than shorter ones. Increases in loaded weight (or more specifically the weight-to-power ratio) are particularly detrimental in situations where trucks are unable to maintain prevailing traffic speeds or are unable to accelerate as rapidly as may be desired, for example, in overtaking or merging maneuvers. The marginal effect of each truck is reduced as the proportion of trucks in the traffic stream is increased.

Although the precise effects on capacity have not been established for tractor-semitrailers versus twins, 45-ft versus 48-ft semitrailers, or trucks 96 in. wide versus those 102 in. wide, the higher weight-to-power ratios (carriers are not generally increasing tractor horsepower as they switch to more heavily loaded twins) and the increased length of twins and 48-ft semitrailers imply that capacity will be reduced. Nevertheless, the effects of each vehicle are likely to be small, not only because the length and weight differentials are small but also because operations of these vehicles are concentrated on superior types of highways, those on which traffic is less affected by large-truck operations. Countering these small unit degradations is the reduction in the number of trips required to transport a given cargo quantity. Overall, increased use of these wider and longer trucks is unlikely to significantly affect highway operations, and therefore is not expected to increase pressures to build new highways or upgrade existing ones.

Closely related to the capacity issue is the impact that large trucks have on the overall quality of flow in the traffic stream. From the perspective of the individual driver, the quality of flow is determined largely by the ability to maintain the desired speed, the freedom to maneuver, and the absence of perturbations requiring speed or lane changes. Large trucks more seriously degrade flow quality than most other vehicle types. Increased truck length is always a detrimental factor, but the most pronounced impact results from insufficient power to maintain prevailing speeds.

As the speed differential between slowly moving trucks and higher-performance vehicles increases, the trucks are more frequently overtaken. As a result, trailing vehicles must brake or pass more often and, in the composite, suffer greater delays. Further exacerbating the problem is the increased difficulty of passing longer and wider trucks, particularly on two-lane roadways. Within freeway merge areas, entering trucks may slow or block the free entry of trailing vehicles and may precipitate braking and forced lane changes of main-line vehicles. Similar effects may result when heavily loaded trucks make freeway lane changes. The presence of long trucks also tends to impede the merging and lane-change operations of others, thereby reducing their freedom to maneuver.

In comparison with conventional tractor-semitrailers, twins, 48-ft semitrailers, and 102-in. wide trucks intensify the detrimental effects of large trucks on the quality of flow. However, the effects, which are quite small for the anticipated size differentials, have been difficult to quantify by on-the-road measurements (Appendix E). The potentially adverse effects are mitigated by reductions in the number of trips necessary because of the increased capacities of these larger vehicles and by their concentration on superior highways, where large trucks have generally been found to be less disruptive.

In summary, the increased weight of twins, 48-ft semitrailers, and 102-in. wide trucks implies that they will be unable to accelerate as rapidly and to maintain speed on upgrades as effectively as 45-ft semitrailers do. When the effect of weight is coupled with the effect of increased length of twins and 48-ft semitrailers, these large trucks will more severely affect traffic operations and degrade the quality of flow than do conventional tractor-semitrailers. Nevertheless, the effects of each truck will be small and, because combination-truck traffic will be reduced by the increased cargo capacity of the new trucks, the net impact is considered to be insignificant.

Summary Points: Highway Capacity and Quality of Flow

- **Twins versus 45-ft semitrailers**   Twins will cause a small degradation due to increased length and weight. Systemwide effects are likely to be insignificant.
- **48-ft versus 45-ft semitrailers**   48-ft semitrailers will cause a small degradation due to increased length and weight. Systemwide effects are likely to be insignificant.
- **102-in. versus 96-in. width**   102-in. wide vehicles will cause a small degradation due to increased weight. Systemwide effects are likely to be insignificant.

HIGHWAY DESIGN AND CONSTRUCTION

Because of different effects on highway safety, deterioration, or operating efficiency, the nationwide introduction of new truck types with different dimensions and performance characteristics may require that new highways be constructed in a different manner or that existing highways be reconstructed and rehabilitated differently than they would otherwise be. Because highway improvement generally takes several years or more from the beginning of design until the completion of construction, this study was unable to directly observe the effect of twins and other new truck types on highway construction projects initiated since the passage of the 1983 act. Consequently, the study focused on design standards and practices to see whether they are changing or are likely to produce different designs to better accommodate twins and other wider and longer vehicles.

Historically state highway agencies have assumed primary responsibility for adopting highway standards, but generally individual states have been heavily influenced by recommended policies developed by AASHTO. Similarly, for federal-aid highways, the federal government has adopted most AASHTO policies as standards or design guides (Design Standards for Highways, Code of Federal Regulations, Title 23, Part 625). Because AASHTO is instrumental in the writing of key highway standards, the reference point for possible changes to highway standards and practices resulting from the use of new truck types was these AASHTO policies.

As yet, no AASHTO design policies have changed in response to the nationwide introduction of twins or other new truck types, but some changes may ultimately occur. This possibility is discussed for standards and design practices related to highway pavements, bridges, and geometry. Also discussed is the extent to which existing design practices already accommodate the new truck types or whether different designs will be produced if use by the new vehicles is assumed.

Pavement Design Procedures

On the basis of the investigations of this study, no change in pavement design procedures is expected because of the expanded use of twins or other new vehicle types. As shown earlier in this chapter, the AASHTO pavement design procedures (3) as well as those of the Asphalt Institute (4) and the Portland Cement Association (5) are sensitive to different load characteristics and axle configurations and can tailor a design to the expected traffic characteristics, that is, vehicle classification by type and weight.

Whether pavement designs will actually be modified depends on the source of the traffic and weight data that are used as inputs to pavement design. Often, these data are based on measurements taken at permanent truck weigh stations. In such cases, the design process does not really begin to take into account a new vehicle type until it appears on the road. On less costly rehabilitation projects, pavement overlay design will frequently be standardized within a state with some general relationship to traffic volumes and number of heavy trucks but will not be sensitive to the breakdown of heavy trucks by type. Thus, although pavement design can be tailored to specific truck characteristics and loadings, it probably will not change immediately because of the use of twins.

Bridge Design Practices

Neither design standards and procedures nor the resultant designs for bridges and other highway structures need change because of twins or other new vehicle types. Unlike pavement design, bridge design procedures are not very sensitive to differences in traffic composition and in-service vehicle and load characteristics. Instead they are based largely on hypothetical standard loading patterns (*18*). As shown earlier, twins operating at the federal GVW limit produce smaller forces on key bridge components than the standard loading pattern recommended by AASHTO for Interstate bridge design. Moreover, they generally induce smaller forces than comparably loaded 45-ft semitrailers.

Regarding other new vehicle types, the 48-ft semitrailer produces forces no greater than those produced by equally loaded 45-ft semitrailers, and any differences in forces arising from the added wheel track on 102-in. vehicles are inconsequential.

Geometric Standards and Design

Geometric standards specify minimum (or maximum) design values for highway cross-section features (such as lane and shoulder widths) and alignment (horizontal curve radii, slope and length of vertical grades, and sight distances for passing and stopping), including intersections and interchanges. They are influenced to varying degrees by vehicle characteristics and performance, particularly minimum turning radius, offtracking, length, width, braking, and weight-to-power ratio. Highway designers use different standards for different classes of highway depending on the expected use by various vehicle types. For instance, Interstate highways are generally designed to accommodate large trucks, whereas local streets and roads generally are not, even though large trucks occasionally travel on them. For roads of intermediate type, some design features are governed by trucks, and others are not. When trucks govern, generally the designs are not based on worst-case situations, but rather on the characteristics of smaller trucks.

Even on Interstates, geometric features are not necessarily tailored to accommodate all trucks in service at the time of design. A tractor-semitrailer with an overall length of 55 ft, for instance, at present governs the recommended ramp width designs for interchanges despite the common use of longer semitrailer combinations that require somewhat greater widths when turning (*19*). This recommendation is apparently based on a cost-effectiveness perspective that gears designs to the most common trucks and tolerates some vehicle movements that exceed the assumed design condition, in this case those resulting in shoulder encroachments. For similar reasons, geometric improvements to existing highways are not necessarily made to the degree required for new construction or complete reconstruction.

In 1984, AASHTO completed and published a comprehensive revision to its geometric design policies for construction and reconstruction of urban and rural highways, the first revision for some highway classes in almost 20 years (*19*). Because its preparation was essentially complete when the Surface Transportation Assistance Act of 1982 was enacted, the 1984 AASHTO geometric policy guide did not specifically take into account new vehicle types legalized on a nationwide basis by the act. Nevertheless, the set of design vehicles used to develop the standards includes a 102-in. wide twin trailer truck with an overall length of 65 ft, which would include two 27-ft trailers. The largest tractor-semitrailer considered was 102 in. wide with an overall length of 55 ft, which would include a semitrailer length of 40 ft.

As noted previously, the extent to which large trucks govern design geometry varies considerably. The study reviewed the relationships between large truck characteristics and current AASHTO geometric design values logically influenced by truck size and performance.

In summary, there is little likelihood that AASHTO geometric design standards for new construction will be changed because of the nationwide introduction of twins or 102-in. wide vehicles. In general, these vehicles will either have less stringent design requirements than vehicles already in service (e.g., for offtracking) or have already been considered in developing the present standards (e.g., for vehicle width). For the longer 48-ft semitrailers, some change in standards related to turning movements—pavement widening on curves, minimum design for sharpest turns, width for turning roadways, and median openings—may be warranted because these vehicles exceed the requirements of all the current design vehicles. AASHTO's Task Force on Geometric Design is now considering such changes, and some states have already modified their own design policies. The study's survey of state highway agencies found that 14 states (of 48 respondents) had made changes to their geometric design standards and that 4 more were considering changes. In 12 of the 14 states that had made changes so far, minimum turning radii at intersections were increased. Two states introduced larger design vehicles with greater turning requirements.

Further discussion of specific relationships between geometric design and truck characteristics is presented in Appendix L.

Special Highway Rehabilitation or Reconstruction Activities

About one-fifth of the state highway agencies surveyed indicated that they anticipated special rehabilitation or reconstruction work on the designated network or access routes to that network. These states are scattered throughout the country, showing no strong regional orientation.

Increasing minimum turning radii at intersections to better accommodate 48-ft semitrailers was the most commonly cited improvement (six states), followed by lane widening (to 12 ft) or shoulder widening to better accommodate 102-in. wide trucks (three states). Only two states indicated that they had actually completed or firmly programmed such improvements.

Summary Points: Design and Construction

- **Twins versus 45-ft semitrailers** Twins have had no effect on design standards and procedures. Existing pavement design procedures may be adjusted in areas where it becomes apparent that there is heavy use by the new vehicles.
- **48-ft versus 45-ft semitrailers** 48-ft semitrailers have had no effect on bridge and pavement design procedures or construction. There has been some change in geometric design values related to turning movements.
- **102-in. versus 96-in. width** 102-in. wide vehicles have had no effect on bridge and pavement design or construction. There has been no change to geometric design values for new construction, but wider lanes may be required for rehabilitation projects.

ENVIRONMENT

The introduction of new large truck types raises the possibility of adverse environmental effects in two key areas—noise emissions and air quality.

Noise Emissions

Vehicle noise emissions generally increase with increases in GVW, the number of wheels (or axles), and speed. In addition, a number of other factors contribute to noise emissions, including tire design, vehicle shape and configuration, and pavement surface condition (6).

FHWA (20) developed an empirical formula that estimates large-truck noise emissions (in adjusted decibels at a standard distance) given GVW, number of axles, and speed. When a comparison between a 66,000-lb twin trailer truck and a 60,000-lb tractor-semitrailer is made, this formula predicts that the noise emissions of the twins will be only one-tenth of 1 percent greater than those of the tractor-semitrailer, an almost imperceptible difference that is attributable entirely to the higher GVW. However, because the new twins will on average make about 9 percent fewer trips than the tractor-semitrailers they replace, the net effect will be a reduction in large-truck noise emissions. Roughly speaking, the nationwide use of twins will reduce exposure to truck noise emissions in proportion to the expected reduction in combination-truck travel, which is 0.7 percent in 1990 (Chapter 3).

Similarly, 48-ft semitrailers and 102-in. wide trucks will probably reduce overall exposure to large-truck noise, because their use will also reduce the amount of combination-truck travel.

Air Quality

Air pollutant emissions by large trucks are primarily related to vehicle miles traveled; models of these emissions generally do not differentiate between truck configurations or weight classes. Because the use of twins will reduce the amount of combination-truck travel, the introduction of twins is expected to reduce large-truck air pollutant emissions nationwide roughly in proportion to the expected reduction in large-truck vehicle miles, 0.7 percent by 1990 (Chapter 3). For the same reason, the use of longer semitrailers and wider trucks of all types will also reduce overall large-truck air pollutant emissions.

Summary Points: Environment

- **Twins versus 45-ft semitrailers** Twins will reduce exposure to noise and air pollutant emissions nationwide because of vehicle-mile reduction.
- **48-ft versus 45-ft semitrailers** 48-ft semitrailers will reduce exposure to noise and air pollutant emissions nationwide because of vehicle-mile reduction.
- **102-in. versus 96-in. width** 102 in. wide trucks will reduce exposure to noise and air pollutant emissions because of vehicle-mile reduction.

REFERENCES

1. E.J. Yoder and M.W. Witczak. *Principles of Pavement Design*. Wiley-Interscience, New York, 1975.
2. *The AASHO Road Test: Report 5, Pavement Research*. Special Report 61E, HRB, National Research Council, Washington, D.C., 1962.
3. *Guide for Design of Pavement Structures*. American Association of State Highway and Transportation Officials, Washington, D.C., 1986.
4. *Thickness Design—Asphalt Pavements for Highways and Streets*. Asphalt Institute, College Park, Md., Sept. 1981.
5. *Thickness Design for Concrete Highway and Street Pavements*. Portland Cement Association, Skokie, Ill., 1984.
6. *Impacts of Heavy Freight Vehicles*. Road Research Group, Organization for Economic Cooperation and Development, Paris, France, Dec. 1982.
7. *Final Report on the Federal Highway Cost Allocation Study*. FHWA, U.S. Department of Transportation, May 1982.
8. J.B. Rauhut, R.L. Lytton, and M.I. Darter. *Pavement Damage Functions for Cost Allocation*, Vol. 1: Damage Functions and Load Equivalence Factors. FHWA, U.S. Department of Transportation, June 1984.
9. J.A. Deacon. "Load Equivalency in Flexible Pavements." *Proceedings of the Association of Asphalt Paving Technologists*, Vol. 38, 1969, pp. 465-491.
10. *Highway Statistics, 1983*. FHWA, U.S. Department of Transportation, 1983.
11. T.K.F. Wong and M.J. Markow. *Allocation of Life Cycle Highway Pavement Costs*. Massachusetts Institute of Technology, Cambridge, March 1984.
12. *The Feasibility of a Nationwide Network for Longer Combination Vehicles*. FHWA, U.S. Department of Transportation, June 1985.
13. C.H. Ogelsby and R.G. Hicks. *Highway Engineering*. John Wiley and Sons, New York, 1982.

14. H.S. Cohen and J.H. Sinnott. "Pavement and Bridge Impact Analysis Methodology." In *An Investigation of Truck Size and Weight Limits*, Technical Supplement Vol. 6, U.S. Department of Transportation, Sept. 30, 1982.

15. H.G. Downs and D.W. Wallace. *Shoulder Geometrics and Use Guidelines*. NCHRP Report 254. TRB, National Research Council, Washington, D.C., Dec. 1982.

16. *Highway Capacity Manual*. Special Report 209. TRB, National Research Council, Washington, D.C., 1985.

17. A.D. St. John and D.R. Kobett. *Grade Effects on Traffic Flow Stability and Capacity*. NCHRP Report 185. TRB, National Research Council, Washington, D.C., 1978.

18. *Standard Specifications for Highway Bridges*. American Association of State Highway and Transportation Officials, Washington, D.C., 1983.

19. *A Policy for Geometric Design of Highways and Streets*. American Association of State Highway and Transportation Officials, Washington, D.C., 1984.

20. *Statistical Analysis of FHWA Traffic Noise Data*. FHWA, U.S. Department of Transportation, July 1979.

6
Long-Term Monitoring

Government decisions concerning truck size and weight limits, truck safety regulation, and truck taxation have important consequences. These decisions directly influence the productivity of the $100 billion-a-year trucking industry, the public's return on its $30 billion annual expenditure on highway construction and maintenance, and the safety of the roads on which large trucks travel. Yet analyses supporting these decisions have always in the past had to rely on information—about truck use, truck accidents, pavement and bridge deterioration, and trucking industry costs—that was incomplete, outdated, and of unknown validity.

As a result of poor data, decisions must be made with great uncertainty about their impacts, and the balance struck among conflicting concerns (safety, highway performance, productivity) may be far from what it would have been if the consequences of alternative courses had been better known. Decisions may be deferred because taking no action appears the safest course, and they are easy for opponents to attack, leading to protracted controversy. The effectiveness of existing programs and policies cannot be evaluated, so feedback to guide refinements is lost. The history of the debate over enactment and implementation of the 1983 federal law regarding twin trailer trucks provides examples of several of these consequences of poor-quality data.

The purpose of this chapter is to call attention to the need for and value of improved data on truck activity and impacts and to identify some practical improvements to existing data programs, new programs, or special studies on the characteristics and impacts of heavy-truck traffic that would be valuable for helping to answer current policy questions relating to truck size and weight. These recommendations for long-term monitoring are an integral part of the committee's response to Congressional direction for the twin trailer truck study. During the term of this study the trucking industry has only begun its adjustment to the new federal truck size regulations, so many questions concerning the effects of twins will not be finally resolved without long-term monitoring of twins traffic and impacts. Also, the experience during the course of this study with the shortcomings in the data available to support analyses of truck impacts can guide improvements in the government's capability to assess the next round of truck size and weight policy issues—issues that are confronting decision makers today.

Planning for new or revised data programs must be guided by a comparison of the cost to the government and private industry of obtaining the data to the benefit of better information and improved decisions. Clearly, the stakes are high in policy decisions affecting heavy trucks: even marginal improvements in trucking productivity or in the return on the public investment in roads can represent large economic benefits. Therefore substantial public efforts to obtain good information to support these decisions can be justified; and in fact, governments already are devoting substantial resources to collecting data on truck travel, highway accidents, road deterioration, and trucking industry performance. However, as shown in this chapter, there are many opportunities to improve the effectiveness with which these resources are used.

Several groups have recently made or are considering recommendations for improvements to trucking data. These include FHWA, which recently sponsored a study on large-truck safety data needs (1); the American Association of State Highway and Transportation Officials and American Trucking Associations, which have a joint task force on highway issues (2); the Transportation Research Board Committee on Transportation Data and Information Systems (3); the National Highway Safety Advisory Committee (4); and the American Association of State Highway and Transportation Officials, which is sponsoring the Strategic Highway Research Program (5). The number of organizations that are addressing these problems is an indication of the urgent need for improvements to truck data. All these groups have made valuable proposals, and the twin trailer truck study committee's recommendations are intended to complement their efforts.

The need for truck data, the available data resources and their limits, and actions for improving truck data are described in this chapter. In the first section the applications of truck activity data and the types of data required are defined. The basic uses of truck data, the pending and likely future truck size and weight regulatory issues that will require analysis, and the categories of data required for these applications are identified. Next available data resources and their limits are examined. The specific problems and data gaps that past truck-related studies faced are described to illustrate the shortcomings of the available data, and some new truck data programs and new data collection technologies that are already in development are discussed.

In the concluding section recommendations for improving truck data are presented. Several general principles that ought to guide modifications to existing truck data programs or design of new ones are cited, and special studies addressing particular aspects of truck activity, ongoing monitoring and analysis actitivies, and arrangements for better coordination among agencies involved in truck data are proposed.

APPLICATIONS AND TYPES OF DATA REQUIRED

One of the reasons why researchers are often frustrated with the short-comings of truck data programs is that these programs are called on to support an extremely wide range of functions, all of which have special and sometimes conflicting information requirements. The important applications are as follows:

- Planning for future highway capacity needs;
- Setting highway design criteria;
- Projecting pavement repair requirements;
- Enforcing size, weight, safety, tax, and registration regulations;
- Predicting the impacts of changes in taxes, size and weight limits, pollution controls, and safety regulations affecting trucks;
- Allocating cost and revenue responsibility among types of vehicles for designing road user taxes;
- Studying regional economic development;
- In the private sector, supporting marketing and site selection decisions of shippers, carriers, and trucking equipment suppliers;
- Administering the economic regulation of trucking;
- Evaluating the effectiveness of safety, size and weight, and environmental regulations to see whether they are accomplishing their intended purposes; and
- Comparing the safety performance of various vehicle types (e.g., twins), vehicle design features (e.g., brakes), or categories of trucking operations or drivers in research to find methods to control truck safety.

Although the multiple applications of truck data must be kept in mind in designing any new data programs, in this chapter data needs for evaluating existing or new truck size and weight limits are primarily addressed.

Current Truck Size and Weight Issues

Truck size and weight limits have changed frequently in the past, almost always in the direction of allowing larger sizes, and this trend appears likely to continue. Federal and state governments will continue to be confronted with new proposals for changes in the limits, and the task of government regulators will be to keep these changes in step with improvements in highway geometric and structural design, advances in trucking equipment, better safety management of truck fleets, and refinements to truck taxes to reflect the greater cost responsibility of larger vehicles. Truck size and weight and related issues that are today being seriously discussed or analyzed include

● Nationwide use of turnpike doubles, triple trailer combinations, and other larger combinations that now are permitted in only a few states (6);

● Greater use of very heavy trucks (over 80,000 lb gross vehicle weight), coupled with lower axle weight limits (and consequently new kinds of truck configurations), to achieve greater trucking productivity with reduced pavement damage (7);

● Trailers longer than the 48-ft semitrailer that Congress required the states to allow in 1983 (8);

● A revised bridge formula that limits the weight allowed on any group of axles as a function of the spacing between axles according to the load-carrying capacity of the bridge (9);

● The highway cost responsibility of very heavy trucks and new configurations (10);

● The feasibility of a nationwide weight-distance tax—a tax based as directly as possible on the pavement damage actually caused by each vehicle (10); and

● Reforms to improve the uniformity of state regulations regarding registration, taxation, and size and weight (11).

Decisions made on each of these matters will have major consequences for the cost, safety, and convenience of highway travel, so investment in collecting information to support the decisions would certainly have large payoffs.

Data Requirements

Analyzing the costs and benefits of a change in truck size and weight limits requires predicting the impact of the change on roadway wear, congestion and the demand for new capacity, road design requirements, the frequency of traffic accidents, and the cost of transporting freight. To predict these effects, the analyst needs, first, information about current truck travel characteristics and an estimate of how travel will change under the new limits and, second, an understanding of the relationships between truck travel and the impact categories—highway performance, safety, and freight costs. The major specific data elements needed are as follows:

● *Truck travel data*: annual vehicle miles traveled classified by weight, configuration, engine type, and body type of truck; by type and weight of freight carried; by type of carrier; by shipment origin and destination; and by road class, traffic volume, design, and structural condition; and daily and seasonal variations in travel.

● *Truck impact data*: the frequency of accidents for each kind of truck and road condition; information relating volume and composition of truck traffic to highway performance; and the costs of transporting each category of freight by trucks of various dimensions.

A complete data set—one containing travel and impact data disaggregated by all the dimensions just listed—would be prohibitively expensive. Therefore, the problem in planning a truck data program is to assess which data will pay for their cost through improved decision making. The logical starting point for this assessment is to examine the adequacy of available data resources.

AVAILABLE DATA RESOURCES AND THEIR LIMITS

Existing sources and data collection programs relating to truck use, safety, road wear, and the trucking industry are listed and briefly described in the following paragraphs. Then the limitations of the available data are illustrated by examples of problems encountered in two recent major studies concerning truck size and weight policy. Last, proposed data collection programs are mentioned.

Existing Truck Data Programs

Truck Use

Travel data for particular vehicle categories, road classes, and geographical areas are a requirement common to evaluations of safety, road wear, and industry impacts of size and weight regulations; however, the available data are incomplete. The major existing programs include the following:

• The FHWA-sponsored state Vehicle Classification Count and Truck Weight Study Program (12), annual vehicle counts and biennial weight studies conducted by the states and compiled by FHWA since 1969, in which the distribution of traffic by vehicle type (including double trailer counts), weight, and regulatory status of carrier at several hundred sites nationwide is reported. This is the most complete nationwide source for the distribution of traffic by vehicle type and road class. However, the program does not rely on formal sampling techniques, state-level sample sizes (about 12 sites per state) are small, and counting and weighing are confined mainly to rural roads during daylight hours in the summer.

• The Truck Inventory and Use Survey, conducted by the Census Bureau every 5 years (13). In this large survey of the owners of a sample of trucks registered in the United States information is collected on the physical characteristics and uses of the vehicles. Past truck size and weight analyses have relied heavily on this survey, but its validity has sometimes been questioned, as will be described in the following section.

• The Commodity Transportation Survey (14), also conducted by the Census Bureau, which is a survey of a sample of point-to-point shipments of manufactured products. The Census Bureau has in the past considered abandoning this activity for budgetary reasons.

• FHWA's Highway Performance Monitoring System (15), which compiles road design and condition information, travel data, and accident data for a sample of road segments in each state. The state highway agencies collect the data and report it to FHWA. The travel and accident data are incomplete (not all states report them), and accidents are not reported by vehicle class.

• Truck and trailer sales data collected by the Census Bureau (16) and by trade associations (17, 18).

• Other state and local traffic counting programs. States and municipalities frequently conduct traffic studies for planning purposes, but these data usually are too varied and scattered to be of practical systematic use in nationwide studies.

• Vehicle registration files, especially a nationwide file (19) compiled annually by a private firm from the registration records of all the states.

Accidents

The major continuing accident data collection programs include the following:

- Bureau of Motor Carrier Safety accident reports (*20*), which are required of all interstate motor carriers for accidents involving injuries or property damage over $2,000;
- Fatal Accident Reporting System (*21*), maintained by the National Highway Traffic Safety Administration, a file of all police-reported fatal motor vehicle accidents;
- National Accident Sampling System (*22*), also maintained by the National Highway Traffic Safety Administration, detailed accident data for a random sample of accidents in 50 localities nationwide. This data program is concerned with all motor vehicle accidents, so its sample procedures are not suited to estimating relative accident rates of different categories of combination trucks.
- State accident data collection programs. All states maintain a central computerized file of police accident reports. The utility of the various state accident records systems is limited by the lack of uniform accident reporting procedures. In many state accident reports, for example, it is not possible to distinguish a straight truck from a combination vehicle.

None of these accident data programs coordinates collection of accident data with collection of exposure (travel) data. The Bureau of Motor Carrier Safety, for example, compiles detailed information on the age, experience, and other characteristics of truck drivers involved in accidents, but without information on the characteristics of the population of drivers, these statistics reveal nothing about the influence of driver characteristics on accident rates. Linking accident data to exposure data is usually the most uncertain step of accident rate studies.

Road and Bridge Wear

The American Association of State Highway and Transportation Officials' Strategic Highway Research Program has recently begun planning its long-term pavement performance study (*23*). This major study will continuously collect data on pavement condition, axle loading, environment, and maintenance for a sample of road segments over a period of 20 years. Its purpose is to obtain pavement damage functions applicable to actual highway conditions. The study will greatly improve understanding of the relationship of truck size and weight to pavement wear and maintenance cost. Currently, virtually all estimates of the effects of changes in truck traffic or road wear are based on the results of the AASHO Road Test (*24*), a series of trials conducted on a test track in 1958.

Trucking Industry Efficiency

The major source reporting data on costs and finances in the trucking industry is the Interstate Commerce Commission, which collects financial and operating data on regulated trucking firms. The data for individual companies are available to the public. As economic deregulation proceeds, the Commission has proposed to drastically reduce the volume of data collected.

Data Gaps in Past Studies

Incomplete data on trucking activity led to large uncertainties in some results of the Highway Cost Allocation Study (25) and the Truck Size and Weight Study (26). Examples of the data problems faced during these analyses indicate where improvements to data would be valuable.

For the Highway Cost Allocation Study, estimates were needed of numbers of vehicles and miles traveled by vehicle type, axle configuration, and gross weight. The Truck Inventory and Use Survey, conducted by the Census Bureau, was the principal truck data source. The study encountered several major data problems:

● A reliable value for the total population of combination trucks was not available. The Truck Inventory and Use Survey showed a total of 800,000 in 1977, whereas other estimates ranged from 1.2 million to 1.4 million.

● The estimate of total combination-truck miles traveled was proportional to the number of vehicles and so was equally uncertain.

● Distributions of the truck population by axle configuration were also highly uncertain because of problems in the Truck Inventory and Use Survey questionnaire and the unrepresentative coverage of the FHWA Vehicle Classification Count Program.

● Distributions of combination-truck miles traveled by gross weight grouping had to be indirectly imputed because the Truck Inventory and Use Survey contains little weight information.

● The study relied on AASHO Road Test results for estimating pavement wear attributable to the various truck classes. Although this method is generally accepted among highway engineers, it is always a target for criticism because of the difficulty of extrapolating results of narrowly defined test conditions to the full range of real-world situations.

The Truck Size and Weight Study needed a freight flow data base—a description of all freight shipments by commodity, shipment size, mode (including the various combination types and body styles), origin and destination, and route traveled. Data-related difficulties included the following:

• The total number of combination-truck miles was uncertain for the same reason as that in the cost allocation study.

• Data on the distribution of total miles by commodity, origin and destination, and combination type were limited, and estimates of these flows were based on a long string of assumptions. The Commodity Transportation Survey has data on mode (truck and rail), but no information on truck type and reports only on the initial movement (from the factory) of manufactured goods.

• There is no nationwide data source showing in any detail where combination-truck travel occurs—that is, truck miles by major route, by state or region, or by type of combination. The Truck Size and Weight Study assigned mileage on the basis of the origin-destination flows and assumptions about least-cost routes.

• The Truck Size and Weight Study also needed impact relationships to estimate the effects of limit changes on pavement wear, traffic operations, accidents, pollution, and trucking costs. It included a study (27) of the effects of truck size and weight on traffic and safety, but the results were attacked as unreliable (see Appendix F). Little hard data were available on the effect of size limits on unit trucking costs, so the cost relationships were developed mainly on the basis of theoretical assumptions.

The analysis of twin trailer truck impacts for the Twin Trailer Truck Monitoring Study has also been hampered by data shortcomings, especially by gaps in data on the use of twins, accident frequencies, and trucking costs. These difficulties are described in Chapters 3, 4, and 5.

The data problems encountered in these three studies may not have seriously biased their results. However, the large number of assumptions built into their impact estimates weakens the value of these studies to decision makers, and their conclusions can easily be attacked by showing that changes in key assumptions would substantially alter the results.

New or Enhanced Data Collection Programs

Government agencies and private organizations are making progress in solving some of the truck data problems previously described. Important current efforts include the following:

• Coordination of FHWA's annual Vehicle Classification Count and Truck Weight Study Program with its Highway Performance Monitoring System: FHWA's new *Traffic Monitoring Guide* (28) recommends to the states a program for conducting classification counts and weighing at a statistically valid sample of sites linked to roadway and other traffic data at the same sites. Data specifications are compatible with capabilities of automatic counting and weighing devices.

● New data collection methods, such as the automatic weigh-in-motion apparatus already extensively used in several states and the electronic automatic vehicle identification systems now in the experimental stage, may lower the cost of collecting truck activity data and, if so, could greatly increase the quantity and quality of truck activity data. Full implementation of these technologies is some years off, but efforts are under way to test their capabilities and plan how to effectively organize and apply the data they can produce. In particular, the Crescent Study (29), a cooperative effort of eight states, one Canadian province, and several trucking firms, is demonstrating an integrated electronic weigh-in-motion and automatic vehicle identification system for monitoring truck activity.

● A new accident reporting system under consideration by the Bureau of Motor Carrier Safety would replace the current requirement for detailed reporting of all accidents with a sampling procedure that would allow validation of carrier reports (30).

● The University of Michigan National Truck Trip Information Survey (31), sponsored by the American Trucking Associations, the Motor Vehicle Manufacturers Association, and the National Highway Traffic Safety Administration and now in progress, will provide more detailed information on miles traveled by road type, geographic location, time of day, and trailer type than is available from other sources. It is currently planned as a one-time-only study rather than an ongoing program.

● The Strategic Highway Research Program's long-term pavement performance study, described earlier, eventually will allow fundamental improvements in pavement impact estimates.

RECOMMENDATIONS FOR IMPROVING TRUCK DATA

Principles to Guide Design of Truck Data Programs

There are three possible explanations for the shortcomings in the various truck data bases and the difficulties encountered in analysis of truck size and weight policies: lack of resources devoted to data collection and analysis, the complexity of the issues involved, and institutional and organizational obstacles that hinder effective data collection and analysis. However, expenditures on data collection are substantial: no dollar estimates are available, but certainly millions of dollars are spent annually at the federal level on data programs relevant to truck size and weight issues, and larger amounts are spent by state governments. Truck size and weight issues—for example, relationship of size and weight to accident rates or to pavement wear—are certainly complex, but analyses of these questions have historically been constrained simply by absence of data or flaws in research design rather than by these inherent complexities.

Rather than lack of funds or the complexities of the problems, organizational obstacles appear to have been the most important factor explaining continuing data problems and the resulting uncertainty over the impacts of large trucks. To overcome these obstacles, the designers of truck data programs need to keep in mind several general rules:

• Data collection must be designed with the specific policy questions or enforcement activities that it is intended to support in mind. Otherwise, important data elements will be overlooked and money will be wasted collecting unnecessary information.

• Regular communication between data users and producers is essential to ensure that data programs are responsive to needs.

• Performance evelution should be built into the design of any regulatory program. Truck safety and size and weight regulatory programs are likely to fall short of their intended objectives if no data system is in place for measuring compliance and effectiveness.

• The planning and administration of data programs should rely on estimates of the costs and benefits of data collection to help decide what data to collect and to select data collection methods (e.g., whether a survey or a census is necessary or whether a one-time study or ongoing monitoring program is called for).

• Analysts should demonstrate to administrators how better data would help decision making by including sensitivity analyses and confidence intervals in their results and by identifying critical areas where improved data would sharpen study conclusions.

Recommendations for Specific Truck Data Activities

The specific recommendations given in the following sections do not constitute a comprehensive truck data collection program; rather, they are aimed first at improving the organizational structure that supports such data programs and second at filling several of the most critical gaps in the information available today.

Federal Truck Data Collection Responsibility

As truck size and weight policy becomes increasingly a federal concern, the U.S. Department of Transportation (DOT) should take greater responsibility for ensuring the quality and completeness of the data required to guide decisions on federal size and weight limits, truck taxes, and truck safety regulation. In particular, DOT should improve the quality and consistency of data reported through the federal-state cooperative data programs. Most of the major federal highway data programs—including the Highway Performance Monitoring System, the Fatal Accident Reporting System, and the Vehicle Classification Count and Truck Weight Study Program—depend on the states to collect data and report these to DOT. Some of this data reporting is voluntary, and some is mandatory under the rules of the federal-aid highway program; in either case the states vary greatly in the reliability and timeliness of their responses. To improve the situation, DOT should

● Actively monitor and audit the quality of state data submissions and the methods used by the states to produce the data;
● Provide technical expertise to individual states that need help to solve data problems;
● Review its state data requests to see whether any that are now voluntary are essential to DOT's responsibilities and ought therefore to be made mandatory and also to see whether any are of low value and should be dropped;
● Devise some form of financial incentive to partially reimburse states for one-time-only costs of major improvements to their highway data capabilities, especially introduction of weigh-in-motion technology; and
● Set minimum acceptable standards for state compliance with mandatory data submittals, and enforce these standards.

Federal-State-Private Truck Data Forum

DOT should take a lead role in establishing an officially recognized standing organization to provide a forum for communication between truck data users and producers and to guide the development of the various truck activity data resources into a coordinated program. The panel should include representatives of all the major federal data-producing agencies, state governments, industry, researchers, and policymakers. Coordination among the various users and producers of truck data is the only way to attain cost-effective management of the large sums spent annually for highway data collection. The panel should aim for closer cooperation among the following groups in particular:

- The National Highway Traffic Safety Administration and FHWA, to ensure that the former's large-scale safety monitoring programs (the National Accident Sampling System and the Fatal Accident Reporting System) are applicable to the safety analysis needs of the federal highway programs;

- DOT and the states (possibly through participation of the American Association of State Highway and Transportation Officials), to recruit state support and consensus for reforms in the federal-state cooperative data programs;

- Government agencies and industry, to open new possibilities for tapping private data sources through voluntary government-industry programs (such as the current testing of automatic vehicle identification apparatus in the Crescent Study)—private business, especially the trucking industry, is a major supplier of truck data (through reporting to the Census Bureau, the Bureau of Motor Carrier Safety, and the Interstate Commerce Commission and through surveys and interviews in many special studies) and a major user of government statistics; and

- DOT and other federal agencies involved in truck data, especially the Census Bureau, to ensure the continuing collection of data that is vital to most of the transportation analyses that DOT is required to carry out.

The organization of the truck data panel should provide for participation both by high-level officials of the participating organizations and by their technical staffs, for example, through a two-tiered structure involving a DOT advisory committee overseeing working staff groups. All the participating groups should agree to regularly submit their major truck data programs to the panel for review and comment.

State Truck Traffic Data Collection

All state highway agencies should move expeditiously to adopt the truck traffic data collection procedures recommended in FHWA's *Traffic Monitoring Guide (28)*, especially coordination with the Highway Performance Monitoring System and adoption of automated weighing and classification devices. Cooperative pilot programs such as the Crescent Study to test new truck traffic monitoring technologies deserve the active support and participation of the state highway agencies.

The states should adopt consistent formats for recording a core of key information about each highway accident, including a consistent vehicle classification system that identifies, as a minimum, whether a truck involved in an accident is a straight truck, a tractor-semitrailer, or a twin trailer truck.

Extended Monitoring of Twins

FHWA should continue the short-term twin trailer truck monitoring activities begun in this study for at least 4 years until the trucking industry has more fully adjusted to the new federal size limits. Specifically, tracking of twins traffic by carrier class, body type, and road class and of twin trailer truck accident frequency should continue by using existing federal data programs and the special programs in place in several states. FHWA should evaluate and set standards for the quality of the state-collected data in these programs.

Coordination of the Strategic Highway Research Program with Other Data Needs

The designers of the Strategic Highway Research Program's long-term pavement performance study should investigate the feasibility of coordination between the study and the FHWA Highway Performance Monitoring System, should plan for timely analysis of preliminary results, and should adopt a data collection and analysis plan that does not unnecessarily limit the hypotheses about the determinants of road deterioration that can be tested.

Special Studies

DOT-sponsored studies are necessary or should be continued in three areas.

- Development of trucking cost models directly applicable to size and weight policy analysis. The effects on motor carrier costs and productivity are key concerns for analyses of potential changes to size and weight policies, and the lack of detailed cost data and models is always a major source of uncertainty in estimates of benefits of higher limits. The Interstate Commerce Commission has discontinued most of its cost data collection and research activities.

- Determination of the costs to private drivers, in addition to the direct costs of accidents, that are due to the presence of larger and heavier vehicles in the traffic stream. These costs may include time loss due to congestion, inability to pass, or selection of alternative routes so as to avoid truck traffic and motorists' perceived costs from discomfort and inconvenience. Such a study would contribute to understanding the attitudes held by the driving public toward large trucks and what actions could be taken to make large trucks and other vehicles more compatible.

- Determination of the relationships between truck characteristics and accident rates. However, a major special research project dealing with twins safety alone is not warranted. Although the evidence on the relative safety of twins and tractor-semitrailers is not absolutely conclusive, this narrow issue does not have the highest priority among truck safety questions. The recently completed FHWA report *Development of a Large Truck Safety Data Needs Study Plan (1)* specifies the scope of the data collection that would be necessary to reliably and comprehensively examine the relationship of truck type to accident rates. That data effort would be expensive, because the magnitude of the effects to be measured is small compared with the effects of the multitude of external factors that would have to be controlled for in such a study and because existing accident and travel data collection programs would not be sufficiently reliable or detailed to be employed in the study. DOT should undertake the large-truck safety data study only after an explicit evaluation of its cost-effectiveness. Research and data collection on truck safety undertaken by FHWA and by the National Highway Traffic Safety Administration should be coordinated to ensure the most effective departmentwide approach to the problem.

REFERENCES

1. Bellomo-McGee, Inc. *Development of a Large Truck Safety Data Needs Study Plan.* FHWA, U.S. Department of Transportation, 1986 (forthcoming).
2. "ATA, AASHTO Highway Task Forces Plan Meeting, Agenda." *Transport Topics*, July 8, 1985, p. 27.
3. A.E. Pisarski and R.R. Schmitt. "Critical Data Issues and Opportunities in Transportation." *Transportation Research News*, Nov.-Dec. 1984.
4. *Commercial Vehicle Safety: A Report to the Secretary of Transportation by the National Highway Safety Advisory Committee.* National Highway Safety Advisory Committee, Washington, D.C., May 1985.
5. S.M. Schust. "Potential Payoff High for New Highway Research." *AASHTO Quarterly*, Vol. 63, No. 4, Oct. 1984, pp. 4–5.
6. *The Feasibility of a Nationwide Network for Longer Combination Vehicles.* FHWA, U.S. Department of Transportation, June 1985.
7. "Speakers Address Modal Session." *AASHTO Quarterly*, Jan. 1985.
8. "Truck Size and Weight: Automobile Transporters." *Federal Register*, Vol. 49, No. 192, Oct. 2, 1984, p. 38956.
9. "ARTBA Continues to Press for New Bridge Formula." *Better Roads*, April 1984.
10. "Motor Carrier Advisory Committee to Give FHWA Comments on Studies." *Traffic World*, Feb. 4, 1985, p. 33.
11. "Trucking Uniformly Eyed by State Governors, FHWA." *Traffic World*, Jan. 7, 1985, p. 7.

12. P.M. Kent and M.J. Robey. *1975–1979 National Truck Characteristics Report*. FHWA, U.S. Department of Transportation, June 1981.

13. *1977 Census of Transportation: Truck Inventory and Use Survey: United States*. Report TC77-T-52. Bureau of the Census, U.S. Department of Commerce, May 1980.

14. *1977 Census of Transportation: Commodity Transportation Survey*. Bureau of the Census, U.S. Department of Commerce, 1980.

15. *Highway Performance Monitoring System: Field Manual*. FHWA, U.S. Department of Transportation, Sept. 1980.

16. *Current Industrial Reports M37L-Truck Trailers* (monthly). Bureau of the Census, U.S. Department of Commerce.

17. *1984 Van Trailer Size Report*. Truck Trailer Manufacturers Association, Alexandria, Va., Oct. 1984.

18. *Commercial Vehicle Packages 1, 2, and 3* (monthly). Motor Vehicle Manufacturers Association, Detroit, Mich.

19. *National Vehicle Population Profile* (annual). R.L. Polk and Co., Detroit, Mich.

20. *Accidents of Motor Carriers of Property 1983*. Bureau of Motor Carrier Safety, FHWA, U.S. Department of Transportation, Oct. 1984.

21. *Fatal Accident Reporting System 1983*. NHTSA, U.S. Department of Transportation, March 1984.

22. *National Accident Sampling System 1983*. NHTSA, U.S. Department of Transportation, Jan. 1985.

23. *America's Highways: Accelerating the Search for Innovation*. TRB Special Report 202. Transportation Research Board, National Research Council, Washington, D.C., 1984.

24. U.S. Congress. House. Bureau of Public Roads, U.S. Department of Commerce. *Maximum Desirable and Weights of Vehicles Operated on the Federal-Aid Systems*. H. Doc. 354, 88th Congress, 2nd Session, Aug. 1964.

25. *Final Report on the Federal Highway Cost Allocation Study*. FHWA, U.S. Department of Transportation, May 1982.

26. *An Investigation of Truck Size and Weight Limits: Final Report*. U.S. Department of Transportation, Aug. 1981.

27. G.R. Vallette *et al*. *The Effect of Truck Size and Weight on Accident Experience and Traffic Operations*. U.S. Department of Transportation, July 1981.

28. *Traffic Monitoring Guide*. FHWA, U.S. Department of Transportation, June 1985.

29. "Crescent Study Approved." *AASHTO Journal Newsletter*, June 14, 1985.

30. "BMCS Accident Reporting: New System Being Considered." *Commercial Carrier Journal*, Dec. 1984, p. 64.

31. "Up Front." *Commercial Carrier Journal*, May 1985, p. 16.

7

Summary and Conclusions

This concluding chapter will draw together the estimates presented earlier of the various benefits and costs of nationwide legalization of twins in the three areas of trucking productivity, safety, and pavements and other highway impacts. The summary will show that although greater use of twins has reduced the cost of shipping goods by truck, it has also increased some public costs, particularly road pavement wear. Nevertheless, these added costs will be small compared with the shipping cost savings gained. Greater use of twins will have little overall effect on highway safety; however, the safety of trucks in general continues to be a major concern, and many opportunities are at hand for improving the safety of twins and all large trucks.

The first section in this chapter is a summary of the effects of nationwide legalization of twins. Following this is a description of how the benefits and costs are distributed among affected groups and regions and between urban and rural areas. Then the question of the safety of twins, which has been the main point of controversy over expanded use of these vehicles, is put in context as one part of the broad issue of truck safety. Finally, opportunities are described for actions to improve the safety of both twins and combination trucks generally.

EFFECTS OF NATIONWIDE LEGALIZATION OF TWINS

Twin trailer trucks have been in use in every state since 1983, when a federal law required all states to allow twins on their major roads. In 1982 twins were prohibited in 14 states, all in the East. However, they were common in other parts of the country and accounted for about 4 percent of all miles of combination-truck travel. Twins were most extensively used in the Far West, and half of all the twin trailer truck travel nationwide occurred in California. Since 1983, twins travel has grown to 7 percent of combination-truck travel and will reach 11 percent and then stabilize by about 1990. This expanded use of twins is increasing freight productivity and accelerating pavement wear but should not have a net effect on safety. Impacts in each of these three areas are summarized in the following paragraphs.

Twins offer productivity gains because a twin trailer truck has greater volume capacity than a tractor-semitrailer and because the flexibility afforded by having freight loaded into two small trailers rather than one large one allows a truck operator hauling packages or small shipments to reduce the average number of times that each shipment is handled and to avoid circuitous routings. These advantages are valuable to carriers in the segment of the for-hire trucking industry that specializes in multiple small shipments of low-density freight (the general freight common carriers) but usually are not important in the other segments of the industry—the for-hire carriers of truckload-sized shipments and the private fleets operated by firms to carry their own goods exclusively. Therefore nearly all the growth in twin trailer truck traffic is occurring in the general freight common carrier segment, which accounts for only about 15 percent of all combination-truck travel.

Through reduced miles of truck travel and reduced handling, truck operators will save $500 million (1985 dollars) annually (0.5 percent of total intercity trucking costs) once the transition to twins has occurred. The expanded use of twins will save 500 million combination-truck miles annually (0.7 percent of total combination-truck travel) compared with the travel in tractor-semitrailers that would otherwise be required to carry the same freight. The carriers that switch from tractor-semitrailers to twins will attain on average a 9 percent savings in combination-truck miles in their operations. The flexibility of twins is as important as their greater volume capacity in achieving both the mileage and the dollar savings.

Highway safety will be little affected by the expanded use of twins, because the accompanying reduction in combination-truck miles of travel will offset a possible increase in accident involvements per mile traveled. Under identical operating conditions at highway speeds, a twin trailer truck is probably more likely to be involved in an accident than a tractor-semitrailer (that is, twins probably have a higher rate of involvements per mile traveled). This higher accident rate presumably is related to three handling difficulties that are characteristic of twins. First, when twins are steered through an abrupt maneuver such as a sudden lane change to pass another vehicle, the rear trailer may exhibit an exaggerated side-to-side motion often described as a crack-the-whip effect. This phenomenon is known technically as rearward amplification and may result in rollover of the rear trailer. Second, drivers of twins are less able than drivers of tractor-semitrailers to sense impending trailer instability and prevent related accidents. This impaired sensory feedback is the result of the greater number of coupling points in a twin trailer truck (a total of three compared with one in a tractor-semitrailer). To properly control a vehicle the driver must be able to sense the dynamic forces acting on it. Finally, when a twin trailer truck rounds a curve at highway speeds, its rear wheels deviate from the path of the front wheels (offtrack) toward the outside of the curve and may encroach on the opposite lane or the shoulder. Tractor-semitrailers also offtrack in this way, but slightly less so than twins at highway speeds. At slow speeds the offtracking performance of twins is superior to that of tractor-semitrailers. Consequently twins are more maneuverable than tractor-semitrailers in low-speed situations such as driving on city streets.

Estimates of the difference in accident rates between twins and tractor-semitrailers are necessarily imprecise because such comparisons must be made under very similar operating conditions—for example, similar routes, drivers, and times of day—if they are to reflect safety differences between the two vehicles rather than safety effects of the operating conditions. In the three studies comparing twins and tractor-semitrailers by using actual pre-1983 travel and accident experience that did the best job of controlling for the effects of these extraneous factors, the ratios of the accident involvement rate of twins to that of tractor-semitrailers were 0.98, 1.06, and 1.12. In the three most reliable studies that estimated involvement rates in fatal accidents, the ratios of the twins rate to the tractor-semitrailer rate were 0.93, 1.05, and 1.20. Historical data also show that there are no significant differences in severity between accidents involving twins and those involving tractor-semitrailers. Data on twins safety since 1982 are still fragmentary but show small increases in twins involvements that are roughly comparable with their increased share of miles traveled and are not inconsistent with these pre-1983 observations of only slight differences in accident rates between twins and tractor-semitrailers.

The 9 percent reduction in combination-truck miles in operations that are converted from tractor-semitrailers to twins approximately offsets the possibly higher frequency of accident involvements per combination-truck mile that twins exhibit. The net safety impact of expanded use of twins will thus be slightly fewer miles of truck travel with slightly more accidents per mile, resulting in a negligible change in the number of accidents.

Pavement wear on U.S. highways will be accelerated by increased substitution of twins for tractor-semitrailers. Twins typically weigh more than the tractor-semitrailers they replace, their loads are usually distributed less uniformly than tractor-semitrailer loads, and they have four single axles under their trailers rather than the two pairs of closely spaced axles (tandem axles) that support the semitrailer in a tractor-semitrailer. These three characteristics account for the greater wearing effect of twins on asphalt pavement and are only partially offset by the reduction in combination-truck travel due to twins. The net effect after allowance is made for reduced travel is that twins will cause 90 percent more wear on asphalt pavements to carry a given quantity of freight compared with the tractor-semitrailers they replace. On portland cement concrete twins will cause about 20 percent more wear. Systemwide, at the expected 1990 use of twins, the additional wear that twins will cause would cost roughly $50 million annually to repair, or about 2 percent of total annual pavement rehabilitation expenditures by the states.

The use of 102-in. wide trucks and 48-ft long semitrailers, also authorized nationwide in the law that allowed nationwide use of twins, increases pavement wear because these vehicles weigh more on average than the ones they replace. Semitrailers 48 ft long are more likely than shorter semitrailers to override shoulders and curbs during turns, and so will cause some added roadside damage, necessitate some changes in geometric design practices, and will have more accidents on turns. A truck 102 in. wide is more stable than the previously standard 96-in. wide vehicle, a potential safety advantage provided the vehicle is equipped with wider axles matching the width of the body.

In summary (Table 7-1), the 1983 federal law legalizing twins has exerted a substantial influence on equipment selection and operations in the general freight common carrier segment of the trucking industry, and as a result, these carriers have been able to transport freight at a lower cost. The new traffic in twins is accelerating pavement wear, but the added pavement rehabilitation costs will be only one-tenth of the freight cost savings. The growth in the use of twins has not increased highway accident losses, but twins do have certain handling peculiarities that can pose a risk in some circumstances.

DISTRIBUTION OF BENEFITS AND COSTS OF EXPANDED USE OF TWINS

Although in the aggregate the benefits of expanded use of twins exceed the associated costs, these costs and benefits will not affect all parties equally. If current state and federal highway tax structures remain unchanged, then the principal added cost of twins—increased pavement wear—will be borne by all automobile and truck operators, through the higher operating costs that pavement wear causes. The productivity savings

TABLE 7-1　The Effects of Nationwide Legalization of Twin Trailer
Trucks

Use and productivity gains by 1990	
Twins travel	7.8 billion mi/year—10.8 percent of all combination truck travel; up from 3.7 percent in 1982; less-than-truckload carriers account for nearly all growth
Net combination-truck travel savings	500 million mi/year—0.7 percent of total combination-truck travel
Freight cost savings	$500 million/year (from reduced freight handling and reduced mileage)—0.5 percent of intercity truck freight costs
Highway safety impacts	
Handling of twins	Severe rear-trailer sway in response to abrupt steering maneuvers
	Driver's ability to sense impending trailer instability impaired
	Rear wheels deviate more from track of front wheels at highway speed; tracking is better than that of tractor-semitrailer at city street speeds
Accident rates	Twins probably have slightly higher rates than similarly operated tractor-semitrailers on rural roads
Accident severity	No difference between twins and tractor-semitrailers under similar conditions
Systemwide safety	Reduction in travel offsets slightly higher accident rate; therefore net overall effect on safety is small
Impacts on pavement and other highway features	
Pavement	Twins cause 90 percent more pavement wear on asphalt pavement and 20 percent more on portland cement concrete than tractor-semitrailers carrying the same freight
Systemwide pavement cost	$50 million/year increase in pavement rehabilitation cost by 1990—2 percent of total rehabilitation expenditures
Wear of structures, traffic flow, and geometric design requirements	Impacts all negligible

from twins will not all accrue to trucking companies. Substantial savings
will be passed along to shippers, and some increases in wages are possible.
The carriers who are the major users of twins are engaged in a highly
competitive industry, and these competitive pressures will result in somewhat lower freight transportation costs for their customers.

Safety costs will be negligible from the perspective of the change in
the accident risk confronting a typical motorist, the result of slightly fewer
miles of truck travel with slightly more accidents per mile. However, from
the perspective of the individual truck driver in a twin trailer truck who

previously drove a tractor-semitrailer, the accident risk is slightly greater unless the driver is well aware of the particular handling characteristics of twins and is skilled at allowing for these characteristics.

The regional distribution of pavement and safety impacts will be roughly proportional to the distribution of the additional twins travel resulting from the 1983 federal truck size rules. Outside the western states, this added travel will be distributed nearly in proportion to each region's share of nationwide combination-truck travel. Thus the 14 states in the East where twins were prohibited until 1983 account for nearly one-fourth of nationwide combination-truck travel and will receive about the same proportion of the new twins travel. The eastern states where twins had been legal together with the Central and Plains states account for about three-fifths of all combination-truck travel and will receive a little more than that share of the new twins travel. The West and Mountain states account for one-sixth of combination-truck travel and will experience one-ninth of the added twins travel. Total twins travel as a share of all combination-truck travel will be highest in the West and Mountain states, as it was before 1983, but the greatest growth in use of twins relative to the pre-1983 level will be in the East.

The distribution of impacts between urban and rural areas will also depend on the distribution of new twins travel. One-third of the additional twins travel will be on roads in urban areas (about the same as the urban share of all combination-truck traffic). Most of the new urban traffic in twins will be on Interstates. Twins operated by general freight common carriers begin and end their runs at terminals that are usually located in fringe areas, and freight is picked up from shippers and delivered to recipients in one of the two short trailers from the twins or in another vehicle. Because pickup and delivery will more often be done in smaller vehicles, twins will be very uncommon on city streets, and this will help to reduce the number of full-sized tractor-semitrailers in city traffic.

Under slow-speed urban conditions, the safety performance of twins compares more favorably with that of tractor-semitrailers than on rural highways, because twins are the more maneuverable of the two types. Pavement impacts of twins are also mitigated somewhat in urban areas, because urban Interstates have mainly concrete pavements, whereas most rural Interstates are asphalt. The proportions of concrete and asphalt pavement in urban and rural areas vary regionally.

TWINS SAFETY IN THE CONTEXT OF OVERALL TRUCK SAFETY

Although the twins traffic resulting from the 1983 federal law has not increased truck accidents or fatalities, truck safety in general continues to be a serious concern. Public awareness of truck safety and media attention devoted to the topic are intense, and the widely held perception that trucks are a major and growing part of the highway accident problem has been a principal basis for opposition to liberalized truck size rules. Many perceive current truck safety problems as consequences of trends toward more and larger trucks. Indeed, between the late 1950s and the present, combination-truck travel has doubled and average loaded weight has risen 30 percent.

These trends have been accommodated by numerous regulatory actions by all levels of government. Increases in truck traffic and in the dimensions of trucks have occurred in a series of small steps as states amended their truck size regulations and trucking firms gradually upgraded their fleets. Each step of this process, like the step taken in 1983, has proved to be too small to have caused any distinct, identifiable deterioration in safety. Yet, although each step may have influenced safety in ways too small and difficult to observe, today's serious safety problem might be argued to be the cumulative impact of this series of individual steps, each of which appeared innocuous individually. This argument does not stand up to close scrutiny, however. The long-term trend in accidents does not show that truck safety performance has gradually eroded as truck size and weight laws have been liberalized. The trend during the past 50 years in heavy-truck accident involvement rates (as with rates for all vehicles) has been downward—accident involvement rates for intercity freight trucks reported in the 1930s were several times higher than rates typical today. Good quantitative estimates of this decline or of the relative decline compared with accident involvement rates for other vehicles are not possible because nationwide accident statistics have been available only in the past 10 years. The long-term decline in the accident involvement rates of heavy trucks and other vehicles is attributable to the construction of the Interstate system and other improvements in road design, changes in travel patterns, new vehicle designs, and other factors; nonetheless, the trend does not show that increasing truck size has been associated historically with deteriorating truck safety.

The heavy-truck accident involvement rate increased in the late 1970s, fell in the early 1980s, and may be rising again currently. The number of accidents has recently risen markedly. Combination-truck accidents reported to the U.S. Department of Transportation's Bureau of Motor Carrier Safety in 1984 were up 16 percent compared with 1983; combination-truck fatal involvements reported to the Bureau of Motor Carrier Safety were up 8 percent, and combination-truck fatal involvements reported to the National Highway Traffic Safety Administration (a more complete count) were up 6 percent. Many observers have found this trend to be a cause of concern; however, its pattern may be cyclical—the increases in the late 1970s and recently both correspond to periods of economic expansion when more inexperienced drivers are hired, older equipment is used more, and traffic volumes are increasing. Thus the number of combination-truck accident involvements reported in 1984, although above the previous year's level, was about the same as in the peak year of 1979. It is impossible to tell yet whether recent experience represents a departure from the long-term declining trend.

Regardless of the trend, the toll from heavy-truck accidents is high. One highway fatality in nine occurs in an accident involving a heavy truck, and when accident rates for the two categories of vehicles on similar roads are compared, heavy trucks are involved in fatal accidents about twice as often per mile traveled as other vehicles. The rate of involvement of heavy trucks in all (fatal and nonfatal) accidents is lower than that of other vehicles, but this difference is in large part because heavy trucks accumulate a larger share of their travel on roads that are the safest for all vehicles.

Although twins use increases trucking productivity and does not increase systemwide safety risks, it may be possible to develop trucks that are safer than present twins yet are equally productive and perhaps no more wearing to roads. The ultimate limits of vehicle dimensions that can be accommodated safely and cost-effectively have not been established. Truck safety depends not only on what kinds of vehicles are allowed, but also on how these vehicles are operated and maintained, how roads are designed and maintained, and how drivers are trained and licensed. The recommendations that follow identify several promising means for improving truck safety through improvements in each of these components of the truck transportation system.

OPPORTUNITIES FOR IMPROVING TRUCK SAFETY

The federal government, state governments, and truck operators should vigorously pursue the following potential means for improving the safety of twins and trucks generally.

Improved Safety for Twins

Some motor carriers are using a variety of low-cost measures that appear to improve safety for twins. These measures include tighter pintle hook connections between converter dollies and lead semitrailers, balanced load distribution to improve vehicle control, and training and instruction aids to alert drivers to the handling differences between twins and tractor-semitrailers. Industry leaders should make information on these measures available throughout the industry so that other carriers can give full consideration to adopting them.

In the longer term, alternative dolly designs for coupling twin trailers by using double drawbars could provide an opportunity for improving rear-trailer stability. An FHWA-sponsored research study in progress is examining how dolly design affects handling and stability characteristics.

Improved Safety for 102-in. Wide Trucks

The U.S. Department of Transportation should require that the increase in truck body width to 102 in. be matched with increased axle width to take advantage of this opportunity for improved stability.

More Stringent Driver Controls

Driving trucks is a demanding task; interstate truck drivers often accumulate over 100,000 mi per year. The greatest gains in truck safety may lie in stricter requirements for these drivers, including a single national license with uniform standards, stricter enforcement of driving time limits, appropriate physical qualifications, required driving performance monitoring, and training requirements.

Improved Truck Controllability

The handling and braking performance of heavy trucks is greatly inferior to that of passenger cars. There is a need for development of new technology and broader application of existing technology in the design of trucks and trailers for improved controllability. Opportunities for improved performance exist in the following areas:

- Better proportioning of brake torques over the range of loads,
- Antilock-controlled brakes,
- Suspension and load bed layouts that improve basic roll stability of all types of trucks and trailers, and
- Truck and tractor chassis designs that assure stable response to steering.

Safety Responsibility of Size and Weight Legislation

Systematic attention has never been given to requiring safety features in the larger trucks that have been legislatively authorized. The 1983 federal truck size legislation, for example, allowed 102-in. wide trucks without also stipulating that the axles be full width to assure that the potential stability benefits would accrue. Regulators should consider, as a general rule, that changes to truck size regulations that allow increased vehicle productivity be coupled to requirements to upgrade the safety of the vehicles as well, using the potential productivity gain as an incentive for safety gains.

Upgraded Geometric Design of Highways

Although it is not cost-effective to reconstruct all of the nation's highways to accommodate occasional or infrequent use by the largest legal trucks, state highway agencies should periodically reexamine truck volumes and accident statistics to identify locations, such as ramps or interchanges, that are disproportionately prone to truck accidents and take corrective measures where cost-effective. In all rehabilitation and reconstruction projects on the designated network, state highway agencies should emphasize upgrading geometric designs where justified to ensure that the larger trucks can be safely accommodated.

Dedication to Comprehensive Safety Management by Trucking Firms

Many trucking firms have demonstrated that it is possible to reduce and control accident losses through serious management emphasis on safety, which may include screening new drivers, ongoing monitoring and training of all drivers, thorough equipment maintenance and inspection, employment of qualified safety professionals with the authority to carry out a rigorous program, accident data systems that allow progress to be measured and problems to be quickly spotted, and a clear company policy placing safety before short-run cost considerations. All trucking firms should promote and adopt such measures. Small firms and owner-operators will face practical difficulties in establishing comprehensive safety management programs; nonetheless, basic safety management must be recognized as an indispensable component of all trucking operations regardless of size.

More Effective Enforcement of Truck Safety Regulations

The Bureau of Motor Carrier Safety and the responsible state and local agencies must have the resources necessary to do the enforcement jobs assigned to them. Enforcement agencies can use limited resources more efficiently by instituting monitoring programs to evaluate whether their efforts are having the intended safety impacts.

Monitoring Truck Use and Its Effects

Efforts to improve truck safety will be hindered if reliable information is not available to identify safety problems, analyze their causes, and measure the success of actions taken to solve them. Chapter 6 contains recommendations for enhancing capabilities for monitoring truck use and impacts.

Glossary of Trucking and Highway Terms

A number of special terms referring to trucks, the trucking industry, and highways that are used frequently in this report are defined. Trucking terms are not standardized, so, for example, a given piece of equipment may be known by different names in different parts of the country or among different groups involved in the industry.

Terms in italics are defined elsewhere in the glossary.

TRUCK TERMS

COMBINATION TRUCK. A truck comprising two or more detachable units, usually a *tractor* and one or more *trailers* or *semitrailers* (Figure G-1). Combination trucks carry most intercity freight that travels by truck in the United States. They are also used commonly for pickup and delivery and other local trips. About 1.3 million (counted by the number of power units) are in operation, traveling 70 billion mi annually (*1*).

DOLLY or CONVERTER DOLLY. The device most commonly used to couple the trailers of a multitrailer combination. It consists of a frame mounted on an axle with a hook-and-eye connection to the front semitrailer and a *fifth wheel* connection to the rear semitrailer (Figures G-2 and G-3). Dollies for twins have a single axle; dollies for the larger *turnpike doubles* have *tandem axles*. The forward con-

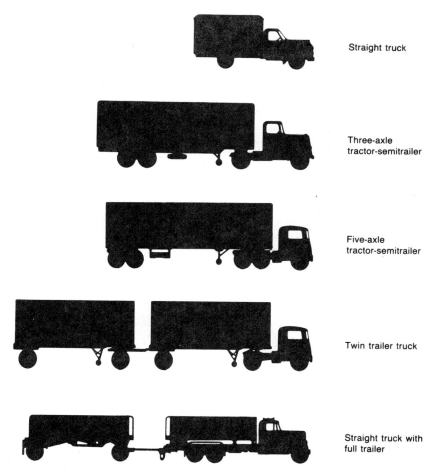

Straight truck

Three-axle
tractor-semitrailer

Five-axle
tractor-semitrailer

Twin trailer truck

Straight truck with
full trailer

FIGURE G-1   Truck types.

nection of the dolly is usually a single eye that attaches to the *pintle hook* on the rear of the front trailer. An uncommon variant design, the B-dolly or double-drawbar dolly, has two parallel drawbars and two hook-and-eye connections to the front trailer (Figure G-3). The connection between front trailer and the B-dolly is rigid, eliminating one articulation point between the two trailers. Some B-dollies incorporate a steering mechanism that allows the dolly axle to pivot during turns, reducing offtracking.

FIGURE G-2　Dolly being connected to rear trailer.

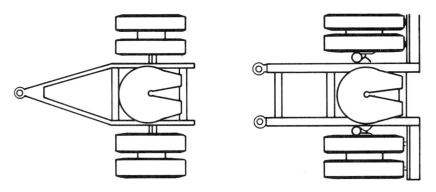

FIGURE G-3　Converter dollies: A-dolly (most common in United States) (*left*), B-dolly (*right*) (*3*).

DOUBLE TRAILER TRUCK or DOUBLE. A *combination truck* with two *trailers*, usually both *semitrailers*. The front of the first semitrailer rests on the rear axles of the *tractor* and the front of the second semitrailer rests on a *dolly*. Other connection arrangements between the two trailers are sometimes used. Several types of double trailer trucks are in common use, classified by the arrangement of axles and the length of the trailers: *twin trailer truck*, *turnpike double*, and *Rocky Mountain double*. The 1983 federal law had no effect on the legality of these last two longer and heavier double trailer trucks.

FIFTH WHEEL. A horizontal circular plate mounted over the rear axle of a *tractor*, with a hole in the center into which a vertical pin under the front end of a *semitrailer* fits to couple the two units together. The fifth wheel is the pivot point between the tractor and semitrailer and bears the weight of the front of the semitrailer.

PINTLE HOOK. A fixed upright hook extending from the rear of the frame of a *trailer* to be used in a *double trailer truck*. An eye at the front end of the *dolly* in a *double trailer truck* hooks to the pintle hook on the front trailer to connect the two units.

PUP. A single short (27 or 28 ft long) *trailer* of the type used in *twin trailer trucks*.

ROCKY MOUNTAIN DOUBLE. *Double trailer truck* that has a three-axle *tractor*, a *tandem-axle semitrailer* 40 to 45 ft long, a single-axle *dolly*, and a second 27- to 28-ft single-axle semitrailer (seven axles in all). It is legal in 16 states.

SEMITRAILER. The most common type of cargo-carrying unit in a *combination truck*, consisting of a frame with either a single axle or a *tandem axle* at the rear. The front of a semitrailer has no axle; it rests on the rear axle of the vehicle in front of it (usually the *tractor*) in the combination, coupled by means of the *fifth wheel*. The body of a semitrailer may be a van (enclosed box), a tank or hopper for carrying liquid or dry bulk commmodities, a flatbed for carrying large objects (logs, machinery, etc.), or one of many other types.

STRAIGHT TRUCK or SINGLE-UNIT TRUCK. A truck with the engine, cab, and freight compartment all on the same frame.

TANDEM AXLE. A pair of closely spaced axles, typically about 4 ft apart (for example, the rear two axles of the *tractor-semitrailer* shown in Figure G-4).

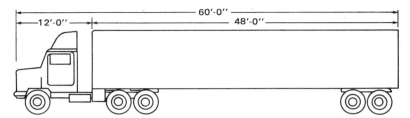

FIGURE G-4   Typical dimensions of a tractor-semitrailer with 48-ft semitrailer.

TRACTOR or TRUCK-TRACTOR. The powered unit of a *tractor-semitrailer* with a cab and engine (almost always a diesel) but no freight compartment. At the rear of the tractor frame is the *fifth wheel* to which a *semitrailer* may be attached. Tractors have one axle in the front and one axle or a *tandem axle* in the rear.

TRACTOR-SEMITRAILER. The most common type of *combination truck*, comprising a *tractor* and one *semitrailer*. The five-axle tractor-semitrailer (three-axle tractor and two-axle semitrailer), typically 50 to 64 ft long and weighing 60,000 to 80,000 lb when loaded, is the most common. The tractor-semitrailer legalized for nationwide use by the 1983 federal law has a semitrailer 48 ft long and 102 in. wide and a typical overall length that can range from 56 to 64 ft (Figure G-4). The longest semitrailer in common use before 1983 was 45 ft.

TRAILER. The cargo-carrying unit in a combination truck; it may be either a *semitrailer* or a full trailer (a trailer with axles at both ends).

TURNPIKE DOUBLE. *Double trailer truck* that has a three-axle *tractor* pulling two *tandem-axle semitrailers*, each typically 45 ft long, coupled by a tandem-axle *dolly* (nine axles in all). It is legal on at least some roads in 13 states.

TWIN TRAILER TRUCK. A *double trailer truck* that has a two- or three-axle *tractor* and two short single-axle *semitrailers*, each usually 27 or 28 ft long, coupled by a single-axle *dolly* (five or six axles in total). These trucks are sometimes called doubles, double bottoms, and western doubles; however, in this report "double trailer truck" and "doubles" always means any *combination truck* comprising a tractor and two *trailers*, which includes twin trailer trucks and longer doubles with seven or more axles. The most common pre-1983 twin trailer truck consisted of a two-axle cab-over-engine tractor drawing two single-axle semitrailers, each 27 ft long and coupled by a single-axle dolly (Figure G-5). The overall length was 65 ft, the maximum legal length in 25 of the 36 states where the vehicle was permitted before 1983 (the other 11 had longer maximums). The width was 96 in., the legal maximum on all roads in 42 states (2) and the federal maximum on the Interstates before 1983. The 1983 federal law permits twins with trailers up to 28 ft long, unlimited overall length, and 102-in. width on Interstates, the federally designated network, and state-selected access roads. The overall length of these twins is now at least 67 ft (Figure G-6). If a conventional tractor is used (engine under a hood forward of the cab), the twin trailer truck may be 3 to 7 ft longer.

TWINS. Twin trailer truck.

HIGHWAY TERMS

AASHO ROAD TEST. A major research project completed in the early 1960s that involved accelerated testing of *flexible* and *rigid pavements* under carefully controlled traffic conditions. Most pavement design in the United States and many other parts of the world is based on the results of this research. The Road Test was conducted by the Highway Research Board (now the Transportation Research Board) under the sponsorship of the American Association of State

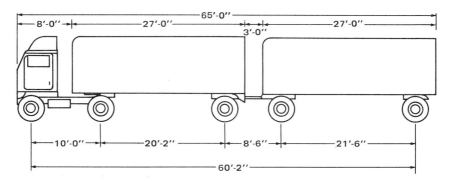

FIGURE G-5   Typical dimensions of pre-1983 twin trailer truck.

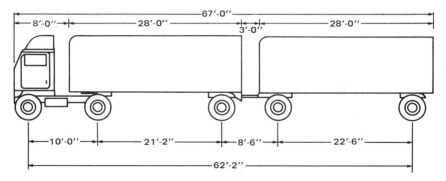

FIGURE G-6 Typical dimensions of twin trailer truck permitted under 1983 federal law. [NOTE: Use of conventional tractor adds 3 to 7 ft to total length.]

Highway Officials (AASHO), since renamed the American Association of State Highway and Transportation Officials (AASHTO).

BRIDGE. Concrete, steel, or wooden highway *structure* over body of water, other highway, railroad, or topographic depression.

CULVERT. Pipe-like drain running transversely underneath a roadway.

EQUIVALENT SINGLE-AXLE LOAD (ESAL). For a given load on a single or *tandem axle*, the number of repetitions of an 18,000-lb single axle that would have the same adverse effect on pavement life.

FEDERAL-AID HIGHWAY. U.S. road owned and maintained by the states or by local governments on which the states may use their shares of the federal funds distributed through the federal-aid highway program for construction, reconstruction, and major maintenance. The 835,000-mi federal-aid highway system represents 40 percent of the miles of paved road in the United States and includes almost all principal intercity routes as well as many major urban roads.

FEDERAL-AID PRIMARY HIGHWAY. One of the system of highways that includes the *Interstates* as well as the next most important class of *federal-aid highways*. The non-Interstate portion of the system comprises 257,000 mi of roads. Although most are constructed to somewhat above-average design standards, federal-aid primaries vary greatly in quality. Eighty percent of non-Interstate primary miles are two-lane undivided roads, and 32 percent have lane widths less than the 12-ft Interstate standard.

FLEXIBLE PAVEMENT. Highway pavement, usually constructed with an asphalt-concrete wearing surface over layers of crushed rock, that distributes its loads to a relatively small area of earth such that distortions or irregularities in the underlying earth or any of the crushed rock layers will be reflected in the wearing surface. Flexible pavements comprise about 50 percent of all *Interstate* highway mileage and over 85 percent of all *federal-aid primary* mileage (excluding Interstates).

GEOMETRIC DESIGN STANDARD. Minimum (or maximum) design value for dimensions of a highway cross-section feature (such as lane and shoulder widths) or alignment feature (such as horizontal curve radius), including dimensions of intersections and interchanges.

INTERSTATE SYSTEM. A 43,000-mi system of the most important *federal-aid highways* connecting all major cities in the country and built, for the most part, to the highest standards of highway design. Most Interstate highways have four or more lanes, a median or barrier separating the two opposing directions of traffic, access only at interchanges by means of ramps so that cross traffic does not interfere with traffic on the highway, lanes 12 ft wide, broad paved shoulders, and curves and slopes gentle enough that vehicles can negotiate them without slowing.

RIGID PAVEMENT. Highway pavement constructed of portland cement concrete that generally possesses sufficient strength and stiffness to distribute its loads over a relatively large area and can bridge over minor irregularities in the underlying earth or supporting material. About 50 percent of *Interstate* highways are constructed of rigid pavement, but it is much less common on other highways. On *federal-aid primary highways* (excluding Interstates) rigid pavement comprises less than 15 percent of the total mileage.

STRUCTURE. Highway bridge or viaduct over a body of water, railroad, other highway, topographic depression, or urban development. *Culverts* are structures.

TRUCKING INDUSTRY TERMS

BREAKBULK OPERATION. Freight handling operation performed at some terminals in which shipments from smaller terminals are consolidated for more efficient *line-haul* travel or where, in the reverse operation, consolidated shipments destined for smaller terminals are sorted and routed.

COMMON CARRIER. A *for-hire* trucking company that offers transportation services to the general public according to published rates regulated by the *Interstate Commerce Commission (ICC)*. Common carriers are required to offer service on equal terms to all shippers in the geographic areas that they are permitted to serve.

CONTRACT CARRIER. A *for-hire* trucking company that specializes in hauling goods according to terms specified in contracts with individual shippers (traditionally a small number). Since 1980 distinctions between *ICC*-regulated contract and *common carriers* have eroded as common carriers have sought more contract business and as the restrictions on the types and numbers of shippers that contract carriers can deal with have been dropped.

FOR-HIRE CARRIER. Firm whose principal business is to provide trucking services carrying the goods of others. For-hire carriers and *private carriers* are the two major components of the *trucking industry*.

GENERAL FREIGHT COMMON CARRIER. A *common carrier* authorized by the *ICC* to carry general freight, a regulatory commodity classification that includes nearly everything except large shipments of certain special commodities (special commodities include petroleum products, heavy machinery, refrigerated products, motor vehicles, building materials, forest products, household goods, and other specific commodities defined by ICC). This classification is nearly equivalent to *LTL carrier*. The major business of nearly all general freight common carriers is LTL operations, but most also carry truckload (TL) freight and a few specialize in TL freight. General freight common carriers include most of the largest *for-hire* trucking firms.

INTERSTATE COMMERCE COMMISSION (ICC). Federal government agency that regulates *for-hire carriers* engaged in interstate commerce except carriers that haul only certain exempt commodities (unprocessed agricultural commodities and seafood). For-hire carriers that operate entirely within a single state and *private carriers* (provided they do not infringe on the ICC definition of for-hire carriage) are not regulated. The ICC regulates who may enter the for-hire trucking industry, the rates a carrier may charge, the commodities each carrier can haul, the routes and territories it may serve, procedures for shippers' claims against carriers, insurance requirements, and other aspects of trucking businesses. Since the Motor Carrier Act of 1980, regulation in all these areas has been considerably relaxed.

LESS-THAN-TRUCKLOAD (LTL) CARRIER. A *for-hire carrier* that specializes in hauling LTL freight, small shipments of a size such that several can make up the full load of one truck. An LTL carrier must have a network of terminals located throughout its service area, a local *pickup and delivery fleet*, and a fleet of *combination trucks* for *line haul*. Larger LTL carriers usually also have one or more *breakbulk* terminals.

LINE HAUL. Movement of freight between origin and destination terminals (as distinguished from *pickup and delivery* between terminals and shippers and receivers).

OWNER-OPERATOR. An individual who owns and operates his own truck as a business. Traditionally owner-operators have lacked *ICC* authorization to operate on their own account and so have specialized in hauling exempt commodities or in leasing their truck and labor to ICC-authorized carriers. With deregulation, owner-operators can more easily obtain operating authority or lease themselves to *private carriers*.

PICKUP AND DELIVERY FLEET . Vehicles and drivers who haul freight from local shippers to the terminal or from the terminal to local receivers.

PRIVATE CARRIER. Firm whose principal business is manufacturing, mining, trade, or some other industry that operates its own trucks to transport its own goods.

REGULATED CARRIER. Usually, a firm that is subject to the regulations of the *Interstate Commerce Commission* (although nearly all trucking firms are subject to one extent or another to regulation by a variety of federal and state government agencies).

TON-MILE. The movement of 1 ton of freight 1 mi, a measure of the output of a freight transportation operation. If 100 trucks each carrying a 10-ton load travel 1,000 mi each, they have in total traveled 100,000 truck-mi or vehicle-mi, carried 1,000 tons of freight, and produced 1 million ton-mi of freight transportation.

TRUCKING INDUSTRY. All businesses that operate trucks, including both *private carriers* and *for-hire carriers*. *Combination-truck* traffic on U.S. roads is divided roughly equally between for-hire and private carriers.

TRUCKLOAD (TL) CARRIER. A carrier that specializes in TL freight, a single shipment of which constitutes the full load of a truck. A TL carrier normally picks up a load in the *line-haul* vehicle at the shipper's dock and delivers it directly to the receiver in the same truck, so the carrier does not handle the freight at its own terminals. Roughly 85 percent of all *combination-truck* travel is TL freight carriage, including nearly all *contract carriers*, *private carriers*, and *common carriers* other than the *LTL carriers*.

REFERENCES

1. *Highway Statistics 1983*. FHWA, U.S. Department of Transportation, 1984.
2. J. Galligan and D.M. DiNunzio. ''Guide to Trucking Rules and Regulations.'' *Commercial Carrier Journal*, April 1983.
3. *Doubles: Loss Prevention Data Sheet*. Liberty Mutual Insurance Company, Boston, Mass., 1984.

Appendix A
Sections of Highway Laws Relating to
Truck Size and Weight

SURFACE TRANSPORTATION ASSISTANCE ACT OF 1982
Public Law 97-424, 97th Congress, Jan. 6, 1983 (96 Stat. 2097)

*   *   *   *   *   *   *   *

VEHICLE WEIGHT, LENGTH, AND WIDTH LIMITATIONS

SEC. 133. (a) Section 127 of title 23 of the United States Code is amended to read:

"§ 127. Vehicle weight limitations—Interstate System

''(a) No funds authorized to be appropriated for any fiscal year under provisions of the Federal-Aid Highway Act of 1956 shall be apportioned to any State which does not permit the use of the National System of Interstate and Defense Highways within its boundaries by vehicles with a weight of twenty thousand pounds carried on any one axle, including enforcement tolerances, or with a tandem axle weight of thirty-four thousand pounds, including enforcement tolerances, or a gross weight of at least eighty thousand pounds for vehicle combinations of five axles or more. However, the maximum gross weight to be allowed by any State for vehicles using the National System of Interstate and Defense Highways shall be twenty thousand pounds carried on one axle, including enforcement tolerances, and a tandem axle weight of thirty-four thousand pounds, including enforcement tolerances, and with an overall maximum gross weight, including enforcement tolerances, on a group of two or more consecutive axles produced by application of the following formula:

$$W = 500 \left(\frac{LN}{N - 1} + 12N + 36 \right)$$

where W equals overall gross weight on any group of two or more consecutive axles to the nearest five hundred pounds, L equals distance in feet between the extreme of any group of two or more consecutive axles, and N equals number of axles in group under consideration, except that two consecutive sets of tandem axles may carry a gross load of thirty-four thousand pounds each providing the overall distance between the first and last axles of such consecutive sets of tandem axles is thirty-six feet or more: *Provided*, That such overall gross weight may not exceed eighty thousand pounds, including all enforcement tolerances, except for those vehicles and loads which cannot be easily dismantled or divided and which have been issued special permits in accordance with applicable State laws, or the corresponding maximum weights permitted for vehicles using the public highways of such State under laws or regulations established by appropriate State authority in effect on July 1, 1956, except in the case of the overall gross weight of any group of two or more consecutive axles, on the date of enactment of the Federal-Aid Highway Amendments of 1974, whichever is the greater. Any amount which is withheld from apportionment to any State pursuant to the foregoing provisions shall lapse. This section shall not be construed to deny apportionment to any State allowing the operation within such State of any vehicles or combinations thereof which the State determines could be lawfully operated within such State on July 1, 1956, except in the case of the overall gross weight of any group of two or more consecutive axles, on the date of enactment of the Federal-Aid Highway Amendments of 1974. With respect to the State of Hawaii, laws or regulations in effect on February 1, 1960, shall be applicable for the purposes of this section in lieu of those in effect on July 1, 1956. With respect to the State of Michigan, laws or regulations in effect on May 1, 1982, shall be applicable for the purposes of this subsection.

"(b) No State may enact or enforce any law denying reasonable access to motor vehicles subject to this title to and from the Interstate Highway System to terminals and facilities for food, fuel, repairs, and rest."

* * * * * * * *

PART B—COMMERCIAL MOTOR VEHICLE LENGTH LIMITATION

LENGTH LIMITATIONS ON FEDERALLY ASSISTED HIGHWAYS

SEC. 411.(a) No State shall establish, maintain, or enforce any regulation of commerce which imposes a vehicle length limitation of less than forty-eight feet on the length of the semitrailer unit operating in a truck tractor-semitrailer combination, and of less than twenty-eight feet on the length of any semitrailer or trailer operating in a truck tractor-semitrailer-trailer combination, on any segment of the National System of Interstate and Defense Highways and those classes of qualifying Federal-aid Primary System highways as designated by the Secretary, pursuant to subsection (e) of this section.

(b) Length limitations established, maintained, or enforced by the States under subsection (a) of this section shall apply solely to the semitrailer or trailer or trailers and not to a truck tractor. No State shall establish, maintain, or enforce any regulation of commerce which imposes an overall length limitation on commercial motor vehicles operating in truck-tractor semitrailer or truck tractor semitrailer, trailer combinations. No State shall establish, maintain, or enforce any regulation of commerce which has the effect of prohibiting the use of trailers or semitrailers of such dimensions as those that were in actual and lawful use in such State on December 1, 1982. No State shall establish, maintain, or enforce any regulation of commerce which has the effect of prohibiting the use of existing trailers or semitrailers, of up to twenty-eight and one-half feet in length, in a truck tractor-semitrailer-trailer combination if those trailers or semitrailers were actually and lawfully operating on December 1, 1982, within a sixty-five-foot overall length limit in any State.

(c) No State shall prohibit commercial motor vehicle combinations consisting of a truck tractor and two trailing units on any segment of the National System of Interstate and Defense Highways, and those classes of qualifying Federal-aid Primary System highways as designated by the Secretary pursuant to subsection (e) of this section.

(d) The Secretary is authorized to establish rules to implement the provisions of this section, and to make such determinations as are necessary to accommodate specialized equipment (including, but not limited to, automobile transporters) subject to subsections (a) and (b) of this section.

(e)(1) The Secretary shall designate as qualifying Federal-aid Primary System highways subject to the provisions of subsections (a) and (c) those Primary System highways that are capable of safety accommodating the vehicle lengths set forth therein.

(2) The Secretary shall make an initial determination of which classes of highways shall be designated pursuant to paragraph (1) within 90 days of the date of enactment of this section.

(3) The Secretary shall enact final rules pursuant to paragraph (1) no later than two hundred and seventy days from the date of enactment of this section and may revise such rules from time to time thereafter.

(f) For the purposes of this section, "truck tractor" shall be defined as the noncargo carrying power unit that operates in combination with a semitrailer or trailer, except that a truck tractor and semitrailer engaged in the transportation of automobiles may transport motor vehicles on part of the power unit.

(g) The provisions of this section shall take effect ninety days after the date of enactment of this title.

(h) The length limitations described in this section shall be exclusive of safety and energy conservation devices, such as rear view mirrors, turn signal lamps, marker lamps, steps and handholds for entry and egress, flexible fender extensions, mudflaps and splash and spray suppressant devices, load-induced tire bulge, refrigeration units or air compressors, and other devices, which the Secretary may interpret as necessary for safe and efficient operation of commercial motor vehicles, except that no device excluded under this subsection from the limitations of this section shall have by its design or use the capability to carry cargo.

ACCESS TO THE INTERSTATE SYSTEM

SEC. 412. No State may enact or enforce any law denying reasonable access to commercial motor vehicles subject to this title between (1) the Interstate and Defense Highway System and any other qualifying Federal-aid Primary System highways, as designated by the Secretary, and (2) terminals, facilities for food, fuel, repairs and rest, and points of loading and unloading for household goods carriers.

ENFORCEMENT

SEC. 413. The Secretary, or, on the request of the Secretary, the Attorney General of the United States, is authorized and directed to institute any civil action for injunctive relief as may be appropriate to assure compliance with the provisions of this title. Such action may be instituted in any district court of the United States in any State where such relief is required to assure compliance with the terms of this title. In any action under this section, the court shall, upon a proper showing, issue a temporary restraining order or preliminary or permanent injunction. In any such action, the court may also issue a mandatory injunction commanding any State or person to comply with any applicable provision of this title, or any rule issued under authority of this title.

*   *   *   *   *   *   *   *

COMMERCIAL MOTOR VEHICLE WIDTH LIMITATION

SEC. 416.(a) No State other than the State of Hawaii, shall establish, maintain, or enforce any regulation of commerce which imposes a vehicle width limitation of more or less than 102 inches on any segment of the National System of Interstate and Defense Highways, or any other qualifying Federal-aid highway as designated by the Secretary of Transportation, with traffic lanes designed to be a width of twelve feet or more; except that a State may continue to enforce any regulation of commerce in effect on April 6, 1983, with respect to motor vehicles that exceed 102 inches in width until the date on which such State adopts a regulation of commerce which complies with the provisions of this subsection.

(b) Notwithstanding the provisions of this section or any other provision of law, certain safety devices which the Secretary of Transportation determines are necessary for safe and efficient operation of motor vehicles shall not be included in the calculation of width.

(c) Notwithstanding the provisions of this section or any other provisions of law, a State may grant special use permit to motor vehicles that exceed 102 inches in width.

(d) Notwithstanding any other provision of law and in accordance with the provisions of this section, a State shall have authority to enforce a commercial vehicle width limitation of 102 inches on any segment of the National System of Interstate and Defense Highways, or any other qualifying Federal-aid highway as designated by the Secretary of Transportation, with traffic lanes designed to be a width of twelve feet or more.

(e) The provisions of this section shall take effect on April 6, 1983.

TANDEM TRUCK SAFETY ACT OF 1984
Public Law 98-554, 98th Congress, Oct. 30, 1984

TITLE I

SHORT TITLE

SEC. 101. This title may be cited as the "Tandem Truck Safety Act of 1984".

EXEMPTION FROM LENGTH REQUIREMENTS

SEC. 102. Section 411 of the Surface Transportation Assistance Act of 1982 (49 U.S.C. App. 2311) is amended by adding at the end thereof the following new subsection:

"(i)(1) If the Governor of a State, after making the consultations specified in paragraph (2) of this subsection, determines that any specific segment of the National System of Interstate and Defense Highways is not capable of safety accommodating motor vehicles having the lengths set forth in subsection (a) of this section or motor vehicle combinations described in subsection (c) of this section, the Governor may notify the Secretary of such determination and request that the Secretary exempt such segment from one or both of such subsections.

"(2) Before making such notification, the Governor shall consult with units of local government within the State in which the specific segment of such System is located, as well as the governor of any State adjacent to that State that might be directly affected by such exemption. As part of such consultations, consideration shall be given to any potential alternative route that—

"(A) can safely accommodate motor vehicles having the lengths set forth in subsection (a) of this section or motor vehicle combinations described in subsection (c) of this section; and

"(B) serves the area in which such segment is located.

"(3) The Governor shall transmit with such notification specific evidence of safety problems that supports such determination and the results of consultation regarding any alternative route under paragraph (2) of this subsection.

"(4)(A) If the Secretary determines, upon request by a Governor under paragraph (1) of this subsection or on the Secretary's own initiative, that any segment of the National System of Interstate and Defense Highways is not capable of safely accommodating motor vehicles having the lengths set forth in subsection (a) of this section or motor vehicle combinations described in subsection (c) of this section, the Secretary shall exempt such segment from one or both of such subsections. Before making such determination, the Secretary shall consider any possible alternative route that serves the area in which such segment is located.

"(B) The Secretary shall make such determination within a period of 120 days after the date of receipt of notification from a Governor under paragraph (1) of this subsection or the date on which the Secretary initiates action under this paragraph, as the case may be, with respect to such segment. If the Secretary determines that such determination will not be made within such time period, the Secretary shall immediately notify the Congress and shall furnish the reasons for the delay, information regarding the resources assigned, and the projected completion date, for any such determination.

"(C) The Secretary shall make such determination only after affording interested parties notice and the opportunity for comment. Any exemption granted by the Secretary under this paragraph before the date on which final rules are issued under subsection (a) of this section shall be included as part of such final rules. Any such exemption granted on or after such date shall be published as a revision of such rules.''.

EXEMPTION FROM WIDTH REQUIREMENTS

SEC. 103. Section 416 of the Surface Transportation Assistance Act of 1982 (49 U.S.C. App. 2316) is amended—

(1) by redesignating subsection (e) as subsection (f); and

(2) by inserting after subsection (d) the following new subsection:

"(e)(1) If the Governor of a State, after making the consultations specified in paragraph (2) of this subsection, determines that any specific segment of the National System of Interstate and Defense Highways is not capable of safely accommodating motor vehicles having the width set forth in subsection (a) of this section, the Governor may notify the Secretary of such determination and request that the Secretary exempt such segment from such subsection for the purpose of allowing the State to impose a width limitation of less than 102 inches for vehicles (other than buses) on such segment.

"(2) Before making such notification, the governor shall consult with units of local government within the State in which the specific segment of such System is located, as well as the Governor of any State adjacent to the State that might be directly affected by such exemption. As part of such consultations, consideration shall be given to any potential alternative route that—

"(A) can safely accommodate motor vehicles having the width set forth in subsection (a) of this section;

"(B) serves the area in which such segment is located.

"(3) The Governor shall transmit with such notification specific evidence of safety problems that supports such determination and the results of consultation regarding any alternative route under paragraph (2) of this subsection.

"(4)(A) If the Secretary determines, upon request by a Governor under paragraph (1) of this subsection or on the Secretary's own initiative, that any segment of the National System of Interstate and Defense Highways is not capable of safely accommodating motor vehicles having the width set forth in subsection (a) of this section, the Secretary shall exempt such segment from such subsection for the purpose of allowing the State to impose a width limitation of less than 102 inches for vehicles (other than buses) on such segment. Before making such determination, the Secretary shall consider any possible alternative route that serves the area in which such segment is located.

"(B) The Secretary shall make such determination within a period of 120 days after the date of receipt of notification from a Governor under paragraph (1) of this subsection or the date on which the Secretary initiates action uder this paragraph, as the case may be, with respect to such segment. If the Secretary determines that such determination will not be made within such time period, the Secretary shall immediately notify the Congress and shall furnish the reasons for the delay, information regarding the resources assigned, and the projected completion date, for any such determination.

"(C) The Secretary shall make such determination only after affording interested parties notice and the opportunity for comment. Any exemption granted by the Secretary under this paragraph before the date on which final rules are issued under subsection (a) of this section shall be included as part of such final rules. Any such exemption granted on or after such date shall be published as a revision of such rules.".

CONFORMING AMENDMENTS

SEC. 104.(a) Section 411(a) of the Surface Transportation Assistance Act of 1982 (49 U.S.C. App. 2311(a)) is amended—

(1) by striking out "No" and inserting in lieu thereof "Except as provided in subsection (i) of this section, no";

(2) by inserting "(other than a segment exempted under subsection (i) of this section)" after "Highways"; and

(3) by striking out "Secretary," and inserting in lieu thereof "Secretary of Transportation (hereinafter in this part referred to as the 'Secretary'),".

(b) Section 411(c) of the Surface Transportation Assistance Act of 1982 (49 U.S.C. App. 2311(c)) is amended by inserting ''(other than a segment exempted under subsection (i) of this section)'' after ''Highways''.

(c) Section 412 of the Surface Transportation Assistance Act of 1982 (49 U.S.C. App. 2312) is amended by inserting ''(other than any segment thereof which is exempted under section 411(i) or 416(e) of this title)'' after ''Highway System''.

(d) Section 416(a) of the Surface Transportation Assistance Act of 1982 (49 U.S.C. App. 2316(a)) is amended—

(1) by striking out ''No'' and inserting in lieu thereof ''Except as provided in subsection (e) of this section, no''; and

(2) by inserting ''(other than a segment exempted under subsection (e) of this section)'' after ''Highways''.

(e) Section 416(d) of the Surface Transportation Assistance Act of 1982 (49 U.S.C. App. 2316(d)) is amended—

(1) by inserting ''(other than a segment exempted under subsection (e) of this section)'' after ''Highways''; and

(2) by striking out ''with traffic lanes designed to be a width of twelve feet or more''.

DESIGNATION OF HIGHWAYS SUBJECT TO WIDTH LIMITATION

SEC. 105. Section 416(a) of the Surface Transportation Assistance Act of 1982 (49 U.S.C. App. 2316(a)) is amended—

(1) by inserting after ''more'' the second place it appears the following: '', or any other qualifying Federal-aid Primary System highway designated by the Secretary if the Secretary determines that such designation is consistent with highway safety''; and

(2) by adding at the end of such section the following new sentence: ''After the date of the enactment of this sentence, any Federal-aid highway (other than any Interstate highway) which was not designated under this subsection on June 5, 1984, may be designated under this subsection only with the agreement of the Governor of the State in which the highway is located.''

REASONABLE ACCESS

SEC. 106. Section 412 of the Surface Transportation Assistance Act of 1982 (49 U.S.C. App. 2312) is amended— (1) by inserting ''(a)'' after ''Sec. 412.''; and

(2) by striking out the period at the end thereof and inserting in lieu thereof the following: ''and for any truck tractor-semitrailer combination in which the semitrailer has a length not to exceed 28 1/2 feet and which generally operates as part of a vehicle combination described in section 411(c) of this Act.

''(b) Nothing in this section shall be construed as preventing any State or local government from imposing any reasonable restriction, based on safety considerations, on any truck tractor-semitrailer combination in which the semitrailer has a length not to exceed 28 1/2 feet and which generally operates as part of a vehicle combination described in section 411(c) of this Act.''.

Appendix B
Implementation of the Designated Network

A summary of the extent, conditions, and administration of the network of roads open to twins and longer and wider semitrailers is given. The characteristics of this network of roads have a dominant influence on the productivity, safety, and highway impacts of the new federal size limits. The descriptions cover the three categories of roads over which trucks of the dimensions authorized by the Surface Transportation Assistance Act of 1982 (enacted in 1983) may travel:

● The federally designated network, including the Interstates and portions of the federal-aid primary system selected by the Secretary of Transportation;

● Specific access routes and roads within access-distance limits determined by the states in order to comply with the law's requirement for reasonable access to the federally designated network; and

● Additional routes independently designated by the states (that is, without compulsion by any federal law or regulation) for use by the larger trucks. These routes may be on the federal-aid primary system, other federal-aid roads, or non-federal-aid roads and in some cases have more restrictive limits than those applying on the federally designated network (for example, an overall length limit may apply).

The last category includes roads that were open to twins, 48-ft semitrailers, or 102-in. wide trucks before the new federal law, and also roads opened to these vehicles by some states in response to the federal law.

233

When enacting legislation to comply with the federal limits, several states chose to uniformly apply the federal limits on all state-administered roads or on all public roads (subject in many states to local government restrictions), presumably motivated by the complexity of administering two distinct sets of truck size limits for different collections of roads.

In the first section that follows, the extent of the federal and state networks is described. Then the physical characteristics of these roads (geometric design features, pavement types, and traffic volumes), the administration of the federal and state networks, and access provisions are outlined. Finally, the degree to which the network and access rules are restricting use of twins and the other federally authorized vehicles is assessed.

The designated network probably will undergo some significant revisions in the next several years. The existing federal network is still under review; the Secretary of Transportation is empowered to delete or (with state concurrence) add routes; the 1984 amendments provide a means for states to petition to have segments removed from the network; and a number of states have instituted procedures for ongoing designation of additional through routes (beyond the federally designated roads) and access routes for use by twins, 48-ft semitrailers, or 102-in. wide vehicles. If the historical pattern of development of size and weight regulations continues, it is likely that the miles of roads open to these larger trucks will increase in the future; therefore the size and weight regulatory scheme described here is still rapidly evolving.

EXTENT

Federally Designated Network

The federal network open to twins, 48-ft long semitrailers, and 102-in. wide vehicles comprises 182,000 mi of roads, including the entire 43,000-mi Interstate system and 139,000 mi of federal-aid roads other than Interstates, 54 percent of non-Interstate federal-aid primary road miles (Table B-1).[1]

---

[1]Road mileage quantities are those reported by the state highway agencies in a survey undertaken in 1985 by the American Association of State Highway and Transportation Officials in support of the Twin Trailer Truck Monitoring Study, supplemented by mileage reported by FHWA (1). The states reported about 3,000 mi of roads other than federal-aid primaries or Interstates on the federally designated network, contrary to the provisions of the law creating the network. These roads, apparently included by oversight, have since been dropped from the network, reclassified as primaries, or switched from the federal to the state network (2).

TABLE B-1   Federally Designated Network

Region	Interstate Miles[a]	Other Federal-Aid Primary (FAP) Roads Designated[b]	
		Miles	Percent of All Other FAP Miles
California	2,400	1,900	17
Other Western and Mountain	9,200	27,800	72
Central and Plains	16,700	87,400	74
East			
No pre-1983 twins	8,700	7,800	15
Pre-1983 twins	5,600	11,000	32
U.S. total	42,600	136,000	53

[a]All Interstates are part of the designated network.

[b]In addition, approximately 3,000 mi of non-federal-aid primary roads were inadvertently included in the 1984 federal network. Adjustments in process will render the entire federally designated network primary routes.

SOURCE: FHWA [*Highway Statistics (1)*] and survey of state highway agencies by AASHTO.

The fraction of primary roads (other than Interstates) included in the federal network varies from nearly 100 percent in 15 states to less than 10 percent in each of 13 states (Figure B-1). Except for Alaska, the states with less than 10 percent of primary miles federally designated are in the East, and twins were banned in 10 of the 13 before 1983. Conversely, 12 of the 15 states that have virtually all their federal-aid primaries in the federal network are west of the Mississippi.

State-Designated Routes

In addition to the federal network, 1.2 million mi of roads are now open to twin trailer trucks at least 65 ft long and 102 in. wide (Table B-2). Most of these roads were open to 65-ft by 96-in. twins before 1983, and the nationwide mileage open to twins at the standard width (96 in. before 1983, 102 in. afterwards) has changed very little. Regional changes, however, have been large—in the East from less than 10,000 mi open to 96-in. twins before 1983 to 101,000 mi today (Table B-3), including 68,000 mi of state-designated routes (mostly in Mississippi). In the remainder of the United States, the mileage open to twins at the standard width has actually declined slightly (Table B-3), because some states have not permitted 102-in. wide vehicles on all roads where twins had operated before 1983.

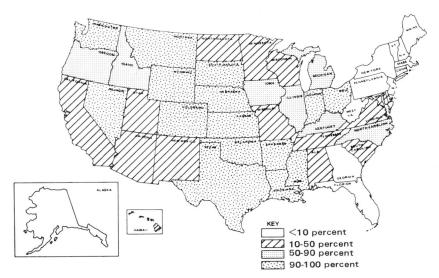

FIGURE B-1 Fraction of non-Interstate federal-aid primary road miles included in federally designated network.

Adding the state-designated routes to the federally designated network increases from 15 to 23 the number of states with virtually all federal-aid primary road miles open to twins 65 ft long and 102 in. wide. However, 65-ft by 102-in. twins are barred on substantial portions of the road systems of all but 13 states (Figure B-2).

In most states the roads open to 48-ft by 102-in. semitrailers are the same as those open to 102-in. twins (Figure B-3).However, in a few eastern states (Georgia, Maine, Rhode Island, and Wisconsin) restrictions on 48-ft by 102-in. semitrailers are much less stringent than those on twins, and three western states (California, Idaho, and New Mexico) with few restrictions on twins refuse to allow 48-ft by 102-in. semitrailers on most roads.

CHARACTERISTICS

The physical characteristics (lane width, prevalence of divided highways, pavement type, and traffic volume) of the federally designated network and the portions of the state-designated routes open to 65-ft by 102-in. twins that are federal-aid primaries are described. (The Interstate and

TABLE B-2 Federally Designated and Additional State-Designated Through Roads Open to Twins 102 in. Wide and 65 ft Long by Road System, 1985

Road System	Miles (× 1,000)			Percentage of Total Miles	
	Total in Road System	Federally Designated Network	Additional State-Designated Routes	Federal- and State-Designated Routes	Open to 96-in. × 65-ft Twins in 1982
Interstate	43	43	1	100	79
Other federal-aid primary	257	136	23	62	57
Other federal-aid	533	3	183	35	41
Non-federal-aid	3,044	1	993	32	34
Total	3,877	182	1,200	36	37

SOURCE: FHWA (*1*) and survey of state highway agencies by AASHTO.

TABLE B-3 Federally Designated and Additional State-Designated Through Roads Open to Twins 102 in. Wide and 65 ft Long by Region, 1985

	Miles (× 1,000)			Percentage of Total Miles	
Road System	Total in Road System	Federally Designated Network	Additional State-Designated Routes	Federal- and State-Designated Routes	Open to 96-in. × 65-ft Twins in 1982
California	174	4	170	100	100
Other Western and Mountain	700	38	303	49	55
Central and Plains	1,829	105	660	42	48
East					
No pre-1983 twins	713	17	1	3	0
Pre-1983 twins	462	17	66	18	2
Total	3,877	182	1,199	36	37

SOURCE: FHWA (1) and survey of state highway agencies by AASHTO.

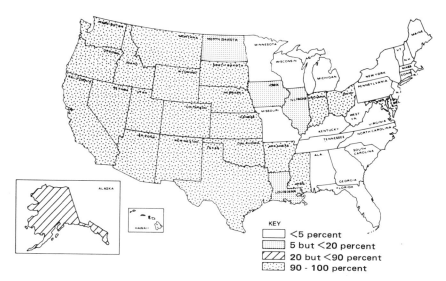

FIGURE B-2   Fraction of all public roads open to twins 102 in. wide and 65 ft long in 1985.

primary portions carry the preponderance of heavy-truck travel on the networks and are the roads for which the available data on characteristics are the most complete.) Lane width and divided highway design are indicators of the overall quality of geometric design of the roads. They are related to the safety of the larger combination trucks, and have been critical concerns in the controversies surrounding the establishment of the designated network. The type of pavement is a key determinant of the road wear costs of changes in truck traffic on the designated roads. Traffic volumes are directly related to all safety and highway maintenance and operations impacts and are perhaps a more meaningful measure than road miles of the extent of the network of roads open to twins compared with the U.S. road system as a whole.

The estimates of road miles by lane width, divided versus undivided, pavement type, and traffic volume described in the following paragraphs are derived from information collected by FHWA from some states during the development of the designated network, responses to the survey of the states conducted for this study, and published tabulations of road characteristics compiled by FHWA (1). These sources are incomplete and in many instances it was necessary to rely on rough approximations to

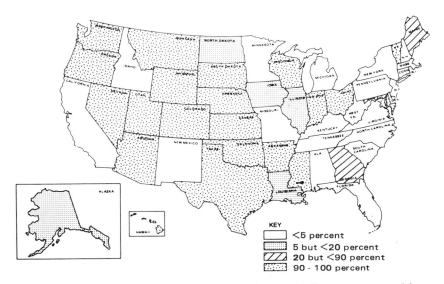

FIGURE B-3 Fraction of all public roads practically open to combinations with a semitrailer 102 in. wide and 48 ft long in 1985.

Lane Width

Lanes 12 ft wide are standard for all new federal-aid construction and are considered adequate for safety under all traffic conditions. All but a few miles of the Interstate system have lanes at least 12 ft wide. Of the miles of state or federally designated roads on federal-aid primaries other than Interstates, 24 percent have lanes less than 12 ft wide and 10 percent less than 11 ft (Table B-4). For comparison, 31 percent of all non-Interstate primary road miles have lanes less than 12 ft wide, so the network roads appear to be of somewhat above-average geometric design. When Interstates are added to other primaries, the fraction of designated miles with lanes less than 12 ft wide falls to 19 percent.

produce the estimates (for example, assuming that the distribution of pavement types of the designated federal-aid primary roads in a state is the same as the distribution for all federal-aid primaries in that state). Nonetheless, at the regional level, the estimates are a reasonable guide to the characteristics of the network.

TABLE B-4 Characteristics of the Federally Designated Network and Primary Portions of State-Designated Networks Open to Twins

Region	Non-Interstate Lane Width		Non-Interstate Divided Highway (%)	Rigid Pavement (% of miles)	
	<11 ft (% of miles)	<12 ft (% of miles)		Interstate	Non-Interstate
California	13	28	19	75	9
Other Western and Mountain	10	28	6	17	1
Central and Plains	9	21	12	59	13
East					
No pre-1983 twins	16	25	21	49	6
Pre-1983 twins	15	26	18	45	8
U.S. total	10	24	12	47	9

NOTE: Percentages are estimates derived from incomplete information.
SOURCE: Reports of state highway agencies, unpublished tabulations of the Highway Performance Monitoring System, and FHWA (1).

The fraction of designated miles with lanes less than 12 ft wide is fairly uniform among the regions, but lanes less than 11 ft wide are more prevalent (as a fraction of total designated miles) in the East (Table B-4).

Most of these narrower roads have obtained designated status either because they are in a state that has elected to open all its main roads to 65-ft by 102-in. twins or because they are short segments necessary for defining connected routes within the network.

Divided Highways

Virtually all Interstate mileage consists of divided highway with full access control. An additional 35,000 mi of primaries is divided and of this, 17,000 mi has partial or full access control. Most of these divided primaries are on the federal- or state-designated networks, so about one-third of designated primary mileage (including Interstates) is controlled-access divided highway. In several eastern states most of the non-Interstate routes on the network are divided highways.

Pavement Type

Rigid (portland cement concrete) pavements constitute 20,000 mi (47 percent) of the Interstates and 15,000 mi (9 percent) of the non-Interstate designated primaries (Table B-4). For comparison, 10 percent of all non-Interstate primary road miles have rigid pavements. Most portland cement concrete pavements on the network are in the Central and Plains region.

The preponderance of road miles on the designated primaries consists of flexible (asphalt) pavements classified as high-type (with a combined surface and base pavement thickness of 7 in. or more), but 22,000 mi is low- or intermediate-type with thinner pavements.

Traffic Volumes

The Interstates and the federal- and state-designated portions of the primaries constitute only 10 percent of the 2 million mi of paved roads in the United States, but they account for about half of all vehicle miles of travel and three-fourths of all combination-truck travel. Roughly an additional one-fifth of all vehicle travel and 5 percent of combination-truck travel occur on the other roads that the states have opened to 65-ft by 102-in. twins.

ADMINISTRATION

Federal

Federal responsibilities for administration of the designated network are limited to the initial selecting of routes, modifying of the network, enforcing state compliance with the federal law's reasonable-access requirement, and overseeing state activities relating to the roads that are funded with federal aid.

Additions to the federal network require approval of the state in which they are located, and states can petition to have segments of the Interstate deleted. Through 1985 no significant changes had been made in the federal network as it was originally published in 1984, although FHWA continued to review it (3) and some roads not on the primary system that were accidentally included in the original network were transferred from federal to state-designated status. In the AASHTO survey of state highway agencies, six states reported that they are considering requesting deletion of Interstate routes from the network, but none had done so. In New York City, where concerns about unsafe Interstate segments on the network first arose, the larger combination trucks have been restricted to use of some Interstates during off-peak hours only.

FHWA has not taken formal action against any state for failure to comply with the access requirement of the federal law and has stated its preference for allowing the states wide latitude in this regard (4). It has, however, participated informally in settling disputes between states and truck operators over access.

Through its administration of the federal-aid highway program, FHWA is encouraging the states to improve the routes on the federally designated network, to upgrade their truck traffic and accident data collection programs to allow identification of authorized trucks and identification of the location of accidents, and to use these data to spot potential hazards. FHWA has declared these activities to be a program emphasis area in the administration of the federal-aid highway program (5).

State

The states have full responsibililty for maintaining the roads of the federally designated network and enforcing size and weight limits on them, as on any federal-aid road. The states also have authority over setting size and weight limits off the federal network and making provision for access to the federal network.

With the creation of the federal network, each state was faced with the problem of administering two sets of size and weight rules, each applicable to separate portions of its highway system, unless the state chose to open all its roads to the federally authorized vehicles. Thirteen states have chosen the latter course, and 37 are enforcing two sets of limits. In the state highway agency questionnaire, the states were asked how they administered this system of dual regulations, specifically:

- Their overall opinions on whether the new federal limits have made size and weight enforcement more or less difficult,
- How routes were selected to be placed on the state-designated network or to be nominated for the federal network,
- How truck operators are informed of which routes are open to the twins and longer tractor-semitrailers,
- How the limits are enforced and the level of enforcement activity,
- Special efforts required for maintenance of the designated routes, and
- Provisions for access routes.

Despite the apparent complexity of enforcing dual limits, most states appear not to be seriously concerned by the requirement. Only 14 responded that size and weight enforcement had been made more difficult by the new federal law, and 7 actually reported that enforcement had been simplified, presumably through improved uniformity with neighboring states. Regarding selection of routes for the network, just 8 states have conducted special studies to determine criteria for including roads on the networks. For selecting additional through routes (other than access routes) for the network, 13 states have established formal procedures.

To inform truck drivers which routes are open to twins and longer tractor-semitrailers, 22 of the 37 states with dual limits publish a map showing designated routes, whereas only 3 post signs to indicate the routes. In several states the routes are not identified by any means other than published verbal descriptions.

Regarding enforcement, 15 states reported issuing more than one citation per month for twins or a longer and wider tractor-semitrailer on a road where it was not permitted. In the East, about half of these citations have been for twins; in the remainder of the country almost all have been for the longer or wider tractor-semitrailers. Twins off the network are usually visually identified by police, but most citations for semitrailer length or width have apparently occurred at weigh stations or when the vehicle was stopped for some other violation. Despite the difficulty of visually distinguishing 48-ft long and 102-in. wide semitrailers, no state said that it requires length or width to be marked on the vehicle.

Special maintenance activities on the designated networks are described in Chapter 5; provisions for access routes are described in the following section.

STATE ACCESS PROVISIONS

The 1983 act provided that no state could deny reasonable access between the designated network and terminals and facilities for food, fuel, repair, and rest. In its final rule implementing the act, FHWA did not define this requirement beyond the language of the legislation except to stipulate that the state must give information on request about its access provisions. FHWA commented that it would allow the states to establish their own individual access rules but would monitor their policies for conformity with the act.

Between 1983 and 1985 all states but one enacted some form of access provision, although the restrictiveness varied greatly from state to state (Table B-5). In 8 states virtually all roads were opened to all vehicles authorized by the 1983 act and in 12 others practical restrictions were minimal (Table B-6). In most of these, twins and 48-ft semitrailers had been legal before 1983, but new legislation was required for 102-in. wide vehicles.

The remaining states adopted one or both of two mechanisms for defining access privileges (Table B-6):

- A provision allowing vehicles of the federally authorized dimensions on any road within a specified number of miles from the designated network and
- A procedure for carriers or shippers to apply for access from the designated network to a specified location over a specified route.

The variations on these two approaches developed by the individual states have been extremely diverse. Important differences among the states include the following:

- The methods of defining access: Twenty-three states permit access by right within a specified distance of the designated network, 23 states require truck operators to apply for access permission, and 15 combine the two approaches (Table B-6).
- Additional restrictions on access: In several states access may be further limited to state highways or specified interchanges only, may apply to some but not all of the federally authorized vehicle dimensions, or may be confined to off-peak hours.

TABLE B-5 State Access Provisions

Region and State	General Access Limit (miles)	Other Provisions
East: no pre-1983 twins		
Alabama	1 (temporary)	As of May 1985 the state legislature had taken no action on reasonable access; access is from designated interchanges only
Connecticut	0.5	Special requests for access beyond limit
District of Columbia	—	Special requests
Georgia	1	Special requests for access beyond limit
Maine	0.5–3	Urban, 0.5 mi; rural, 0.3 mi; special request from local agency for access beyond limit
Massachusetts	—	Special requests (certain roads may be restricted during peak hours)
New Hampshire	—	Special requests, but generally not to exceed 2 mi
New Jersey	—	Special requests
North Carolina	3	3 mi for services, unlimited access for terminals
Pennsylvania	0.2	Lane widths must be at least 12 ft; special requests for access beyond limit
Rhode Island	1–3	Rural, 1 mi along two-lane highways, 3 mi along four-lane highways; urban, 1 mi; special requests otherwise
South Carolina	1	General access along four-lane highways in rural areas and along highways with 12-ft lanes in urban areas; special requests otherwise
Vermont	0.5	Special requests for access beyond limit; 0.5 mi general access from designated interchanges only
Virginia	0.5	General access subject to local approval; special requests for access beyond limit
West Virginia	2	Special requests for access beyond limit
East: pre-1983 twins		
Delaware	—	Special requests
Florida	1–3	Rural, 1 mi along a two-lane highway, 3 mi along a four-lane highway; urban, 1 mi along a highway with 12-ft lanes, special requests for access beyond limit
Kentucky	5	—
Maryland	—	—
Mississippi	Unlimited	Shortest practical route (no application necessary)

NOTE: The restrictions described apply to twins, 48-ft semitrailers, or 102-in. wide vehicles, but not necessarily to all three.

Region and State	General Access Limit (miles)	Other Provisions
New York	0.3	Special requests for access beyond limit
Tennessee	—	Special requests (shortest reasonable route)
Central and Plains		
Arkansas	Unlimited	Except specific roads with temporary weight restrictions (exceptions are rare)
Illinois	5	Access highway must be a state route or be approved by a local government
Indiana	Unlimited	Generally allowed unless otherwise posted (restrictions are rare)
Iowa	3–10	Interstate system, 5 mi
		Access to and from designated routes extends to all roads and streets within connected cities on the network and within the following distances from such cities:
		City Population — Distance (mi)
		Less than 2,500 — 3
		2,500–25,000 — 4
		25,000–100,000 — 6
		100,000–200,000 — 8
		Over 250,000 — 10
		Local governments may restrict truck usage on streets under their jurisdiction
Kansas	Unlimited	—
Louisiana	3	—
Michigan	5	On state routes only
Minnesota	—	Special requests
Missouri	10	Access may be limited by bridge weight limits
Nebraska	Unlimited	All U.S. and state routes
North Dakota	10	Special requests for access beyond limit
Ohio	Unlimited	—
Oklahoma	—	Determined on a case-by-case basis by Highway Patrol
South Dakota	Unlimited	Local jurisdictions may petition state to restrict access; none has done so
Texas	Unlimited	Unless otherwise posted
Wisconsin	5	—
Other Western and Mountain		
Alaska	25	Local ordinances may restrict vehicles authorized by Surface Transportation Assistance Act of 1982 on some roads within limit

NOTE: The restrictions described apply to twins, 48-ft semitrailers, or 102-in. wide vehicles, but not necessarily to all three.

TABLE B-5 *continued*

Region and State	General Access Limit (miles)	Other Provisions
Arizona	Unlimited	—
California	0.5	0.5 mi for services from designated interchanges; terminal access by request to local agency
Colorado	Unlimited	—
Hawaii	Unlimited	—
Idaho	Unlimited	Kingpin to rear axle restriction of 39 ft for all semitrailers except on federally designated network
Montana	Unlimited	—
Nevada	Unlimited	Local jurisdiction restrictions may apply, but none is in effect
New Mexico	20	—
Oregon	—	Application to local agency (restrictions are rare in practice)
Utah	Unlimited	Recreation canyon roads excepted
Washington	Unlimited	Unless otherwise posted
Wyoming	Unlimited	—

NOTE: The restrictions described apply to twins, 48-ft semitrailers, or 102-in. wide vehicles, but not necessarily to all three.
SOURCE: FHWA (4) and survey of state highway agencies by AASHTO.

TABLE B-6 States Classified by Type of Access Rule Employed

Type of Access Rule	Region			East	
	California	Other Western and Mountain	Central and Plains	No Pre-1983 Twins	Pre-1983 Twins
All miles or virtually all miles open to federally authorized vehicles		Arizona Hawaii Montana	Kansas Nebraska Ohio Texas		Mississippi
Some restrictions in principle, but very broad access rule or very localized restrictions only		Colorado Nevada Oregon Utah Washington Wyoming	Arkansas Indiana Oklahoma South Dakota	North Carolina	Maryland
Access by distance limit and by special application	California		Illinois Iowa North Dakota	Connecticut Georgia Maine Pennsylvania Rhode Island South Carolina Vermont Virginia West Virginia	New York Florida
Access within a specified distance limit only		Alaska New Mexico	Louisiana Michigan Missouri Wisconsin	Alabama	Kentucky
Access by special application only		Idaho	Minnesota	District of Columbia Massachusetts New Hampshire New Jersey	Tennessee Delaware

• To whom the access privilege applies: In eight states only the person who applies for access has permission to use the route; in the other states with access application procedures, once access is approved, the route is open to all vehicles.

• Effective duration of access permission: In four states access permission may be for a limited time only, and in the District of Columbia access is by trip permit only.

• Time and dollar cost of applying for access: In at least three states a truck operator must pay a fee to apply for access, and six states admitted that the average time to process an application is 1 month or more.

• Local involvement in approving access: Thirteen states reported that local governments have some involvement in reviewing access applications, and in 9 of these local authorities have veto power over requests.

The states with the most active programs of accepting and reviewing access applications are Florida, Massachusetts, New York, Pennsylvania, Tennessee, and Virginia. These states had received a total of 1,700 applications (at state or local government offices) for specific routes as of May 1985 and are the only states that reported receiving more than 100 requests. Virginia leads in the number of requests denied, with 179 applications rejected, mainly because the roads involved had poor alignment or narrow lanes. The states reported that the majority of applications are from large LTL general freight common carriers; a few come from private carriers.

Describing the extent and condition of the access routes is extremely difficult because the state access-distance limits encompass many thousands of short road segments. Describing access routes is further complicated by the lack of any important distinction in some states between an access route and a segment of the state-designated network of through roads. An access road connecting at both ends to designated roads and open to all vehicles of the authorized dimensions with no time limit is equivalent to a segment of the state-designated network. Nevertheless, a few generalizations appear to be supported by the limited responses of the states to questions in the survey by the American Association of State Highway and Transportation Officials concerning the characteristics of access routes:

• The total mileage of access routes is substantial because of the mileage covered by the access-distance limits. Of the 12 states that provided an estimate of the total mileage within their access-distance limits, 6 reported in excess of 10,000 mi each. There will be light twins traffic on most of these roads because they do not lead to any important freight traffic destination.

• Access routes granted through special application tend to be short, averaging 3.3 mi each in the five states for which data are available.

• Access routes are most commonly arterial roads in rural areas, although, as would be expected, in states where the designated network is extensive, access routes are more likely to be local streets and roads in urban areas.

RESTRICTIVENESS

In appearance, the various route restrictions, access rules, and administrative procedures that govern the operation of twins, 48-ft semitrailers, and 102-in. wide vehicles appear to form a confusing and burdensome set of regulations that might be expected to have an important effect on the extent of use of these vehicles. However, in interviews conducted for this study, large motor carriers using twins report that except for isolated circumstances, route restrictions have not prevented them from employing twin trailer trucks advantageously. In addition, judging from the responses to the highway agency survey, only a minority of states regard the truck size rules as a serious new enforcement burden. There are five reasons for this apparent contradiction:

• The routes open to twins and larger semitrailers, because they include all the Interstates and most primary roads, account for a large share of all heavy-truck traffic.

• Attitudes of state and local governments toward the larger vehicles and the stringency of enforcement of the regulations, which vary greatly among jurisdictions, influence the degree of restriction imposed on the larger vehicles as much as the written regulations do. Thus, some states (e.g., Missouri and North Carolina) have placed only limited mileage on the designated network but have interpreted access privileges so broadly that the larger vehicles are in practice allowed on nearly all roads. Although most carriers interviewed insisted that they followed the letter of the law regarding access as they understood it, several reported a noticeable variability from state to state in efforts to enforce network restrictions.

• Many states expressed greater concern over the potential operational problems of 48-ft semitrailers than those of either twins or 102-in. wide vehicles. In several of these states (e.g., California, Idaho, and New Mexico) twins are free to travel on virtually all roads but 48-ft semitrailers are substantially restricted.

• Maintaining a fleet of both twins and tractor-semitrailers is an inefficient mode of operation for an LTL general freight carrier. Therefore, once the decision has been made to convert to twins, a carrier will prefer to use them as much as possible, taking circuitous routes to avoid gaps in the network and sometimes violating restrictions.

● Initial disputes between states or local governments and truck operators in many areas have been resolved over 3 years of experience with the new size and weight rules through negotiation and increased familiarity and acceptance of twins and larger tractor-semitrailers.

Despite the generally unrestrained use of twin trailer trucks in most parts of the country, the restrictions, where they do exist, can have substantial local impact. Carriers report these major problems:

● Inability to reach terminals because of access restrictions: The 16 carriers interviewed reported that some terminals are inaccessible to twins in 10 states: Alabama, Connecticut, Florida, Georgia, Maine, Massachusetts, New Jersey, New York, Pennsylvania, and Vermont. However, in nearly all cases, the terminals involved are small, and over time, access arrangements have been worked out for many terminals that were initially blocked.

● Circuitous routing on the designated network: If the most direct route between two points is closed to twins, the carrier must either operate twins extra miles over designated roads or serve the route with a conventional tractor-semitrailer. Examples of routes not on the network that have necessitated circuitous routing include US-15, the major north-south route through central Pennsylvania, and US-78 in Alabama, the main road between Birmingham and Memphis.

● The Connecticut state requirement for a special operator's permit for twin trailer truck drivers: Connecticut is the only state with such a law, which requires the driver to go to the state to take a special driving test to qualify for the permit. The law initially disrupted New England operations for many carriers, but many have by now had their drivers take the test and receive the license.

● The time and paperwork burden of applying for access, especially in those states where local governments have a strong role in approving access. Carriers report applications taking a year to process in extreme instances, but these problems are largely transitional and are being resolved with time.

In summary, the evidence from the carrier interviews and the state surveys indicates that the impact of the network and access restrictions may be characterized as follows:

● The restrictions will ultimately have little impact on the amount of travel by twin trailer trucks in nearly all parts of the country.

• The restrictions have slowed introduction of twins in some areas, but this impact is lessening with time.

• Even in the Northeast, where restrictions are the most stringent and twins use is lightest, carriers cite the characteristics of the freight markets they serve rather than state regulations as the primary factor determining how much they use twins.

• Network and access restrictions may have an effect on the extent of use of 48-ft long semitrailers and 102-in. wide vehicles.

Restrictions on these vehicles are more severe than those on twins in many states. A few carriers have chosen to purchase new twin trailer trucks at the 96-in. width, in part because of concerns about state restrictions.

REFERENCES

1. *Highway Statistics* (annual). FHWA, U.S. Department of Transportation, 1982, 1983, 1984.
2. "Deletion of Non-Federal-Aid Primary Routes From the National Network for Commercial Motor Vehicles." *Federal Register*, Vol. 50, No. 217, Nov. 8, 1985, pp. 46425-46426.
3. "Truck Size and Weight; Advance Notice of Proposed Rulemaking." *Federal Register*, April 1, 1985, pp. 2825-12827.
4. "Truck Size and Weight." *Federal Register*, June 6, 1984, pp. 23310–23311.
5. *Program Emphasis Areas—Fiscal Year 1986*. FHWA Notice N1000.6. FHWA, U.S. Department of Transportation, Aug. 8, 1985.

Appendix C
Use Characteristics and Cost Impacts:
Literature Review

The economic strength of the incentives to individual trucking firms of switching from tractor-semitrailers to twin trailer trucks is an important determinant of the potential growth in the use of twins. The literature is reviewed from the aspects of (a) the economic advantages of twin trailer trucks, (b) the carriers that will be attracted to twins, (c) the potential market penetration, and (d) the total estimated economic benefit to users.

FAY/TRAFFIC DISTRIBUTION SERVICES STUDY (1)

As part of the Truck Size and Weight Study, the Fay/Traffic Distribution Services (Fay/TDS) study was commissioned to examine the use of twins in the states permitting them. The study used a variety of indirect sources of information to determine the economic incentives for operating twin trailer trucks. The sources included carrier interviews, weigh station statistics, and comparisons of prices among regions and firms with higher and lower percentages of twins use.

Operating Efficiencies

Although the report recognized the benefits of increased cubic capacity, the authors stressed the advantages of reduced handling and circuity. In addition to greater cubic capacity, twins have four key advantages over tractor-semitrailers in increasing operating efficiency:

- Two 28-ft trailers can hold four "marks," whereas a semitrailer can hold only two. (A mark is a single shipment, usually weighing 5,000 to 10,000 lb, that can be delivered without handling over a loading dock.)
- In normal less-than-truckload (LTL) operations, deliveries can be made from the individual 28-ft trailers operated separately rather than unloading the shipment from a long semitrailer into a smaller truck.
- With use of twins, shipments headed to two different terminals in the same general direction can often avoid being handled at an intermediate breakbulk point.
- Because the amount of handling and breakbulk operations are reduced, delivery times and shipment distances can be reduced.

Use of twins also increases some costs. The extra equipment has higher capital costs, the tare weight is increased (which reduces shipping capacity), and the mix of tractor-semitrailers and twins in a fleet can cause balance problems. The imbalance can be considerable between some terminal pairs. For example, Atlanta, as a distribution center in the Southeast, generates inbound truckload shipments, but sends LTL shipments outbound. If a terminal operator had mostly tractor-semitrailers inbound and twins outbound, the fleet would become unbalanced unless there were substantial movement of empty trailers between terminals. In such situations, the terminal operator would be more likely to opt for one trailer configuration. In the case of high-density inbound shipments, a tractor-semitrailer would probably minimize overall costs.

Market Penetration

On the basis of a review of some terminal operations in the East and discussions with individual terminal operators, the report estimated that twins might penetrate only 5 to 10 percent of the total eastern fleet of general commodity trucks because of fleet balance problems. This compares with an existing market share in the Pacific Coast states of 33 percent; hence the report estimates that ultimate market penetration of twins in eastern states might range from 10 to 30 percent of that of tractor-semitrailers.

Type of Carriers Benefitting

Although the carrier interviews indicated that the benefits of twins accrue mostly to LTL shippers, some private carriers in the West use twin trailer trucks as well. Private carriers with lightweight shipments (such as paper products) and carriers moving retail or grocery-type merchandise to individual stores rely on twins partly because of the operating efficiencies due to reduced handling.

Cost Advantages

Shipping rates in the West and in firms with higher percentages of twins were not lower than those in comparable regions or firms, and as a result the Fay/TDS researchers were unable to document shipper savings. Carrier interviews revealed that many terminal operators in eastern states were interested in, and in some cases enthusiastic about, twins. Nonetheless the operators believed that they would not know the actual cost savings until they had experimented with them for a few years. As a result of these findings, the report did not attempt to quantify the benefits that would accrue to a firm as a result of shifting to twins.

In estimating the economic incentives of twin trailer trucks, the report drew on a cost study by the California Public Utilities Commission to estimate the higher running costs of twin trailer trucks. The Public Utilities Commission estimated the cost of operating different truck configurations. Cost components were broken down according to initial cost, salvage value, insurance, tags, licenses, fuel consumption, maintenance, and labor cost. By adding the various cost components for different configurations (tractor and 40-ft semitrailer in the case of the tractor-semitrailer, and tractor, dolly, and 27-ft trailers in the case of the twins) the report estimated that twins have a cost per truck mile that is roughly 11 percent higher than that of a tractor-semitrailer. Labor costs were estimated to be about 11 percent higher and maintenance costs about 16 percent higher.

FARRELL (2)

Information about the actual cost advantages of twin trailer trucks is difficult to obtain because of its proprietary nature. However, without giving bottom-line figures, the author, a representative of a trucking firm, agreed with the benefits identified in the Fay/TDS report and pointed out an additional one as well. Twins are attractive to LTL firms that operate in low-traffic-density markets. A smaller trailer can be more easily filled to capacity in widely dispersed geographic areas and dispatched directly to its destination. The reduced circuity also makes smaller shipments more attractive because they can be handled competitively. These low-density markets are more characteristic of western than eastern states, which may indicate that eastern carriers would be less inclined to use twins. However, for firms with smaller market shares in the East, the low-density advantage might also provide an inroad into a competitor's market.

JUNG (3)

Jung gave a brief essay on the economic benefits of twin trailer trucks and pointed to their two basic advantages: the flexibility of reducing the handling of small shipments and the greater cubic capacity for lighter-density products. Using a single shipment of 13,000 lb as an example, the author estimated that being able to direct the shipment as one trailer of a twin trailer configuration for part of the trip and bypassing a cross-dock operation when the trailers were separated reduced the overall cost of the shipment by about 25 percent.

In reviewing the cubic capacity benefits, the report cited a 1969 study by A.T. Kearny. This study of 108 terminals in 33 states estimated that in about one-half of all trailer loads, the trailer reaches its volume capacity before it reaches its weight capacity (it "cubes out"). The Kearny study estimated that overall general freight costs could be reduced 4 percent by increasing the volume capacity of standard rigs.

SELVA AND KOLINS (4) AND KOLINS (5)

Selva and Kolins estimated line-haul costs for general commodity tractor-semitrailers, twin trailer trucks, and triple trailer trucks by updating the cost curves developed in Highway Research Record (HRR) 127 (6). The cost curves in HRR 127 were, in turn, updates from the cost curves developed from 1956 Interstate Commerce Commission data in Highway Research Bulletin 301 (7). In order to update the HRR 127 cost curves to 1981 costs, line-haul costs for three component areas (repairs and servicing, indirect costs, and depreciation and overhead) were inflated to 1981 dollars by multiplying by the ratio of 1981 to 1964 costs for these same categories. Because 1981 Interstate Commerce Commission data were not available for these costs, the 1981 costs were estimated by extrapolating from pre-1979 ICC data. Fuel costs were reestimated by developing a model of fuel efficiency for tractor-semitrailers and twins. Labor costs were updated on the basis of a survey of labor costs by Trucking Management, Inc. Tire wear for tractor-semitrailers and twins was estimated with a model that accounted for axle loads, vehicle horsepower, and miles driven annually. The total estimated costs per mile for tractor-semitrailers and twins are given in Table C-1. The productivity gains resulting from a shift to twins from tractor-semitrailers were estimated in the report discussed next.

Kolins (5) estimated the benefits in reduced line-haul costs resulting from a shift in freight from tractor-semitrailers to twin trailer trucks, assuming that twin trailer trucks with a gross vehicle weight of 80,000 lb

TABLE C-1 Fully Allocated Line-Haul Cost Estimates, 1981 (4)

Gross Vehicle Weight (lb × 1,000)	Cost Estimates (cents/mile)						
	Repairs and Servicing	Indirect and Overhead	Depreciation and Interest	Fuel	Wages	Tires and Tubes	Total
Tractor-Semitrailers							
29	12.80	41.60	17.44	24.73	38.05	3.38	138.00
44	15.78	42.80	17.44	26.82	38.05	3.38	144.27
60	18.97	44.14	17.44	29.00	38.05	3.38	150.98
80	22.96	45.45	17.73	31.80	38.05	4.83	160.82
Twins							
29	12.80	41.60	19.44	24.20	39.04	3.38	140.46
44	15.78	42.80	19.44	26.22	39.04	3.38	146.66
60	18.97	44.14	19.44	28.38	39.04	3.38	153.35
80	22.96	45.45	19.73	31.08	39.04	4.83	163.09
85	24.03	45.78	20.02	31.76	39.04	5.64	166.27

and an overall length of 65 ft would be permitted nationwide. The analysis was made for specific traffic corridors and within specific regions in order to identify the effects on carrier costs in those regions with either lower permitted gross vehicle weights (73,280 lb), a prohibition against twins use, or both.

Methodology

Kolins (5) relied on data from seven large LTL general freight common carriers giving details on a sample of 6,500 dispatches (details include payload weight, shipment density, and type of vehicle). From dispatch data Kolins estimated the average density of shipments (in pounds per cubic foot) in order to estimate the potential payload advantages of twins. These potential shifts were applied to the estimated line-haul costs developed in the preceding study to develop the actual reduction in costs per ton-mile. For example, 60 percent of general freight carried in the Southeast was lighter than 13.4 lb/ft^3. On the basis of a reported trailer utilization rate of 85 percent, the report estimates that the average twin trailer truck payload would increase 2,055 lb over the average payload of a 45-ft semitrailer.

Market Penetration

The analysis by Kolins (5) was limited to specific corridors and regions to demonstrate the effects of the lower weight limits in the barrier states and the prohibition against twin trailer trucks in the eastern states. However, Kolins provided a rough estimate of the total truck miles of travel affected by allowance of twins nationwide. On the basis of a 1969 A.T. Kearney report, 47.5 percent of common carrier freight shipped was reported to be constrained by the then-existing trailer size limits. When this figure is multiplied by the American Trucking Associations estimate that LTL general freight common carriers account for 34.4 percent of all intercity tonnage, it implies that roughly 16 percent of all truck miles would be affected [(0.475 × 0.344) = 16].

Carriers Affected

The Kolins report (5) was limited to LTL general commodity common carriers. Estimates were not made of the potential benefits of twin trailer trucks to other kinds of trucking firms.

Cost Advantages

By estimating the increase in average payload weight and relying on the line-haul cost estimates in Table C-1, Kolins estimated that in the Northeast, Southeast, and Southwest, the combined effect of increasing gross vehicle weights to 80,000 lb and allowing twin trailer trucks nationwide would be to reduce line-haul costs between 16.6 and 19.5 percent/ton-mile (Table C-2). This cost reduction was estimated by using the average shipment of common carrier freight within each region; hence it implies that the cost reductions apply to the average line-haul cost of the firm. The shift from 45-ft semitrailers at 80,000 lb to twins at 80,000 lb has nearly as large an impact (from 13.6 to 16.8 percent reduction in cents per ton-mile). Most common carrier freight would cube out before gaining the advantages of the increased weight limit; hence most of the advantages result from increased trailer capacity.

NCHRP REPORT 198 (8)

The effects on trucking costs and pavement damage of a variety of changes in truck size and weight limits were discussed in NCHRP Report 198. Allowing 27-ft twin trailers to operate nationwide at 80,000 lb gross vehicle weight was estimated to reduce trucking costs by $1.5 billion annually (1979 dollars).

Methodology

The study first developed a commodity-flow model based largely on data from the Commodity Transportation Survey in the 1972 Census of Trans-

TABLE C-2   Reduction in Fully Allocated General Freight Motor Carrier Line-Haul Costs (5)

Truck Size and/or Weight Limit Change	Reduction in Costs (%) by Region		
	Northeast	Southeast	Southwest
Tractor-semitrailer[a] (73,280 lb) to twin trailer truck (80,000 lb)	19.5	18.1	16.6
Tractor-semitrailer (80,000 lb) to twin trailer truck (80,000 lb)	16.8	15.9	13.6

[a]Semitrailer is 45 ft long.

portation. The network model has one node in each state except in California, Texas, Pennsylvania, and New York, which each have two. The hypothetical network is somewhat more extensive than the Interstate system, particularly in the western states. The effect of allowing twin trailer trucks nationwide was estimated by assuming that most light-density freight in trucks loaded to cubic capacity would be shipped in twin trailer trucks if permitted by law. The savings to the industry were estimated by comparing the cost per ton-mile of tractor-semitrailers with that of the more efficient twins. The line-haul costs were developed in part from those in NCHRP Report 141 (9), which in turn updated HRB Bulletin 127 (6), which had in turn updated HRB Bulletin 301 (7), which relied on 1956 Interstate Commerce Commission data.

Cost Benefits

The benefits in this study derived solely from reduced line-haul costs. The potential benefits of reduced circuity and reduced terminal costs were not estimated. The study only provided cost curves for selected vehicle types. However, one example given for freight with a weight of 10 lb/ft^3 shows that moving a comparable amount of freight in twins would reduce costs per ton-mile by about 9 percent.

Carriers Affected and Market Penetration

Rather than estimating the benefits to specific freight carriers, this study estimated the aggregate impact on the trucking industry by assuming that most light-density cargo (12 lb/ft^3) in tractor-semitrailers loaded to capacity would shift to twin trailer trucks. The density of various commodities was estimated from a survey of trucking firms. The percent distribution of commodity tonnage and origin and destination were estimated from the 1972 Census of Transportation and other sources.

Some restrictions were placed on the shift in commodities. Household goods and agricultural commodities were assumed to be relatively unaffected by the availability of twin trailer trucks. Even though household shipments are light in density, most movers use the same truck for shipment as for pickup and delivery. Twin trailer trucks were thought to be too cumbersome to be attractive to movers of household goods. In addition, most agricultural commodities are moved by independent owner-operators. Because these truckers need rigs flexible enough to handle a wide variety of shipments, the study assumed that independents would prefer to operate tractor-semitrailers.

In addition, the shift of commodities to various alternative truck types was assumed to parallel the distribution of such shipments in areas of the country where they were already permitted. Thus the distribution of shipments by truck type in the West was used as a basis for estimating the shifts of commodities to twin trailer trucks nationwide. The hypothesized shift in commodities is shown in Table C-3. Despite these restrictions, the hypothetical shift in commodities may tend to overstate the shifts that would actually occur. The model assigns shipments by total capacity available. That is, it assigns full truckloads of several types of commodities found in tractor-semitrailers to twins and assumes that the full capacity of the twins would be used as well. The report noted that the payloads assigned by the model were higher than the payloads measured at truck weigh stations.

Because the report estimated the benefits by an aggregate shift in commodities, the impact on the different carriers was not estimated. The report did not provide detailed estimates of the effects on total vehicle miles of travel (VMT) but did estimate that twin trailer truck travel will increase by 2.98 billion vehicle-mi.

TRUCK SIZE AND WEIGHT STUDY (10–13)

The Surface Transportation Assistance Act of 1978 directed the Secretary of Transportation to undertake a study of truck size and weight limits. The study, completed in 1981, investigated a number of scenarios involving greater uniformity in size and weight regulations. One scenario involved permitting twins (65 ft in overall length and 80,000 lb) in all states on the entire primary system.

TABLE C-3   Estimated Increase in Ton-Miles of Twin Trailer Truck Travel by Commodity (6, Tables 13 and 19)

Commodity	Estimated Share of Existing Ton-Miles[a] (%)	Projected Share (%)
Textiles	0.9	30
Pulp	3.2	20
Furniture	0.8	5
Light manufactured goods	1.3	35
General freight	17.5	50

[a]Base projections include unspecified amount of travel in turnpike doubles.

Cost Reductions

The cost advantage of shifting to twins was estimated by first developing average carrier costs from 1977 Interstate Commerce Commission statistics. Private carrier costs were estimated with data collected from individual firms. These costs were adjusted to allocate capital costs across both terminal and line-haul operations. Line-haul labor costs for twin trailer trucks were increased 5 percent and maintenance costs 16 percent per truck mile based on the estimates from the Fay/TDS study (1) (see earlier discussion of Fay/TDS estimates). Fuel cost per truck mile was increased 3 percent based on the Transportation Systems Center's own models. When converted to ton-miles, these adjustments indicated that carriers in the Northeast shifting to twins would reduce their line-haul costs costs by 12 percent.

In addition, in the Truck Size and Weight Study it was assumed that terminal costs would be reduced. The Fay/TDS study, although stressing the potential benefits of reduced handling, had been unable to document the actual cost reductions. In the Truck Size and Weight Study it was assumed that these costs would be reduced by 10 percent per ton handled. Based on the reductions in line-haul and terminal handling costs, the study cost model projected that twins provided aggregate cost savings of about 11 percent for LTL common carriers compared with carrying the same freight in conventional (45-ft) semitrailers.

Carriers Benefitting

To simplify the analysis, in the Truck Size and Weight Study it was assumed that only LTL carriers would shift to twins. LTL carriers transport the low-density cargoes and have high terminal costs that make the cost reductions of twins most attractive. The cost models developed for other carriers also showed potential benefits when carriers were moving low-density cargoes. However, on the basis of the assumption that the greatest overall benefit comes from cross-dock handling—most advantageous to LTL firms—it was assumed that only LTL light-density cargoes would shift to twin trailer trucks.

Travel Affected

The Truck Size and Weight Study projected the effect of legalizing twins in the eastern states by comparing estimated 1985 long-distance (interstate) travel with and without changes in size and weight regulations. The study used 1985 as a baseline year under the assumption that the changes in size and weight limits effective in 1981 would not filter through the fleet until 1985. The use of 1985 as a base year served mainly to provide a hypothetical future year that allows some time for the industry to adapt to changes in federal and state regulations. The estimated truck miles of travel in the 1985 base case—assuming no changes in size and weight limits after 1981—involved an extensive and complex set of adjustments to 1977 Truck Inventory and Use Survey data and other data sources. These adjustments indicated that by 1985 twins would travel about 3.7 billion vehicle-mi of interstate travel. They would account for 8.1 percent of all interstate combination-truck travel and 34 percent of all general commodity LTL travel (Table C-4).

In projecting the use of twins with uniform weights of 80,000 lb and 65-ft lengths, it was also assumed that travel would be permitted on the entire primary network. The Surface Transportation Assistance Act of 1982 (enacted in 1983) did not require that all primary highways be open to twins, so in some eastern states, travel will be more limited than the Truck Size and Weight Study projections. Allowing twins use nationwide would increase VMT to 6.4 billion mi and increase the share of total truck

TABLE C-4   Truck Size and Weight Study Projections of Increased Long-Distance Twins Traffic (*10*, *12*)

Projections	Twins	All Trucks	General Commodity LTL	Twins Share of Travel	
				All Trucks (%)	LTL (%)
Base case					
Truck-miles[a]					
($\times 10^9$)	3.7	45.4	10.8	8.1	34.1
Ton-miles[b]					
($\times 10^9$)	27.4	518.4	72.5	5.3	37.7
Uniform limit[c]					
Truck-miles					
($\times 10^9$)	6.4	44.0	10.2	14.5	62.7
Ton-miles					
($\times 10^9$)	47.8	517.8	71.9	9.2	66.4

NOTE: Truck Size and Weight Study excluded short-range traffic, which accounts for 44 percent of truck miles. Long-distance travel included projections for entire primary system (including Interstates) (*12*, Table 2-4).
[a]From Truck Size and Weight Study (*9*, Table 4-2); data in this table are for loaded vehicles only and have to be multiplied by 1.32 to expand to total truck-miles. Base-case projections assume no change in truck size and weight limits after 1981.
[b]From Truck Size and Weight Study (*7*, Table D-6).
[c]Uniform limit assumes 65-ft overall length and 80,000-lb gross vehicle weight. Forecast does not include shift in traffic from rail to truck.

miles of travel to 14.5 percent. The share of general commodity LTL travel would increase to 66.4 percent (Table C-4).

The increased twins travel projected by the model was restricted in some regions. The use of twins by LTL carriers in the eastern states formerly prohibiting their use was restricted to 50 percent of the VMT that these vehicles could win on a cost basis alone. In the base case the model predicted a level of twins use in the Northeast that greatly exceeded the proportion in the 1977 Truck Inventory and Use Survey. Restricting the growth in travel to 50 percent kept these proportions more in line. The same rule was applied to most of the eastern states (Regions 1, 3, and 5 in Figure C-1).

Economic Benefits

The combined effects of greater use of twins and higher weight limits produced shipper cost savings of $2.1 billion (1977 prices). Of this, $1.6 billion was attributable to the shift of LTL freight to twins due to the assumed lower handling costs and line-haul savings from the greater cubic capacity.

FIGURE C-1   Truck Size and Weight Study analysis regions (*10*). [NOTE: Alaska and Hawaii were excluded from the analysis.]

The forecasts were produced by developing a network data base of freight shipments, estimating the cost of each shipment for alternative truck configurations, and assigning the shipments to the least-cost legal configuration (assuming that carrier cost savings would be passed on to shippers).

The forecast benefits did not include the potential diversion of freight from rail to truck. In the case of a shift of light-density commodities—those most likely to shift to twin trailers—such effects would be minimal.

The present value of the cost savings resulting from legalized twins would be approximately $30 billion (1980 prices). This estimate excluded the impact associated with traffic injuries and fatalities, air quality, and shipper benefits due to improved services (shorter shipping times) from carriers that would not be reflected in lower freight rates.

ANDERSON (14)

Anderson analyzed the aggregate impact of the 1983 act on the truck and rail transportation industry. Although the study did not provide details for its estimates, it suggested that the legislation will mostly benefit LTL carriers or carriers of light-density shipments. Operating costs per cubic foot for twin 27-ft trailers were estimated to decline 17 percent compared with those for a 45-ft semitrailer. The operating cost of 28-ft twins would decline by 24 percent. These benefits do not include those resulting from reduced handling and circuity.

GENERAL ACCOUNTING OFFICE (15)

The General Accounting Office summarized the impact of the 1983 act on the trucking industry by comparing the increased tax burden placed on heavy trucks with the productivity gains achievable through heavier permitted weights and operation of twin trailer trucks.

Cost Advantages

Because twin trailer trucks have greater capacity, the economic benefits will accrue to carriers of light-density cargoes. The potential cost advantages were not estimated; other productivity estimates made by Selva and Kolins (4) and Anderson (14) were cited.

Carriers Benefitting

The General Accounting Office estimated that 44 percent of all interstate ton-miles by LTL carriers before 1982 was constrained by the physical size of trailers. This estimate was derived from the projections of travel and commodity density by the Truck Size and Weight Study (*10-13*). In contrast, only 9 percent of truckload shipments would cube out before reaching the weight limit. For this reason, the General Accounting Office estimated that LTL carriers would be the primary beneficiaries of the 1983 act.

AMERICAN TRUCKING ASSOCIATIONS (*16*)

The American Trucking Associations argued that the U.S. Department of Transportation overestimated the productivity benefits resulting from the 1983 act. The Department of Transportation estimated that the productivity savings resulting from eliminating the "barrier-state" weight limits, allowing twins in the East, and increasing trailer length and width would total $4.94 billion annually (before taxes). The American Trucking Associations countered that the total benefits would be only about half as much ($2.63 billion before taxes).

The American Trucking Associations contended that the Department of Transportation overestimated the productivity impact of twins for two reasons: first, the number of vehicle miles affected was inflated by use of an overly high empty mileage assumption and, second, the cost of the vehicle travel eliminated was too high.

The Department of Transportation, drawing on the Truck Size and Weight Study, first estimated the impact of twins on truck travel by calculating the loaded miles affected by the greater carrying capacity. This estimate was then inflated by the assumption that these vehicles travel empty 32 percent of the time. The American Trucking Associations, relying on a 1977 study by the Interstate Commerce Commission, countered that the carriers most likely to be affected by twins (regulated firms using vans) have an empty mileage rate on Interstate highways of only 10 percent.

In addition, the American Trucking Associations argued that Department of Transportation assumed that the vehicle mileage eliminated averages $4.65 per mile. In contrast, American Trucking Associations assumed an average cost per mile of $2.68 based on its own estimate of vehicle operating costs (*4*).

SYSTEM DESIGN CONCEPTS, INC. (17)

The impact of limiting the Truck Size and Weight Study model to the Interstates was documented. Provision was made for access on primary highways (up to 15 mi). The study estimated that allowing twins on the Interstate would decrease total truck travel by 0.6 percent (or by 758 million truck-mi). This would result in a total freight cost reduction of $1,672 million (1980 dollars). Total twin trailer truck travel would increase by 1.65 million mi by 1985.

REFERENCES

1. Gordon Fay Associates, Inc., and Traffic Distribution Services, Inc. "Carrier, Market and Regional Cost and Energy Trade-offs." In *An Investigation of Truck Size and Weight Limits*, Tech. Suppl. Vol. 7, Part II, Appendix E, U.S. Department of Transportation, 1982.
2. J. Farrell. "Marketing and Cost Impacts of Double Trailers." Presented at 63rd Annual Meeting of the Transportation Research Board, Washington, D.C., 1984.
3. C.J. Jung, Jr. *The Economics of Twin Trailers*. University of Richmond, Richmond, Va., 1969.
4. R. Selva and R. Kolins. *The Impact of Gross Vehicle Weights on Line Haul Trucking Costs: 1981 to 1985*. American Trucking Associations, Washington, D.C., 1981.
5. R. Kolins. *General Freight Common Carrier Productivity and the Liberalization of Truck Size and Weight Statutes*. American Trucking Associations, Washington, D.C., 1981.
6. *Line-Haul Trucking Costs and Weighing Vehicles in Motion*. Highway Research Record 127. HRB, National Research Council, Washington, D.C., 1966.
7. *Line-Haul Trucking Costs in Relation to Vehicle Gross Weights*. HRB Bulletin 301. HRB, National Research Council, Washington, D.C., 1961.
8. R. J. Hansen Associates, Inc. *State Laws and Regulations on Truck Size and Weight*. NCHRP Report 198. Transportation Research Board, National Research Council, Washington, D.C., 1979.
9. *Changes in Legal Vehicle Weights and Dimensions*. NCHRP Report 141. Highway Research Board, National Research Council, Washington, D.C., 1973.
10. D. Maio. "Carrier, Market and Regional Cost and Energy Trade-offs." In *An Investigation of Truck Size and Weight Limits*, Tech. Supp. Vol. 7, Part I, U.S. Department of Transportation, 1982.
11. R. Kochanowski and D. Sullivan. "Truck and Rail Cost Effects of Truck Size and Weight Limits." In *An Investigation of Truck Size and Weight Limits*, Vol. 2, U.S. Department of Transportation, 1980.

12. J. Mergel and M. Nienhous. "Truck Traffic Forecasts and TS&W Limit Scenario Analysis Methods." In *An Investigation of Truck Size and Weight Limits*, Tech. Supp. Vol. 4, U.S. Department of Transportation, 1982.

13. *An Investigation of Truck Size and Weight Limits: Final Report*. U.S. Department of Transportation, Aug. 1981.

14. D. Anderson. *Special Study: The Surface Transportation Assistance Act of 1982: Carrier and Shipper Impacts*. Data Resources, Inc., Washington, D.C., 1983.

15. *The Surface Transportation Assistance Act of 1982: Comparative Economic Effects on the Trucking Industry*. Report GAO/ICE-84-2. General Accounting Office, April 1984.

16. *Analysis of the Department of Transportation's Claim of the Benefits Accruing to the Trucking Industry from the Surface Transportation Assistance Act of 1982*. American Trucking Associations, Inc., Washington, D.C., July 1983.

17. System Design Concepts, Inc. *Additional Truck Size and Weight Analyses: Impact of Allowing Doubles on the Full Interstate System and Using Only the Bridge Formula (B) to Limit Gross Weight*. Office of the Secretary, U.S. Department of Transportation, April 1982.

Appendix D
Truck Handling and Stability:
Literature Review

A review and evaluation are presented of research on the safety-related handling and stability properties of large trucks that may be different for twins or for longer, wider semitrailers than for conventional combination trucks. The properties reviewed are

- Offtracking,
- Response to steering,
- Sensory feedback,
- Braking,
- Oscillatory sway,
- Rollover in steady turns,
- Yaw stability in steady turns.

In the sections that follow, each characteristic is defined, its relationship to safety is explained, and the research on how twins and longer, wider tractor-semitrailers differ from conventional vehicles in respect to the characteristic is summarized. For twins, the discussion is based on trucks equipped with single-drawbar dollies, the usual U.S. practice (see Glossary). A final section discusses the sensitivity of handling and stability performance to dolly design.

OFFTRACKING

When a vehicle turns, the path of each rearward tire does not coincide with that of the corresponding forward tire. This phenomenon is termed offtracking. At low speeds, the rear tires track inward, toward the center of the curved path. The amount of low-speed offtracking is commonly expressed either in terms of the maximum swept-path width, which is the maximum distance separating the outermost tire path (outward tire of steering axle) from the innermost tire path (inward tire of rearmost axle), or the maximum distance between the inward tires on the forward and rear axles. At high enough speeds, the rear tires track outward, away from the center of the curved path. The amount of high-speed offtracking is commonly expressed by the maximum distance between the paths of the outward tires on the forward and rear axles.

Although the safety implications of vehicle offtracking are not well established, one view is that "greater offtracking of the vehicle in turning movements can be highly significant from the viewpoint of safety" (1). When the vehicle is making sharp turns under low-speed conditions, such as at intersections, the amount of offtracking can be quite large. If the pavement edge radius and lane width are inadequate, the turning truck is forced to encroach on other lanes, possibly cutting across the pavement edge as well. The result may be damage to the roadside and its appurtenances as well as congestion and delay to motorists. Accidents can also be the result of such situations but, because of the low speeds, they are not likely to be severe ones. Under high-speed operations, offtracking may result in lane and roadside encroachments and may reduce the clearance between adjacent vehicles. Because the amount of high-speed offtracking is typically quite small, it is unlikely to pose a significant accident hazard except on fairly sharp turns and at excessive speeds, such as might be encountered on freeway exit ramps. Offtracking-induced collisions with curbs, guardrails, or other vehicles are potentially dangerous in this situation because of the high speed.

Under low-speed operations, computer simulations reveal that the swept path is significantly increased by increases in both the number and length of trailing units (more correctly, the wheelbases of the units) (Figure D-1). Twins perform significantly better than tractor-semitrailers in low-speed operations because the detrimental effect of the second trailer of the twins is more than offset by the greater semitrailer length of the tractor-semitrailer. For example, under a rather severe, 90-degree, 35-ft radius turn, the swept path of a pair of 28-ft twins is about 4 ft less than that of a 45-ft, cab-behind-engine tractor-semitrailer and about 2.5 ft less than that of a 45-ft, cab-over-engine tractor-semitrailer (3,pp. 29-37).

Under high-speed operations, offtracking increases with increases in the number of trailing units and with speed. For a given configuration, high-speed offtracking is a maximum for trailer lengths in the range of 25 to 30 ft (Figure D-1). The combination of these two factors accounts for the superior high-speed offtracking characteristics of tractor-semitrail-

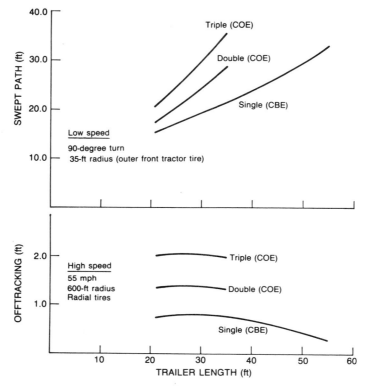

FIGURE D-1   Effect of trailer length and truck configuration on offtracking behavior (2). [NOTE: Double-trailer and triple-trailer offtracking and swept path are plotted versus the length of each individual trailer in the combination. Thus the offtracking for twin 27-ft trailers is found at the point on the "Double" curve above 27 ft on the horizontal axis. (COE = cab-over-engine tractor, CBE = cab-behind-engine tractor.)]

ers. For the specific conditions shown in Figure D-1, a tractor-semitrailer with a 45-ft semitrailer offtracks approximately 0.8 ft less than a pair of 28-ft twins. For trucks having bias-ply rather than radial tires, this difference is approximately 70 percent greater (2), or about 1.4 ft.

For the offtracking behavior illustrated in Figure D-1, it is assumed that lateral forces are not offset by any superelevation of the road cross section in the turn. Although the relationship of offtracking to superelevation apparently has not been documented in the literature, presumably high-speed (outward) offtracking is very slight for all the vehicles considered here on a properly superelevated curve at normal operating speeds.

One of the particular concerns about the operation of 48-ft semitrailers is the increase in low-speed offtracking. For a right-angle, 35-ft radius turn, the swept-path width for the typical tractor-semitrailer with a 48-ft semitrailer exceeds that for the 45-ft semitrailer by about 1.5 ft (3). On a 58-ft radius, 180-degree turn, the design semitrailer now used in California for designated-network highways (102 in. wide and 48 ft long) sweeps a path 5.7 ft wider than did the design vehicle in use before enactment of the Surface Transportation Assistance Act of 1982 (4). Under high-speed operations, an increase in the semitrailer length from 45 to 48 ft has a very slight beneficial effect (Figure D-1).

Wider trucks occupy more roadway space on curved sections just as they do on straight sections, but the width does not affect offtracking behavior. The main effect of wider trucks is reduced lateral clearance, which increases the likelihood of offtracking-induced collision.

In summary, increased use of twins will improve low-speed offtracking but will degrade high-speed offtracking, a reversal of the effects of increased use of 48-ft semitrailers. With respect to offtracking, conditions for twins are critical on freeway exit ramps, whereas for 48-ft semitrailers, at-grade intersections present the critical situation. Wider trucks slightly exacerbate the consequences of offtracking, primarily as a result of reduced lateral clearances.

RESPONSE TO STEERING

With articulated vehicles, abruptly applied steering movements induce transient motions in trailing units that differ from those of the tractor. Response of the trailer lags behind that of the tractor, an oscillating pattern may be superimposed over the trace of the trailer, and lateral accelerations experienced by the trailer may be amplified in relation to those experienced by the tractor. Such transient behavior, if sufficiently severe, may precipitate rollover or other critical reflections of instability and loss of control.

Desirable truck response characteristics include a minimal trailer response time, quick damping of induced trailer oscillations, and little or no amplification of lateral acceleration. Numerous prior investigations have established a fundamental understanding of the effect of truck configuration on transient behavior.

Jindra (5) employed a simplified linear model in a theoretical study of the handling characteristics of 70,000-lb, five-axle twins. The vehicles, assumed to be traveling at constant velocity, were subjected to a stepped steering input, and the lateral dynamic response (primarily the yaw angle of the rear trailer body) was simulated.

Jindra's work was extended and refined by Hazemoto (6), Mallikarjunarao and Fancher (7), Fancher (8), and Ervin et al. (2). In general, assumptions of linearity were retained, but limited field testing was conducted for model calibration and validation. Among the initial steering maneuvers that have been investigated were both single and double lane changes and other collision avoidance maneuvers. A variety of twins have been investigated, ranging from 5 to 11 axles and from 70,000 to about 150,000 lb gross truck weight.

From this work, there is a consensus that improved vehicle transient response results from the following:

- Reduced number of trailing units,
- Increased length of trailer or trailers,
- More rigid dolly connection,
- Increased tire cornering stiffness,
- Placement of more lightly loaded or empty trailer in rearmost position as well as elimination of overloading of rearmost trailer,
- Reduced vehicle speeds, and
- Loading such that centers of gravity are located at the same position for each trailer.

Possible effects of the following vehicle design variables on transient response are either in dispute or are insignificant:

- Length of the dolly tongue,
- Location of tractor fifth wheel with respect to its drive axle, and
- Distance between the axle and the aft-mounted tow point on the semitrailer.

Ervin et al. (2) have made direct comparisons between the tractor-semitrailer with a 45-ft semitrailer and 27-ft twins. For a lane-change maneuver at 55 mph, the measure of merit was the amplification ratio, the ratio between maximum lateral acceleration of the rearmost trailer and that of the tractor. Amplification ratios were found to be 1.0 for the tractor-semitrailer and about 2.5 for the twins. Also evaluated was the maximum width of an object in the roadway at a specified distance ahead that could be cleared at a velocity of 55 mph without rollover. The widths were found to be about 8 ft for the tractor-semitrailer and about 3 ft for the twins. These investigators concluded that rearward amplification behavior is a substantial safety issue for multiple-trailer vehicles.

Ervin et al. (2) also addressed the link between accident patterns and the rearward-amplification behavior of multiple-trailer vehicles. They observed, "The accident record is known to contain various examples of multiple-trailer configurations which have suffered an extraordinarily high incidence of accidents in which only their rearmost trailer has overturned." Obviously implied is that rearward amplification intensifies the lateral acceleration of the rearmost trailer with the result that its rollover threshold is reached before that of other units in the train.

The literature has not been directed to the effect of either increased truck width or of increased semitrailer length on trailer response to abruptly applied steering. Any effects of increased use of 102-in. wide trucks and 48-ft semitrailers are likely to be inconsequential.

In summary, trucks of different configuration are unlikely to respond much differently to gradually applied steering changes. When the turning maneuver must be abrupt, however, the poorer transient response of twins in comparison with that of tractor-semitrailers has been documented.

SENSORY FEEDBACK

Forces acting on drivers of single-unit vehicles typically mirror those acting on the vehicle. The driver is thus able to quickly sense impending instabilities such as rollover and sliding and to take corrective action as may be required. Drivers of combination trucks, on the other hand, are somewhat isolated from their trailing units. They may be unable to sense impending sliding, rollover, or even bouncing of these units until it is too late to take effective corrective action.

The difference between single-unit vehicles and combination trucks derives from two sources—delayed trailer response to driver steering and loss in ability to transmit forces at points of articulation. The problem is particularly acute for multiple-trailer combinations, primarily because of the increased number of articulation points and the use of single pintle-hook couplings, which are unable to effectively transmit roll moments from one unit to the next.

Although impaired sensory feedback is not a matter that has been intensively scrutinized, control problems have been documented. For example, drivers in a series of twins rollover tests were reported to have often been unaware of a rollover until it was observed in their rearview mirror (9). On the basis of another series of rollover tests, installation of "a roll warning device or a roll sensitive driver seat suspension" was suggested as a means for increasing driver awareness of impending rollover (10).

Direct comparisons of twins and tractor-semitrailers, of longer and shorter tractor-semitrailers, and of wider and narrower combination trucks have yet to be undertaken. Nevertheless, sensory feedback is almost certainly more seriously impaired for twins than for tractor-semitrailers. Hence, drivers of twins are less well able to take effective corrective action when forces acting on trailing units become critical. Little or no difference is expected as a result of small length or width changes.

BRAKING

The two major components of braking performance are stopping distance and vehicle controllability. Stopping distance is the distance between the point of brake application and the final resting position, and controllability is the ability both to maintain directional control and to avoid instabilities such as jackknifing and trailer swing during the braking maneuver.

Stopping distance is influenced by many factors, including the available friction at the tire-pavement interface, the distribution of loads on the individual axles (including wheel load shifts during braking), and characteristics of the vehicle braking system. Ideally, the braking system should deliver consistently high torque at each tire, maintained in a manner preventing lockup. On brake application, initiation of braking torque should proceed from the rearmost to the steering axle so that tension is induced in the trailer couplings. On brake release, sequencing should proceed in the reverse direction. In either event, however, the elapsed time before all brakes are actuated must be minimal for the shortest possible stopping distance.

Vehicle controllability during braking is related to lockup of the wheels on one or more of the axle sets. When pneumatic tires lock up, or cease to rotate, they are unable to produce the lateral forces necessary for directional stability and control. When lockup occurs on the wheels of the steering axle, the vehicle is unsteerable and cannot be directed along a curved path or around an obstacle. When lockup occurs on the wheels of the tractor's rear axle or on the wheels of a dolly's axle, the tractor or dolly is unstable in yaw; the ensuing rapid rotational motion is commonly termed jackknifing. Finally, if the wheels of the rearmost trailer axle lock up, that end of the trailer swings outward, a condition commonly termed trailer swing.

Although problems of brake fade and inadequate maintenance and adjustment of brakes are important during normal stopping and slowing maneuvers, any effects of truck configuration are likely to be significant only for emergency or evasive braking. For this reason, most comparisons of configuration effects are limited to emergency braking.

An FHWA research program has provided limited data for comparing the relative braking performance of twins and tractor-semitrailers. Field tests of in-use vehicles simulated emergency stopping from a speed of 20 mph: the measure of merit was the distance traveled from the point of brake application to the point of rest. In 1955 and again in 1963, twins required approximately 22 percent greater distance in which to stop than tractor-semitrailers (*1*). The reported differential was reduced to 5 percent in 1974 (*11*). The average twin trailer truck weighed from 6,000 to 10,000 lb more than the average tractor-semitrailer in these tests, a factor contributing to but not completely explaining the differences in stopping distance. Deficiencies in brake adjustment and maintenance were generally noted, but possible differential effects between twins and tractor-semitrailers were not examined.

Both twins and a tractor-semitrailer with a 45-ft semitrailer were subjected to the field braking tests reported by Kibbee (*12*). The measures of merit were stopping distance and stability (ability to remain within a 12-ft lane). Speeds were varied from 20 to 55 mph, and the tests were made on both dry and wet surfaces at three levels of gross weight ranging from empty to a fully loaded weight of 70,000 lb. The trucks were new, as were the brakes and tires, and the braking systems were carefully prepared and adjusted before and during testing. Pavement surface skid resistance characteristics were excellent.

It was concluded (*12*) that "though minor differences in performance of the two combinations were evidenced in the results of the tests, the vehicles essentially performed equally in both stopping ability and stability." In every test on dry surfaces, however, the stopping distance for tractor-semitrailers was less than that for twins. For the more critical, higher-speed, wet-surface stops, tractor-semitrailers were superior for the tests of fully loaded vehicles, twins were superior for the tests of half-loaded vehicles, and results were mixed for the tests of empty vehicles.

Field braking tests performed at Utica, Michigan, and reported by Nelson and Fitch (*13*) have often been cited in the literature. Although this was primarily an investigation of the braking performance of longer combination trucks—40-ft twins and 27-ft triples—limited data were also collected on the 40-ft tractor-semitrailer and the 27-ft twins. Tests were conducted on a level surface that was in relatively good condition under both dry and wet conditions. As is common, brakes were properly adjusted before testing.

Results of the Nelson and Fitch stopping distance measurements do not indicate any consistent difference between the performance of twins and of tractor-semitrailers (Table D-1). However, the number of tests was quite limited and the results were quite variable (note the "replicate"

TABLE D-1   Stopping Distances from Utica Testing (13)

| Braking System | Pavement Condition | Speed (mph) | Twins | | Tractor-Semitrailer | |
			Gross Vehicle Weight (lb × 1,000)	Stopping Distance (ft)	Gross Vehicle Weight (lb × 1,000)	Stopping Distance (ft)
Service	Dry	50	55.7	160	—	—
			55.7	187	62.4	197
			69.2	212	—	—
			81.8	160	—	—
Emergency	Dry	50	—[a]	—[a]	—[a]	—[a]
Service	Wet	35	55.7	94	62.4	105
			5.7	140	62.4	112
Emergency	Wet	35	55.7	235	62.4	195
			55.7	261	62.4	227

NOTE: Dashes indicate that no data were available.
[a]Reported distances were extrapolated.

twins stopping distances using service brakes on the wet roadway). Apparently, no particular controllability problems were observed, but, as in the Kibbee (12) tests, drivers were instructed to modulate the brakes or make steering adjustments in order to maintain controllability and minimize hazard.

Stopping distance measurements collected in Utah showed that twins required slightly greater stopping distances than tractor-semitrailers (14). Although stability during braking was similar for the two types of trucks on dry pavements, twins were more stable than tractor-semitrailers on wet roadways.

The Utah tests were conducted at approach speeds from 20 to 40 mph on a pavement having excellent frictional properties. The largest number of replicate tests were performed on dry pavements at 30 and 40 mph. Under these conditions, the average stopping distances for twins and tractor-semitrailers were 58.5 ft and 53.1 ft, respectively, at 30 mph and 94.9 ft and 89.6 ft, respectively, at 40 mph. Possible effects of the difference in gross vehicle weight (77,140 lb for twins and 69,500 lb for tractor-semitrailers) were not investigated.

Mercer et al. (15) conducted comparative field tests of the braking behavior of single, double, and triple combinations. A significant finding was that both brake application and release times increase as the number of trailing units increases. These investigators concluded that the braking performance of combination trucks with standard 27-ft or 45-ft semitrailers was less than ideal but could be improved by the use of current technology.

Ervin et al. (2) have also addressed the possible effects of truck configuration on braking performance. The general conclusion was that stopping distance is unlikely to vary with configuration. However, hypotheses were advanced that (a) stopping distances may be increased as trailer length is shortened because of greater amounts of axle load transfer during deceleration, (b) brake transmission time (to the rearmost axle) may be increased as the number of trailers is increased, and (c) the likelihood of truck instability due to wheel lockup increases as the number of articulation points increases.

Little attention has been given to possible effects of semitrailer length on the performance of tractor-semitrailers in emergency braking situations. To the extent that longer semitrailers imply longer wheelbases, a slight improvement in stopping capability can be expected. Larger deceleration rates can be achieved without rear wheel lockup because less wheel load is shifted from rear to forward axles during braking (2). The increased payload expected with longer semitrailers could also be consequential. However, the possible effect of vehicle weight on stopping distance has not been established; for example, field tests have shown no consistent differences between 53,000-lb and 70,000-lb tractor-semitrailers (12). Increases in truck width, although they imply greater weights, are not likely to alter emergency braking performance.

In summary, the braking performance of twins apparently matches that of tractor-semitrailers, at least when the braking system is properly designed and the brakes are well maintained and adjusted. No significant change in braking is expected with increased use of 48-ft long semitrailers and 102-in. wide combination trucks.

OSCILLATORY SWAY

Oscillatory sway is a condition in which trailing units of a combination vehicle demonstrate a low-amplitude lateral oscillation. Usually transient in nature, oscillatory sway can be initiated by small steering adjustments and magnified by such factors as crosswinds and uneven pavement.

The study of oscillatory sway has not advanced to the point at which possible effects of such characteristics as the number and length of trailers are well understood. However, on the basis of a limited number of observations of in-service operations, sway of twins appears to be of small amplitude and unlikely to affect the accident risk to the truck (14-16).

Driver inexperience, lack of training, and physical and mental fatigue have been identified as contributing factors to the occurrence of sway. Also identified as contributing factors are slack in the hitch connections, poorly lubricated fifth wheels, misalignment of suspensions and axles, use of radial or worn tires, short trailer wheelbases, loading that produces either an empty rear trailer or one that is more heavily loaded than the leading trailer, and high truck speeds (*17*).

In summary, oscillatory sway in twins is not considered to be a significant safety hazard. At the same time, twins have a greater propensity to sway than tractor-semitrailers, an effect that can be countered by driver training, no-slack hitches, proper trailer loading, and properly maintained equipment. Sway of longer tractor-semitrailers or of wider trucks has not been identified as a potential safety problem.

ROLLOVER IN STEADY TURNS

Rollover is a particularly severe form of instability, usually caused by excessive speeds of vehicles operating on curved paths. It results when the overturning moment due to centrifugal force exceeds the weight-related restoring moment. In articulated vehicles, the rearmost unit is normally the first and perhaps the only unit to roll over. In addition to excessive speeds and sharp turns, rollover is promoted by high centers of gravity, narrow wheel tracks, and inadequate roadway superelevation.

The linkage between roll stability and highway safety is a rather clear one. Vehicles having lower rollover thresholds will roll over more frequently than other vehicles, and their safety record will be so blemished. Perhaps no better correlation exists between the accident record and the performance (stability and control) characteristics of large trucks than that between rollover involvement and the nominal level of roll stability (*2*).

Full-scale field tests have identified specific vehicle factors that promote rollover stability, including increased spring stiffness, increased spring-base width, reduced trailer suspension lash, and increased coupling stiffness both in fifth-wheel and converter-dolly connections (*9,10*). Evidence from computer simulations suggests little difference in the roll stabilities of twins and tractor-semitrailers under steady or "static" turning maneuvers (*2*). Wider trucks, on the other hand, offer significant improvement in roll stability if the axle length and spring-base width are increased to match the bed width (*2*). Increased semitrailer length is not likely to affect roll stability.

In summary, a significant improvement in roll stability, and consequently safety, can be realized by the use of 102-in. wide trucks having longer axles and greater spring-base widths. Under steady turning maneuvers, roll stability is similar for twins and tractor-semitrailers and is unaffected by length of the trailing units.

YAW STABILITY IN STEADY TURNS

Yaw instability or divergence describes a condition in which the heading of a turning vehicle increasingly diverges from the desired direction of travel, typically resulting in spinout for straight trucks and jackknifing for articulated vehicles. The process can be described in the following way.

When a vehicle traverses a curved path, the centrifugal effect causes an increase in the loads on the outside tires and a decrease in those on the inside. Because of the nonlinear sensitivity of tire cornering stiffness to vertical load, the net effect of this outward shifting is to reduce the ability of each axle to resist lateral forces without sliding. Because of peculiarities in the fore and aft roll stiffness distribution of truck suspension design, the effect of lateral load shifts is greater at the rear axle of a straight truck or tractor than at the front. The rear straight-truck or tractor axle thus has a tendency to slide first, and when it does, the vehicle spins out or jackknifes. Yaw stability is affected by numerous factors such as speed and center of gravity of the loaded vehicle, superelevation and radius of the roadway, friction available at the tire-pavement interface, and peculiarities of the vehicle tires and suspension system.

The yaw stability problem has been expressed as one that involves only the tractor's understeer characteristic. Because this characteristic is not directly related to the number, length, and width of trailing units, the yaw stabilities of twins, tractor-semitrailers with 48-ft semitrailers, and 102-in. wide trucks are not appreciably different from those of tractor-semitrailers with 45-ft semitrailers (2).

DOLLY DESIGN

The preceding sections describe the handling and stability characteristics of twins equipped with single-drawbar dollies (A-dollies). Other dolly designs are possible that would alter the handling and stability of twins.

For example, the double-drawbar B-dolly (see Glossary, Figure G-3) eliminates one articulation point between trailers and apparently reduces rearward amplification, the likelihood of rear trailer rollover, and oscillatory sway. Double-drawbar dollies can increase low-speed offtracking, but some versions incorporate a steering mechanism to counteract this tendency (18,19). Compared with the single-drawbar dolly, such B-dollies are heavier, more costly to buy and maintain, and possibly more difficult to hitch. An ongoing FHWA-sponsored research study, Techniques for Improving the Dynamic Ability of Multitrailer Combination Vehicles, should provide better data on the improvement of control and stability through dolly design. Another ongoing study, Heavy Vehicle Weights and Dimensions, by the Road and Transportation Association of Canada, may shed further light on the handling properties of twins and the effect of dolly design.

REFERENCES

1. *Review of Safety and Economic Aspects of Increased Vehicle Sizes and Weights.* FHWA, U.S. Department of Transportation, Sept. 1969.
2. R.D. Ervin, R.L. Nisonger, C.C. MacAdam, and P.S. Fancher. *Influence of Size and Weight Variables on the Stability and Control Properties of Heavy Trucks*, Vol. 1. Report FHWA-RD-83-029. University of Michigan Transportation Research Institute, Ann Arbor, March 1983.
3. M.D. Freitas. "Safety of Twin Trailer Operations. In *Proceedings, 28th Annual Conference*, American Association for Automotive Medicine, Morton Grove, Ill., 1984.
4. *1983 Truck Turn Study.* Office of Project Planning and Design, California Department of Transportation, Sacramento, Nov. 1983.
5. F. Jindra. *Handling Characteristics of Tractor-Trailer Combinations.* SAE Paper 650720. Society of Automotive Engineers, Warrendale, Pa., Oct. 1965.
6. T. Hazemoto. *Analysis of Lateral Stability for Doubles.* SAE Paper 730688. Society of Automotive Engineers, Warrendale, Pa., June 1973.
7. C. Mallikarjunarao and P. Fancher. *Analysis of the Directional Response Characteristics of Double Tankers.* SAE Paper 781064. Society of Automotive Engineers, Warrendale, Pa., Dec. 1978.
8. P.S. Fancher. *The Transient Directional Response of Full Trailers.* SAE Paper 821259. Society of Automotive Engineers, Warrendale, Pa., Nov. 1982.
9. A.M. Billing. *Rollover Tests of Double Trailer Combinations.* Report TVS-CV-82-114. Transport Technology and Energy Division, Ministry of Transportation and Communications, Downsview, Ontario, Canada, Dec. 1982.
10. R.N. Kemp, B.P. Chinn, and G. Brock. *Articulated Vehicle Roll Stability: Methods of Assessment and Effects of Vehicle Characteristics.* TRRL Report 788. U.K. Transport and Road Research Laboratory, Crowthorne, Berkshire, England, 1978.
11. P.A. Winter. *Brake Performance Levels for Trucks and Passenger Cars.* Bureau of Motor Carrier Safety, FHWA, U.S. Department of Transportation, 1974.
12. L.C. Kibbee. *Report of Truck Brake Tests Conducted for the Virginia Twin Trailer Study Commission.* Virginia Highway Users Association, March 1969.
13. R.E. Nelson and J.W. Fitch. *Optimum Braking, Stability and Structural Integrity for Longer Truck Combinations.* SAE Paper 680547. Society of Automotive Engineers, Warrendale, Pa., 1968.
14. D.E. Peterson and R. Gull. *Triple Trailer Evaluation in Utah.* Report UDOT-MR-75-4. Utah Department of Transportation, Salt Lake City, Sept. 1975.

15. W.R.J. Mercer, J.R. Billing, and M.E. Wolkowicz. *Test and Demonstration of Double and Triple Trailer Combinations*. Report TVS-CV-82-109. Transport Technology and Energy Division, Ministry of Transportation and Communications, Downsview, Ontario, Canada, Aug. 1982.

16. *Report of the Twin Trailer Study Commission to the Governor and the General Assembly of Virginia*. Senate Doc. 14. Department of Purchase and Supply, Richmond, Va., 1970.

17. E.C. Mikulcik. *Hitch and Stability Problems in Vehicle Trains*. University of Calgary, Alberta, Canada, Nov. 6, 1973.

18. *The Feasibility of a Nationwide Network for Longer Combination Vehicles*. FHWA, U.S. Department of Transportation, June 1985.

19. R.D. Ervin, P.S. Fancher, and T.D. Gillespie. *An Overview of the Dynamic Performance Properties of Long Truck Combinations*. University of Michigan Transportation Research Institute, Ann Arbor, 1984.

Appendix E
Traffic Operations: Literature Review

The efficiency and safety of the flow of traffic on a road may be altered by the presence of large trucks. The literature is reviewed that examines the effects of trucks on eight important factors influencing traffic flow: speed, passing, freeway merging and lane changing, splash and spray, aerodynamic buffeting, blockage of view, lateral placement, and level of service and capacity. These eight are the principal mechanisms by which changes in truck size or configuration might affect traffic operations.

SPEED

In comparison with most other vehicles, large heavily laden trucks accelerate slowly and experience difficulty in maintaining speeds on upgrades. When trucks travel more slowly than the prevailing traffic, the speed differential not only suppresses the average travel speed, intensifies passing requirements, and reduces highway capacity but also increases the risk of accidents (1–4).

The speeds of large trucks have been subjected to extensive investigation by using both simulation techniques and in-service monitoring. In brief, general findings of these investigations include the following:

- The primary vehicle characteristic affecting acceleration and speed performance of large trucks is the weight/power ratio (2,5–8).

● The magnitude of truck speed reduction on upgrades is dependent not only on truck performance but also on driver skill, entry speed, and the length and severity of grade (6,8–11).

● On upgrades that are long or steep or both, the speed of heavy trucks is reduced to a minimum, termed creep or sustained speed, which for a typical heavy truck is about 10 to 25 mph, depending on gradient (6,8,11,12).

● The speed of large trucks on downgrades is highly variable, but heavily laden trucks travel at reduced speeds on severe downgrades, sometimes approaching creep conditions, in order to maintain vehicle control (11,13).

● Loaded trucks travel more slowly than empty ones, an effect that is magnified on upgrades (13).

● On extended highway segments, large trucks have historically operated at lower speeds than automobiles, the difference diminishing both as average gradient becomes smaller and as speed-limit controls become more restrictive (7,14,15). Following implementation of the nationwide 55-mph speed limit, trucks and automobiles began to travel at the same average speeds on straight, level segments of main rural highways (16) but large-truck speeds continued to lag behind automobile speeds on urban freeways (17).

● The extent to which large trucks suppress average traffic speeds depends on numerous factors, including the volume of both trucks and other vehicles, desired speeds of other vehicles, desired and attainable speeds of trucks, and the availability of passing opportunities. Although such effects have not been examined extensively except in conjuction with capacity investigations, increased delay and reduced speed have been documented on predominantly two-lane highways (5,11), on multilane highways (13), and at signalized intersections (18).

In addition to the foregoing work, limited comparisons have found that twins travel somewhat more slowly than tractor-semitrailers. For example, drivers reported that the minimum speeds they were able to sustain on a section of Interstate 80 in Utah and Nevada averaged 2.4 mph less for twins than for tractor-semitrailers. For a section of Interstate 15 in Utah, the differential in average minimum speeds was reported to be 4 mph, again with twins traveling more slowly (19). On three other Interstate upgrades investigated in another study, the speed advantage of tractor-semitrailers varied from a minimum of 2.8 mph on a 1.5-mi, 3-percent gradient to a maximum of 8.0 mph on a 1-mi, 5-percent gradient (2). A third study of 14 predominantly multilane sites found the average speed of tractor-semitrailers to exceed that of twins by approximately 3 mph (13). On upgrades with loaded trucks, the difference was quite pronounced—loaded tractor-semitrailers traveled approximately 13 mph faster than loaded twins.

Differences in the speed performance of twins and tractor-semitrailers are attributed to possible differences in their weights, aerodynamic properties, and available horsepower.

The ability of a truck to maintain speed on a grade is profoundly influenced by its weight. The power required to maintain a given speed, to a first approximation, varies inversely with the vehicle weight (13).

Moving twins encounter more air resistance than tractor-semitrailers, especially with crosswinds, and are therefore less able to sustain high speeds. The effect is attributed both to the second gap (between the two trailers) and to the increased overall length. Because of their better aerodynamic shape, cab-behind-engine tractors encounter less air resistance than do cab-over-engine tractors [Table E-1 (20)].

The inhibiting effect of weight on speed as well as the effect of aerodynamic and other resistances can be countered by increasing the horsepower available at the drive axles. Although information available in the open literature is sketchy, no differences have been recorded in the horsepower ratings of twins and tractor-semitrailers (21,22). In interviews conducted for this study, carriers indicated that they had not changed their tractor power specifications when they began purchasing twin trailer trucks to replace tractor-semitrailers (see Chapter 3).

As truck width increases from 96 to 102 in. or semitrailer length increases from 45 to 48 ft, increased air resistance and increased loaded weight are likely to contribute to lower truck speeds on severe upgrades. However, the magnitude of these effects has not been documented in the open literature, and they could be offset by use of higher-powered tractors.

TABLE E-1   Aerodynamic Characteristics of Selected Trucks (20)

Configuration	No. of Tractor Axles	Cab Type[a]	Length of Van Trailer (ft)	Effective Flat Plate Area (ft^2)[b]	
				No Crosswind	Crosswind at 20-Degree Relative Angle
Tractor-semitrailer	2	COE	27	81	118
Tractor-semitrailer	3	COE	40	85	145
Tractor-semitrailer	3	CBE	40	85	119
Twins	2	COE	27	93	156
Triple	2	COE	27	108	199

[a]COE denotes cab over engine and CBE, cab behind engine.
[b]Effective full-scale flat-plate area is the product of the drag coefficient and the reference frontal area. Air resistance is directly proportional to this effective frontal area.

In summary, large trucks travel more slowly than other vehicles on both upgrades and the more severe downgrades. Although the upgrade effect reflects reduced performance due primarily to larger weights, speed reductions on downgrades result from a deliberate attempt by the driver to maintain vehicle control. On level, tangent sections of highway controlled by a 55-mph speed limit, truck and automobile speeds are comparable. On grades where maximum power is required to maintain speeds, twins travel more slowly than tractor-semitrailers, on average, a consequence of their larger weight and increased air resistance. Under similar conditions, 102-in. wide trucks and 48-ft tractor-semitrailers are likely to travel more slowly than their smaller counterparts.

PASSING

Superior quality of traffic flow (that is, the absence of any inhibition of each vehicle's movement by the presence of other vehicles on the road) requires that drivers be able to maintain their desired speeds of travel. In mixed traffic streams in which the distribution of actual speeds may have a large variance, faster vehicles must have frequent opportunities to easily pass or overtake slower vehicles. Generally, as the demand for passing increases and the opportunity and ease of passing decrease, delays to impeded vehicles increase and the quality of flow decreases. However, the degree of passing difficulty is influenced by many factors, including

- The volumes or flow rates of the traffic mix;
- The presence or absence of opposing traffic (two-lane versus multilane facilities);
- The distribution of speeds (as determined by desired speeds of travel and by vehicle characteristics and the length and severity of grades);
- The clear sight distance available to passers on two-lane, two-way roadways (as determined primarily by highway geometry);
- Acceleration capability of the passer, including the effects of grade; and
- Size of overtaken vehicles.

Because of their reduced ability to accelerate and to maintain speed, large trucks are more likely to impede traffic flow and, if passing opportunities are limited, may delay higher-performance vehicles. On two-lane, two-way highways, their increased bulk restricts the sight distance of following vehicles and their increased length intensifies the difficulty of safely completing or aborting a passing maneuver.

The effect of large trucks on passing impedance is much more significant on two-lane, two-way highways than on multilane highways. Although the primary factor is the reduction of passing opportunities due to the presence of opposing traffic, grades are frequently more severe on two-lane highways and sight-distance restrictions assume a critical role in passing behavior.

Extensive investigations of the behavior of automobiles in passing large trucks on two-way, two-lane rural highways have been reported by Trout-beck (23–25). Among the findings of greatest relevance to the current investigation are the following:

● Drivers of following vehicles initiated passing maneuvers closer to automobiles than to trucks, but when they were passing trucks, the initiation distance was independent of truck length and configuration.

● Difficulty of the passing manuever increased as the length of the overtaken vehicle increased. In particular, mean passing times and distances were found to be about 6 percent greater for a 65-ft tractor-semi-trailer than for a 52-ft tractor-semitrailer. Passing vehicles have also been observed to accelerate over a longer period of time when passing longer trucks (26).

● Behavior in passing a 69-ft twin trailer truck was not significantly different from that in passing a tractor-semitrailer of the same length. Furthermore, drivers familiar with the twin did not pass in a more conservative manner than those unfamiliar with this truck type.

Troutbeck also examined the delay caused by slower-moving vehicles in the traffic stream. In comparison with 52-ft trucks, increased unit delays for 65-ft trucks were collectively countered by the reduced number of trucks required to transport the same volume of cargo.

As summarized by Larson and Hanscom (2), other studies examining primarily longer doubles and triples have found evidence of

● Delays occasioned by the use of doubles and triples on two-lane highways,
● Reticence of drivers to pass longer vehicles in spite of available gaps of sufficient size to permit safe passing,
● Increased time to pass longer trucks, and
● Volume effects on passing opportunity and comfort.

Large trucks are less disruptive on multilane facilities because the opportunity to pass is not reduced by limited sight distances and the presence of opposing traffic. For example, little or no delay to automobiles on four-lane freeways was reported when the one-directional automobile volumes remained below 1,500 vehicles per hour and all slow trucks remained in the right lane (27). The likelihood of delay on upgrades increases, however, with increases in the volumes of both automobiles and trucks. More of the faster-moving vehicles are delayed, both because of reduced opportunity to change lanes and because of temporary lane blockage as increasing numbers of trucks pass other trucks. When there is an acceptable gap, trucks have been observed to pass slower-moving vehicles even though other traffic in the passing lane will be delayed (28).

The empirical study by Hanscom sheds additional light on the influence of large trucks on multilane passing behavior (13). In comparison with following empty trucks, vehicles following loaded trucks on upgrades experienced greater delays, suffered greater speed reductions, approached from the rear more rapidly, and passed with greater relative speed. Also compared were the relative effects of twins and tractor-semitrailers. Although vehicles following twins approached from the rear more rapidly and passed at higher relative speeds, significant differences in following vehicle speeds and delays were not observed. Apparently, traffic volumes were not sufficiently great at the study sites to seriously inhibit the ability to pass by changing lanes.

The effects of longer semitrailers are similar to those of twins, deriving primarily from the combination of increased length and heavier loading. Because the length and weight increases are smaller between a 45-ft and a 48-ft tractor-semitrailer than between a 45-ft tractor-semitrailer and twins, any detrimental effect of 48-ft tractor-semitrailers is expected to be of less significance than that of twins.

The operation of wider trucks is likely to intensify the difficulties of passing, particularly on two-lane roadways. The increased width not only reduces the sight distance of following motorists but also increases the gross vehicle weight, reducing truck speeds on upgrades and increasing the required number of overtakings. In a recent examination of the effect of wider trucks (in which trucks much wider than 102 in. were considered) on passing behavior on two-lane rural highways, it was found that increased truck width had the following observable effects: increased distance between the slow-moving truck and trailing vehicles, decreased lateral separation between the truck and the passing vehicle, decreased distance between the road edge and the passing vehicle, and reduced discrimination by the passer between acceptable and unacceptable gaps to opposing vehicles (29). These behavioral changes were considered to be reasonable but, because they are small for a width increment from 96 to 102 in., they were not considered to compromise highway safety.

In summary, the reduced speeds of large trucks, particularly on upgrades, increase the number of overtakings by higher-performance vehicles. If frequent opportunities to pass safely without delay are not available, the overall quality of flow diminishes. The increased articulation of twins has little or no effect on passing behavior, and the slightly increased passing times and distances due to small length differentials in comparison with conventional tractor-semitrailers are likely to be offset by a reduction in the number of trucks necessary to transport a given cargo quantity. The primary detrimental effect of both twins and 48-ft tractor-semitrailers derives from performance decrements resulting from larger weight/power ratios. The heavier weights that accompany wider trucks are also likely to increase the required number of passing maneuvers. Although very wide trucks adversely affect passing behavior, this effect for 102-in. wide trucks versus 96-in. wide trucks is not likely to compromise highway safety.

FREEWAY MERGING AND LANE CHANGING

Operational effects of large trucks are less significant on freeways than on other highway types. On freeways, merging is the one maneuver most likely to be adversely affected by the presence of large trucks. The length and limited accelerative capability of large trucks may increase their difficulty in finding a suitable gap in which to merge without interrupting the flow of either mainline or ramp traffic. When a truck is operating at reduced speed in the outer lane of a freeway, the length of the truck combined with a possible backup of closely trailing vehicles may tend to block the entry of merging vehicles.

Limited evidence has been recorded of difficulty experienced by larger combinations in finding suitably sized gaps in which to merge and of disruption to mainline traffic (30,31). However, attempts to quantify these effects have failed to identify significant differences between vehicles of different lengths and weights (13,29). This neutral finding may have been due to methodological shortcomings: nevertheless, until more definitive data indicate otherwise, there is no reason to suspect that minor increases in truck length and weight, such as might result from more extensive use of twins, 48-ft semitrailers, and 102-in. wide trucks, will have a significantly adverse effect on merging maneuvers.

Although merging and lane changing are similar maneuvers, there are subtle differences that may be important. In particular, the reversal of steering in lane changing, if done rapidly, is more likely to have a whiplike effect on trailing units. In addition, increases in truck length and width may impair the rearward view of the driver as well as his ability to judge the safety of a lane change.

In one limited study, tractor-semitrailers precipitated the sudden slowing of following cars in 12 percent of their observed lane-change maneuvers:

corresponding percentages for twins and triples were 15 and 45 percent, respectively (29). In other literature on large trucks, at the most only casual mention is made of the operational effects of lane changes by large trucks.

In summary, although the results of past operational studies are inconclusive, there is no indication that merging and lane changing would be seriously disrupted by increasing use of twins, longer semitrailers, and wider trucks.

SPLASH AND SPRAY

Under adverse environmental conditions, motor vehicles in motion splash water, slush, and snow, typically in moderately large droplets or chunks. In addition, some of these droplets or chunks strike the undercarriage or tires and are broken up into a cloud or mist of fine particles, called spray. Depending on the nature and extent of the spray, the vision of following and passing motorists, as well as those whom the truck is passing, may be severely impaired, increasing not only the difficulty of the driving task but the degree of hazard as well. Large trucks create more critical splash and spray conditions than smaller vehicles because they displace more moisture from the road surface, develop air-flow patterns more conducive to spray formation, and release the moisture cloud at a higher elevation above the road surface.

Despite similarities in their shape and bulk, twins and tractor-semitrailers may generate different quantities and patterns of spray. In particular the increased length of twins is likely to increase the time during which the vision of passing motorists may be impaired and may affect the magnitude of air turbulence as well, and the flow of air at the additional gap between the two trailers may provide an additional source for the generation of spray clouds. On the other hand, the tandem axles of the tractor-semitrailer generate larger and denser spray clouds. Water drops propelled from the pavement surface are more likely to be atomized as they impact on the surface of the rotating, adjacent tire and are recirculated between the tires of a tandem set.

Because of the complexity of the splash-and-spray phenomenon, full-scale field tests are normally employed in evaluating truck-configuration effects. Notable among the earlier tests were those conducted at Fort Stockton, Texas, under the auspices of the Western Highway Institute (32). The severity of the splash and spray generated by tractor-semitrailers and twins when operated under rather carefully controlled test conditions was visually rated by observers using a five-point scale that ranged from unsatisfactory to satisfactory. Not only was the twin trailer truck found to be superior to the tractor-semitrailer by each of seven observers, but it was judged to be the best among the 11 different trucks that were evaluated.

On the basis of tests conducted at Madras, Oregon, in 1974, the amount of spray generated by twins has also been reported to be less, by approximately 20 percent, than that generated by a conventional tractor-semitrailer (33). It is unfortunate with respect to the current inquiry that the tests at Madras used a 40-ft semitrailer rather than 27- or 28-ft twin trailers. In any event, the Madras finding is weakened because of uncontrolled variations in water puddling, wind direction and speed, and in truck path and speed, and because insufficient data were available on the test date to establish a meaningful comparison.

Specific deficiencies of the Madras tests were corrected in later, more refined testing at Fort Stockton (20). Among the 11 trucks tested were tractor-semitrailers with 40-ft van trailers (both cab-over-engine and cab-behind-engine tractors) and twins with 27-ft van trailers. Although the degree to which visibility was degraded by splash and spray was different for the several truck types, the investigators concluded that the differences were not substantial considering the order of resolution and accuracy of the measurements. In the specific comparison of twins and tractor-semitrailers other confounding effects included limited number of tests, rather large variability in test results, and differences in truck loading. Nevertheless, test data showed that visibility was more severely impaired by tractor-semitrailers than by twins.

Longer tractor-semitrailers are likely to slightly aggravate the splash and spray problem. Larger quantities of water are displaced by their heavier weight, and the passing motorist remains under the influence of the spray cloud for an increased period of time. However, these differences are not large and are likely to be inconsequential for the replacement of 45-ft by 48-ft semitrailers.

Wider trucks are likely to generate small increases in spray because of their heavier loads and the displacement of larger air masses. Further intensifying the problem is the slight reduction in the distance between adjacent vehicles in the traffic stream. A beneficial consequence of the use of all larger vehicles is a reduction in the number of expected trips and hence the exposure of other motorists to spray clouds.

These limited testing programs, as well as more subjective assessments of others (19,34), indicate that the disruption and hazard due to splash and spray will be reduced by increased use of twins. Although the effects of wider trucks and longer semitrailers on splash and spray have not been documented in the open literature, they are likely to be small and inconsequential.

AERODYNAMIC BUFFETING

The aerodynamic forces acting on a vehicle are suddenly altered when the vehicle passes a large truck traveling in an adjacent lane, whether in the same or the opposite direction. Unless appropriate steering adjustment is made, a potentially hazardous lateral displacement may result. The disturbance is exacerbated when (a) the lateral separation between the two vehicles is small, (b) the difference in speeds between the vehicles is small, (c) the disturbed vehicle is large but of low density (such as a truck-camper), (d) the truck is large and its shape contributes to aerodynamic disturbance, and (e) the disturbed vehicle is on the leeward side of the truck in a crosswind (35).

For similar cab styles and trailer types, the only differences between twins and tractor-semitrailers that are likely to influence the amount of aerodynamic buffeting include the increased length of twins and the gap between the two trailers. Length is the only potentially distinguishing factor between 45- and 48-ft semitrailers. When the disturbed vehicle is on the leeward side of the truck in a crosswind, increased truck length increases the time during which the disturbed vehicle is shadowed from the ambient wind and increases the potential lateral displacement, if uncorrected, as well. Although the presence of the second gap in twins creates an added disturbance under crosswind conditions, the peak lateral displacement remains similar in magnitude to that induced by a tractor-semitrailer and the added disturbance is of little consequence. When there is no crosswind, the performances of twins and tractor-semitrailers are similar (20).

Increasing truck width has two potentially adverse aerodynamic effects: the lateral separation between adjacent vehicles is reduced and the disturbance of the air at the front of the moving truck is increased. Both with and without crosswinds, these effects have been found to be negligible for a width increase from 96 to 102 in. (29,35,36).

In summary, the increased lengths of twins and 48-ft semitrailers and wider truck bodies have potentially adverse effects on aerodynamic buffeting. The effects are sufficiently small to be considered negligible, however, for the small length and width differentials under consideration.

BLOCKAGE OF VIEW

One of the potentially adverse safety impacts of large trucks is that they may block the line of sight of nearby motorists, temporarily depriving them of information essential to safe vehicle operation. Unfortunately, no accident information is available with which to assess the possible gravity of this problem. The few studies that have examined truck blockage of view have focused on model development and an analysis of the effects of sign and signal location (*37–40*). The results do not highlight the effects of increasing truck size, nor are they applicable to the broad range of situations and conditions in which restrictive sight distances may be hazardous. Furthermore, they do not account for counteractions taken by the alert motorist—such as speed reductions and lane changes—which prevent serious line-of-sight disruption.

LATERAL PLACEMENT

The safe movement of traffic requires lanes of sufficient width to minimize the probability of inadvertent out-of-lane excursions and to provide comfortable and safe clearances between meeting and passing vehicles with no more than minor lateral displacements from their desired paths of travel. Large trucks are more likely than smaller vehicles to exceed lane boundaries simply because they occupy larger proportions of the available lane width and hence have a smaller margin for accommodating random deviations in their paths of travel. Furthermore, not only is the lateral displacement greater when automobiles meet or pass trucks than when they meet or pass other automobiles—a consequence both of the reduced ability to accurately detect the position of the truck (*41*) and of perception of greater hazard (*29*)—but also the greater truck width reduces body clearances. An anticipated consequence of the operation of wide trucks on narrow roadways is therefore a reduction in highway safety.

Some of the more salient results of past research, conducted primarily to establish lane-width standards for two-lane roads, are as follows:

Lateral placement

- Vehicles travel further from the centerline as lane width increases (*42,43*), as shoulder width increases up to at least 3 or 4 ft (*42–44*), and as shoulders are improved in type (*42–44*).
- Vehicles travel further from the centerline during the day than at night (*42*), when meeting other vehicles (*42,44*), and, at least for narrow pavements, when volume increases (*44*).
- Trucks travel considerably closer to the pavement edge than cars and slightly closer to the centerline (*42,43*).

Vehicle body clearance

● Body clearances are increased as lane width increases (*44*) and with increases in shoulder width and improvement in shoulder type (*42*).

● Body clearances are greater when automobiles meet other automobiles than when they meet trucks. They are smallest when trucks meet other trucks on roadways having narrow lanes or inadequate shoulders or both (*42*).

● Body clearances are less for passing maneuvers than for meetings (*44*).

Shoulder encroachments

● Shoulder encroachments increase rapidly when total pavement width decreases below 22 ft (*44*).

● Shoulder encroachments are more frequent when the shoulder is paved and is similar in appearance to the traffic lanes (*42,43*), but their frequency is reduced by the provision of pavement-edge stripes (*42*).

● Trucks encroach on shoulders more frequently than automobiles (*42–44*).

Unfortunately, few investigations have directly examined the influence of truck width and configuration on lateral displacement and body clearances. Early speculation was that small changes in truck width, such as that from 96 to 102 in., would generate large changes in the lateral displacement of meeting and passing vehicles (*41*). Recent measurements on a two-lane rural road, however, indicated reduction in the mean separation of only 3 to 4 in. when truck width increased from 96 to 102 in. (*29*). Possible effects of truck configuration, particularly those associated with oscillatory sway, have not been documented.

Although it is generally acknowledged that accident rates decrease as lane width increases (*45*), the interactive effects of lane width and the nature and extent of truck traffic have not been established. Current accepted design standards regard 12-ft lanes to be adequate for accommodating 102-in. wide trucks and permit 11-ft lanes under low-speed conditions except where large volumes of truck traffic are anticipated (*46*). On narrow roads with sharp curves, the length of a semitrailer rather than its width is the critical dimension determining interference with oncoming traffic, because length determines offtracking (see Appendix D).

If the shoulder width is inadequate, the presence of parked trucks can also lead to critical intervehicle clearance conditions and the swerving of passing vehicles. Although the extent to which passing drivers shy away from parked trucks has not been established, design guidelines suggest that shoulder width is ample if the truck clears the pavement edge by a minimum distance of 1 ft, preferably 2 ft (*46*). Thus, to accommodate trucks of 102-in. rather than 96-in. width, the design shoulder width would be increased by 6 in. An even smaller increase has been recommended for non-Interstate highways in rural areas (*47*). Increased use of wider trucks on high-type highways is not likely to result in critical parking conditions because current design standards are based on 102-in. wide trucks.

In summary, reduced body clearances, reduced pavement-edge clearances, and increased lateral displacement of adjacent vehicles are anticipated as a result of the substitution of 102-in. wide trucks for 96-in. trucks. However, the changes will be small and are unlikely to have a significantly adverse effect on highway safety under normal road conditions. The use of longer tractor-semitrailers is not expected to alter the lateral placement of vehicles traveling in adjacent lanes: twins may do so but only to the extent that they are more prone than tractor-semitrailers to oscillatory sway.

LEVEL OF SERVICE AND CAPACITY

Highway capacity is a measure of the maximum traffic flow rate, usually expressed in vehicles per hour, that can reasonably be accommodated by a specific segment of highway. When the highway is operating under capacity conditions, the quality of flow is poor; speeds are low, delays may be excessive, and opportunities for maneuvering are severely constrained. The quality of flow improves continuously as the volume becomes less than that at capacity. Traffic engineers collapse the flow-quality continuum into six distinct level-of-service increments, labeled A through F. The flow quality is superior under level-of-service A: movement is virtually unaffected by other vehicles in the traffic stream. Flow quality deteriorates as the level of service progresses from A to E. The maximum volume that can be accommodated at level-of-service E is that which has been termed capacity. Operations are unstable and the flow rate is reduced at level-of-service F. Delays become excessive and movement can be characterized as stop-and-go.

Because of their increased lengths and lower acceleration and speed-maintenance capabilities, the presence of large trucks in a traffic stream depresses the roadway capacity and reduces the level of service. The effect of each large truck is measured in terms of passenger-car equivalents, the number of passenger cars that has the same impact on flow quality as one truck. Passenger-car equivalents are complex functions not only of truck characteristics but also of the total traffic volume, truck volume, and the nature of the highway element (for example, intersections versus open-road conditions, number of lanes, merging sections, and gradient). The largest detrimental effects of large trucks on level of service and capacity are observed on two-lane upgrades with restricted opportunity for passing.

According to the most authoritative source (48), the effects of trucks operating on open-road segments are more severe for two-lane than for multilane highways and for terrain with greater relief, as shown by the passenger-car equivalents of trucks:

| | Truck Passenger-Car Equivalent by Terrain | | |
Lane Configuration	Level	Rolling	Mountainous
Two-lane	2.0–2.2	4.0–4.5	7.0–12.0
Multilane	1.7	4.0	8.0

The effects on long, steep upgrades, which must be examined on an individual basis, are more pronounced for upgrades having larger gradients when trucks make up a smaller percentage of the total traffic stream (Table E-2). For at-grade intersections, the passenger-car equivalent for combination vehicles is typically 2.0, with adjustments being made for gradient at unsignalized locations.

The Highway Capacity Manual (48) considers the population of large trucks as one group of vehicles, and its lack of specificity precludes examination of the effects of individual truck types. Although such individual effects have not been comprehensively reported in any other authoritative design guide, the effects of truck length, speed, weight/power ratio, and type have been demonstrated.

TABLE E-2 Effect of Gradient and Percentage of Trucks on Passenger-Car Equivalents of Trucks: Extended Four-Lane Freeway Upgrades (48)

| | Passenger-Car Equivalent by Percentage of Trucks | | | |
Gradient (%)	5	10	15	20
0	2	2	2	2
1	3	3	3	3
2	6	5	4	4
3	7	6	5	5
4	9	8	7	7
5	11	8	8	8
6	12	9	9	9

Using a deterministic model, Huber has demonstrated the effects of vehicle length on passenger-car equivalents for free-flowing, multilane conditions (49). As the effective truck length (measured in a standing queue from the rear of the preceding vehicle to the rear of the subject vehicle) increases from 60 to 75 ft, the passenger-car equivalent increases in the range of 6 to 25 percent, depending primarily on the method for defining equivalency.

Intuitively, reduced speeds of large trucks are likely to more seriously degrade flow quality than their increased length. Some evidence to this effect is indicated from the two-lane, two-way upgrade simulations of St. John and Kobett (11). Rather dramatic increases in passenger-car equivalents were observed as a result of decreases in the free-flow speed of impeding trucks, and the marginal effect of each truck was diminished as trucks made up a greater proportion of the traffic stream (Table E-3).

One important truck characteristic that affects speed performance (and therefore passenger-car equivalents) on grades is the weight/power ratio. According to the Highway Capacity Manual procedures for analyzing level of service on multilane upgrades, the truck population is classified by performance attributes into one of three categories—light, typical, or heavy. The approximate average weight/power ratios for these three categories are, respectively, 100, 200, and 300 lb/hp. Passenger-car equivalents generally increase as truck performance decreases, an effect that is magnified as the grade becomes steeper (Table E-4).

Recent investigations conducted in support of FHWA's Highway Cost Allocation Study examined passenger-car equivalents for 14 different vehicle types categorized according to the FHWA visual procedures for the Highway Performance Monitoring System case study. Although certain anomalies are present in the data, the passenger-car equivalents on rural highways (50) generally increased as the number of axles on combination trucks increased and as the upgrades became steeper (Table E-5).

TABLE E-3 Effect of Truck Speed and Concentration on Passenger-Car Equivalents of Trucks (11)

Low Volume Truck Speed (mph)	Passenger-Car Equivalent by Percentage of Trucks	
	8–9	18–21
50	7	3
40	16	9
30	29	17
20	51	32

TABLE E-4 Effect of Gradient and Truck Type on Passenger-Car Equivalents of Trucks: Extended Four-Lane Freeway Upgrades with 15 Percent Trucks (48)

Gradient (%)	Passenger-Car Equivalent by Type of Truck		
	Light (100 lb/hp)	Medium (200 lb/hp)	Heavy (300 lb/hp)
0	2	2	2
1	2	3	4
2	2	4	5
3	4	5	7
4	4	7	9
5	5	8	13
6	5	9	18

TABLE E-5 Effect of Highway Type, Gradient, and Number of Combination-Truck Axles on Passenger-Car Equivalents of Trucks: Extended Upgrades and Traffic Level-of-Service C (50)

No. of Lanes	Lane Position	Gradient	Passenger-Car Equivalent by No. of Axles			
			3	4	5	6+
Two	—	Flat	2.1	1.1–1.6	1.1–2.1	2.1
		Moderate	6.2	1.3–2.6	2.5–5.1	10.2
		Steep	22.1	13.4–20.7	22.3–24.5	25.1
Four	Median	Flat	1.5	2.8–5.7	3.4–3.5	3.5
		Moderate	1.8	1.2	1.2–1.5	1.8
		Steep	4.0	5.2–6.8	8.5–8.9	9.2
Four	Outside	Flat	4.2	1.6	3.6–5.0	1.4
		Moderate	1.5	2.0–2.3	3.4–3.6	3.7
		Steep	4.7	7.8	8.4–10.8	11.1

Apparently no definite examination of the effects on level of service and capacity of replacing tractor-semitrailers with twins, 45-ft semitrailers with 48-ft semitrailers, or 96-in. wide trucks with 102-in. wide trucks has yet been undertaken. However, the increased length of twins and 48-ft semitrailers as well as the heavier loading of all of these trucks imply a greater unit degradation in flow quality by these vehicles than by the shorter and narrower vehicles. Countering this undesirable effect is a reduction in the number of trips necessary to transport a given quantity of cargo. The net effect of this trade-off is unknown.

300

REFERENCES

1. J.C. Glennon. An Evaluation of Design Criteria for Operating Trucks Safely on Grades. In *Transportation Research Record 312*, HRB, National Research Council, Washington, D.C., 1970, pp. 93–112.
2. E.E. Larson and F.R. Hanscom. *Traffic Operational Impact of Large Trucks; a Literature Review*. Transportation Research Corporation, Haymarket, Va., Oct. 1984.
3. R.E. Scott and J. O'Day. *Statistical Analysis of Truck Accident Involvements*. Report DOT-HS-800-627. University of Michigan Highway Safety Research Institute, Ann Arbor, Dec. 1971.
4. C.M. Walton and O. Gericke. *An Assessment of Changes in Truck Dimensions on Highway Geometric Design Principles and Practices*. Center for Highway Research, University of Texas, Austin, 1981.
5. P.F. Everall. *Social Benefits from Minimum Power-Weight Ratios for Goods Vehicles*. TRRL Report LR 291. U.K Transport and Road Research Laboratory, Crowthorne, Berkshire, England, 1969.
6. G.F. Hayhoe and J.G. Grundmann. *Review of Vehicle Weight/Horsepower Ratio as Related to Passing Lane Design Criteria*. Report PTI 7806. Pennsylvania Transportation Institute, University Park, Oct. 1978.
7. J.E. Leisch and J.P. Leisch. New Concepts in Design-Speed Application. In *Transportation Research Record 631*, TRB, National Research Council, Washington, D.C., 1977, pp. 4–14.
8. C.M. Walton and C.E. Lee. Characteristics of Trucks Operating on Grades. In *Transportation Research Record 631*, TRB, National Research Council, Washington, D.C., 1977, pp. 23–30.
9. P.Y. Ching and F.D. Rooney. Discussion of "Effect of Trucks, Buses, and Recreational Vehicles on Freeway Capacity and Service Volumes." In *Transportation Research Record 699*, TRB, National Research Council, Washington, D.C., 1979, pp. 24–25.
10. *Highway Capacity Manual*. Special Report 87. Highway Research Board, National Research Council, Washington, D.C., 1965.
11. A.D. St. John and D.R. Kobett. *Grade Effects on Traffic Flow Stability and Capacity*. NCHRP Report 185. TRB, National Research Council, Washington, D.C., 1978.
12. M. Forsythe et al. *Accident and Traffic Operations Implications of Large Trucks*. BioTechnology, Inc., Falls Church, Va., Sept. 1975.
13. F.R. Hanscom. *The Effect of Truck Size and Weight on Accident Experience and Traffic Operations*, Vol. 2: Traffic Operations. Report FHWA/RD-80/136. BioTechnology, Inc., Falls Church, Va., July 1981.
14. *Highway Statistics*. FHWA, U.S. Department of Transportation, 1975.
15. A.A. Gadallah. "Driver Response to Voluntary and Mandatory Speed Limits." *Traffic Engineering*, Vol. 46, No. 3, March 1976, pp. 32–35.

16. *Special Speed Monitoring Survey: Trucks and Buses.* Voluntary Truck and Bus Fuel Economy Improvement Program, NHTSA, U.S. Department of Transportation, March 1979.

17. E.L. Seguin et al. *Urban Freeway Truck Characteristics.* Report FHWA/RD-83/033. Institute for Research, State College, Pa., June 1983.

18. T.H. Yurysta and H.L. Michael. Effect of Commercial Vehicles on Delay at Intersections. In *Transportation Research Record 601*, TRB, National Research Council, Washington, D.C., 1976, pp. 59–65.

19. D.E. Peterson and R. Gull. *Triple Trailer Evaluation in Utah.* Report UDOT-MR-75-4. Utah Department of Transportation, Salt Lake City, Sept. 1975.

20. D.H. Weir, J.F. Strange, and R.K. Heffley. *Reduction of Adverse Aerodynamic Effects of Large Trucks*, Vol. 1: Technical Report. Report FHWA-RD-79-84. Systems Technology, Inc., Hawthorne, Calif., Sept. 1978.

21. *Review of Safety and Economic Aspects of Increased Vehicle Sizes and Weights.* FHWA, U.S. Department of Transportation, Sept. 1969.

22. G.R. Vallette, H. McGee, and J.H. Sanders. *The Effect of Truck Size and Weight on Accident Experience and Traffic Operations*, Vol. 4: Truck Exposure Classification by Size and Weight. Draft Final Report. BioTechnology, Inc., Falls Church, Va., May 1979.

23. R.J. Troutbeck. Effect of Overtaken Vehicle Speed and Length on Overtaking Behavior on Two-Lane Rural Roads. *Traffic Engineering and Control*, Vol. 23, No. 6, June 1982, pp. 318–328.

24. R.J. Troutbeck. *Overtaking Behavior Around Road Trains: An Extrapolation of Observed Behavior.* AIR 197-12. Australian Road Research Board, Nunawading, Victoria, 1980.

25. R.J. Troutbeck. *The Effect of Height and Configuration of the Overtaken Vehicle and the Use of a 'Long Load' Sign on Overtaking Behavior.* AIR 197-9. Australian Road Research Board, Nunawading, Victoria, April 1979.

26. T.D. Sherard. "The Safety and Operating Characteristics of Big Trucks." Presented at the Society of Automotive Engineers Northwest Section Meeting, April 1971.

27. L. Newman and K. Moskowitz. Effect of Grades on Service Volume. In *Transportation Research Record 99*, TRB, National Research Council, Washington, D.C., 1965, pp. 224–243.

28. A.D. St. John et al. *Freeway Design and Control Strategies as Affected by Truck and Traffic Regulations.* Report FHWA-RD-75-42. Midwest Research Institute, Kansas City, Mo., April 1975.

29. E.L. Seguin et al. *The Effects of Truck Size on Driver Behavior.* Report FHWA/RD-81/170. The Institute for Research, State College, Pa., March 1982.

30. *Triple Trailer Study in California.* California Business and Transportation Agency, 1972.

31. *Operational Characteristics of 100-Foot Double Trailer/Tractor Operations in Michigan.* Michigan Department of State Highways and Transportation, Lansing, Dec. 1976.

32. *Splash and Spray Characteristics of Trucks and Truck Combinations*. Research Committee Report 5. Subcommittee on Splash and Spray, Western Highway Institute, San Francisco, Calif., May 1, 1973.

33. T.E. Ritter. *Truck Splash and Spray Tests at Madras, Oregon*. Report AR-955. Southwest Research Institute, San Antonio, Tex., Oct. 1974.

34. W.R.J. Mercer, J.R. Billing, and M.E. Wolkowicz. *Test and Demonstration of Doubles and Triple Trailer Combinations*. Report TVS-CV-82-109. Transport Technology and Energy Division, Ministry of Transportation and Communications, Downsview, Ontario, Canada, Aug. 1982.

35. D.H. Weir, R.H. Hoh, and G.L. Teper. Driver-Vehicle Control and Performance in the Presence of Aerodynamic Disturbances from Large Vehicles. In *Transportation Research Record 520*, TRB, National Research Council, Washington, D.C., 1974, pp. 1–12.

36. G.J. Brown and G.R. Seeman. *An Experimental Investigation of the Unsteady Aerodynamics of Passing Highway Vehicles*. Development Sciences, Inc., May 1972.

37. P. Abramson. "Blockage of Signs by Trucks." *Traffic Engineering*, Vol. 41, No. 7, April 1971, pp. 18–26.

38. G.F. King and H. Lunenfeld. *Development of Information Requirements and Transmission Techniques for Highway Users*. NCHRP Report 123. TRB, National Research Council, Washington, D.C., 1971.

39. G.F. King, P. Abramson, and C. Duerk. Truck Blockage of Signals. In *Transportation Research Record 597*, TRB, National Research Council, Washington, D.C., 1976, pp. 1–9.

40. G.F. King. *Guidelines for Uniformity in Traffic Signal Design Configurations*, Vol. 1: Final Report. KLD Report 58. KLD Associates, Inc., Huntington Station, N.Y., July 1977.

41. R.M. Michaels and L.W. Cozan. "Perceptual and Field Factors Causing Lateral Displacement." *Public Roads*, Vol. 32, No. 11, Dec. 1963, pp. 233–240.

42. A. Taragin. Driver Behavior as Related to Shoulder Type and Width on Two-Lane Highways. In *HRB Bulletin 170*, Highway Research Board, National Research Council, Washington, D.C., 1958, pp. 54–76.

43. M.D. Shelby and P.R. Tutt. Vehicle Speed and Placement Study. In *HRB Bulletin 170*, Highway Research Board, National Research Council, Washington, D.C., 1958, pp. 24–50.

44. A. Taragin. "Effect of Roadway Width on Vehicle Operation." *Public Roads*, Vol. 24, No. 6, Oct.-Dec. 1945, pp. 143–160.

45. H.H. Bissell et al. "Roadway Cross Section and Alinement." In *Synthesis of Safety Research Related to Traffic Control and Roadway Elements*, Vol. 1. Report FHWA-TS-82-232. FHWA, U.S. Department of Transportation, Dec. 1982.

46. *A Policy on Geometric Design of Highways and Streets*. American Association of State Highway and Transportation Officials, Washington, D.C., 1984.

47. J.B. Saag and J.E. Leisch. *Synthesis of Information on Roadway Geometric Causal Factors*. Report FHWA/PL/007. Jack E. Leisch and Associates, Evanston, Ill. Jan. 1981.

48. *Highway Capacity Manual*. Special Report 209. TRB, National Research Council, Washington, D.C., 1985.

49. M.J. Huber. Estimation of Passenger-Car Equivalents of Trucks in Traffic Stream. In *Transportation Research Record 869*, TRB, National Research Council, Washington, D.C., 1982, pp. 60–70.

50. W.D. Cunagin and C.J. Messer. *Passenger Car Equivalents for Rural Highways*. Report FHWA/RD-82/132. H.G. Whyte Associates, Inc., Gary, Ind.; Texas Transportation Institute, College Station, Dec. 1982.

Appendix F
Accident Rates of Twins:
Literature Review

Descriptions are presented of 15 studies comparing accident rates of twin trailer trucks or other double trailer trucks with rates of tractor-semitrailers, and the collective results of these studies are summarized. Then a review is given of research aimed at identifying factors in the operating environment (the characteristics of roads, carriers, and drivers) that, along with vehicle configuration, can influence observed differences in accident rates among classes of trucks.

COMPARATIVE ACCIDENT RATES

Scott and O'Day (1)

Data furnished by the Indiana Toll Road Commission were used to compare the accident experiences of tractor-semitrailers and double trailer trucks (mainly turnpike doubles) operating on the Indiana Toll Road during 1966–1970. Of the two truck types, tractor-semitrailers were much more extensively used than doubles, and doubles experienced only 14 accident involvements. After determining that the upper 95-percent confidence limit for the doubles accident rate was below the estimate for tractor-semitrailers, the authors concluded that doubles had a significantly lower accident involvement rate than tractor-semitrailers. They suggested that the special

304

permit requirements placed on doubles use might have influenced their performance.

A second deficiency of this study, in addition to the limited exposure of doubles, was that doubles were not identified specifically by the toll records. After soliciting the opinion of toll road officials, the authors concluded that the number of doubles was equivalent to the sum of the number of six-axle commercial vehicles and one-fourth of the number of "special oversized or unusual vehicles."

Although this is not a pivotal study and its results may have been biased by limited use and uncertain identification of doubles, it was among the first to demonstrate that larger doubles can be operated reasonably safely on turnpikes.

FHWA Review (2)

In a comprehensive review of the safety and economic aspects of increased vehicle size and weight, FHWA solicited accident and exposure data from two large interstate motor carriers operating in western states, Consolidated Freightways (1964–1968) and Pacific Intermountain Express (1965–1968). Because each carrier made significant use of both tractor-semitrailers and twins, possible bias from an inadequate exposure base was eliminated. Although statistical tests were not employed, the accident record of twins was obviously superior to that of tractor-semitrailers.

The FHWA-reported finding of the superiority of twins is seriously weakened by failure to identify similarities and differences in the operational environments of the two truck types and by failure to validate the carrier-reported data.

Because both carriers are rather large, it can be assumed that they served diverse markets and possibly employed the two truck types in different ways, on different roadway environments, or in different geographical areas. Available information is too incomplete to judge whether the accident differences that were attributed to truck configuration might have been due instead to other uncontrolled factors. A second consideration is whether the data may have been reported in ways best serving the self-interests of the carriers. This caveat is perhaps too frequently issued and too infrequently tested, but it nevertheless raises questions in interpreting the significance of carrier-reported data.

Carrier-reported accident data were found to be unreliable in a study reported by Campbell and Carsten (3):

> When the accident rates for the study fleets were tabulated it became clear that there were large differences in completeness of reporting.

> Some large Common carriers reported accident rates for their intercity
> tractors that were very much in line with the predicted levels. . . .
> Other Common carriers, however, reported rates for intercity tractors
> that were so low as to strain credibility. . . . An examination of the
> accident data on a case by case basis for one fleet showed that we
> had received reports on only those accidents that met the BMCS
> threshold. . . . Minor accidents were left out entirely, yet the same
> company later released figures indicating a far greater number of
> accidents.

> The tabulation of rates for municipal fleets revealed similar variation
> in data quality. . . .

> Many fleets, fearing damage to their reputations if data were leaked,
> were clearly reluctant to report all their accidents. Others found the
> collection of the data to be too much of a burden on their time. But
> whatever the reasons the data were clearly too unreliable to perform
> their intended purpose. . . .

Fleischer and Philipson (4)

The University of California Traffic Safety Center conducted a study
primarily to evaluate both the available data base and associated statistical
techniques for analyzing commercial vehicle accidents. The roadway system for which data were accumulated consisted of all Interstate, U.S.,
and state roads (and certain adjacent county roads as well) in two areas
of California, one centered on Sacramento and the other on Los Angeles.
The study period extended for about 12 months during 1975–1976, and
the accident data base was built primarily from 3,000 California Highway
Patrol accident reports. Commercial vehicles were divided into a number
of subsets on the basis of their configuration, number of axles, and vehicle
weight. For each subset, both direct and "induced" exposure estimates
were made. The direct estimates involved linear extrapolations of basic
commercial vehicle count data obtained from average annual daily traffic
(AADT) and truck weight studies. The induced estimates were based on
assumptions relative to other data obtained from the accident reports themselves.

The most prevalent twins and tractor-semitrailer subsets included
five-axle trucks weighing in excess of 25,000 lb. For these, the vehicle
involvement rates (per million vehicle miles) for accidents of all types
were larger for tractor-semitrailers than for twins, and there were rather
large differences between the two different techniques for estimating
exposure (4):

Vehicle Weight (lb)	Vehicle Involvement Rate by Type of Exposure			
	Direct		Induced	
	Twins	Tractor-Semitrailer	Twins	Tractor-Semitrailer
25,001–60,000	0.83	1.8	0.95	1.2
60,001 or more	1.4	2.1	0.99	1.0

The authors were unable to determine which of the two techniques yielded the more accurate estimates.

The primary deficiency of the foregoing comparisons is probably the uncertainty in the truck exposure estimates, although there is no convincing evidence of bias toward either twins or tractor-semitrailers. Because police accident reports were used, there was doubtless an underrepresentation of property-damage-only accidents in the accident data base. Although reported accident involvement rates would then be smaller than actual ones, validity of the truck configuration comparisons might not be seriously undermined. Finally, control was not made for the wide range in road types and locations, a deficiency whose impact on the validity of the comparison is unknown.

Campbell and Carsten (3)

In this comprehensive study designed to evaluate the safety consequences of Federal Motor Vehicle Safety Standard 121, Air Brake Systems, determination of the accident experiences of tractor-semitrailers and twins was a by-product of the main investigation.

For nationwide intercity operations, the ratio of the fatal accident involvement rate of twins to that of tractor-semitrailers was found to be 1.46 (1976–1978 accident data from NHTSA's Fatal Accident Reporting System). Differences were even more pronounced in the comparisons of casualty (nonfatal and fatal) accident involvement rates for nationwide intercity ICC-authorized carrier operations. Here, the ratio of twins rate to tractor-semitrailer rate was found to be 2.64 [1976–1977 Bureau of Motor Carrier Safety (BMCS) accident data]. The authors concluded that twin trailer trucks appeared to be overinvolved in both injury and fatal accidents in comparison with tractor-semitrailers.

Following a review of data published later by the Bureau of the Census, Campbell (5) determined that the original exposure estimates for twins were too low, thereby inflating their estimated accident involvement rates. By chance, the method used to obtain a representative sample for the purpose of studying brakes had underrepresented regions of the country within which the majority of twins was registered. Campbell concluded that, except for data for 1977 model-year tractors, the Campbell and Carsten study (3) should not be used to compare accident involvement rates for twins and tractor-semitrailers.

For 1977 model-year tractors used in intercity operations throughout the nation during 1977 and 1978, the fatal-accident involvement rates for twins and tractor-semitrailers were 2.8 and 5.9 fatal-accident involvements per 100 million vehicle-mi, respectively. For 1977 model-year tractors used in intercity operations of ICC-authorized carriers throughout the nation during 1977, the casualty accident involvement rates for twins and tractor-semitrailers were 40.6 and 52.5 casualty-accident involvements per 100 million vehicle-mi, respectively.

Although these data show a distinct superiority in both the fatal- and casualty-accident experiences of twins, the sample from which twins accident rates were estimated was too limited to yield conclusive findings. Not only were twins involved in only 14 fatal accidents and 82 casualty accidents, but the nationwide exposure estimates were apparently based on the operations of only about 90 twins, each recorded for only 2 days during the last 4 months of 1978.

Popoff (6)

Twins and tractor-semitrailers were compared on the basis of 1980 involvements in all types of accidents on the provincial highways of Saskatchewan. The accident data base was constructed from police accident reports, and exposure estimates were obtained from the Planning Branch of the Department of Highways and Transportation. The overall accident involvement rate for twins was less than that for tractor-semitrailers, but although he concluded that there was no overinvolvement of twins, Popoff cautioned that the twins sample was small and subject to statistical variance.

Popoff also observed that twins had a large incidence of single-vehicle accidents. He noted that additional in-depth study would be required to ascertain whether the operational characteristics of twins were responsible for this pattern.

Iowa Department of Transportation (7)

In support of its investigation of the impact of 65-ft twins on highway safety in Iowa, the Iowa Department of Transportation collected accident and exposure data from 15 major interstate carriers. Based on 1974 operations, the average accident rates were reported to be 3.02 and 2.57

accidents per million vehicle miles for tractor-semitrailers and twins, respectively. The total number of accidents for each vehicle type exceeded 1,000, and the difference in accident rates between the two vehicle types was judged to be not significant. The average fatality rates were reported to be 3.81 and 6.17 deaths per 100 million vehicle-mi for tractor-semitrailers and twins, respectively. Because of the relative sparsity of fatalities (14 for tractor-semitrailer accidents and 34 for twins accidents), however, the difference in fatality rates was judged to be not significant.

Because of inadequate documentation, assessment of the possible validity of these accident rates is impossible. Unknowns include the regions served by the several carriers, the kinds of highways over which the trucks were operated, and all other characteristics of the operating environment. Furthermore, there is no indication of attempts having been made to validate the carrier-reported data.

The Iowa investigation also included some limited accident data for Iowa and for Missouri as well as accident data that had been previously published elsewhere. An inquiry to transportation officials in 28 states where 65-ft twins had been operating generated 12 responses to the effect that no increase in accidents had been noticed following state legalization of 65-ft twins. Responses from the remaining 16 states were either not submitted or were classified "unknown." It was concluded that 65-ft twins had not been shown to be less safe than conventional tractor-semitrailers.

Chirachavala and O'Day (8)

The accident data for this study were taken from accidents reported to BMCS for 1977, and exposure estimates were based on the 1977 Truck Inventory and Use Survey of the Bureau of the Census. By limiting the analysis to intercity operations of ICC-authorized carriers, it was possible to devise roughly comparable results of accidents and travel from the two data sources.

Perhaps the most significant finding was that the overall accident involvement rates for tractor-semitrailers and twins were essentially the same. In addition to vehicle configuration, two other factors were examined in depth—trailer type and trip length. Using multivariate analysis techniques, these investigators found that all pairwise interactions among these three factors were significant in explaining accident rates but that the most important single factor was trip length, followed in order of importance by trailer type and configuration. This finding emphasizes the necessity for controlling for the effects of other significant factors in configuration studies.

The primary weakness of this study results from the data that were employed. The BMCS accident data are carrier reported and may be subject to reporting bias. In addition, accidents involving intrastate carriers and noncasualty accidents involving property damage totaling less than $2,000 are not reported. The study findings would have been strengthened by a separate analysis of casualty accidents, those likely to have been most accurately reported by the involved carriers. The 1977 Truck Inventory and Use data are a small sample, containing fewer than 300 twins. Efforts to estimate nationwide quantities from this sample have been difficult and controversial. Chirachavala and O'Day emphasized that the absolute values of the accident rates that they reported were not well determined but suggested that the rates would be meaningful for comparative purposes.

In summary, this study is methodologically sound and comprehensive. Although its findings are weakened by inadequacies in the accident and exposure data, the effect of these inadequacies is less important for the kinds of comparative analyses conducted than for determination of absolute accident rates.

Glennon (*9*)

On two occasions, Glennon has compared for purposes of litigation the accident experiences of tractor-semitrailers and twins when each type was operated under nearly identical roadway and environmental conditions. Because the principal findings of the two studies were similar, only those of the more recent and more thorough investigation are reported here. Accident and exposure data were furnished by Consolidated Freightways for approximately 305,000 matched-pair runs of tractor-semitrailers and twins during 1976–1980. Each pair of vehicles was operated on the same day and over identical routes—predominantly in midwestern states. Although some two-lane and city roads were included, the routes were largely Interstates and other main interurban highways.

The small difference in accident involvement rate (Table F-1) was determined to be not statistically signficant. When tractor-semitrailers and twins were compared on the basis of average number of injuries per accident, no statistically significant difference was observed between the two truck types.

The Glennon investigation is noteworthy for its extraordinary control for the effects of variables other than configuration. Not only were roadway and environmental conditions similar for the two configurations, but subsequent testing also revealed similar driver age and accident experience as well as similar proportions of day and night operations. Maintenance

TABLE F-1 Accident Data for Consolidated Freightways Matched-Pair Analysis (9)

Truck Type	No. of Accidents of All Types	Vehicle Miles of Travel ($\times 10^6$)	Accident Involvement Rate per Million Vehicle Miles
Tractor-semitrailer	198	107.6	1.84
Twins	211	107.6	1.96

and operational practices as well as equipment purchasing specifications were nearly identical for the two truck types.

Glennon's study has been faulted in legal proceedings concerning twin trailer trucks on the grounds that the study unnecessarily excluded some of the available semitrailer travel and accident data in the procedure followed to select the matched pairs of twins and tractor-semitrailers runs that formed the basis for comparisons (10). This criticism is valid insofar as the analysis apparently failed to attain the minimum possible statistical uncertainty in its estimates with the data available, but the procedure did not bias the twins-versus-tractor-semitrailers comparison either against or in favor of twins.

Glennon's principal finding of similarity in the accident experiences of tractor-semitrailers and twins generally applies to large general commodity carriers transporting mixed freight in over-the-road operations on main highways. Because the analysis offers no insights into the effects of operational environment on the relative accident experiences of tractor-semitrailers and twins, the extent to which the finding can be generalized to other types of operations is unknown.

Yoo, Reiss, and McGee (11)

The primary purpose of the study by Yoo, Reiss, and McGee was to compare accident and severity rates of tractor-semitrailers and twins. The roadway system of interest included 97,000 rural roads and urban freeways in California. Accident data for 1974 were obtained from the California Highway Patrol. Because of uncertainties in the reporting of property-damage-only accidents, only the study's results concerning casualty accidents are described in this summary. The total vehicle miles of travel for twins and tractor-semitrailers were developed from FHWA estimates for all state roads and California Department of Transportation estimates for California state highways. This total was apportioned to the two vehicle types on the basis of their relative appearance at 15 vehicle counting stations located throughout the state.

On the basis of their complete analysis, the investigators concluded that there was no statistically significant difference in the total accident rates but that the operation of twins resulted in a significantly larger number of deaths per million vehicle miles of travel ("As Reported" data in Table F-2).

One questionable assumption in developing exposure estimates was that the relative proportions of tractor-semitrailers and twins on the study roadways (98 percent rural) were the same as the averages at 15 counting stations (73 percent rural). An alternative assumption not investigated in the study is that the relative proportions on the study roadways were the same as the average at the 11 rural counting stations. When exposure estimates are recomputed in accordance with this second assumption, the twins accident record relative to that of tractor-semitrailers is improved (Table F-2). Although the second method for computing exposure is intuitively appealing because of its use of rural classification data to characterize composition of the traffic stream on the predominantly rural study network, a proper choice between the two methods would have required the acquisition and analysis of additional field data.

Possible differences in the predominant operational environments for the two truck configurations were not investigated. However, because of the extensive use of twins in California, such differences might be expected to be of less significance than in other states within which the use of twins might be more specialized. Unfortunately, the unique character of the

TABLE F-2 Relative Accident Experience on Rural Roads and Urban Freeways in California (*11*)

Accident Measure per Million Vehicle Miles	Ratio of Accident Rate for Twins Versus That for Tractor-Semitrailers	
	As Reported	Adjusted[a]
Vehicle involvements		
Casualty accidents	1.04	0.94
Nonfatal injury accidents	1.03	0.93
Fatal accidents	1.16	1.05
Casualties	1.02	0.92
Nonfatal injuries	1.00	0.90
Deaths	1.42[b]	1.28

[a]Data from the four urban counting stations were disregarded in the exposure calculations.
[b]Deaths per million vehicle miles was the only measure in which the difference between twins and tractor-semitrailers was found to be statistically significant.

population of twins in California prevents unqualified extrapolation of the findings of this and other California studies to other regions.

BMCS Report (*12*)

BMCS has conducted three special surveys of a panel of interstate carriers known to operate twins in an attempt to document their safety experiences. For both tractor-semitrailers and twins, each carrier provided information on number of vehicles operated, vehicle miles of travel, number of accidents, number of injuries, number of deaths, and amount of property damage. The three studies covered the periods of 1969–1973, 1974–1976, and 1977–1980 and produced one of the largest of the available data bases. Altogether 12 carriers participated in the surveys but only 3 were represented in all studies. Gross accident rates for the 12-year period are not particularly useful because they mask (a) extreme variability among the responses of the individual carriers, (b) unknown effects of the varying operational environments, and (c) large size differences among the carriers. The gross accident rates per million vehicle miles from these special surveys are as follows (*12*):

	Accident Rate by Truck Type	
Accident Type	*Twins*	*Tractor-Semitrailer*
Casualty	0.56	0.82
Death	0.053	0.055

In an attempt to control for unknown but possibly significant external effects, further analysis of the BMCS carrier panel data has been conducted specifically for the Twin Trailer Truck Monitoring Study. The accident experiences of twins and tractor-semitrailers were first compared for each carrier in each of the three reporting periods. Of the total of 21 carrier periods, complete data were available for only 16. This number was further reduced by selecting the 10 carrier periods for which the annual mileage per vehicle was similar for the two truck configurations. In the six cases thus eliminated, the carriers reported drastically different annual utilization for the two truck types (annual miles per twin were from 64 percent to 454 percent higher than annual miles per tractor-semitrailer in the same carrier period), and accident rates were typically much greater for that truck type with the smaller annual utilization (Figure F-1). Presumably the difference in annual mileage between tractor-semitrailers and twins in these six cases reflects very different operating conditions for the two

314

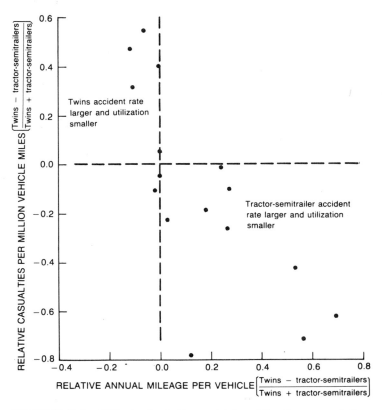

FIGURE F-1   Effect of relative vehicle utilization on relative casualty rate (*12*).

vehicle types. In the remaining 10 carrier periods, twins exhibited slightly higher accident rates per million vehicle miles than tractor-semitrailers:

	Accident Rate by Truck Type	
		Tractor-
Accident Type	*Twins*	*Semitrailer*
Casualty	0.65	0.60
Death	0.059	0.049

The significance of this finding is tempered by possible carrier reporting biases and by imprecision in the attempt to control for confounding effects of different operational environments. Further, there is doubtless a regional bias because twins have been operated more extensively in midwestern and western states than elsewhere. Finally, the average rates conceal the wide variability observed among the reporting carriers.

Graf and Archuleta (13)

Another California study was undertaken in response to the 1982 Surface Transportation Assistance Act and the need for a more accurate understanding of the relative accident experience of three types of large trucks: straight trucks, single-trailer combination trucks, and double-trailer combination trucks. Nearly all single-trailer combination trucks in California are tractor-semitrailers, and nearly all double-trailer combination trucks are twins. Comparisons were limited to 18 road segments (totaling 716 mi in length) selected so that each included a truck weigh site to maximize accuracy of the exposure estimates. A large accident data base was developed for the 5-year study period (1979–1983) from the Statewide Integrated Traffic Records System of the California Highway Patrol: Altogether there were 3,961 single-trailer accident involvements and 1,294 double-trailer involvements.

In comparing single-trailer and double-trailer combination trucks, little overall difference was found in their total accident involvement rates and in their casualty-accident involvement rates. Double-trailer combination trucks, on the other hand, exhibited fatal-accident involvement rates approximately 25 percent greater than those of single-trailer combinations, a finding diminished in significance by sample-size limitations (the data include only 40 double-trailer fatal involvements).

Separate comparisons were also made between rural and urban segments and between freeway and nonfreeway segments. Results of this second-tier analysis were not revealing, and the authors attached little significance to those differences in accident involvement rates that were in apparent contradiction to the general findings summarized earlier. A larger data base, particularly one containing more nonfreeway segments, might have enabled more definitive findings regarding the effects of location and highway type on the relative accident experience of single and double trailers.

When the travel and accident experience at the sites is aggregated by simply summing involvements and vehicle miles at all the sites for each vehicle type and computing rates as the ratio of the sum of involvements to the sum of miles traveled, the resulting ratios of double-trailer to single-trailer involvement rates are as follows:

	Fatal Accidents	Casualty Accidents	All Accidents
Rural segments (12 sites)	1.06	1.11	1.24
Urban segments (6 sites)	2.21	0.78	0.76

However, the 18 sites are not a random sample of California roads (they are sites where travel data happen to be available), and any method of aggregating the results at each site is to some extent arbitrary.[1] The simple summation method just described has the drawback that if double-trailer travel is distributed differently among the road segments than is single-trailer travel, the ratios of rates reflect not only differences between the two vehicle types but also differences among the road segments that influence accident rates. For example, if double trailers and single trailers were equally safe but double trailers traveled a larger fraction of their miles on roads that are dangerous for all vehicles, then double trailers would have the higher accident rate.

One method of aggregating sites that is unaffected by differences between vehicle types in the distribution of travel among the road segments is to compute a weighted average accident rate for each vehicle type, with the weight assigned to each site equal to the total double-trailer plus single-trailer miles traveled at that site. With this method of aggregation, the ratios of double-trailer to single-trailer involvement rates are as follows:

	Fatal Accidents	Casualty Accidents	All Accidents
Rural segments	0.93	1.03	1.12
Urban segments	2.29	0.82	0.79

These ratios are a better indication of the relative safety of twins and tractor-semitrailers than the ratios resulting from the simple summation of sites shown earlier. Although use of other weights could also be defended, this method of aggregation has several advantages: the comparative rates are not affected by differences in the roads on which double trailers and single trailers travel, greater weight is given to sites where statistical uncertainty in the accident rates is less, and more weight tends to be given to roads with greater combination-truck traffic.

---

[1] Another basis for comparison would be the number of sites at which the double-trailer all-accidents involvement rate was higher than the single-trailer rate. Among the 12 rural sites, doubles had the higher rate at 6. Among the 6 urban sites, the doubles rate was higher at 1.

317

Perhaps the major strength of the study by Graf and Archuleta is its attempt to control for possible confounding effects of the operating environment by focusing on the 18 specific road segments and presenting comparative accident and exposure statistics for each segment. In addition, the sample size was relatively large, and care greater than that normally exercised was taken to assure accurate exposure estimates. Inability to distinguish between semitrailers and full trailers and between trailer body types is an unfortunate limitation of the study. Confidence in the validity of the study findings would be strengthened had the exposure estimates been based on volume and classification information collected during the entire 5-year period rather than for only 1 year. Finally, statistical testing might have proven useful for isolating actual truck configuration effects from possibly spurious accident patterns.

Despite its limitations, this study adds valuable insight into the comparative safety effects of tractor-semitrailer and twins operations.

Manning (14)

In reviewing Idaho's experience with extra-length combination trucks, Manning presented accident rates on rural state highways during 1982. For both Interstate and non-Interstate highways, multitrailer vehicles (twins, longer doubles, and triple-trailer combination trucks) were less frequently involved in injury accidents (ratio of multitrailer to single-trailer accident rates of approximately 0.78). At the same time, multitrailer units were more frequently involved in accidents of all levels of severity. The ratios of multitrailer to single-trailer accident rates (all accidents) were approximately 1.28 and 1.44 for Interstate and non-Interstate highways, respectively.

Because the longer doubles and triples were restricted to designated routes and controlled by a special permit process, their contribution to the multitrailer accident experience is likely to have been greater on Interstate than on non-Interstate highways. The smaller twins, which had been allowed on all state highways for many years, are likely to have dominated the non-Interstate statistics.

Because of the brevity of Manning's presentation and the fact that the accident rates of twins were not isolated, the importance of the 1982 Idaho accident statistics to the current critique is difficult to assess. Perhaps of more importance was the observation that operation of the twins was "relatively compatible with highways through mountainous terrain and with most of the newer access ramps."

Zeiszler (15)

In many ways, the Zeiszler study was similar to the later study by Yoo, Reiss, and McGee (11). The roadway system consisted of rural roads and incorporated freeways in California. Accident rates were based on casualty accidents occurring during the latter half of 1972 and identified in the statewide accident record system. Vehicle travel estimates were obtained from the Design Department of the Division of Highways.

In the comparison of involvement rates for casualty accidents, there was little difference between twins and tractor-semitrailers (Table F-3). Zeiszler concluded that both twins and tractor-semitrailers were under-represented in the accident pattern and that "the double is at least as safe as the tractor semi-trailer."

Zeiszler's findings must be considered somewhat weaker than those of Yoo, Reiss, and McGee. The study period was smaller, and the exposure estimates are more suspect. In particular, it was apparently assumed, without verification, that "each vehicle type travels an equal number of miles." Such an assumption confounded the task of establishing absolute accident rate levels and reduced the validity of comparisons between the two truck types. Like the study by Yoo, Reiss, and McGee, possible differences in the operational environments were not investigated.

Vallette et al. (16)

One of the most ambitious studies of the relative safety of tractor-semi-trailers and twins was performed by BioTechnology, Inc. (BioTech) for FHWA. Designed as a comprehensive investigation of the impact of truck size, weight, and configuration on highway safety, accident and exposure data were collected over a 1½-year period during 1976 to 1978 for 1,058 mi of roadway in six states. Evaluation of the configuration issue was dominated by sites in California and Nevada.

TABLE F-3 Accident and Exposure Data for Rural Roads and Incorporated Freeways in California (15)

Truck Type	Vehicle Miles of Travel ($\times 10^6$)	No. of Casualty Accidents	Involvement Rate in Casualty Accidents per Million Vehicle Miles
Twins	686	352	0.51
Tractor-semitrailer	1,300	609	0.48

A major finding was that twins had a significantly larger total accident involvement rate than tractor-semitrailers. However, no statistically significant differences were evident in the involvement rates for casualty accidents. Because of the controversial nature of its principal findings, the BioTech study has generated heated debate and critical review. One such review was conducted by the Transportation Systems Center (*17*), which found that the BioTech conclusion that twins had a substantially larger accident involvement rate than tractor-semitrailers was reasonable and that known biases in the data base were probably not great enough to invalidate this result. At the same time, the Center concluded that "the BioTech report has serious deficiencies in presentation of basic data, documentation of methods, and major findings."

A second, independent review was performed by Midwest Research Institute (*18,19*). This review alleged a large number of critically substandard aspects of the BioTech work. By far the most damaging claim was that the exposure data on which rate calculations were based "contained flaws and biases of a magnitude so large as to render these data essentially useless." The specific criticisms are detailed and multiple but in general may be summarized as follows:

- Data on which exposure calculations were based were often collected at locations not representative of travel conditions throughout the accident segment.
- Much of the exposure data was collected for travel in a single direction, but many sites demonstrated distinct and significant directional biases.
- The exposure data were not based on a sample that represented long-term average conditions, and appropriate procedures were not employed to eliminate temporal biases, including day and night and seasonal effects.
- Raw vehicle classification data on which exposure estimates were based required adjustments to eliminate bias due to the varying number of axles on different vehicle types: these necessary adjustments were not made.
- Errors and inconsistencies in the vehicle classification data base and incompatibilities with manual classification data collected by California suggest considerable difficulty in generating an accurate vehicle classification profile from the photographic record, as attempted by BioTech.

The review concluded by rejecting the BioTech finding that twins had demonstrated a substantially larger accident involvement rate than tractor-semitrailers.

Midwest Research Institute's examination of the raw classification count data base and the overall thoroughness of its review add weight to its principal finding relative to the contradictory conclusion of the Transportation Systems Center. The two independent reviews concurred, however, in their documentation of deficiencies sufficiently serious to suggest that the BioTech study did not meet the standards of reasonable scientific inquiry. Therefore, the BioTech findings are judged to be of little or no validity and to offer no insight into the relative safety of twins and tractor-semitrailers.

Arthur D. Little, Inc. (20)

A study done in 1974 has sometimes been cited in evaluations of the truck configuration issue. In particular, accident and exposure data for Ohio Turnpike operations were analyzed and reported as follows (20):

> Direct inquiries to the Ohio Turnpike Commission yielded accident data that corroborated the Indiana experience. From January 18, 1960 through August, 1973, tandem trailer units have accumulated a total of 36,667,000 miles on the Ohio Turnpike and have been involved in 28 accidents, yielding a rate of 0.76 accident per million vehicle miles. In contrast, the rate for all trucks on this turnpike (based on 1968-72 data) is 1.39 accidents per million vehicle miles.

Unfortunately, this information is of limited utility because there is no definition of "truck" and a comparable accident rate for tractor-semitrailers was not determined. Although it may be justifiably concluded that doubles were more safely operated on the Ohio Turnpike than the entire population of trucks, this may reflect less on the safety of the doubles configuration and more on the conditions of their operation. Doubles operations were permitted only by established trucking companies and only by drivers who were approved on the basis of safety record.

Results of the Arthur D. Little study have not been added to the summary in Table F-4 simply because comparative accident rates for both tractor-semitrailers and doubles were not determined.

Summary

The relative accident rates of twins and tractor-semitrailers as reported by the several studies are extremely variable and conflicting: the rate for twins ranged from about one-half that for tractor-semitrailers to several times as large (Table F-4). Perhaps such a large difference should not be surprising: the trucks often differed with respect to such important characteristics as the number of axles and trailer type, they were operated on a range of highway types in different geographical regions, and the data were often limited both in accuracy and quantity. Thus, selectivity is demanded in judging which of the results from prior studies are most useful.

Four of the studies with obvious limitations are the following:

● Scott and O'Day (*1*): The doubles population on the Indiana Toll Road was not representative of the small twins, and accidents involving doubles were very small in number.

● FHWA review (*2*) and Iowa Department of Transportation (*7*): Documentation was insufficient for a reasonable evaluation and interpretation of carrier-reported data, and apparently no effort was made to validate these data.

● Vallette et al. (*16*): Study findings can be discounted largely because the exposure estimates were found to be unreliable.

Of the remaining studies, the most valuable are those in which attempts have been made to minimize the obscuring effects of the operating environment. The most reliable studies in this regard are the following:

● Chirachavala and O'Day (*8*): Reasonable similarity between roadway types, temporal distribution of operations, commodity types and densities, and carrier operating practices was achieved by limiting comparisons to intercity operations of van trailers by ICC-authorized carriers.

● Glennon (*9*): Matched-pair study design, concentration of movements on main intercity highways, and validation of similar day and night distribution of operations and similar driver age and operational experience indicate exceptional control for effects of operating environment.

● Yoo, Reiss, and McGee (*11*): Although no effort was made to control for possible differences in the operating environments for the two truck configurations, in the aggregate such differences are likely to be small in California because of the extensive use of a wide variety of twins there.

● BMCS (*12*): The BMCS data are much less amenable to control for effects of operating environment than the foregoing three studies. However, limitation to over-the-road movements by carriers operating both twins and tractor-semitrailers and similarly utilizing the two truck types (as suggested by similar annual mileage per vehicle) suggests reasonable similarity in operational missions, carrier operating practices, and roadway types.

● Graf and Archuleta (*13*): Control for possible effects of operating environment was achieved by the analysis of 18 distinct roadway segments for which reliable accident and exposure estimates could be made.

TABLE F-4 Summary of Comparative Accident Rate Investigations

Data Source	Date	Ratio of Vehicle Involvement Rate of Twins Versus That of Tractor-Semitrailers			Comments
		Fatal Accidents	Casualty Accidents	All Accidents	
Indiana Toll Road Commission (1)	1966–1970	—	—	0.49	Limited data, five-axle twins not evaluated
Consolidated Freightways, western states (2)	1964–1968	—	—	0.60	Insufficient documentation, unvalidated carrier data
Pacific Intermountain Express, western states (2)	1965–1968	—	—	0.79	Insufficient documentation, unvalidated carrier data
Main roads, two areas of California (4)	1975–1976	—	—	0.46–0.99	Possible operational differences, uncertain exposure estimates, findings preliminary
Nationwide intercity, 1977 model-year tractors (3)	1977–1978	0.48	—	—	Limited data
Nationwide intercity, ICC-authorized carriers, 1977 model-year tractors (3)	1977	—	0.77	—	Limited data
Provincial highways, Saskatchewan (6)	1980	—	—	0.82	Limited data, possible operational differences, findings preliminary
Interstate carriers (7)	1974	1.62	—	0.85	Insufficient documentation, unvalidated carrier data
Nationwide intercity van trailers, ICC-authorized carriers (8)	1977	—	—	0.98	
Consolidated Freightways, nationwide (9)	1976–1980	—	—	1.06	
Rural roads and urban freeways, California (adjusted) (11)	1974	1.05	0.94	—	
Rural roads and urban freeways, California (as reported) (11)	1974	1.16	1.04	—	

Data Source	Date	Ratio of Vehicle Involvement Rate of Twins Versus That of Tractor-Semitrailers			Comments
		Fatal Accidents	Casualty Accidents	All Accidents	
Nationwide interstate carriers (12)	1969–1980	1.20[a]	1.08[b]	—	Possible operational differences, five-axle twins not evaluated separately, insufficient documentation
Rural roads, California (13)	1979–1983	0.93	1.03	1.12	
Urban roads, California (13)	1979–1983	2.29	0.82	0.79	
Rural state highways, Idaho (14)	1982	—	0.78[c]	1.28–1.44[c]	
Rural roads and incorporated freeways, California (15)	1972	—	1.06	—	Questionable exposure estimates, possible operational differences
Urban freeways, California and Nevada[d] (16)	1976–1977	—	0.93	1.81	Unreliable exposure estimates
Rural freeways, California and Nevada[d] (16)	1976–1977	—	2.88	2.07	Unreliable exposure estimates
Urban nonfreeways, California and Nevada[d] (16)	1976–1977	—	1.11	4.60	Unreliable exposure estimates
Rural nonfreeways, California and Nevada[d] (16)	1976–1977	—	6.15	4.73	Unreliable exposure estimates

NOTE: The shaded portion of this table contains those studies that were generally better designed and executed and that had the most reliable results.

[a]Ratio of average number of deaths per million vehicle miles for 10 carrier periods.

[b]Ratio of average number of casualties per million vehicle miles for 10 carrier periods.

[c]Twins category includes all trucks and truck-tractors with two or more trailers.

[d]May have included additional states.

Results of these five studies indicate a much smaller difference between the accident involvement rates of twins and tractor-semitrailers than does the range of results from the entire collection of studies.

Of the remaining six studies identified in Table F-4, only three presented findings in apparent contradiction with the foregoing—Fleischer and Philipson (4), Campbell and Carsten (3), and Manning (14). None of these incorporated adequate control for operational effects, and each suffered from one or more other deficiences such as inadequate sample size, inadequate documentation, and questionable exposure estimates. In two of the three studies (3,4), the comparison of twins and tractor-semitrailers was simply an incidental by-product of the main investigation. Accordingly, the apparent contradiction between these three studies and the most reliable studies cited earlier is not compelling.

EFFECTS OF OPERATING ENVIRONMENT

The accident experience of large trucks is greatly influenced by the environment within which they are operated. Because the predominant operating environments of tractor-semitrailers and twins have been different in response both to their unique operational capabilities and to governmental regulation and control, accident comparisons must attempt to isolate the effects of truck configuration from those of the operating environment.

Characteristics of the operating environment that influence the accident experience of large trucks include the following:

1. Highway type
   a. The death rate and the casualty accident involvement rate are greater for two- and three-lane highways than for freeways (21).
   b. The total accident involvement rate is greater for non-federal-aid highways than for federal-aid highways (2).
   c. The total accident involvement rate is greater for rural two-lane primary highways than for rural Interstate highways (22).
   d. Accidents on two-lane rural highways are more severe than those on four-lane rural highways (23).
   e. Accidents on undivided rural highways are more severe than those on divided rural highways (24).
   f. The odds of occurrence of a high-severity injury are greater on conventional highways than on freeways or expressways (25).
2. Highway location
   a. The total accident involvement rate is greater on urban highways than on rural highways (2).

    b. The death rate and casualty-accident involvement rate are greater for rural highways than for urban highways (*21*).

    c. Accidents on rural highways are more severe than those on urban highways (*23*).

3.   Time of day: Nighttime accidents are more severe than daytime accidents (*22,24*).

4.   Trip distance: Fatal- and injury-accident involvement rates are greater for local movements than for intercity movements (*3*).

5.   Cab style

    a. The fatal-accident involvement rate is greater for cab-over-engine tractors than for conventional tractors (*3*).

    b. Accidents involving cab-over-engine tractors are significantly more likely to result in a fatality or major injury than those involving conventional tractors (*25*).

6.   Fleet size: The fatal-accident involvement rate is greater for small fleets than for large fleets (*3*).

7.   Carrier type: Fatal- and injury-accident involvement rates are greater for ICC-authorized carriers than for nonauthorized carriers (*3*).

8.   Driver age: Younger truck drivers are involved in a disproportionately high percentage of accidents (*26*).

Historically, the operations of twins and tractor-semitrailers have differed in many ways, of which the following may have been reflected either directly or indirectly in the accident records. In comparison with tractor-semitrailers,

- Twins have made slightly more extensive use of multilane highways (*8,17*); A greater proportion of twins mileage has been accumulated on divided highways (*8*);
- A slightly greater proportion of twins mileage has been in long-range operations (*8,27*);
- Twins use has been more geographically concentrated, particularly in western and midwestern states (*8,27*);
- Twins have utilized a larger proportion of cab-over-engine tractors and a much smaller proportion of short and medium-sized conventional tractors (*8,27,28*);
- Twins use has been somewhat more uniformly distributed throughout the 24 hr of the day, and a greater proportion of their mileage has been accumulated during the night (*8,29*);
- Twins have been more extensively utilized as indicated by a larger annual per-vehicle mileage (*8,12,27*);
- Twins have been more heavily laden (*2,28,30-33*);

● A larger proportion of twins mileage has been with van trailers and a smaller proportion with tanker and platform trailers (8); and

● Twins have carried a larger share of mixed cargo (general freight) and a much smaller share of heavy cargo (8).[1]

Most prior studies have failed to adequately separate the effects on accident patterns of truck configuration from those of the operational environment. As a result, it is often unclear whether the reported accident patterns are more a consequence of configuration or of different operational environments.

A preliminary assessment of the interactive effects of truck configuration and operational environment has been reported by Chirachavala and O'Day (8). Interactive effects of configuration, trip length, and trailer type were investigated. Trip length was found to be the most important of the three factors in explaining variations in accident rates, followed in decreasing order of importance by trailer type and truck configuration. All pairwise interactions among the three variables were also found to be significant. Although, as the authors suggested, nonsampling errors may have influenced these results, significant interactive effects are readily apparent:

| | Ratio of Twins Involvement Rate Versus Tractor-Semitrailer Involvement Rate by Trip Length | |
Trailer Type	Local	Intercity
Van	0.41	0.98
Tanker	—	1.43
Flatbed	—	2.47

Twins were much safer in pulling van trailers for local trips, whereas tractor-semitrailers were much safer in pulling flatbed trailers for intercity movements.

As a second illustration of interactive effects, data presented by BMCS (12) were subjected to further analysis. For the 16 carrier periods for which complete data were available, there was large variation not only in the relative accident experience of twins and tractor-semitrailers but also

---

[1]The exception is California, where twin tankers are commonly used for petroleum products, twin platforms or flatbeds are routinely used for agricultural products, and twin dump trailers are often used for rock, gravel, and other bulk commodities. See Tables 3-6 and 3-7 in Chapter 3.

in the annual vehicle utilization (miles per vehicle per year). The influence of relative vehicle utilization on relative accident rates is shown in Figure F-1. Although there is much scatter in the data, the overall tendency is obvious: The configuration that demonstrated the better accident experience was the one that was more extensively utilized.

To the extent that variations in annual mileage per vehicle may reflect variations in operational environment, these results, like those of Chirachavala and O'Day, support the conclusion that the relative safety of twins and tractor-semitrailers depends on the operational environment.

REFERENCES

1. R.E. Scott and J. O'Day. *Statistical Analysis of Truck Accident Involvements.* Report DOT-HS-800-627. University of Michigan Highway Safety Research Institute, Ann Arbor, Dec. 1971.

2. *Review of Safety and Economic Aspects of Increased Vehicle Sizes and Weights.* FHWA, U.S. Department of Transportation, Sept. 1969.

3. K.L. Campbell and O. Carsten. *Fleet Accident Evaluation of FMVSS 121.* Report UM-HSRI-81-9. University of Michigan Highway Safety Research Institute, Ann Arbor, March 1981.

4. G.A. Fleischer and L.L. Philipson. *Statistical Analyses of Commercial Vehicle Accident Factors*, Vol. 2: Summary Report. Report DOT-HS-803-419. Traffic Safety Center, University of Southern California, Los Angeles, Feb. 1978.

5. K.L. Campbell. Testimony in *Center for Auto Safety et al. v. Elizabeth H. Dole et al.*; *Consolidated Freightways et al. v. Elizabeth H. Dole et al.*, 83-3885 and 84-0136, U.S. District Court for the District of Columbia, affidavit dated Feb. 23, 1984.

6. A.J. Popoff. *Heavy Truck Involvement in Traffic Accidents.* Traffic Safety Engineering Branch, Saskatchewan Highways and Transportation, Regina, Saskatchewan, Canada, Nov. 1982.

7. *Sixty-Five Foot Twin Trailers on Iowa Highways: Perspective.* Division of Planning, Iowa Department of Transportation, Ames, April 1975.

8. T. Chirachavala and J. O'Day. *A Comparison of Accident Characteristics and Rates for Combination Vehicles with One or Two Trailers.* Report UM-HSRI-81-41. University of Michigan Highway Safety Research Institute, Ann Arbor, Aug. 1981.

9. J.C. Glennon. "Matched Pair Analysis." *Consolidated Freightways Corporation v. Larson et al.*, 81-1230, U.S. District Court, Middle District of Pennsylvania, Aug. 12, 1981.

10. Office of the Attorney General, Commonwealth of Pennsylvania. "Defendants' Post-Trial Proposed Findings of Fact and Conclusions of Law." *Consolidated Freightways Corporation v. Larson et al.*, 81-1230, U.S. District Court, Middle District of Pennsylvania, Aug. 12, 1981.

328

11. C.S. Yoo, M.L. Reiss, and H.W. McGee. *Comparison of California Accident Rates for Single and Double Tractor-Trailer Combination Trucks*. Report FHWA-RD-78-94. BioTechnology, Inc., Falls Church, Va., March 1978.

12. *Safety Comparison of Doubles Versus Tractor-Semitrailer Operation*. Bureau of Motor Carrier Safety, FHWA, U.S. Department of Transportation, June 1983.

13. V.S. Graf and K. Archuleta. *Truck Accidents by Classification*. California Department of Transportation, Sacramento, Feb. 1985.

14. D.V Manning. "Idaho's Experience with Extra Length Combinations." Presented at Meeting of American Association of State Highway and Transportation Officials, Denver, Colo., Oct. 3, 1983.

15. R. Zeiszler. *Accident Experience of Double Bottom Trucks in California*. Operational Analysis Section, California Highway Patrol, Sacramento, April 1973.

16. G.R. Vallette et al. *The Effect of Truck Size and Weight on Accident Experience and Traffic Operations*, Vol. 3: Accident Experience of Large Trucks. Report FHWA-RD-80-137. BioTechnology, Inc., Falls Church, Va., July 1981.

17. *Technical Evaluation of the BioTechnology, Inc. Study "The Effect of Truck Size and Weight on Accident Experience and Traffic Operations."* Transportation Systems Center, U.S. Department of Transportation, Cambridge, Mass., July 1981.

18. W.D. Glauz. *Analysis of BioTechnology Report*. Midwest Research Institute, Kansas City, Mo., undated.

19. W.D. Glauz and D.W. Harwood. Large Truck Accident Rates: Another Viewpoint. In *Transportation Research Record 1038*, TRB, National Research Council, Washington, D.C., 1985, pp. 17–25.

20. Little, A.D., Inc. *The Safety of High Gross Weight Trucks*. Massachusetts Construction Industry Council, May 1974.

21. R.N. Smith and E.L. Wilmot. *Truck Accident and Fatality Rates Calculated from California Highway Accident Statistics for 1980 and 1981*. Report SAND82-7066. Sandia National Laboratories, Albuquerque, N. Mex., Nov. 1982.

22. A.E.S. Radwan. *Characteristics of Heavy Truck Accidents*. Report JHRP-76-18. Joint Highway Research Project, Engineering Experiment Station, Purdue University, West Lafayette, Ind., June 1976.

23. J. Hedlund. *The Severity of Large Truck Accidents*. National Center for Statistics and Analysis, NHTSA, U.S. Department of Transportation, April 1977.

24. T. Chirachavala, D.E. Cleveland, and L.P. Kostyniuk. Severity of Large-Truck and Combination-Vehicle Accidents in Over-the-Road Service: A Discrete Multivariate Analysis. In *Transportation Research Record 975*, TRB, National Research Council, Washington, D.C., 1984, pp. 23–36.

25. L.L. Philipson, P. Rashti, and G.A. Fleischer. *Statistical Analyses of Commercial Vehicle Accident Factors*, Vol. 1: Technical Report, Part 1. Report

DOT-HS-803-418. Traffic Safety Center, University of Southern California, Los Angeles, Feb. 1978.

26. J.P. Eicher, H.D. Robertson, and G.R. Toth. *Large Truck Accident Causation*. Report DOT-HS-806-300. National Center for Statistics and Analysis, NHTSA, U.S. Department of Transportation, July 1982.

27. K.L. Campbell et al. *Tractor-Trailer Combinations: National Estimates of Their Distribution and Use, Based on the 1977 Truck Inventory and Use Survey*. Report UMTRI-83-14. Transportation Research Institute, University of Michigan, Ann Arbor, April 1983.

28. G.R. Vallette, H. McGee, and J.H. Sanders. *The Effect of Truck Size and Weight on Accident Experience and Traffic Operations*, Vol. 4: Truck Exposure Classification by Size and Weight. Draft Final Report. Bio-Technology, Inc., Falls Church, Va., May 1979.

29. D. Mactavish and D.L. Neumann. *Vehicle Classification Case Study for the Highway Performance Monitoring System*. Office of Highway Planning, FHWA, U.S. Department of Transportation, Aug. 1982.

30. D.E. Peterson and R. Gull. *Triple Trailer Evaluation in Utah*. Report UDOT-MR-75-4. Utah Department of Transportation, Salt Lake City, Sept. 1975.

31. F.R. Hanscom. *The Effect of Truck Size and Weight on Accident Experience and Traffic Operations*, Vol. 2: Traffic Operations. Report FHWA-RD-80-136. BioTechnology, Inc., Falls Church, Va., July 1981.

32. P.M. Kent and M.T. Robey. *1975-1979 National Truck Characteristics Report*. Office of Highway Planning, FHWA, U.S. Department of Transportation, June 1981.

33. D.L. Neumann and P. Savage. *Truck Weight Case Study for the Highway Performance Monitoring System (HPMS)*. Office of Highway Planning, FHWA, U.S. Department of Transportation, June 1982.

Appendix G
Accident Severity Literature Review and Analysis of Bureau of Motor Carrier Safety Accident Reports

In addition to accident involvement rates, relative accident severity is an essential component of comparisons of the accident patterns of twins and tractor-semitrailers. Even given a situation for which the total accident involvement rates are equivalent, one or the other of the two configurations may be more frequently involved in more severe types of accidents and would therefore be labeled as the more "hazardous" of the two. In this appendix various measures of accident severity are discussed. Then prior studies comparing the severity of accidents involving twins with that of accidents involving tractor-semitrailers are reviewed. Finally, an original analysis of accident severity based on Bureau of Motor Carrier Safety (BMCS) accident reports is presented.

SEVERITY MEASURES

Analysis of accident severity is complicated by absence of a commonly accepted measure of severity. For the purposes here, the more severe accidents are considered to be those with more deaths, more injuries, or more vehicles involved. A second complicating factor is that there is no commonly accepted collective severity measure for a set of accident data. Either of two acceptable approaches has been used. The first examines the distribution of accident types by severity level. For example, a commonly used indicator is the fraction of all accidents that results in casualty.

The second approach expresses the average consequences of an accident, for example, the average number of deaths per accident.

For either of these two collective measures, the preferred base is the complete set of accidents, that is, the set that contains accidents of all severity levels. Unfortunately, most accident data bases have deficiencies in this regard, particularly with respect to property-damage-only accidents. For example, according to Najjar (1), only 39 percent of the accidents in the 1979 BMCS accident file were classified as property damage only in contrast to an estimate of 72 percent from the 1979 National Accident Sampling System truck accident investigations. A similar problem has been reported by Smith and Wilmot (2): The reporting level for property-damage-only accidents in California has been only about 40 percent.

An alternative base, the set of casualty accidents, yields such measures as the fraction of all casualty accidents that results in death or the average number of deaths per casualty accident. Although this base yields more reliable estimates, proper interpretation of the results is much more complicated. The situation deemed more hazardous on the basis of the average number of deaths per casualty accident is not necessarily more hazardous on the basis of the average number of deaths per accident at all severity levels.

PRIOR STUDIES

In the limited number of studies in which accident severity has been expressed by deaths or by fatal accident involvements, twins accidents have usually been found to be more severe than those of tractor-semitrailers (Table G-1). In the remaining studies that document the average accident consequence, no consistent difference emerges in the severities of accidents of tractor-semitrailers versus those of twins (Table G-2).

The remaining comparisons evaluate severity by the distribution of accidents by severity level, and all include injury accidents in the severity measure. Although results are mixed and the information base is small, there is some indication that tractor-semitrailer accidents may be more likely to result in injury (Table G-3).

The foregoing summary suggests that

● There are more deaths in the average twins accident than in the average tractor-semitrailer accident,

● A larger proportion of twins accidents result in death than do tractor-semitrailer accidents, and

● A larger proportion of tractor-semitrailer accidents result in nonfatal injury than do twins accidents.

TABLE G-1 Comparative Accident Severity: Deaths per Accident or Fatal Accident Frequency

Base Data	Type of Severity Measure	Accident Severity by Truck Type		Source
		Twins	Tractor-Semitrailer	
1969, nationwide, BMCS	Average number of deaths per accident (all severities)	0.047	0.044	Scott and O'Day (3)
1969–1980, nationwide, BMCS special survey, 10 carrier periods	Average number of deaths per accident (all severities)	0.086	0.076	BMCS (4)
1969, nationwide, BMCS	Average number of deaths per accident with automobiles (all severities)	0.071	0.058	Scott and O'Day (3)
1974, California, rural roads and urban freeways	Average number of deaths per casualty accident	0.130	0.095	Yoo, Reiss, and McGee (5)
1974, 15 interstate carriers	Average number of deaths per accident (all severities)	0.024	0.013	Iowa Department of Transportation (6)
1973–1974, nationwide, BMCS, residential or business, four or more lanes	Odds of fatality to automobile occupant in automobile-truck accidents (all severities)[a]	0.10	0.07	Hedlund (7)
1973–1974, nationwide, BMCS, rural, four or more lanes	Odds of fatality to automobile occupant in automobile-truck accidents (all severities)[a]	0.19	0.12	Hedlund (7)
1973–1974, nationwide, BMCS, residential or business, two lanes	Odds of fatality to automobile occupant in automobile-truck accidents (all severities)[a]	0.12	0.06	Hedlund (7)
1973–1974, nationwide, BMCS, rural, two lanes	Odds of fatality to automobile occupant in automobile-truck accidents (all severities)[a]	0.19	0.22	Hedlund (7)
1977, nationwide, BMCS, ICC-authorized carriers, intercity vans	Fraction of accidents (all severities) that result in death	0.086	0.075	Chirachavala and O'Day (8)

[a]Ratio of the number of automobile-truck accidents in which one or more automobile occupants were killed to the number of automobile-truck accidents in which no automobile occupant was killed.

TABLE G-2 Comparative Accident Severity: Injuries, Casualties, or Vehicles per Accident

Base Data	Type of Severity Measure	Accident Severity by Truck Type		Source
		Twins	Tractor-Semitrailer	
1969, nationwide, BMCS	Average number of injuries per accident with automobiles (all severities)	0.74	0.64	Scott and O'Day (3)
1969, nationwide, BMCS	Average number of injuries per accident (all severities)	0.56	0.51	Scott and O'Day (3)
1972, California, rural roads and incorporated freeways	Average number of casualties per casualty accident	1.66[a]	1.55[a]	Zeiszler (9)
1972, California, rural roads and incorporated freeways	Average number of involved vehicles per casualty accident	2.29[a]	2.24[a]	Zeiszler (9)
1976–1980, nationwide, Consolidated Freightways	Average number of casualties per accident (all severities)	0.23	0.23	Glennon (10)
1974, California, rural roads and urban freeways	Average number of casualties per casualty accident	1.54	1.57	Yoo, Reiss, and McGee (5)
1969–1980, nationwide, BMCS special survey, 10 carrier periods	Average number of casualties per accident (all severities)	0.82	0.98	BMCS (4)

[a]Approximate.

These findings, however, are inconclusive for the following reasons:

• Many of the reported differences between twins and tractor-semitrailers were not found to be statistically significant;

• Completeness of many of the data bases, particularly the property-damage-only accident components, is suspect;

• The number and overall quality of the investigations are limited; and

• Attempts to control for the influence of the operating environment in the relative accident severity investigations were either limited or nonexistent.

TABLE G-3 Comparative Accident Severity: Nonfatal Injury or Casualty Frequency

Base Data	Type of Severity Measure	Accident Severity by Truck Type		Source
		Twins	Tractor-Semitrailer	
1977, nationwide, BMCS, ICC-authorized carriers, local vans	Fraction of accidents (all severities) that result in nonfatal injury	0.48	0.73	Chirachavala and O'Day (8)
1976–1977, predominantly California	Fraction of single-vehicle accidents (all severities) that result in casualty to truck occupant	0.21	0.28	Vallette et al. (11)
1977, nationwide, BMCS, ICC-authorized carriers, local vans	Fraction of accidents (all severities) that result in casualty	0.59	0.77	Chirachavala and O'Day (8)
1975–1976, two areas of California, freeways and expressways	Fraction of accidents (all severities) that result in major casualty to automobile occupant	0.10	0.12	Philipson, Rashti, and Fleischer (12)
1977, nationwide, BMCS, ICC-authorized carriers, intercity vans	Fraction of accidents (all severities) that result in nonfatal injury	0.52	0.60	Chirachavala and O'Day (8)
1977, nationwide, BMCS, ICC-authorized carriers, intercity vans	Fraction of accidents (all severities) that result in casualty	0.60	0.68	Chirachavala and O'Day (8)
1975–1976, two areas of California, conventional two-way roads	Fraction of accidents (all severities) that result in major casualty to automobile occupant	0.16	0.14	Philipson, Rashti, and Fleischer (12)
1976–1977, predominantly California	Fraction of multiple-vehicle accidents (all severities) that result in casualty to occupant not in truck	0.33	0.25	Vallette et al. (11)
1976–1977, predominantly California	Fraction of multiple-vehicle accidents (all severities) that result in casualty to truck occupant	0.18	0.11	Vallette et al. (11)

This last point is worthy of further mention because operational environment most likely exerts a strong influence on relative accident severity. Chirachavala et al. (*13*) have documented an attempt to identify some of these effects by using data drawn from the 1980 BMCS data base for accidents in over-the-road operations. Two severity measures were employed: the fatality ratio, defined as the ratio of the number of fatal accidents to the number of nonfatal accidents, and the injury ratio, defined as the ratio of the number of injury accidents to the number of property-damage-only accidents.

Results generally support the previous findings that twins accidents are more likely to involve death and that a greater proportion of tractor-semitrailer accidents involve injury (Tables G-4 and G-5). Notable exceptions exist, however, particularly the increasing injury severity of twins involvements in wet or snowy conditions. But the primary point, supported also by Hedlund (*7*), is simply that the operating environment has a definite effect on the relative severity of accidents involving twins and tractor-semitrailers. Because the literature on relative severity of such accidents is inconclusive, an original analysis was conducted for the Twin Trailer Truck Monitoring Study. This analysis is presented next.

TABLE G-4   Influence of Roadway, Environment, and Accident Type on Fatality Ratio (*13*)

| Roadway Type | Environment | Fatality Ratio by Accident Type | | | |
| | | Single-Vehicle Accident | | Collision with Automobile | |
		Twins	Tractor-Semitrailer	Twins	Tractor-Semitrailer
Rural, undivided	Dry Day	0.031	0.023	0.222	0.150
	Night		0.040		0.261
	Wet/snowy		0.022		0.147
Rural, divided	Dry Day	0.042	0.034	0.186	0.102
	Night		0.049		0.148
	Wet/snowy		0.021		0.064
Urban	Dry Day	0.080	0.014	0.036	0.035
	Night		0.042		0.106
	Wet/snowy		0.019		0.049

TABLE G-5   Influence of Roadway, Environment, and Accident Type on Injury Ratio (*13*)

| Roadway Type | Environment | Fatality Ratio by Accident Type | | | |
| | | Single-Vehicle Accident | | Collision with Automobile | |
		Twins	Tractor-Semitrailer	Twins	Tractor-Semitrailer
Rural, undivided	Dry				
	Day	0.75	1.01	2.35	2.55
	Night	0.74	1.31	2.32	3.29
	Wet/snowy	0.78	0.98	2.44	2.46
Rural, divided	Dry				
	Day	0.48	1.14	1.28	2.54
	Night	1.44	1.28	3.79	2.86
	Wet/snowy	0.98	0.80	2.57	1.77
Urban	Dry				
	Day	0.27	0.50	2.01	2.63
	Night	0.28	0.54	2.12	2.86
	Wet/snowy	0.64	0.55	4.77	2.91

ANALYSIS OF BMCS REPORTS

The basis for this investigation was accident reports submitted to the Bureau of Motor Carrier Safety by motor carriers of property in interstate or foreign commerce. In accord with Federal Motor Carrier Safety Regulations, a report must be filed whenever a reportable accident occurs that involves a motor vehicle engaged in the interstate, foreign, or intrastate operations of a motor carrier subject to the regulation. Accidents must be reported if they result in death, bodily injury requiring off-scene medical treatment, or damage to all property of $2,000 or more.

The data analyzed consisted of accidents that had been reported during the 6-year period of 1976–1981. These are the only years for which the necessary data were available in computer-compatible format. To mitigate sample-size limitations that often plague the analysis of traffic accident data, annual data were aggregated to form a single 6-year data set. The risk of ignoring possible temporal effects during this period was judged to be small in comparison with the advantages of the aggregated data.

To control for possible confounding effects of body type, number of axles, level of accident reporting, loaded weights, and commodity type, comparisons were limited to five-axle trucks of both types carrying general freight in van trailers and operated by carriers authorized by the Interstate

Commerce Commission. To control for operating environment influences, the data were partitioned into 32 categories, representing all combinations of four regions[1] (California, Other Western and Mountain, Central and Plains, and East), four highway types (two-lane, undivided four or more lanes, divided four or more lanes, and ramps), and two land uses (rural and urban).

The 1976–1981 data contained a total of 25,066 accidents that met the criteria established and for which the necessary data were available. The distribution of these accidents between the two truck types and among the 32 operating environment cells is shown in Table G-6. In Table G-7 several measures are used to summarize the severity of accidents involving twins and tractor-semitrailers for the entire data set.

Detailed statistical comparisons were limited to two severity measures: the fraction of all reported accidents that resulted in injury and the fraction of all reported accidents that resulted in death. The null hypothesis being tested was that twins accidents involved injury (or death) with a frequency equal to that of tractor-semitrailer accidents. The statistical procedures, patterned after those of Campbell (14), involved comparing the observed number of twins injury (or fatal) accidents with the expected number, calculated assuming a proportion of injury (or fatal) involvement identical to that of tractor-semitrailers. Individual calculations, performed for each of the 32 operating-environment cells, were summed to provide the necessary aggregate measures (Table G-8).

Overall, twins were involved in 7.5 percent fewer injury accidents (statistically significant) and 15.0 percent fewer fatal accidents (not statistically significant) than would be expected if their involvement proportions had been identical to those of tractor-semitrailers (Table G-9). The difference in injury involvement was attributable primarily to accidents on four-or-more lane divided highways in rural areas. Regional differences, if any, were not pronounced.

One of the most notable differences between twins and tractor-semitrailer accidents is in the frequency with which two or more vehicles are involved. Altogether, 59 percent of the tractor-semitrailer accidents involved multiple vehicles while only 44 percent of the twins accidents were similarly classified—a statistically significant difference at a level of significance of 0.05 using the Z-test. After the possible effects of the operating environment were controlled for, a similarly pronounced difference re-

---

[1]The Other Western and Mountain region included Montana, Wyoming, Colorado, New Mexico, and all westerly states except California. The East region included New York, Pennsylvania, West Virginia, Kentucky, Tennessee, Mississippi, and all easterly states. Remaining contiguous states made up the Central and Plains region.

TABLE G-6 Accidents Involving Five-Axle Vans Carrying General Freight and Operated by ICC-Authorized Carriers

| | | No. of Accidents by Land Use | | | |
| | | Rural | | Urban | |
Region	Highway Type	Twins	Tractor-Semitrailer	Twins	Tractor-Semitrailer
Central and Plains	Four or more lanes, divided	365	4,560	85	2,066
	Four or more lanes, undivided	6	167	14	631
	Two lanes	92	1,864	28	1,076
	Ramps	26	407	20	354
Other Western and Mountain	Four or more lanes, divided	243	588	23	120
	Four or more lanes, undivided	7	19	8	40
	Two lanes	85	196	22	65
	Ramps	10	32	8	29
California	Four or more lanes, divided	102	179	35	89
	Four or more lanes, undivided	3	4	8	41
	Two lanes	26	38	13	29
	Ramps	10	14	9	13
East	Four or more lanes, divided	8	4,723	2	1,827
	Four or more lanes, undivided	1	200	2	500
	Two lanes	14	1,865	2	1,338
	Ramps	1	425	1	288

SOURCE: Bureau of Motor Carrier Safety accident data, 1976–1981.

TABLE G-7 Severity of Accidents Involving Twins and Tractor-Semitrailers: All Highway Types, Locations, and Regions

Accident Base	Measure	Severity	
		Twins	Tractor-Semitrailer
All severities[a]	Avg. no. of deaths	0.071	0.075
	Avg. no. of casualties	0.90	1.06
	Fraction involving death	0.059	0.061
	Fraction involving injury	0.55	0.61
	Fraction involving casualty	0.61	0.67
Casualty only[b]	Avg. no. of deaths	0.12	0.11
	Avg. no. of injuries	1.36	1.48
	Avg. no. of casualties	1.48	1.60
	Fraction involving death	0.097	0.092
	Fraction involving injury	0.90	0.91
	Fraction involving casualty	1.00	1.00

NOTE: The accident totals of this table exceed those of Table E-1 because accidents with incomplete coding of highway type, location, and/or region are included here.
[a]Accident totals: twins, 1,329; tractor-semitrailer, 25,493.
[b]Accident totals: twins, 812; tractor-semitrailer, 16,993.

mained—twins were involved in about 19 percent fewer multivehicle accidents than would be expected if their involvement proportions had been identical to those of tractor-semitrailers (Table G-10). With the possible exception of accidents occurring on ramps or in California, this general pattern was observed in both rural and urban areas, in all geographic regions, and for all highway types.

Further comparisons were undertaken to ascertain whether the reduced severity of twins accidents could be partially explained by their less frequent involvement in multivehicle collisions. Those accidents involving only a single vehicle were found to have been generally less severe for twins than single-vehicle accidents were for tractor-semitrailers: twins were involved in 14.0 percent fewer injury accidents (statistically significant) and 20.9 percent fewer fatal accidents (not statistically significant) than would be expected if their involvement proportions had been identical to those of tractor-semitrailers (Table G-11). The reduced severity of single-vehicle twins accidents was generally observed in both rural and urban areas, in all geographic regions, and for all highway types. For multivehicle accidents, on the other hand, those involving twins appeared to have been slightly more severe than those involving tractor-semitrailers, but generally the differences were small and in only one instance was a statistically significant difference observed (Table G-12).

Automobile-truck accidents, a subset of multivehicle accidents, were analyzed separately to ascertain whether twins and tractor-semitrailers

TABLE G-8 Comparison of Observed and Expected Frequencies of Injury Accidents Involving Twins

Land Use and Highway Type	Region	Fraction of Tractor-Semitrailer Accidents Involving Injury	Twins Accidents		
			Total No.	No. Involving Injury	
				Observed	Expected
Rural					
Four or more lanes, divided	California	0.637	102	63	64.9
	Central and Plains	0.602	365	197	219.6
	East	0.618	8	2	4.9
	Other Western and Mountain	0.568	243	128	138.0
Ramps	California	0.571	10	5	5.7
	Central and Plains	0.590	26	13	15.3
	East	0.638	1	0	0.6
	Other Western and Mountain	0.500	10	5	5.0
Four or more lanes, undivided	California	0.250	3	2	0.8
	Central and Plains	0.611	6	4	3.7
	East	0.630	1	0	0.6
	Other Western and Mountain	0.526	7	5	3.7
Two lanes	California	0.737	26	9	19.2
	Central and Plains	0.582	92	55	53.6
	East	0.594	14	5	4.3
	Other Western and Mountain	0.531	85	38	45.1

Land Use and Highway Type	Region	Fraction of Tractor-Semitrailer Accidents Involving Injury	Twins Accidents Total No.	No. Involving Injury Observed	No. Involving Injury Expected
Urban					
Four or more lanes, divided	California	0.708	35	24	24.8
	Central and Plains	0.667	85	55	56.7
	East	0.678	2	2	14
	Other Western and Mountain	0.633	23	12	14.6
Ramps	California	0.692	9	4	6.2
	Central and Plains	0.703	20	13	14.1
	East	0.632	1	0	0.6
	Other Western and Mountain	0.517	8	3	4.1
Four or more lanes, undivided	California	0.585	8	6	4.7
	Central and Plains	0.674	14	9	9.4
	East	0.640	2	1	1.3
	Other Western and Mountain	0.625	8	6	5.0
Two lanes	California	0.414	13	6	5.4
	Central and Plains	0.596	28	19	16.7
	East	0.596	2	2	1.2
	Other Western and Mountain	0.415	22	14	9.1
Total			1,279	707	764.3

TABLE G-9 Observed and Expected Frequencies of Injury and Fatal Accidents Involving Twins

Variable	Category	Total No. of Accidents	Injury Accidents Number Observed	Injury Accidents Number Expected	Injury Percent Difference[a]	Injury Chi-Squared	Fatal Accidents Number Observed	Fatal Accidents Number Expected	Fatal Percent Difference[a]	Fatal Chi-Squared
All	All	1,279	707	764	7.5	8.74[b]	78	92	15.0	1.78
Location	Rural	999	531	589	9.9	11.15[b]	70	80	12.2	1.00
	Urban	280	176	175	−0.4	0.01	8	12	33.9	1.27
Region	California	206	119	132	9.6	2.26	16	14	−11.1	0.13
	Central and Plains	636	365	389	6.2	3.63	30	39	23.7	2.23
	East	31	12	19	36.8	6.62[b]	0	2	100.0	2.58
	Other Western and Mountain	406	211	225	6.0	1.35	32	36	10.4	0.30
Highway type	Four or more lanes, divided	863	483	525	8.0	6.94[b]	47	57	18.0	1.57
	Four or more lanes, undivided	49	33	29	−13.4	1.13	3	4	21.0	0.17
	Two lanes	282	148	158	6.6	1.30	28	28	0.4	0.00
	Ramps	85	43	52	17.0	3.08	0	2	100.0	2.28

[a]100[(expected − observed)/expected].
[b]Denotes statistically significant difference at a level of significance of 0.05.

TABLE G-10   Observed and Expected Frequencies of Multivehicle Accidents Involving Twins

Variable	Category	Total No. of Accidents	Number Observed	Number Expected	Percent Difference[a]	Chi-Squared
All	All	1,279	563	692	18.7	45.62[b]
Location	Rural	999	392	492	20.4	33.10[b]
	Urban	280	171	200	14.5	13.44[b]
Region	California	206	136	128	−6.0	0.90
	Central and Plains	636	268	365	26.6	58.74[b]
	East	31	9	18	49.9	10.84[b]
	Other Western and Mountain	406	150	181	17.1	7.25[b]
Highway type	Four or more lanes, divided	863	371	484	23.4	51.23[b]
	Four or more lanes, undivided	49	33	34	2.7	0.08
	Two lanes	282	120	136	11.5	2.94
	Ramps	85	39	39	−0.2	0.00

[a]100[(expected − observed)/expected].
[b]Denotes statistically significant difference at a level of significance of 0.05.

TABLE G-11 Observed and Expected Frequencies of Injury and Fatal Single-Vehicle Accidents Involving Twins

Variable	Category	Total No. of Accidents	Injury Accidents				Fatal Accidents			
			Number		Percent Difference[a]	Chi-Squared	Number		Percent Difference[a]	Chi-Squared
			Observed	Expected			Observed	Expected		
All	All	716	338	393	14.0	13.79[b]	28	35	20.9	1.28
Location	Rural	607	292	338	13.7	11.37[b]	26	32	18.0	0.83
	Urban	109	46	55	15.8	2.46	2	4	46.2	0.74
Region	California	70	29	40	27.8	5.19[b]	5	5	28	0.00
	Central and Plains	368	184	196	5.9	1.35	7	14	50.8	3.49
	East	22	7	12	40.4	4.08[b]	0	1	100.0	1.26
	Other Western and Mountain	256	118	145	18.9	8.36[b]	16	15	−7.7	0.06
Highway type	Four or more lanes, divided	492	242	274	11.6	6.62[b]	21	24	14.3	0.40
	Four or more lanes, undivided	16	8	8	−6.3	0.05	1	2	45.0	0.39
	Two lanes	162	72	84	14.5	3.05	6	8	27.5	0.52
	Ramps	46	16	27	41.8	9.95[b]	0	1	100.0	0.77

[a] 100[(expected − observed)/expected].
[b] Denotes statistically significant difference at a level of significance of 0.05.

TABLE G-12 Observed and Expected Frequencies of Injury and Fatal Multivehicle Accidents Involving Twins

Variable	Category	Total No. of Accidents	Injury Accidents				Fatal Accidents			
			Number		Percent Difference[a]	Chi-Squared	Number		Percent Difference[a]	Chi-Squared
			Observed	Expected			Observed	Expected		
All	All	563	369	356	−3.6	1.06	50	50	−0.2	0.00
Location	Rural	392	239	240	0.6	0.02	44	42	−4.6	0.08
	Urban	171	130	116	−12.3	4.77[b]	6	8	23.5	0.40
Region	California	136	90	89	−0.8	0.01	11	9	−19.9	0.25
	Central and Plains	268	181	180	−0.7	0.02	23	22	−6.1	0.08
	East	9	5	6	21.0	0.94	0	1	100.0	0.72
	Other Western and Mountain	150	93	81	−15.2	3.07	16	18	13.0	0.28
Highway type	Four or more lanes, divided	371	241	241	0.2	0.00	26	28	8.4	0.17
	Four or more lanes, undivided	33	25	20	−15.4	3.36	2	2	−2.9	0.00
	Two lanes	120	76	71	−25.5	0.60	22	18	−21.7	0.82
	Ramps	39	27	23	−6.4	1.18	0	2	100.0	1.37

[a] 100[(expected − observed)/expected].
[b] Denotes statistically significant difference at a level of significance of 0.05.

TABLE G-13 Observed and Expected Frequencies of Automobile-Truck Accidents Involving Twins Resulting in Injury or Death to Automobile Occupant

Variable	Category	Total No. of Automobile-Truck Accidents	Injury Accidents				Fatal Accidents			
			Number		Percent Difference[a]	Chi-Squared	Number		Percent Difference[a]	Chi-Squared
			Observed	Expected			Observed	Expected		
All	All	417	276	278	0.8	0.04	40	38	−5.8	0.12
Location	Rural	280	172	181	5.2	1.17	34	31	−8.0	0.18
	Urban	137	104	97	−7.6	1.65	6	6	4.7	0.01
Region	California	95	64	66	2.4	0.09	8	6	−34.0	0.46
	Central and Plains	206	142	143	0.9	0.03	19	18	−6.8	0.09
	East[b]	—	—	—	—	—	—	—	—	—
	Other Western and Mountain	116	70	69	−0.9	0.01	13	14	7.3	0.04
Highway type	Four or more lanes, divided	265	172	180	4.2	0.81	18	20	11.0	0.72
	Four or more lanes, undivided	26	22	19	−18.3	2.06	2	1	−88.9	0.79
	Two lanes	95	63	61	−3.2	0.13	20	15	−31.2	1.37
	Ramps	31	19	19	−0.1	0.00	0	1	100.0	1.12

[a]100[(expected − observed)/expected]. No differences were statistically significant at a level of significance of 0.05.
[b]Data for East omitted in this analysis.

differed with respect to the infliction of injury or death on automobile occupants. Differences between truck types were small and in no case statistically signficant (Table G-13).

This limited investigation of accident severity yields no information about the frequency or rates of twins and tractor-semitrailer accidents. What it does suggest is that, given an accident event, it was less likely to have been a severe one if twins rather than a tractor-semitrailer was involved. The difference in accident severity between the two configurations was small, however, and dependent on accident type: single-vehicle accidents involving twins were somewhat less severe than those involving tractor-semitrailers but a reversed—though not statistically significant—pattern was indicated for multivehicle accidents.

REFERENCES

1. D.V. Najjar. *A Comprehensive Approach to Truck Accident Data*. National Center for Statistics and Analysis, NHTSA, U.S. Department of Transportation, Aug. 1981.
2. R.N. Smith and E.L. Wilmot. *Truck Accident and Fatality Rates Calculated from California Highway Accident Statistics for 1980 and 1981*. Report SAND82-7066. Sandia National Laboratories, Albuquerque, N. Mex., Nov. 1982.
3. R.E. Scott and J. O'Day. *Statistical Analysis of Truck Accident Involvements*. Report DOT-HS-800-627. University of Michigan Highway Safety Research Institute, Ann Arbor, Dec. 1971.
4. *Safety Comparison of Doubles Versus Tractor-Semitrailer Operation*. Bureau of Motor Carrier Safety, FHWA, U.S. Department of Transportation, June 1983.
5. C.S. Yoo, M.L. Reiss, and H.W. McGee. *Comparison of California Accident Rates for Single and Double Tractor-Trailer Combination Trucks*. Report FHWA-RD-78-94. BioTechnology, Inc., Falls Church, Va., March 1978.
6. *Sixty-Five Foot Twin Trailers on Iowa Highways: Perspective*. Division of Planning, Iowa Department of Transportation, Ames, April 1975.
7. J. Hedlund. *The Severity of Large Truck Accidents*. National Center for Statistics and Analysis, NHTSA, U.S. Department of Transportation, April 1977.
8. T. Chirachavala and J. O'Day. *A Comparison of Accident Characteristics and Rates for Combination Vehicles with One or Two Trailers*. Report UM-HSRI-81-41. University of Michigan Highway Safety Research Institute, Ann Arbor, Aug. 1981.
9. R. Zeiszler. *Accident Experience of Double Bottom Trucks in California*. Operational Analysis Section, California Highway Patrol, Sacramento, April 1973.

10. J.C. Glennon. "Matched Pair Analysis." *Consolidated Freightways Corporation v. Larson et al.*, 81-1230, U.S. District Court, Middle District of Pennsylvania, Aug. 12, 1981.

11. G.R. Vallette et al. *The Effect of Truck Size and Weight on Accident Experience and Traffic Operations*, Vol. 3: Accident Experience of Large Trucks. Report FHWA-RD-80-137. BioTechnology, Inc., Falls Church, Va., July 1981.

12. L.L. Philipson, P. Rashti, and G.A. Fleischer. *Statistical Analyses of Commercial Vehicle Accident Factors*, Vol. 1: Technical Report, Part 1. Report DOT-HS-803-418. Traffic Safety Center, University of Southern California, Los Angeles, Feb. 1978.

13. T. Chirachavala, D.E. Cleveland, and L.P. Kostyniuk. Severity of Large-Truck and Combination-Vehicle Accidents in Over-the-Road Service: A Discrete Multivariate Analysis. In *Transportation Research Record 975*, TRB, National Research Council, Washington, D.C., 1984, pp. 23–36.

14. B.J. Campbell. *Seat Belts and Injury Reduction in 1967 North Carolina Automobile Accidents*. Highway Safety Research Center, University of North Carolina, Chapel Hill, Dec. 1968.

Appendix H
Driver Survey Questionnaire

TRUCK DRIVER OPINION SURVEY
OPERATION AND SAFETY OF TWIN TRAILER TRUCKS

Transportation Research Board

I. DRIVER

1. Your age: _____ (years)

2. How long have you been driving any type of combination truck? _____ (years)

3. How long have you been driving twin trailer trucks? _____ (years)

4. Have you received formal training in the operation of combination trucks? _____ Yes _____ No

   If yes, about how many hours of formal training have you received in the operation of:
   a. Twin trailer trucks: behind-the-wheel
                           training: _____ (hours)
                           classroom, demonstrations,
                           films, etc.:   _____ (hours)

b. Other combination behind-the-wheel
training: _____ (hours)
classroom, demonstrations,
films, etc.:   _____ (hours)

If you have had formal training, where have you received it? (check the one that applies)

_____ Mainly from current or past employers
_____ Mainly from others (schools, military, etc.)

5. Approximately how many miles each year do you drive a combination truck? _____ (miles/year)

6. Approximately what percentage of the miles you drove in the past year were in twins? _____(%)

II. AREA OF OPERATIONS

1. In what regions of the country do you most frequently drive?

_____ Southwest   _____ South Central   _____ Southeast
_____ Northwest   _____ North Central   _____ Northeast

2. On what types of highway do you accumulate most of your driving mileage?

_____ Rural, undivided high-   _____ Urban, undivided streets
ways   or roads
_____ Rural, divided highways   _____ Urban, divided high-
(Interstates, turnpikes,   ways (Interstates, ex-
etc.)   pressways, etc.)

3. When you drive twins or 48-foot semitrailers, how do you tell if the routes you choose follow the special roads designated for these trucks by the states? (check all that apply)

_____ The company assigns my routes.
_____ I use maps or guide books showing the allowed roads.
_____ In the areas where I drive, these trucks are allowed on all roads.
_____ Other (describe: _____)

III. EMPLOYMENT

1. What best describes your employment status?

_____ Owner-operator
_____ Carrier employee
_____ Other (describe: _____)

2. What type of carrier is the company you currently drive for?

_____ Common
_____ Contract
_____ Private
_____ Exempt
_____ Other (describe: _____)

3. About how large is the trucking operation of the company you drive for?

_____ Small—fewer than 50 tractors operated at all locations
_____ Medium—50 to 500 tractors operated at all locations
_____ Large—more than 500 tractors operated at all locations
_____ Don't Know

IV. TYPE OF TWIN TRAILER TRUCK
Describe the twin trailer truck you have *most frequently* operated.

1. Total number of axles on the tractor and trailers (count a tandem axle as two axles): _____ (number)

2. Number of axles on the tractor alone (count a tandem axle as two axles): _____ 2 _____ 3 _____ 4

3. Overall vehicle length: _____ (feet)

V. COMPARISON WITH TRACTOR-SEMITRAILER

1. Have you operated a tractor-semitrailer truck within the past 5 years?

_____ Yes _____ No

If your answer is "No," please skip the next four questions and proceed to Section VI.

2. Describe the tractor-semitrailer truck you have *most frequently* operated.

a. Total number of axles on the tractor and trailer (count a tandem axle as two axles): _____ (number)

b. Overall vehicle length: _____ (feet)

3. Answer the following questions by checking the most appropriate space:

	Twin	No Difference	Semi	Don't Know
a. If you had the choice on your current job, which truck would you prefer to drive?	_____	_____	_____	_____
b. Which truck is safer to operate?	_____	_____	_____	_____
c. Which truck performs better on the road?	_____	_____	_____	_____
d. Which truck creates less splash and spray on wet or slushy pavements?	_____	_____	_____	_____

4. By checking the most appropriate space, compare the ease of operating a twin trailer truck and a tractor-semitrailer truck in each of the following situations:

	Twins Easier	No Difference	Semis Easier	Don't Know
a. Merging onto freeway	_____	_____	_____	_____
b. Lane change on freeway	_____	_____	_____	_____
c. Passing slow vehicles on freeway	_____	_____	_____	_____
d. Passing slow vehicles on 2-lane road	_____	_____	_____	_____
e. Stopping quickly in emergency	_____	_____	_____	_____
f. Controlling truck in emergency braking	_____	_____	_____	_____

g. Controlling loaded truck on long, steep downgrade _____ _____ _____ _____

h. Maintaining speed on long, steep up-grade _____ _____ _____ _____

i. Operating on city streets _____ _____ _____ _____

j. Turning sharp cor-ners _____ _____ _____ _____

k. Operating on steep, curved off-ramps _____ _____ _____ _____

l. Operating on slick pavement _____ _____ _____ _____

m. Operating on very rough pavement _____ _____ _____ _____

n. Operating under se-vere crosswinds _____ _____ _____ _____

o. Operating truck having poorly ad-justed brakes _____ _____ _____ _____

p. Operating truck having worn or mis-matched tires _____ _____ _____ _____

q. Operating empty truck _____ _____ _____ _____

r. Hitching and un-hitching a trailer _____ _____ _____ _____

5. By checking the most appropriate space, compare how often twin trailers and tractor-semitrailers are associated with the following situations:

	More Often With Semis	No Difference	More Often With Twins	Don't Know
a. Trailer swaying on open roadway	_____	_____	_____	_____
b. Magnified trailer movement in re-sponse to abrupt steering	_____	_____	_____	_____

c. Difficulty detecting quickly when a trailer starts an unusual motion _____ _____   _____ _____

d. A trailer appears like it is about to roll over _____ _____   _____ _____

e. The truck feels like it is about to jack-knife _____ _____   _____ _____

f. Brake malfunction _____ _____   _____ _____

g. Hitch malfunction _____ _____   _____ _____

h. Following motorists hesitate to pass on 2-lane roadways _____ _____   _____ _____

i. Passing motorists pull in too quickly _____ _____   _____ _____

j. Vehicles approaching on 2-lane roads encroach on shoulder _____ _____   _____ _____

k. Poor trailer load distribution interferes with handling _____ _____   _____ _____

l. Difficulty seeing rear of the truck _____ _____   _____ _____

VI. YOUR OVERALL OPINIONS ABOUT TWINS

1. Are you satisfied with the handling and performance properties of twin trailer trucks?

_____ Yes   _____ Maybe   _____ No   _____ Don't Know

2. What, if any, are your recommendations for improving the handling and performance properties of twin trailer trucks?

3. Are you satisfied with the safety of twin trailer trucks?

_____ Yes   _____ Maybe   _____ No   _____ Don't Know

4. What, if any, are your recommendations for improving the safety of twin trailer trucks?

VII. OTHER TRUCKS

1. Have you operated a tractor-semitrailer with a 48-foot semitrailer?

   _____ Yes   _____ No   _____ Don't Know

   If your answer is "Yes," how does its performance and safety compare with 40 or 45-foot semitrailers?

2. Have you operated a 102-inch wide combination truck?

   _____ Yes   _____ No   _____ Don't Know

   If your answer is "Yes," how does its performance and safety compare with 96-inch wide combination trucks?

Appendix I
Pavement Effects of Different Vehicle Weights, Weight Distributions, and Axle Arrangements—An Example

In this example an illustration is given of how changes in gross vehicle weight (GVW), weight distribution, and axle arrangement can individually alter a truck's effect on pavement wear and pavement life. Then an illustration is given of the effect of all these changes combined.

A 60,000-lb tractor-semitrailer is used for the base case. This is the vehicle that is typical of the type of truck that can be replaced by a twin trailer truck. Changes to the base case, which are evaluated in the example, are characteristic of those that would be expected if the base tractor-semitrailer were replaced by a twin trailer truck.

The effect on pavement wear is estimated in terms of 18,000-lb equivalent single-axle loads (ESALs) by using the American Association of State Highway and Transportation Officials (AASHTO) pavement design procedures (*1*). Assumed design values for the AASHTO load-equivalency factors are as follows: $p_t = 2.5$, $D = 9$ in., and $SN = 3$. Axle loads are given in thousands of pounds.

1. Base case (60,000-lb tractor-semitrailer)

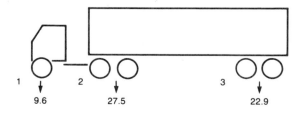

1   2   3

9.6   27.5   22.9

356

	ESALs by Axle or Axle Group			
Pavement Type	1 Single	2 Tandem	3 Tandem	Total
Flexible	0.10	0.52	0.27	0.89
Rigid	0.07	0.79	0.37	1.23

2. Base plus 6,000 lb [weight distribution between tandem axles (ratio of front tandem load to rear tandem load) and axle arrangement unchanged]

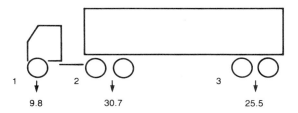

a. No adjustment for fewer trips

	ESALs by Axle or Axle Group				
Pavement Type	1 Single	2 Tandem	3 Tandem	Total	Percent Increase over Base
Flexible	0.11	0.77	0.39	1.27	43
Rigid	0.08	1.26	0.58	1.92	56

b. Adjusted for 9 percent fewer trips

Assume: Because of higher payloads and greater operating flexibility, the heavier vehicle will need just 0.91 as many trips (or vehicle miles) to carry the same total payload as the lighter truck. This assumption is consistent with the expected mileage of twins compared with the tractor-semitrailer trucks they replace (Chapter 3).

Pavement Type	Total ESALs (unadj.)	Adjustment Factor	Adjusted Total ESALs	Percent Increase over Base
Flexible	1.27	0.91	1.16	30
Rigid	1.92	0.91	1.75	42

3. Base with less uniform weight distribution (GVW and axle arrangement unchanged)

Assume: Ratio of front tandem load to rear tandem load changes from 1.20 to 1.32; steering axle load unchanged.

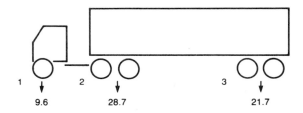

	ESALs by Axle or Axle Group				
Pavement Type	1 Single	2 Tandem	3 Tandem	Total	Percent Increase over Base
Flexible	0.10	0.60	0.22	0.92	3
Rigid	0.07	0.95	0.29	1.31	7

4. Base case with twin trailer truck axle arrangement (GVW and weight distribution unchanged)

Assume: Axle arrangement changed to five single axles, the usual twin trailer truck arrangement.

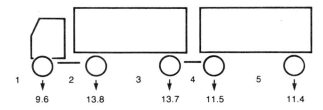

	ESALs by Axle or Axle Group						
Pavement	_1_	_2_	_3_	_4_	_5_		_Percent Increase_
Type	_Single_	_Single_	_Single_	_Single_	_Single_	_Total_	_over Base_
Flexible	0.10	0.38	0.37	0.20	0.20	1.25	40
Rigid	0.07	0.32	0.32	0.15	0.15	1.01	(18)

5. Effect of combination of higher weight, less uniform weight distribution, and different axle arrangement

Note: All changes from base case as described previously except that ratio of heaviest to lightest tandem-axle load was used to first calculate the total loads on axles 2 and 3 and on axles 4 and 5, and then these total loads were divided between single axles to match typical weight distributions of twins between heaviest and lightest single-axle load, excluding the steering axle (ratio equals 1.58).

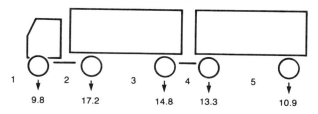

a. No adjustment for fewer trips

	ESALs by Axle or Axle Group						
Pavement	_1_	_2_	_3_	_4_	_5_		_Percent Increase_
Type	_Single_	_Single_	_Single_	_Single_	_Single_	_Total_	_over Base_
Flexible	0.11	0.86	0.50	0.34	0.17	1.87	110
Rigid	0.08	0.84	0.45	0.28	0.12	1.77	44

b. Adjusted for 9 percent fewer trips

Note: In this example the cumulative effect of higher weight, less uniform weight distribution, and a different axle arrangement is greater than the sum of the individual changes. This result occurs because changes to weight distribution and axle arrangement alter the incremental impact of the added 6,000 lb of weight as well as the impact of the original 60,000 lb. Also, dividing a tandem axle unevenly between the two single axles to match typical weight distributions of twins increases the effect on pavement wear.

Pavement Type	Total ESALs (unadj.)	Adjusted Factor	Adjusted Total ESALs	Percent Increase over Base
Flexible	1.87	0.91	1.70	91
Rigid	1.77	0.91	1.61	31

TABLE I-1 Summary

	Flexible Pavement		Rigid Pavement	
Case	Total ESALs	Percent Increase over Base	Total ESALs	Percent Increase over Base
Base (60,000-lb tractor-semi-trailer)	0.89	—	1.23	—
Base plus 6,000 lb				
No adjustment for fewer trips	1.27	43	1.92	56
Adjusted for 9 percent fewer trips	1.16	30	1.75	42
Base with less uniform weight distribution	0.92	3	1.31	7
Base with axle arrangement of twin trailer truck	1.25	40	1.01	(18)
Base plus all of the foregoing (66,000-lb twin trailer truck)				
No adjustment for fewer trips	1.87	110	1.77	91
Adjusted for 9 percent fewer trips	1.70	91	1.61	31

REFERENCE

1. *Guide for Design of Pavement Structures*. American Association of State Highway and Transportation Officials, Washington, D.C., 1986 (in preparation).

Appendix J
Effects of Twins and Other Large Trucks on Bridges and Culverts

Bridges are complex structures that are designed in widely differing ways and constructed with a variety of materials. Generally, every bridge consists of three principal elements: a substructure (the piers, abutments, and other foundation structures that support the bridge from the ground); a superstructure (the girders, trusses, or arches that rest on the substructure and support the bridge deck); and finally the bridge deck or roadway. Each of these elements must be sized to accommodate not only traffic loads but also the dead load of the structure and various environmental loads (such as wind, earthquakes, or thermal forces). As bridge spans increase in length, dead load as a proportion of the total load increases, so that for bridges with very long spans (e.g., 1,000 ft) only about 20 percent of the load-bearing capacity of main structural members is required to carry the live load (1).

U.S. highway bridges are usually designed in accord with specifications developed by the American Association of State Highway and Transportation Officials (AASHTO) (2). These specifications require that bridges withstand a hypothetical, standardized loading pattern with a safety factor against collapse. In addition, the specifications require that component steel members and connections be designed to withstand the number of load repetitions over the expected life of the bridge to prevent fatigue failures.

The hypothetical truck loading patterns used for bridge design bear little resemblance to those of real trucks in service in terms of axle configurations and loads but are intended to envelop the effects of all in-service truck types loaded within legal axle and gross vehicle weight (GVW) maximums. They cover the case of a single truck on the bridge span as well as that of multiple trucks simultaneously occupying a bridge span. Safety factors are used so that the stresses in bridge components that would be induced by these hypothetical loads are well below the stresses that would cause unacceptable deformation or loss of serviceability.

AASHTO standards recommend a standard truck loading pattern designated as HS 20-44 for Interstate highway bridges and a minimum loading pattern designated as HS 15-44 for other highways that may carry heavy-truck traffic. Altogether, four standard truck loading patterns are specified in the AASHTO standards (Table J-1). About 87 percent of Interstate highway bridges are currently designed to accommodate the HS 20-44

TABLE J-1   Standard AASHTO Truck Loading Patterns

Designation	Loading Pattern[a]	Percent of Federal Aid System Bridges[b]	
		Interstate	Other Primary
HS 20-44		86.8 (or greater)	41.6 (or greater)
HS 15-44		8.9	23.0
H 20-44			
H 15-44		2.0 (or less)	28.3 (or less)

[a]In accordance with AASHTO specifications (2). Loading patterns are given in thousands of pounds.
[b]Data from Truck Size and Weight Study (1).

loading pattern or greater, and about 65 percent of the bridges on federal-aid primary highways (excluding Interstates) are designed to accommodate at least the HS 15-44 or HS 20-44 loading patterns (Table J-1).

Assuming that a bridge is not subjected to loads in excess of its design load and is properly maintained, bridge design procedures suggest that the main structural members can withstand virtually unlimited load repetitions without excessive deformation or distress. For steel bridge components where fatigue cracking is of particular concern, load repetitions cannot be ignored, but design procedures and field investigations indicate that small changes in traffic volumes have no practical effect on fatigue life provided a bridge is properly maintained and not subjected to loads that induce greater forces than the design load. For example, AASHTO specifications for steel bridges on major highway routes require a fatigue analysis that distinguishes between just two levels of truck traffic volume, above and below 2,500 average daily trucks in each direction. An inspection of 140 deficient bridges by Berger (3) supports this relative insensitivity to truck volumes. It found no evidence that fatigue wear resulted from repeated truck loadings at or below the design loading. Instead Berger attributed the observed fatigue failures to inadequate maintenance, poorly designed connections, and repeated overloads.

Because twins and other truck types authorized by the Surface Transportation Assistance Act (STAA) of 1982 are expected to decrease truck volumes to less than what would otherwise have occurred, the key issue with respect to bridge design and use is how the maximum forces induced by these vehicles compare with the maximum forces induced by the standard truck loading patterns. Secondarily, how do they compare with the maximum forces induced by the vehicles they replace? If they are less than the design load forces on an existing bridge, no change in service life is expected nor are restricted use or retrofits to increase load-bearing capacity necessary. If the maximum forces induced by the new vehicles are also less than the maximum forces induced by the vehicles they replace, the new vehicles can clearly be used on any bridge currently used by the existing vehicle types without acceleration of fatigue deterioration.

Rigorous comparison of the forces induced by different loading patterns must be based on specific bridge designs, but simplifying assumptions are possible. Jung and Witecki (4) proposed a simplified method for making such comparisons and Whiteside et al. in NCHRP Report 141 (5) extended this method to provide not only an expedient means to make these comparisons but also a procedure to assess whether operation of the new vehicles is permissible without added strengthening when the forces and stresses that would be induced exceed those of the design load. Within limits such overstress use may be permissible but will increase the long-term possibility of fatigue failure, therefore reducing useful service life.

EFFECTS ON BRIDGE SUBSTRUCTURES

The methods of Jung and Witecki and Whiteside et al. focus on the bridge superstructure; they disregard the substructure because the dimensioning of substructure components is primarily dictated by the weight of the structure itself and site conditions; changes in the traffic loading have little or no effect on new designs or existing bridge substructures. This being the case, the introduction of twins and other STAA truck types, particularly without an increase in GVW limits, will not affect the design or deterioration of the bridge substructure.

EFFECTS ON BRIDGE SUPERSTRUCTURES

For superstructure, this study compared the maximum forces induced by fully loaded (80,000-lb) twins, tractors with 45-ft semitrailers, and the HS 20-44 and HS 15-44 standard loading patterns for a range of longitudinal bridge span lengths for simply supported beams in a manner similar to that used by Jung and Witecki and Whiteside et al. Because of the added space between tandem axles, tractors with 48-ft semitrailers produce forces that are no greater than those induced by tractors with 45-ft semitrailers at equal GVWs.

Up to span lengths of about 90 ft, the loads of individual trucks govern design, that is, produce the maximum bending moments and shear forces. In this span-length range, the fully loaded twins and tractor-semitrailers induce forces below those of the HS 20-44 standard load and near or below those of the HS 15-44 load for span lengths below 60 ft (Figure J-1). For simply supported spans between 60 and 90 ft, the bending moments of the twins and the tractor-semitrailers exceed those of the HS 15-44 standard load, with the forces induced by twins being somewhat less than those of the tractor-semitrailer. For span lengths over 90 ft, multiple vehicle loads generally govern design, but the AASHTO HS standard loading patterns (expressed in terms of a point load and a uniform load per lineal foot for multiple vehicles) cannot be directly compared for specific vehicle types. Nevertheless, twins and tractor-semitrailers were compared by using multiple-vehicle loading patterns similar to those em-

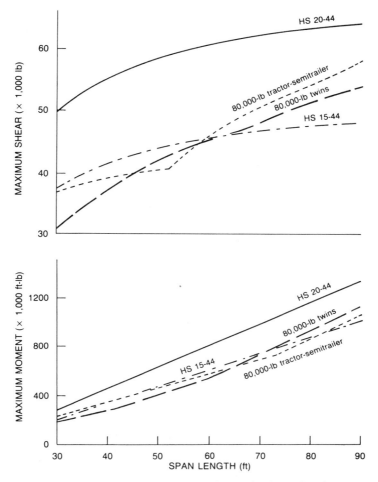

FIGURE J-1   Maximum live-load forces in short simple spans (one lane).

ployed by AASHTO in developing earlier standard loads[1] (Figure J-2).

---

[1]The comparisons used multiple-truck loading patterns similar to those from the 1935 AASHTO bridge specifications: the design truck at maximum load preceded and followed by similar trucks at three-quarters of the maximum load with a spacing of 30 ft between the rear axle of a truck and the front axle of a following truck. See Appendix B of the AASHTO bridge specifications (2).

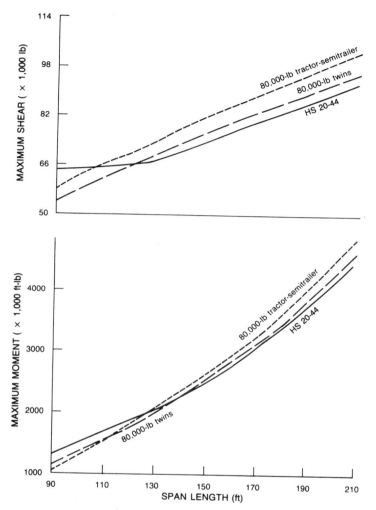

FIGURE J-2 Maximum live-load forces in long simple spans
(one lane) from multiple vehicle loads. [NOTE: Multiple vehicle
loads generally govern design over this span-length range. Because the HS 20-44 multiple vehicle load is expressed in terms
of a uniform load per lineal foot, it should not be directly compared with the moments and shear forces induced by assumed
multiple truck loading patterns for twins and tractor-semitrailers.
See accompanying text.]

These comparisons indicate that the forces induced by multiple twin trailer trucks are close to, but somewhat less than, the forces created by multiple tractor-semitrailers.

For transverse floor beams, fully loaded twins, like fully loaded tractor-semitrailers, induce forces well below those of the HS 20-44 and HS 15-44 standard loading patterns. Design of these members is governed by maximum wheel loads. The HS 20-44 and HS 15-44 wheel loads (one-half the maximum axle load) are 16,000 and 12,000 lb, respectively, whereas 80,000-lb twins and tractor-semitrailers have maximum wheel loads of just 8,000 to 10,000 lb. Wider 102-in. trucks will slightly reduce the bending forces in transverse members compared with 96-in. trucks, but this reduction is too small to affect the design of new bridges or the life of existing bridges.

Similar conclusions about the effects of twins relative to the effects of semitrailer trucks can be reached by applying bridge formulas used to regulate large-truck axle loads and spacings. Various simplified formulas have been developed that seek to put different vehicle configurations on a common footing with respect to the forces they create on a wide range of bridge types. Because they are based on basic principles of structural mechanics, such bridge formulas should produce results consistent with those of Figures J-1 and J-2. The U.S. bridge formula [(6); 23 USC 127] and the Ontario (Canada) bridge formula (4) relate the maximum permissible load on any group of axles to the total load, number of axles, and axle spacings:

U.S. bridge formula:

$$W = 500 \{[LN/(N - 1)] + 12N + 36\}$$

where
  W = maximum load carried on any group of two or more consecutive axles (lb),
  L = distance between the extremes of an axle group (ft), and
  N = number of axles in the group under consideration.

Ontario bridge formula:

$$W = 20 + 2.07B_m - 0.0071B_m^2$$

where

W = maximum load carried on any group of two or more consecutive axles and

B_m = equivalent base length (the distance over which W must be equally distributed to generate the same maximum bending moments in main bridge beams, girders, and trusses). B_m equals Kb, where b is the distance in feet between the extremes of an axle group, and K is a coefficient between about 0.9 and 1.75 that depends on the distribution of axle weights.

Typical fully loaded twins and 45-ft semitrailers satisfy both formulas for all axle combinations; tractor-semitrailers more closely approach the formula maximum loads for the most critical axle combinations than do twins.

EFFECTS ON BRIDGE DECKS

Like bridge superstructures, bridge decks are designed to withstand standard truck loading patterns (2). The foregoing comparisons of the forces induced on superstructure components by typical fully loaded twins and tractor-semitrailers and the AASHTO standard truck loading patterns are generally applicable to bridge decks as well. For concrete slabs, for example, maximum wheel loads govern design (5), and as noted earlier, the maximum wheel loads of 80,000-lb twins are about the same as those of 80,000 lb tractor-semitrailers and well below those of the HS 20-44 and HS 15-20 standard loading patterns. For orthotropic steel decks, AASHTO permits lower wheel loads for the HS 20-44 loading pattern (12,000 lb instead of 16,000 lb) but this is still well above the maximum wheel load (about 10,000 lb) of a fully loaded twin.

Thus no change in bridge deck design should result from the nationwide introduction of twin trailer trucks or longer tractor-semitrailers; that is, standard truck loads that would be used for fully loaded tractors with 45-ft semitrailers will also accommodate twin trailer trucks and longer tractor-semitrailers. Wider 102-in. trucks may produce different bridge deck stresses than the 96-in. trucks they replace, but the magnitude of these differences is inconsequential.

The deterioration of existing bridge decks, which are usually constructed of reinforced concrete, is a major problem throughout the United States, probably the most critical problem related to bridge rehabilitation and repair (7). Bridge deck deterioration results primarily from corrosion when deicing salts are used, although traffic loads may accelerate such deterioration (8). The U.S. Department of Transportation in its highway cost allocation study concluded that bridge deck repair costs should be assigned to vehicle classes without regard to weight or axle configuration (7).

EFFECTS ON CULVERT DETERIORATION

Like bridges, culverts are constructed in a variety of ways with different materials, including reinforced-concrete box culverts, large arches, and both reinforced-concrete and corrugated metal pipes. The primary causes of culvert deterioration and failure are corrosion, mechanical abrasion, and improper construction. Nevertheless, they must be structurally able to resist live load stresses induced by traffic as well as dead load stresses induced by the weight of their earth cover. Live load stresses become significant only when the depth of earth over the culvert (fill depth) is small. The stresses become so large at low fill depths that it is common to specify some minimum depth, often 2 ft, in order to eliminate unreasonable structural requirements. For greater depths, dead load stresses due to overburden assume greater significance. In fact, according to current design procedures, live load is neglected when the fill depth is 8 ft or more (2).

Thus, the structural design of culverts normally incorporates traffic loading only when the fill depths are in the range of 2 to 8 ft. The traffic loading is specified, as for bridge design, by a hypothetical but standard truck loading pattern. Load repetitions are not considered, and an unlimited number of applications can theoretically be tolerated for properly designed and constructed culverts. Progressive structural deterioration caused by traffic loading is not anticipated.

For the design of culverts on roads likely to accommodate heavy-truck traffic, the standard design truck loadings are at least as severe as those of legally operated tractor-semitrailers and twins. Therefore, load-induced deterioration of properly designed culverts is not expected with 80,000-lb tractor-semitrailers or twins, even with unlimited applications. Moreover, the use of longer 48-ft semitrailers and wider 102-in. axles on trucks loaded at the legal maximum weight will not change the stresses because they are created by only one single axle or tandem axle at a time and small changes in wheel spacing on an axle are of little consequence.

However, a small differential effect between twins and tractor-semitrailers, although not treated in design, arises from differences in axle configuration, that is, the use of single axles on twins and the use of tandem axles on tractor-semitrailers. A relevant measure of this effect is the average intensity of vertical loading on top of the culvert (2). The difference between single and tandem axles, each loaded to its legal maximum, is significant only at low fill depths. As fill depth increases, not only does the difference between single and tandem axles diminish but also the dead load effects of the overburden become dominant (Figure J-3). The single axle of the twin induces larger stresses in the culvert only for low fill depths.

The frequency distribution of depths of fill over culverts in service is unknown. However, even within the range in which truck configuration effects may be significant, properly designed and constructed culverts are not expected to suffer traffic-load-induced deterioration from legally loaded

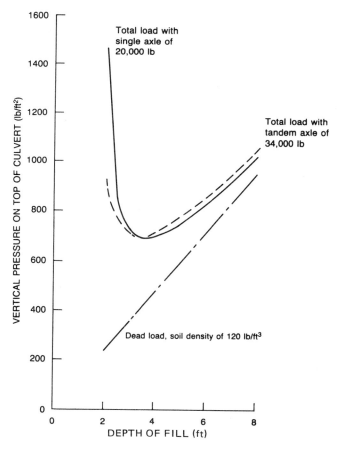

FIGURE J-3   Effect of axle configuration on culvert loading.

tractor-semitrailers or twin trailer trucks. The changing mix of the truck fleet is therefore unlikely to adversely affect culvert performance and serviceability.

REFERENCES

1. *An Investigation of Truck Size and Weight Limits.* U.S. Department of Transportation, Aug. 1981.
2. *Standard Specifications for Highway Bridges.* American Association of State Highway and Transportation Officials, Washington, D.C. 1983.
3. R.L. Berger. *Extending the Service Life of Existing Bridges by Increasing Their Load Carrying Capacity.* Byrd, Tallamy, McDonald and Lewis, Washington, D.C., June 1978.
4. F.W. Jung and A.A. Witecki. *Determining the Maximum Permissible Weights of Vehicles on Bridges.* Ministry of Transportation and Communications, Downsview, Ontario, Canada, Dec. 1971.
5. R.E. Whiteside et al. *Changes in Legal Vehicle Weights and Dimensions: Some Economic Effects On Highways.* NCHRP Report 141. TRB, National Research Council, Washington, D.C., 1973.
6. *Maximum Desirable Dimensions and Weights of Vehicles Operated on the Federal-Aid Systems.* Bureau of Public Roads, U.S. Department of Commerce, Aug. 1964.
7. *Final Report on the Federal Highway Cost Allocation Study.* U.S. Department of Transportation, May 1982.
8. *Durability of Concrete Bridge Decks.* NCHRP Synthesis of Highway Practice 57. TRB, National Research Council, Washington, D.C. 1979.

Appendix K
Effects of Twins and Other Large Trucks on Highway Shoulders and Roadside Appurtenances

The possible effects of twins and other STAA trucks on highway shoulders and roadside appurtenances are discussed.

EFFECTS ON HIGHWAY SHOULDERS

Two shoulder types are considered: (a) full-strength paved shoulders and (b) gravel, turf, and thinly paved shoulders.

Full-Strength Paved Shoulders

Highway shoulders are constructed in a variety of ways, usually with paved, gravel (or other granular material), or turf surfaces. Increasingly, highway agencies are choosing to pave shoulders, most often using a flexible pavement (even when the travel lanes are constructed of a rigid pavement), but paved shoulders are often not constructed to the same design standard as that of adjacent travel lanes. When paved shoulders and adjacent lanes are constructed in the same manner, the occasional use of the shoulder by twins for parking is unlikely to increase the rate of shoulder deterioration to any measurable or practical degree. Similarly, minor shoulder encroachments by moving trucks are unlikely to increase shoulder deterioration because travel lanes and shoulders are constructed in nearly the same manner.

Gravel, Turf, and Thinly Paved Shoulders

When paved shoulders and adjacent lanes are not constructed in the same manner, the added destructive effect of use by twins for parking may be sufficient to accelerate shoulder deterioration. The extent to which this phenomenon will occur depends on the paved shoulder design and the frequency of heavy truck parking.

For gravel and turf shoulders as well as paved shoulders without adequate structural support, minor encroachments of moving trucks onto shoulder edges can cause breakup of the pavement at the edge of the travel lane and erosion, rutting, or breakup of the shoulder surface. Without corrective maintenance, these types of deterioration can produce a severe edge drop condition, which is a difference in level between the travel lanes and the shoulder edge that poses a safety hazard to motorists. The study examined the likelihood that twins and other STAA truck types compared with narrower 45-ft semitrailers might accelerate this problem because of performance characteristics or added width, which would increase the frequency of minor shoulder encroachments.

With regard to truck performance, the most critical characteristic is high-speed offtracking. Offtracking is the phenomenon in which the path of the rearward portion of a vehicle in a steady turn does not coincide with that of the forward portion, and at higher speeds, offtracking tends to be an outward movement of the rear end. Ervin et al. (*1*) examined high-speed offtracking for a variety of large vehicle types and found that it was only significant for severe turning movements such as may occur when a vehicle enters a freeway ramp at excessive speed. Although Ervin et al. reported greater high-speed offtracking for twins than for tractors with either 45- or 48-ft semitrailers (Appendix D, Figure D-1), this degree of offtracking is still not large enough to be a significant factor in shoulder deterioration, especially because it only occurs when the vehicle is being driven in a hazardous manner in which rollover is an imminent threat.

With respect to added vehicle width, available evidence indicates that it may increase the likelihood of shoulder encroachments by heavy trucks, but the evidence is not definitive about encroachment extent or frequency. In reviewing literature on lane width and vehicle lateral placement, for instance, Saag and Leisch (*2*) reported that on two lane roads in situations involving opposing cars or opposing trucks, drivers use the added lane width mostly to increase clearances between vehicles until vehicle clearances of 4 to 5 ft are reached. After that point, further increases in lane width are allocated mostly toward increasing the shoulder clearance. These findings suggest that drivers of wider trucks in similar situations would tend to subtract the added vehicle width from their shoulder clearance rather than the clearance with an opposing vehicle, making a shoulder encroachment more likely. Similar adjustments to shoulder clearances might be made on two-lane and multilane highways in passing situations, but again available research results do not indicate what the frequency of resulting shoulder encroachments might be.

EFFECTS ON ROADSIDE APPURTENANCES

The key issue related to roadside appurtenances is the possibility of low speed collisions between trucks and highway signing, guardrails, curbs and traffic channelization islands at intersections and interchange ramps where trucks are making turning maneuvers. These collisions result in increased maintenance costs or reconstruction to higher geometric standards (see Appendix L). They are especially a product of the inward offtracking of rear trailers that occurs at low speeds. Ervin et al. (1) and Freitas (3,pp. 29–38) investigated low-speed offtracking for various large truck configurations and found that twins performed much better than tractors with 45-ft semitrailers, whereas tractors with 48-ft semitrailers experienced a signficant increase in offtracking (see Appendix D, Figure D-1). The added width of 102-in. wide trucks further aggravates any problems induced by offtracking. This is a particular concern for tractors with 48-ft semitrailers, but no research results are available that relate increases in truck offtracking or width to the frequency of roadside encroachments or damage of roadside appurtenances.

REFERENCES

1. R.D. Ervin, R.L. Nisonger, C.C. MacAdam and P.S. Fancher. *Influence of Size and Weight Variables on the Stability and Control Properties of Heavy Trucks*. Transportation Research Institute, University of Michigan, Ann Arbor, March 1983.
2. J.B. Saag and J.E. Leisch. *Synthesis of Information on Roadway Geometric Causal Factors*. Jack E. Leisch and Associates, Evanston, Ill., Jan. 1981.
3. M.D. Freitas. "Safety of Twin Trailer Operations." In *Proceedings of the 28th Annual Conference*, American Association for Automotive Medicine, Arlington Heights, Ill., Oct. 1984.

Appendix L
Relationships Between Geometric Design and Large-Truck Characteristics

Summarized in this appendix are relationships between large trucks and 13 key highway design features.

PAVEMENT WIDENING ON CURVES

To account for offtracking, in which a vehicle's rear wheels follow a different path from that of the front wheels, and driver difficulty in steering, the American Association of State Highway and Transportation Officials (AASHTO) recommends pavement widening on curves under certain circumstances defined by lane width, curve radius, and design speed. AASHTO recommendations are based on a procedure that takes into account vehicle width and offtracking characteristics. Because it notes that offtracking characteristics do not vary greatly between different large-truck types at design speeds of 30 to 60 mph, AASHTO bases its values on the characteristics of an 102-in. wide single-unit truck but suggests modest increases when tractor-semitrailer traffic is significant. Because twins offtrack less severely than the 45-ft semitrailers already in widespread use when the AASHTO standard was developed and the AASHTO design trucks have widths of 102 in., changes to AASHTO guidelines on pavement widening are unlikely for either twins or 102-in. wide trucks generally. However, a tractor with a 48-ft semitrailer, as shown in Appendix D, offtracks more than a tractor with a 45-ft semitrailer and any of the design trucks used for developing the AASHTO standards. As a

376

consequence, reconsideration of these design values may be warranted to account for the tractor with 48-ft semitrailer.

MINIMUM DESIGN FOR SHARPEST TURNS

At-grade intersections must sometimes be designed to permit low-speed turning in the minimum possible space. For these situations, AASHTO provides prototype design details based on the turning characteristics of the design trucks, with the most severe condition resulting from the off-tracking of a tractor-semitrailer with an overall length of 55 ft (consistent with a 40-ft semitrailer). Because the offtracking of the tractor-semitrailer with 48-ft semitrailer will exceed this design condition, additional design details for sharp turns based on trucks with poorer offtracking performance may be warranted. No change will be required because of twins.

WIDTH FOR TURNING ROADWAYS

Intersection roadways and interchange ramps used by trucks making turning movements should ideally accommodate these trucks without their having to make excursions onto adjacent shoulders or curbs. To do this, the roadway width must at the least accommodate the width of the vehicle and an additional allowance for offtracking. AASHTO recommends minimum turning roadway widths for conditions governed by large-truck traffic based on the characteristics of an 102-in. wide tractor-semitrailer with an overall length of 50 ft (consistent with a 35-ft semitrailer), except for one lane roadways with provision for passing stalled vehicles, on which a single-unit truck is used as the design vehicle. Although some pre-1983 in-service vehicles, as well as the longest AASHTO design truck, have worse offtracking characteristics and would require greater widths, AASHTO did not let these vehicles govern the design recommendations, apparently because it was believed that such a policy would not be cost-effective and that occasional excursions onto shoulders were permissible. As noted previously, for pavement widening on curves, twins will not exacerbate this situation, but tractors with 48-ft semitrailers will. Consequently, reconsideration of AASHTO design recommendations for minimum widths of turning roadways may be warranted.

MEDIAN OPENINGS

Highway designers provide median openings at intersections and driveway entrances on divided highways to permit crossing and turning movements. Ideally, the opening should be large enough to permit large vehicles to turn without encroaching on adjacent lanes, medians, or shoulders, but larger openings may result in erratic maneuvering by smaller vehicles. Although not prescribing minimum openings, AASHTO design policy recognizes that designers must balance these factors on the basis of anticipated traffic characteristics and indicates that some lane encroachments by large trucks may be permissible. Twins will not exacerbate this problem, but tractors with 48-ft semitrailers will because of their greater offtracking than that of existing AASHTO design vehicles.

STOPPING SIGHT DISTANCE

Minimum stopping sight distance is the distance required by a vehicle traveling at or near the design speed of a highway to stop before it strikes a stationary object in its path. This distance is used by designers in determining acceptable vertical and horizontal alignment; it depends on vehicle braking performance as well as on a number of other factors such a road surface friction, driver eye height, object height, and driver reaction time. AASHTO design values for minimum stopping sight distance are based on passenger-car braking characteristics. Although trucks require longer stopping sight distances, AASHTO notes that the greater driver eye height in trucks tends to compensate for these longer stopping distances. After studying this issue, Olson et al. (1) recently concluded that trucks require shorter stopping sight distances than automobiles for locked-wheel stops and about 10 percent greater distances than automobiles for a controlled stop without wheel lockup. Because the AASHTO design values for minimum stopping sight distances are not based on trucks per se, the introduction of new truck types is generally unlikely to affect current design values.

PASSING SIGHT DISTANCE

Minimum passing sight distance is the distance required on a two lane road for a vehicle to safely pass a slower vehicle without a possible collision with an oncoming vehicle in the opposing traffic lane. Designers use minimum passing sight distance to ensure that two lane highways provide reasonable opportunities for passing, and traffic engineers consider passing sight distance requirements in determining proper placement of legal passing zone signing and marking. Passing sight distance depends on a number of factors, including the length of both vehicles involved in a passing maneuver. AASHTO bases its minimum passing sight distance values on a passing maneuver involving only passenger cars, although longer distances are required when either or both of the vehicles are trucks.

As a result, no change in AASHTO minimum passing sight distances is expected unless AASHTO adopts a new rationale for these distances, but the introduction of longer trucks does modestly increase actual safe passing sight distance requirements for maneuvers involving these longer trucks. Typically, a twin trailer truck with 28-ft trailers is about 5 ft longer than a tractor-semitrailer with a 45-ft semitrailer. When a passenger car going 60 mph passes a 65-ft long twin trailer truck going 50 mph, a passing sight distance of 2,940 ft is required, about 50 ft more than if it passes a truck 60 ft long or about 630 ft more than if it passes a passenger car (the AASHTO standard is 2,300 feet).[1]

INTERSECTION SIGHT DISTANCE

Intersections should provide sufficient sight distance so that approaching vehicles can adjust speed or stop if necessary and so that previously stopped vehicles can accelerate and cross or turn without conflict. Of these only the sight distance for crossing or turning from a stop is affected by vehicle characteristics other than braking, specifically vehicle length and acceleration. AASHTO recommends no minimum standard for intersection sight distance to accommodate the crossing or turning maneuvers, but does provide estimated sight distance requirements for various design vehicles, including a tractor-semitrailer with an overall length of 55 ft for crossing and a passenger car for turning. No specific guideline is provided for the longer twin trailer truck design vehicle with an overall length of 65 ft, but designers can use AASHTO formulas to calculate specific design values. For instance, as reported by AASHTO (3), to cross a 40-ft roadway, a truck 65 ft long needs a sight distance of about 1,115 ft, about 40 ft (4 percent) longer than the sight distance needed for a truck 55 ft long with the same acceleration.

LENGTH OF AUXILIARY TURNING LANES

Auxiliary turning lanes should be long enough to allow turning vehicles to enter and decelerate and must provide storage space while these vehicles are waiting for turning opportunities. The AASHTO design policy identifies the factors that designers should take into account, including truck traffic, in determining the length of turning lanes; but it does not rec-

---

[1]Calculations based on a procedure described by Walton and Gericke (2) with the following assumptions: car length of 19 ft, initial manuevering time of 4.5 sec, average acceleration of 1.5 mph per second, and distance traversed by opposing vehicle equal to two-thirds of the distance traveled in left lane by the passing vehicle.

ommend specific values for lane length. The introduction of longer trucks, twins and tractors with 48-ft semitrailers may tend to increase the need for longer turning lanes at locations with substantial truck traffic. Indirectly, current AASHTO design guidelines can take this into account, so that no change to AASHTO guidelines is necessary.

CRITICAL LENGTH OF GRADES

When operating on long steep grades, heavy trucks cannot maintain prevailing traffic speeds, potentially disrupting traffic flow and creating safety hazards. The extent of speed loss depends on the weight-to-power ratio of the truck, its speed at the beginning of the grade, the degree (or percent) of vertical grade, and the length of grade. To limit speed reductions to no more than 10 mph, AASHTO recommends maximum grade lengths based on a truck with a weight-to-power ratio of 300 lb/hp. Generally, weight-to-power ratios have dropped over the past 30 years, and although the introduction of twins and longer semitrailers may reverse this trend slightly, no change in the AASHTO standard appears likely.

LANE WIDTH

Travel lanes should be wide enough to accommodate the width of vehicles in the traffic stream with clearances on either side to prevent encroachments onto adjacent lanes or shoulders. Although vehicle widths can be easily determined, minimum side clearances depend on a number of factors whose interaction is not fully understood—traffic volume and composition, width and use of adjacent lanes or shoulders, and driver behavior, particularly the lateral positioning of a vehicle relative to the lane centerline. AASHTO uses design trucks with 102-in. widths and recommends lane widths of 12 ft on Interstates and on high-speed arterial highways with large traffic volumes, the type of highway that is often included on the designated network where 102-in. wide trucks may legally operate. Lanes widths of 11 ft are permitted on lower-speed urban arterials and on rural arterials with both low traffic volumes (less than 400 vehicles per day) and design speeds of 50 mph or less. Because the 12-ft standard is widely accepted as an appropriate lane width for high-speed traffic that includes 102-in. vehicles and because AASHTO requires this for virtually all highways that might commonly be used for high-speed truck traffic, no change in the AASHTO standard for lane width appears likely.

SHOULDER WIDTH

Shoulders provide a place for vehicles to park during emergency situations. As shoulders increase in width, the possibility that a stopped vehicle will interfere with traffic flow or cause a safety hazard decreases. On rural highways AASHTO recommends minimum shoulder widths ranging from 4 ft, which cannot fully accommodate the parking of either a truck or a passenger car, to 12 ft, which can easily accommodate a 102-in. wide truck. The recommendations are keyed principally to traffic volume, reflecting the belief that as traffic volumes increase, the possibilities for both vehicle emergencies and adverse safety and traffic-related consequences from parked vehicles on shoulders increase. Because of this rationale and the fact that the standards already consider 102-in. wide trucks, no change in the AASHTO recommendations for shoulder width is expected.

REST AREAS

AASHTO recommends truck parking layouts in Interstate rest areas based on a tractor-semitrailer with a total length of 55 ft (4). The introduction of longer twin trailer trucks and tractor-semitrailers may lead to a reconsideration of this recommendation because these vehicles require greater space. However, because trucks with greater space requirements than a 55-ft long tractor-semitrailer were in common use before the nationwide legalization of twins and tractors with 48-ft semitrailers, it is not clear whether this change is of sufficient magnitude for AASHTO to change its design guidelines.

GUARDRAILS

Guardrails are intended to stop or redirect vehicles that run off the roadway. Because these devices are designed to withstand passenger car impacts, not truck impacts, the introduction of new truck types is not expected to cause a change in design standards.

REFERENCES

1. P.L. Olson, D.E. Cleveland, P.S. Fancher, L.P. Kostyniuk and L.W. Schneider. *Parameters Affecting Stopping Sight Distance*. NCHRP Report 270. TRB, National Research Council, Washington, D.C., June 1984.

382

2. C.M. Walton and O. Gericke. *An Assessment of Changes in Truck Dimensions on Highway Geometric Design Principles and Practices.* Center for Highway Research, University of Texas, Austin, 1981.

3. *A Policy of Geometric Design of Highways and Streets.* American Association of State Highway and Transportation Officials, Washington, D.C., 1984.

4. *A Guide on Safety Rest Areas for the National System of Interstate and Defense Highways.* American Association of State Highway and Transportation Officials, Washington, D.C., 1968.

Study Committee
Biographical Information

KENNETH W. HEATHINGTON, *Chairman*, is Associate Vice President for Research for the University of Tennessee Statewide Administration, Executive Director of the University of Tennessee Research Corporation, and Professor of Civil Engineering. He received his bachelor's and master's degrees from the University of Texas and a Ph.D. from Northwestern University. He has held positions with the Continental Oil Company, the Texas Highway Department, and the Illinois Division of Highways and has been Assistant Professor and Associate Professor at Purdue University. Dr. Heathington became Director of the University of Tennessee Transportation Center in 1972, leaving there in 1979 to become Associate Administrator for Highway Safety Programs at the National Highway Traffic Safety Administration. He rejoined the Transportation Center in 1980 and in 1983 became Associate Vice President for Research. He has been Chairman of the TRB Transportation Systems Planning and Administration Group Council, a member of the TRB Regular Technical Activities Division Council, and the TRB Special Projects Division Council. He is a member of Chi Epsilon, Tau Beta Pi, Sigma Xi, TRB, American Society of Civil Engineers, Institute of Transportation Engineers, American Society of Engineering Education, Society of Research Administrators, and various other organizations.

ROBERT G. ADAMS is Deputy Director for Highway Maintenance and Transportation Operations at the California Department of Transportation.

383

He received a bachelor's degree in civil engineering from the University of Minnesota. After joining the California Department of Transportation as an engineer, he held the positions of Assistant Director of Financial Management, Chief of the Division of Project Development, and Chief of the Division of Highways with the department. He is a member of the American Society of Civil Engineers.

CHARLES N. BRADY is Staff Director of Legislative Affairs with the American Automobile Association. He was Director of the AAA Highway Department until assuming his present position. He is a member of the National Motor Carrier Advisory Committee, the National Committee on Uniform Traffic Laws and Ordinances, a former member of the National Highway Traffic Safety Advisory Committee, the TRB Task Force on Truck Size and Weight, and was Chairman of the Highway Users Federation Transportation and Energy Advisory Panel.

THOMAS W. BROWNE has recently retired as Vice President of United Parcel Service, Inc. He has held positions with the Pennsylvania Railroad and was a transportation consultant before joining United Parcel Service as the Manager of Florida Operations. He also held the positions of Upstate New York District Manager and Midwest Customer Service Representative at United Parcel Service.

WILLIAM N. CAREY, JR., retired as Executive Director of the Transportation Research Board in 1980. He had served as a member of the staff of the Highway Research Board and TRB from January 1946. Educated in civil engineering at the University of Minnesota, Mr. Carey served with the U.S. Army Corps of Engineers constructing military airfields during World War II. He has served on several landmark highway research projects including the WASHO Road Test in Idaho (as director) and the AASHO Road Test project in Illinois (as chief engineer for research). Mr. Carey served as Assistant to the Director and Deputy Director before being named Executive Director of the Highway Research Board in 1966.

RALPH V. DURHAM is the Director of the Safety and Health Department of the International Brotherhood of Teamsters. He also serves as President of Teamsters Local Union 391 in Greensboro, North Carolina. Mr. Durham was formerly a member of the National Highway Safety Advisory Committee, the North Carolina Governor's Committee for the National Safety and Health Act, and the National Advisory Committee on the Occupational Safety and Health Administration. He currently serves on the National Driver Register Advisory Committee, the FHWA National

Motor Carrier Advisory Committee, and the National Hazardous Materials Advisory Committee.

ROBERT D. ERVIN is Assistant Head of the Engineering Research Division at the University of Michigan Transportation Research Institute. He received his bachelor's degree from the University of Detroit and a master's degree from Cornell University. Mr. Ervin was Mechanical Engineer at Atomic Power Development Associates before joining the University of Michigan Highway Safety Research Institute in 1969 (later the Transportation Research Institute). He held the positions of Research Associate, Associate Research Scientist, and Research Scientist at the Institute before assuming his current position.

JOHN W. FULLER is Professor of Economics, Geography, and Urban and Regional Planning at the University of Iowa. He received a bachelor's degree from San Diego State University and a Ph.D. in economics from Washington State University. He joined the Wisconsin Department of Transportation, where he held the positions of Chief of Economic Analysis, Chief of the Policy and Goal Analysis Section, and Director of the Environmental and Policy Analysis Bureau. Dr. Fuller was a member and Secretary of the Wisconsin Highway Commission and has been a Lecturer in the Graduate School of Business of the University of Wisconsin, Deputy Executive Director of the National Transportation Policy Study Commission, and Director of the Institute of Urban and Regional Research at the University of Iowa. He administers the Legislative Extended Assistance Group for the Iowa legislature. He is a member of the Iowa Governor's Land Use Advisory Committee, Iowa Department of Transportation Transit Advisory Committee, and numerous professional associations.

WILLIAM D. GLAUZ is the Director of the Engineering and Materials Sciences Department at the Midwest Research Institute in Kansas City, Missouri. He received a bachelor's degree from Michigan State University and a master's degree and a Ph.D. in engineering sciences from Purdue University. Dr. Glauz is chairman of the TRB Committee on Methodology for Evaluating Highway Improvements, and a member of the TRB Committees on Traffic Law Enforcement and Motor Vehicle Size and Weight. He is also a current or past member of the Society of Engineering Science, American Institute of Aeronautics and Astronautics, American Association for the Advancement of Science, Institute of Transportation Engineers, and American Society of Civil Engineers.

RONALD L. HUTCHINSON is a consulting engineer. After receiving a bachelor's degree in civil engineering from Duke University, he held various positions with the U.S. Army Corps of Engineers Ohio River Division Laboratories and the Waterways Experiment Station, from which he retired as Chief of the Pavement Systems Division. He has been an active member of the American Society of Civil Engineers, American Concrete Institute, Society of American Military Engineers, and TRB Rigid Pavement Committee.

MARGARET HUBBARD JONES is an experimental psychologist and Professor Emerita of Human Factors at the University of Southern California. She received her bachelor's degree from Vassar College, master's degree from Hobart College, and a Ph.D. from the University of California at Los Angeles. She has been an instructor at the University of Alabama and Washington State University and was Research Psychologist at the University of California at Los Angeles before joining the University of Southern California. Dr. Jones is a member of the TRB Committee on Vehicle User Characteristics and chairman of the Subcommittee on the Aging Driver. She has recently been a member of the Committees on Pedestrians and on Operator Education and Regulation. She is a member of the Human Factors Society and the International Ergonomics Association and is a fellow of the American Psychological Association. She is on the editorial boards of *Accident Analysis and Prevention*, *The Journal of Safety Research*, and *The Traffic Safety Evaluation Research Review*.

JOHN H. LEDERER is a partner in the firm of DeWitt, Sundby, Huggett and Schumacher, S.C. He received a degree in law from the University of Wisconsin. He was a law clerk to the Honorable Walter Hoffman, U.S. District Judge for Eastern Virginia, before joining DeWitt, Sundby, Huggett and Schumacher. Mr. Lederer is a member of the Dane County Bar Association, American Bar Association, State Bar of Wisconsin, and the Virginia State Bar. He is a specialist in transportation law, commerce clause law, and state regulation.

HUGH W. McGEE is a consulting engineer and a principal in the firm of Bellomo-McGee, Inc. He received his bachelor's, master's and Ph.D. in civil engineering, with an emphasis on transportation, from Pennsylvania State University. Dr. McGee worked with Alan M. Voorhees and Associates, Inc.; BioTechnology, Inc.; and Wagner-McGee Associates, Inc. He is a member of the American Society of Civil Engineers, Institute of Transportation Engineers, the TRB Traffic Control Devices Committee, and several professional societies.

JOHN K. MLADINOV is Executive Deputy Commissioner of the New York State Department of Transportation. He received a bachelor of arts degree from Columbia College, an engineering degree from the Columbia University School of Engineering, and completed graduate work in traffic and planning at Yale University. He held positions with the Washington State Department of Highways, directed the Puget Sound Regional Transportation Study, and has been with the New York State Department of Transportation since 1967. Mr. Mladinov is a member of the Institute of Traffic Engineers, American Public Works Association, National Society of Professional Engineers, and the American Association of State Highway and Transportation Officials.

HAROLD W. MONRONEY is the Director of the Division of Highways at the Illinois Department of Transportation. He received his bachelor's degree from Rose-Hulman Institute of Technology in Terre Haute, Indiana. Mr. Monroney has been with the Illinois Department of Transportation since 1949, holding the positions of Civil Engineer, District Engineer, and various administrative positions before his current position. He is a member of the American Association of State Highway and Transportation Officials Standing Committee on Highways.

NATHANIEL H. PULLING is Project Director of Automotive Safety in the Loss Prevention Research Center of the Liberty Mutual Insurance Company. He received a bachelor's degree from Brown University and a Ph.D. from Harvard University. After 4 years in the U.S. Navy, he became a Research Fellow at Harvard University. In 1967 he joined the Liberty Mutual Insurance Company in his present capacity. Dr. Pulling is a member of the Society of Automotive Engineers, American Society of Mechanical Engineers, American Association for Automotive Medicine, and the Human Factors Society. He has been a member of numerous TRB committees and chaired several of them. Currently he is a member of the Committee on Alcohol, Other Drugs, and Transportation. He is on the Editorial Advisory Board of *Accident Analysis and Prevention*. Dr. Pulling is Adjunct Professor of Mechanical Engineering at Worcester Polytechnic Institute.

BILLY ROSE retired from the North Carolina Department of Transportation in 1986. He received a bachelor's and a master's degree in civil engineering from North Carolina State University and joined the North Carolina Department of Transportation in 1959. He held the positions of Head of the Advanced Planning Department, Assistant State Highway

Administrator, State Highway Administrator and Chief Administrative Officer of the Division of Highways, and Deputy Secretary.

C. MICHAEL WALTON is Professor of Civil Engineering and Associate Director of the Center for Transportation Research at the University of Texas at Austin. He received his B.A. in civil engineering from the Virginia Military Institute and his master's and Ph.D. in civil engineering (transportation) from North Carolina State University. His former administrative and management experience includes Transportation Planning Engineer with the North Carolina State Highway Commission and Transporation Economist with the Office of the Secretary, U.S. Department of Transportation. In addition he has been involved in sponsored research and consulting related to highway and transportation engineering and analysis for approximately 15 years and has authored more than 150 publications in transportation engineering, planning, policy, and economics. In related activities Dr. Walton is a member of the Transportation Research Board, American Society of Civil Engineers, Institute of Transportation Engineers, Operations Research Society of America, and National Society of Professional Engineers. He is chairman of the TRB Committee on Motor Vehicle Size and Weight, past member of the TRB Technical Review Panel for the National Truck Size and Weight Study, and former chairman of the TRB Committee on Transportation Planning Needs and Requirements for Small and Medium-Sized Communities.

MATTHEW W. WITCZAK is Professor of the Department of Civil Engineering at the University of Maryland. He received his bachelor's, master's, and Ph.D. in civil engineering from Purdue University. His previous positions include service with the U.S. Army Corps of Engineers, research engineer with the Asphalt Institute, and Assistant and Associate Professor at the University of Maryland. He is a member of the American Society of Civil Engineers, Association of Asphalt Paving Technologists, American Society for Testing and Materials, and TRB Committee on Pavement Rehabilitation. He is Chairman of the TRB Task Force on Non-Destructive Evaluation of Airfield Pavements. Dr. Witczak received the TRB Burgraff Award in 1967, K.B. Woods Award in 1980, and AAPT Emmons Award in 1975 for outstanding research papers. He is co-author of *Principles of Pavement Design*.